I KINGS
with an
INTRODUCTION TO HISTORICAL LITERATURE

BURKE O. LONG

The Forms of the Old Testament Literature
VOLUME IX
Rolf Knierim and Gene M. Tucker, editors

WILLIAM B. EERDMANS PUBLISHING COMPANY
GRAND RAPIDS, MICHIGAN

For Judy, my wife

255 Jefferson Ave. S.E., Grand Rapids, MI 49503

Printed in the United States of America

Library of Congress Cataloging in Publication Data

Long, Burke O.
I Kings.

(The Forms of the Old Testament literature; v. 9)
Bibliography: passim
1. Bible. O.T. Kings, 1st—Commentaries. I. Title.
II. Title: 1 Kings. III. Title: First Kings. IV. Series
BS1335.3.L66 1984 222'.53066 83-25329
ISBN 0-8028-1920-6

CONTENTS

Abbreviations and Symbols

I. Miscellaneous abbreviations and symbols

ca.	*circa* (about)
cf.	compare
ch(s).	chapter(s)
col(s).	column(s)
Diss.	Dissertation
Dtr	Deuteronomistic
DtrH	Deuteronomistic Historian
DtrR	Deuteronomistic Redactor
ed.	editor(s), edited by; edition
e.g.	for example
esp.	especially
et al.	*et alii* (and others)
Eng. tr.	English translation
Fest.	*Festschrift*
Hebr.	Hebrew
i.e.	*id est* (that is [to say])
LXX	Septuagint
MT	Masoretic Text
n(n).	note(s)
NF, NS	Neue Folge, New Series (in serial listings)
no.	number
NT	New Testament
OT	Old Testament
p(p).	page(s)
par.	parallel (of words or phrases set in parallel)
PN	personal name
RN	royal name
Sam Pent	Samaritan Pentateuch

tr.	translator(s), translated by
v(v).	verse(s)
vol(s).	volume(s)
VS(S)	the ancient version(s), or translation(s), of biblical literature
→	the arrow indicates a cross reference to another section of the commentary.
=	equals, is equivalent to
§(§)	section(s)

II. Publications

AB	Anchor Bible
AfO	*Archiv für Orientforschung*
Alt, *KS*, I, II, III	A. Alt, *Kleine Schriften zur Geschichte des Volkes Israel*
AnBib	Analecta biblica
ANET	J. B. Pritchard, ed., *Ancient Near Eastern Texts Relating to the Old Testament* (3rd ed.; Princeton: Princeton University Press, 1969)
AnOr	Analecta orientalia
ARAB	D. D. Luckenbill, ed., *Ancient Records of Assyria and Babylonia* (2 vols.; Chicago: University of Chicago Press, 1926-1927)
ARE	J. H. Breasted, ed., *Ancient Records of Egypt* (5 vols.; Chicago: University of Chicago Press, 1906-1907)
ARI	A. K. Grayson, *Assyrian Royal Inscriptions* (2 vols.; Wiesbaden: Harrassowitz, 1972-1976)
ASTI	*Annual of the Swedish Theological Institute in Jerusalem*
ATANT	Abhandlungen zur Theologie des Alten und Neuen Testaments
ATD	Das Alte Testament Deutsch
BA	*Biblical Archaeologist*
BASOR	*Bulletin of the American Schools of Oriental Research*
BethM	*Beth Miqra*
Bib	*Biblica*
BJRL	*Bulletin of the John Rylands University Library of Manchester*
BKAT	Biblischer Kommentar: Altes Testament
BWANT	Beiträge zur Wissenschaft vom Alten und Neuen Testament
BZ	*Biblische Zeitschrift*
BZAW	Beihefte zur Zeitschrift für die Alttestamentliche Wissenschaft
CBQ	*Catholic Biblical Quarterly*
Est Bib	*Estudios bíblicos*

EvT	*Evangelische Theologie*
FOTL	The Forms of the Old Testament Literature
FRLANT	Forschungen zur Religion und Literatur des Alten und Neuen Testaments
GKC	*Gesenius' Hebrew Grammar,* ed. E. Kautzsch, tr. A. E. Cowley (2nd ed.; Oxford: Clarendon, 1910)
Gordon, *UT*	C. H. Gordon, *Ugaritic Textbook* (AnOr 38; Rome: Pontificium Institutum Biblicum, 1965)
HKAT	Handkommentar zum Alten Testament
HSAT	*Die heilige Schrift des Alten Testaments* (Kautzsch) (4th ed.; Tübingen, 1922-1923), ed. Bertholet
HSM	Harvard Semitic Monographs
HTR	*Harvard Theological Review*
HUCA	*Hebrew Union College Annual*
IB	*Interpreter's Bible*
ICC	International Critical Commentary
IDB	*Interpreter's Dictionary of the Bible*
IDBSup	Supplementary volume to *IDB*
IEJ	*Israel Exploration Journal*
Int	*Interpretation*
JAOS	*Journal of the American Oriental Society*
JBL	*Journal of Biblical Literature*
JCS	*Journal of Cuneiform Studies*
JNES	*Journal of Near Eastern Studies*
JSOT	*Journal for the Study of the Old Testament*
JSOTSup	Journal for the Study of the Old Testament Supplement Series
JSS	*Journal of Semitic Studies*
KAI	H. Donner and W. Röllig, *Kanaanäische und Aramäische Inschriften* (2nd ed.; 3 vols.; Wiesbaden: Harrassowitz, 1966-1968)
KD	*Kerygma und Dogma*
NEB	*New English Bible*
Or	*Orientalia*
OTL	Old Testament Library
OTS	*Oudtestamentische Studiën*
RB	*Revue biblique*
RGG[3]	*Die Religion in Geschichte und Gegenwart* (3rd ed.; 7 vols.; Tübingen: Mohr, 1957-1965)
RHPR	*Revue d'histoire et de philosophie religieuses*

RISA	G. A. Barton, *The Royal Inscriptions of Sumer and Akkad* (New Haven: Yale, 1929)
RLA	*Reallexikon der Assyriologie* (Berlin and Leipzig, 1932-)
RSV	*Revised Standard Version*
SBLASP	Society of Biblical Literature Abstracts and Seminar Papers
SBLDS	Society of Biblical Literature Dissertation Series
TDOT	G. J. Botterweck and H. Ringgren, eds., *Theological Dictionary of the Old Testament* (Eng. tr.; 12 vols.; Grand Rapids: Eerdmans, 1974-)
ThSt(B)	Theologische Studien (founded and edited by K. Barth)
TLZ	*Theologische Literaturzeitung*
TRu	*Theologische Rundschau*
TTZ	*Trierer Theologische Zeitschrift*
TZ	*Theologische Zeitschrift*
UF	*Ugarit-Forschungen*
VT	*Vetus Testamentum*
VTSup	Vetus Testamentum, Supplements
WMANT	Wissenschaftliche Monographien zum Alten und Neuen Testament
WO	*Die Welt des Orients*
WuD	*Wort und Dienst*
ZAW	*Zeitschrift für die alttestamentliche Wissenschaft*
ZDPV	*Zeitschrift des deutschen Palästinavereins*
ZKTh	*Zeitschrift für Katholische Theologie*
ZTK	*Zeitschrift für Theologie und Kirche*

EDITORS' FOREWORD

THIS BOOK is the third in a series of twenty-four volumes planned for publication throughout the nineteen-eighties. The series eventually will represent a form-critical analysis of every book and each unit of the Old Testament (Hebrew Bible) according to a standard outline and methodology. The aims of the work are fundamentally exegetical, attempting to understand the biblical literature from the viewpoint of a particular set of questions. Each volume in the series will also give an account of the history of the form-critical discussion of the material in question, attempt to bring consistency to the terminology for the genres and formulas of the biblical literature, and expose the exegetical procedure in such a way as to enable students and pastors to engage in their own analysis and interpretation. It is hoped, therefore, that the audience will be a broad one, including not only biblical scholars but also students, pastors, priests, and rabbis who are engaged in biblical interpretation.

There is a difference between the planned order of appearance of the individual volumes and their position in the series. While the series follows basically the sequence of the books of the Hebrew Bible, the individual volumes will appear in accordance with the projected working schedules of the individual contributors. The number of twenty-four volumes has been chosen for merely practical reasons which make it necessary to combine several biblical books in one volume at times, and at times to have two authors contribute to the same volume. Volume XIII is an exception to the arrangement according to the sequence of the Hebrew canon in that it omits Lamentations. The commentary on Lamentations will be published with that on the book of Psalms.

The initiation of this series is the result of deliberations and plans which began some fifteen years ago. At that time the current editors perceived the need for a comprehensive reference work which would enable scholars and students of the Hebrew scriptures to gain from the insights that form-critical work had accumulated throughout seven decades, and at the same time to participate more effectively in such work themselves. An international and interconfessional team of scholars was assembled, and has been expanded in recent years.

Several possible approaches and formats for publication presented themselves. The work could not be a handbook of the form-critical method with some examples of its application. Nor would it be satisfactory to present an encyclopedia of the genres identified in the Old Testament literature. The reference work would have to demonstrate the method on all of the texts, and identify genres only through the actual interpretation of the texts themselves. Hence, the work had to be a commentary following the sequence of the books in the Hebrew Bible (the

Kittel edition of the *Biblia Hebraica* then and the *Biblia Hebraica Stuttgartensia* now).

The main purpose of this project is to lead the student to the Old Testament texts themselves, and not just to form-critical studies of the texts. It should be stressed that the commentary is confined to the form-critical interpretation of the texts. Consequently, the reader should not expect here a full-fledged exegetical commentary which deals with the broad range of issues concerning the meaning of the text. In order to keep the focus as clearly as possible on a particular set of questions, matters of text, translation, philology, verse-by-verse explanation, etc. are raised only when they appear directly relevant to the form-critical analysis and interpretation.

The adoption of a commentary format and specific methodological deliberations imply a conclusion which has become crucial for all the work of form criticism. If the results of form criticism are to be verifiable and generally intelligible, then the determination of typical forms and genres, their settings and functions, has to take place through the analysis of the forms in and of the texts themselves. This leads to two consequences for the volumes in this series. First, each interpretation of a text begins with the presentation of the *structure* of that text in outline form. The ensuing discussion of this structure attempts to distinguish the typical from the individual or unique elements, and to proceed on this basis to the determination of the *genre,* its *setting,* and its *intention.* Traditio-historical factors are discussed throughout this process where relevant; e.g., is there evidence of a written or oral stage of the material earlier than the actual text before the reader?

Second, the interpretation of the texts accepts the fundamental premise that we possess all texts basically at their latest written stages, technically speaking, at the levels of the final redactions. Any access to the texts, therefore, must confront and analyze that latest edition first, i.e., a specific version of that edition as represented in a particular text tradition. Consequently, the commentary proceeds from the analysis of the larger literary corpora created by the redactions back to any prior discernible stages in their literary history. Larger units are examined first, and then their subsections. Therefore, in most instances the first unit examined in terms of structure, genre, setting, and intention is the entire biblical book in question; next the commentary treats the individual larger and then smaller units.

The original plan of the project was to record critically all the relevant results of previous form-critical studies concerning the texts in question. While this remains one of the goals of the series, it had to be expanded to allow for more of the research of the individual contributors. This approach has proved to be important not only with regard to the ongoing insights of the contributors, but also in view of the significant developments which have taken place in the field in recent years. The team of scholars responsible for the series is committed to following a basic design throughout the commentary, but differences of emphasis and even to some extent of approach will be recognized as more volumes appear. Each author will ultimately be responsible for his own contribution.

The use of the commentary is by and large self-explanatory, but a few comments may prove helpful to the reader. This work is designed to be used alongside a Hebrew text or a translation of the Bible. The format of the interpretation of the texts, large or small, is the same throughout, except in cases where the biblical material itself suggests a different form of presentation. Individual books and major literary corpora are introduced by a general bibliography referring to wider information on the subjects discussed, and to works relevant for the subunits of that literary body. Whenever available, a special form-critical bibliography for a specific unit under discussion will conclude the discussion of that unit. In the outline of the structure of units, the system of sigla attempts to indicate the relationship and interdependence of the parts within that structure. The traditional chapter and verse divisions of the Hebrew text are supplied in the right-hand margin of the outlines. Where there is a difference between the Hebrew and English versification the latter is also supplied in parentheses according to the *Revised Standard Version*.

In addition to the commentary on the biblical books, this volume includes an introduction to the major genres found in the Old Testament historical literature and a glossary of the genres discussed in the commentary. Most of the definitions in the glossary were prepared by Professor Long, but some have arisen from the work of other members of the project on other parts of the Old Testament. Each subsequent volume will include such a glossary. Eventually, upon the completion of the commentary series, all of the glossaries will be revised in the light of the analysis of each book of the Old Testament and published as Volume XXIV of the series. The individual volumes will not contain special indices but the indices for the entire series will be published as Volume XXIII.

The editors wish to acknowledge with appreciation the contribution of numerous persons and institutions to the work of the project. All of the contributors have received significant financial, secretarial, and student assistance from their respective institutions. In particular, the editors have received extensive support from their Universities. Without such concrete expressions of encouragement the work scarcely could have gone on. At Claremont, the Institute for Antiquity and Christianity has from its own inception provided office facilities, a supportive staff, and the atmosphere which stimulates not only individual but also team research. Emory University and the Candler School of Theology have likewise provided tangible support and encouragement.

The editors are indebted to Brett Lamberty, William Yarchin, and John Hull, Old Testament graduate students at Claremont Graduate School and research associates for the FOTL project at the Institute for Antiquity and Christianity, for their significant contributions to the editorial process.

ROLF KNIERIM
GENE M. TUCKER

Preface

The chief aim of this book and its successor volume is to present a sustained form-critical analysis of the books of Kings: the whole composition, its parts, and the parts in relation to the whole. Usually biblical scholars stress textual, historical, and philological matters and expend considerable effort in reconstructing earlier stages of development which led to the present Masoretic text. I have reversed the emphasis—not to ignore these matters, for they have been considered at every point, but to focus our attention on the literary features of Hebrew historical narrative. I have also given special attention to forms of historical writing among ancient Israel's neighbors, the better to see the Old Testament as one among several obsessions with the past.

This point of view has meant that the classic categories of form criticism (formal structure, genre, setting, and intention) which underlie this book have been redefined somewhat as befits their application to a substantially unified, singly authored work deriving from the exilic period of Israel's history, after 587 B.C. The reader will notice particularly that I have tried to take "structure" beyond formalism and have discussed aspects of literary art: style, metaphor, imagery, inner associations, and allusions, all parts of a narrative genius which awakens imaginative response in the reader.

The analysis and commentary are based on the Hebrew Masoretic text and coordinated for the reader to the *Revised Standard Version.* Text-critical decisions are not noted unless there were compelling reasons to adopt a reading different from that which underlies the *Revised Standard Version.*

I have selected items for the bibliographies according to the particular aims of the commentary. Listed are works whose primary contributions are to literary and form-critical problems. In addition, the reader will find reference to accessible editions of ancient Near Eastern historical texts and treatments of historiography by recognized specialists.

An author's intellectual debts are probably too numerous and assimilated for individual acknowledgment. Certainly mine are. It is more realistic to express gratitude to special benefactors of time, money, and work space: Bowdoin College for research grants and released time; the Society of Biblical Literature and the School of Theology at Claremont for appointment as the SBL Fellow for 1979; Candler School of Theology at Emory University for tangible support and intellectual excitement during 1982.

I dedicate this book to my wife, Judy. She shares with me the pursuit of individual accomplishment. But she has unselfishly, lovingly, deferred and slowed her own work on those occasions when I took extended leaves from domestic responsibilities.

Burke O. Long

Introduction to Historical Literature

Bibliography

M. Adinolfi, "Storiografia biblica e storiografia classica," *Rivista biblica* 9 (1961) 42-58; B. Albrektson, *History and the Gods* (Lund: Gleerup, 1967); R. Alter, *The Art of Biblical Narrative* (New York: Basic Books, 1981); K. Baltzer, *Die Biographie der Propheten* (Neukirchen: Neukirchener, 1975); G. Barton, *RISA*; W. Berthoff, "Fiction, History, Myth," *The Interpretation of Narrative* (ed. M. W. Bloomfield; Cambridge: Harvard, 1970) 263-87; S. R. Bin-Nun, "Formulas from Royal Records of Israel and of Judah," *VT* 18 (1968) 414-32; E. Blumenthal, "Die Textgattung Expeditionsbericht in Ägypten," in *Fragen an die altägyptische Literatur* (*Fest.* E. Otto; ed. Jan Assmann; Wiesbaden: Reichert, 1977) 85-118; J. H. Breasted, *ARE;* G. Brin, "The Formula X-*ymy* and X-*yôm*: Some Characteristics of Historiographical Writing in Israel," *ZAW* 93 (1981) 183-96; M. Burrows, "Ancient Israel," in *The Idea of History in the Ancient Near East* (ed. R. C. Dentan; New Haven: Yale, 1955) 99-131; H. Cancik, *Grundzüge der Hethitischen und alttestamentlichen Geschichtsschreibung* (Wiesbaden: Harrassowitz, 1976); idem, *Mythische und historische Wahrheit. Interpretationen zu Texten der hethitischen, biblischen und griechischen Historiographie* (Stuttgart: Katholisches Bibelwerk, 1970); G. W. Coats, "The Wilderness Itinerary," *CBQ* 34 (1972) 135-52; idem, *Genesis* (FOTL; Grand Rapids: Eerdmans, 1983); J. B. Curtis, "A Suggested Interpretation of the Biblical Philosophy of History," *HUCA* 34 (1963) 115-23; G. I. Davies, "The Wilderness Itineraries: A Comparative Study," *Tyndale Bulletin* 25 (1974) 46-81; B. Dinur, "The Biblical Historiography of the Period of the Kingdom," in *The Kingdoms of Israel and Judah* (ed. A. Malamat; Jerusalem, 1961) 9-23 (Hebrew); H. Donner and W. Röllig, *KAI*; O. Eissfeldt, *The Old Testament: An Introduction* (tr. P. R. Ackroyd; New York: Harper & Row, 1965) 18-32, 47-56; G. Fohrer, *Introduction to the Old Testament* (tr. D. Green; Nashville: Abingdon, 1968) 51-63, 95-99; N. Frye, *Anatomy of Criticism* (Princeton: Princeton University, 1957) 33-67; C. H. Gordon, *UT;* A. K. Grayson, *Assyrian and Babylonian Chronicles* (Texts from Cuneiform Sources 5; Locust Valley, N.Y.: Augustin, 1975); idem, *ARI*; idem, *Babylonian Historical-Literary Texts* (Toronto: University of Toronto, 1975); idem, "Königslisten und Chroniken," *RLA*; W. W. Hallo, "The Royal Inscriptions of Ur: A Typology," *HUCA* 33 (1962) 1-43; E. Jacob, "Histoire et historiens dans l'Ancien Testament," *RHPR* 35 (1955) 26-35; R. Knierim, "The Vocation of Isaiah," *VT* 18 (1968) 47-68; B. Lewis, *History—remembered, recovered, invented* (Princeton: Princeton University, 1975); M. Lichtheim, *Ancient Egyptian Literature* (3 vols.; Berkeley: University of California, 1973-81); D. D. Luckenbill, *ARAB*; B. Maisler (Mazar), "Ancient Israelite Historiography," *IEJ* 2 (1952) 82-88; A. Malamat, "King Lists of the Old Babylonian Period and Biblical Genealogies," *JAOS* 88 (1968) 163-73; R. Meyer, "Auffallender Erzählungsstil in einem angeblichen Auszug aus der 'Chronik der Könige von Juda,' " in *Festschrift Friedrich Baumgärtel* (ed. L. Rost; Erlanger Forschungen 10; Erlangen: Universitätsbibliothek, 1959) 114-23; G. Misch, *A History of Autobiography in Antiquity* (Cambridge: Harvard, 1950); S. Mowinckel, "Die vorderasiatischen Königs- und Fürsteninschriften," in *Eucharisterion* I (*Fest.* H. Gunkel; ed. H. Schmidt; FRLANT NF 19; Göttingen: Vandenhoeck & Ruprecht, 1923) 278-322; idem, "Israelite Historiography," *ASTI* 2 (1963) 4-26; idem, *Studien zu dem Buche Ezra-Nehemia* II. *Die Nehemia Denkschrift* (Oslo: Universitetsforlaget, 1964); E. Osswald, "Altorientalische Parallelen zur deuteronomistischen Geschichtsbetrachtung," *Mitteilungen des Instituts für Orientforschung* 15 (1969) 286-96; R. H. Pfeiffer, *Introduction to the Old Testament* (New York: Harper & Row, 1941) 374-412; J. R. Porter, "Old Testament Historiography," in *Tradition and Interpretation* (ed. G. W. Anderson; Oxford: Clarendon, 1979) 125-162; J. B. Pritchard, *ANET*; G. von Rad, "The Beginnings of Historical Writing in Ancient Israel," in *The Problem of the Hexateuch and Other Essays* (tr. E. W. Trueman Dicken; New York: McGraw-Hill, 1966) 166-204; idem, "Die Nehemia-Denkschrift," *ZAW* 76 (1964) 176-87; idem, "Theologische Geschichtsschreibung im Alten Testament," in *Gottes Wirken in Israel* (Neukirchen: Neukirchener, 1974) 175-90 (repr. from *TZ* 4 [1948] 161-74); L. Ramlot, "Les généalogies bibliques: Un genre littéraire oriental," *Bible et vie chrétienne* 60 (1964) 53-70; R. Rendtorff, "Geschichtsschreibung im Alten Testament," *Evangelisches Kirchenlexikon* (Göttingen: Vandenhoeck & Ruprecht, 1961); Johannes Schildenberger, *Literarische Arten der Geschichtsschreibung im Alten Testament* (Biblische Beiträge 5; Schweizerisches Katholisches Bibelwerk; Fribourg, 1964); H. H. Schmid, "Das alttestamentliche Verständnis von Geschichte in seinem Verhältnis zum gemeinorientalischen Denken," *WuD* 13 (1975) 9-21; H. Schmidt, *Die Geschichtsschreibung im Alten Testament* (Tübingen: Mohr, 1911); R. Scholes and R. Kellog, *The Nature of Narrative* (New York: Oxford, 1966) 57-69; W. Schultz, "Stilkritische Untersuchungen zur dtr Literatur," *TLZ* 102 (1977) 853-55; John Van Seters, "Histories and Historians of the Ancient Near East: The Israelites," *Or* 50 (1981) 137-95; R. Smend, *Elemente alttestamentlichen Geschichtsdenkens* (ThSt[B] 95; Zurich: EVZ, 1968); E. Sollberger and J. R. Kupper, *Inscriptions royales sumériennes et akkadiennes* (Paris: Cerf, 1971); E. A. Speiser, "The Biblical Idea of History in its Common Near Eastern Setting," *IEJ* 7 (1957) 201-16; idem, "Mesopotamian Historiography," in *The Idea of History in the Ancient Near East* (ed. R. C. Dentan; New Haven: Yale, 1955) 35-76; H. Tadmor and M. Weinfeld, eds., *History, Historiography and Interpretation. Studies in Biblical and Cuneiform Literatures* (Jerusalem: Magnes, 1983); G. W. Trompf, "Notions of Historical Recurrence in Classical Hebrew Historiography," in *Studies in the Historical Books of the Old Testament* (ed. J. A. Emerton; VTSup 30; Leiden: Brill, 1979) 213-29; R. R. Wilson, "The Old Testament Genealogies in Recent Research," *JBL* 94 (1975) 169-89; idem, *Genealogy and History in the Biblical World* (New Haven: Yale, 1977); N. Wyatt, "The Old Testament Historiography of the Exilic Period," *Studia Theologica* 33 (1979) 45-67; idem, "Some Observations on the Idea of History among the West Semitic Peoples," *UF* 11 (1979) 825-32.

HISTORICAL language, whether literal or metaphorical, must have genuinely historical referents. It must refer to persons and objects that really existed and to events that really happened. Therefore, historical literature—by which we mean the range of prose narratives other than the merely practical, such as contracts or business receipts—has as its main characteristic and purpose the recounting of historical reality: the people, objects, and past events of definite time and place.

Of course, matters are more complicated than they may seem at first glance. No historical statement is *purely* referential. There are no "brute facts," for modern or ancient writers. In either case, an author would select, order, interpret, and set matters in relation to each other and to the social traditions of which he or she was a part. Nor would he or she necessarily exclude elements characteristic of fiction from the account. The writer may develop a dramatic plot, or be concerned with metaphor and imaginative description; stereotyped images may add fictional colors to the subject or move the reader to appreciate its legendary or archetypal proportions. In these ways, historical narrative may touch (→) legend, (→) saga, or (→) tale (see "Introduction to Narrative Literature," in G. W. Coats, *Genesis*, 3-10). On the other hand, fiction may incorporate features thought essential to historical narrative, such as chronology or concern with cause-effect relations between events. We must think of literary genres as living creations, bending and melding, one shape flowing into another like a *pas de deux* of cloud and sunshine. The tasks of generic description are to sketch parameters, define constitutive elements against a shifting sky, and retain a sense of the fluid character of language and literary convention.

In this commentary on 1–2 Kings, we understand historical literature as a product primarily of a literate stratum of society, as that kind of narrative prose which is governed by the aim to record people, objects, and events as they really were. Its structure and logic are controlled not so much by aesthetic and imaginative considerations—although these factors may enter in to some degree—as by chronology, direct description, and concern to show cause-effect relationships between events. Speaking aesthetically, one might say that the writer of historical narrative takes pleasure from factuality, regardless of how we moderns might evaluate the use of evidence, argument, or sources.

While some of the OT may for our ears lack a sense of being bound to documentable fact in the way of modern history, much of its prose is nevertheless historical in this literary sense. That is, the Bible manages to resist the label of either fiction *or* history. Its character reflects an "interfusion of literary art with theological, moral, or historiosophical vision" (Alter, 19). The important genres are few in number and may be classified as (1) LIST, (2) REPORT, and (3) developed narrative in the forms of (a) self-contained STORY and (b) more complex continuous, written works of HISTORY. We shall discuss each genre in turn.

BASIC GENRES OF HISTORICAL LITERATURE

A. List

At its simplest, a LIST recounts names or items without any particular principle of order. In more developed forms, the items are ordered systematically by a single main idea or principle. List approaches historical narration when the list maker claims to have reconstructed an order of things as they really existed in the past and as they have relevance to the writer's own present time. For varied examples of lists in the ancient Near East, see Gordon, *UT,* § 17.2; *ANET,* 261-62, 271, 491; Breasted, *ARE* II, §§ 717-45.

A primary OT example with this historical aim is the GENEALOGY, a list of individual or tribal descent from an originating ancestor(s) through intermediate persons down to the last and contemporary person—an unbroken line of biological generation. OT genealogies are numerous and appear variously integrated into wider narrative contexts. We read genealogies of people in 1 Chr 2:1–3:24; Gen

10:1-32; 25:1-4; 22:20-24, and of tribes in Gen 25:13-16, 18. Not represented, except by inference, is a species of genealogy called the KING LIST, which enumerates successive rulers in a particular state. Widely attested in the ancient Near East (see *ANET,* 265-66, 271-72, 564-67; Grayson, "Königslisten"; Malamat), the king list may have been the literary model for Gen 36:31-39. One might compare further the list of "rulers" (*šôpĕṭîm; RSV* "judges") in Judg 10:1-5; 12:7-15, and of "chiefs" in Gen 36:40-43.

From among the many other kinds of lists in the OT, we may cite lists of booty (Num 31:32-40), votive offerings (Exod 35:5b-9; cf. 35:21-29), itinerary (Num 33:5-37; see Coats, "Wilderness"; Davies), and royal mercenaries (2 Sam 23:24-39). Stemming from the time of more centralized rule, we find various administrative lists, probably excerpted from government (→) registers, e.g., tabulations of royal officials (1 Kgs 4:2-6, 7-19), population (Ezra 2; Neh 11:3-36), and cities or towns (Joshua 15–19).

The settings for lists would have been varied, according to their contents and reasons for ordering their subject matter. Their proliferation may have been associated with the monarchy in Israel. All lists, however, seem to presuppose the urge to manage the present by recording names, events, and objects. In a more reflective mode, such records lay claim to the past and justify various lines of continuity with it. Since lists establish connections between past and present, they intend genuine historical recollection and move toward historical writing. For example, see how the OT genealogy might include brief allusions to specific events in the past (Gen 10:8-9, 11, 19, 25), or administrative lists of officials might include other information (1 Kgs 4:11, 15), extraneous to us perhaps, but no doubt pertinent to the writer's own time. In late postexilic times, the genealogy was so important a tool of historical narration that the author of 1–2 Chronicles chose to introduce his work with a sort of world-historical, generation-by-generation prologue (1 Chronicles 1–9).

B. Report

The report is a brief, self-contained narration, usually in third-person style, about a single event or situation in the past. This form of writing is different from the OFFICIAL REPORT, which is represented in narrative as a communication from one person to another, e.g., a messenger reports to the king (2 Sam 11:23-24), or a report in a letter (Ezra 4:12-16; see the Hebrew letter from Lachish, *ANET,* 322). We have in mind a simple account without developed plot or characterization and addressed to a more general audience.

Reports carry diverse contents, naturally, and range in length from the very brief NOTICE to the longer ACCOUNT. We read, for example, in the OT a report of settlement (Judg 1:16-17), of etiological naming (Gen 35:8), and of royal construction works (1 Kgs 7:2-8; 12:25). Authors might report a military campaign (1 Kgs 14:25-26; 2 Kgs 24:20b–25:7) or a conspiracy against the crown (1 Kgs 15:27-30). Outside the OT, see the Siloam Inscription (*ANET,* 321), which simply recounts the carving of a water tunnel. From the many other ancient Near Eastern examples, we may single out Egyptian reports of expeditions (Breasted, *ARE* I, §§ 708-23; II, §§ 119-22; IV, §§ 18-19; Blumenthal). Many of these Egyptian reports appear as the main content of commemorative inscriptions which praise the king or a high official, and in this, are to be compared to reports of a king's deeds contained in Assyrian and Babylonian royal commemorative inscriptions (Grayson, *ARI;* Sollberger; Hallo).

Of course, oral reports might be made by anyone, at any level of society, for many different purposes. However, we may think of the royal courts as the most important societal matrix for encouraging the making and keeping of written reports. Their purposes would have been diverse, depending on content and circumstances of use. Fundamentally, report makers intend to describe in more or less detail what a particular event was and how it took place in order to keep records or legitimate some claim in the time of the writer.

Reports approach more directly the writing of history when they are collected into series. Scholars presume this to have happened in Israel and thus suppose that Israelite and Judahite kings had their scribes keep ANNALS, which are concise records of important events pertaining to an institution such as monarchy or cult. Annals would have comprised a series of reports arranged chronologically year by year. Unfortunately, the OT contains not a single example. Nevertheless, some scholars persist in suggesting that certain historical reports were excerpted from, or based upon, these presumed Hebrew annals (e.g., 1 Kgs 9:15-23; 14:25-28; 1 Kings 6–8). Ancient Near Eastern examples have not survived either, unless one supposes that those royal inscriptions mentioned above were somehow based upon official annals. In Egypt, the closest thing to an annal is found in the very ancient "Palermo Stone" (Breasted, *ARE* I, §§ 76-167).

Another form in which series of reports occur is the CHRONICLE, which, on the basis of examples from late Assyrian and Neo-Babylonian times, may be defined as a prose narration, normally in third-person style, of selected events arranged and dated in chronological order (Grayson, *Chronicles;* idem, "Königslisten"). Unlike commemorative royal inscriptions, chronicles really do intend in the main to summarize and date events over discrete periods of time. In style and content, the distinction between chronicle and king list is sometimes difficult to maintain, since the latter sometimes will include prose narration.

There are no examples of chronicles in the OT. However, the phrases *sēper dibrê hayyāmîm,* "book of things of the days" (frequently in the concluding framework portions of the reigns, e.g., 1 Kgs 14:29; 15:7; etc.), and *sēper dibrê šĕlōmô,* "book of the things of Solomon" (1 Kgs 11:41), and the similar expressions throughout 1–2 Chronicles, may refer to documents of the kind found in Assyria and Babylonia. Only passages such as 2 Kings 25 suggest something like a chronicle, and there the description is much fuller than anything known outside Israel. It is worth noting, finally, that the structured coverage of the Hebrew reigns, whereby events in a particular reign are framed by accession formulas on the one hand and succession formulas on the other, may owe its literary parentage to the Babylonian chronicle form (see full discussion at 1 Kgs 14:21-31). In any event, we lack definitive evidence for the existence of Hebrew chronicles as a genre of historical literature.

C. Historical Story

The historical story is a self-contained narrative mainly concerned to recount what a particular event was and how it happened, but with more literary sophistication than is usually evident in simple reports. Typically, the writer shapes at least a rudimentary plot, i.e., narrative movement from a tension or problem to its resolution. Also, dialogue and dramatic touches may give the writing a certain literary appeal and imaginative quality. In a historical story we may see clearly the varied relationships between history and fiction that the biblical authors present to us. We read of characters and events rooted in plausible time and space, but given contours conceived in the writer's particularizing imagination. The biblical examples range themselves on a spectrum. On the one hand is fiction, which lays a "claim to a place in the chain of causation and the realm of moral consequentiality that belong to history"; on the other hand is "history given the imaginative definition of fiction," in which the "feeling and the meaning of events are concretely realized through the technical resources of prose fiction" (Alter, 32-33, 41). We do not point to social context, as the terms folk, primitive, or "popular history" (Eissfeldt, 50) might suggest. Nor do we seek to lessen the Bible's claim to speak seriously of historical people and events. It is a matter of coming to grips with the literary peculiarity of a type of historical narration. The biblical writer of historical story recalls the past by imaginative reenactment, and with little of the modern reticence about the value of literary artistry in shaping visions of truth.

Clearly it will not always be possible or even useful to distinguish too sharply between historical story and other genres of popular narrative such as (→) legend, (→) tale, or (→) saga. (See "Introduction to Narrative Literature," in G. W. Coats, *Genesis*, 3-10.) The main differences lie not so much in content as in purpose. The author of a historical story does not primarily seek to instruct, entertain, or edify—although the narrative may do any of these. Rather, the aim would be to recount events as they were thought to have occurred and with a feeling for their meaning in the lives of people caught in the ambiguities of human, earthly existence.

OT examples of historical story would include 1 Sam 11:1-11, Saul's selection as king (cf. 1 Kgs 12:1-20), and Judg 9:1-21, Abimelech's rise to power in Israel before there were kings. We may also include those stories in which a prophet plays a major role in the recounted affairs of kings and nations, e.g., 1 Kgs 20:1-43; 22:1-37 (→ prophetic story).

It is possible, perhaps probable, that some OT examples of this genre originated with the folk, and were transmitted orally in popular fashion along with legends, tales, and sagas. For the most part, however, these matters are difficult to see with much clarity, and we are left to consider written stories as associated with the literate scribal classes at work in the royal court and religious institutions. Intentions would have naturally varied somewhat depending on the context of use. In general, the writer of historical story would be mainly interested in recounting how things happened, but on that account not necessarily oblivious to the pleasure to be gained from exploring the artistic and literary imagination, and even on occasion a blatant bias of one kind or another.

D. History

History is an extensive, continuous, written composition made up of various materials, originally oral and/or written, and devoted to a particular subject or historical period. The author describes events presumed to have actually occurred, but assembles his sources—many of which would have been historical stories, lists, reports, and the like—according to some cohering rubric of intelligibility. Thus he will impose structural and thematic connections which unify the work and implicitly or explicitly convey his evaluation of the importance of certain events. Like other forms of historical literature in the Bible, history is inseparable from the fictive powers of an author's literary imagination (see historical story above).

The OT is unrivaled in the ancient Near East for its use of this literary genre. The earliest example may be the "court history of David" (2 Samuel 9–20; 1 Kings 1–2), if one accepts the hypothesis that this material existed independently of its present literary context (see discussion and bibliography at 1 Kings 1–2). Surer examples would be the entire book of Kings and its larger context, the Dtr History Work (Deuteronomy through Kings), if one takes the position of Martin Noth (see full discussion in ch. 1, "Introduction to 1 Kings"). Later Israelite examples would be 1–2 Chronicles (possibly with the addition of Ezra and Nehemiah), and the books of Maccabees.

A particular kind of history writing which is concerned to record events of an individual's life over its duration is BIOGRAPHY (Misch). While the author may give his subject heroic or legendary proportions (→ heroic saga; legend), his composition is ruled by the narration of events in the chronology of a life. The OT offers no examples of genuine biography, although scholars from time to time have incorrectly used the word (e.g., Baltzer). It is doubtful, too, if the designation is suitable to those Egyptian commemorative inscriptions sometimes called royal biography (e.g., Lichtheim).

Finally, we mention the historical MEMOIR, a written first-person account which records incidents in the life of an individual without being a complete biography. The intent is to write about an individual's times, rather than narrate the history of that individual's life. Clear OT examples may be seen in the books of Ezra and Nehemiah (Mowinckel, *Studien;* von Rad, "Nehemia"). Various other texts have been supposed to be memoirs, such as Isaiah 6 (Knierim), but less appropriately.

History is clearly associated with the written, record-keeping functions of the state. In general, we may suppose that in Israel history would have been conceived and composed among those scribes whose business it was to record the affairs of the royal court. Of course, particular examples of a history work, such as the books of Chronicles, or 1–2 Kings, would have their setting in a particular time and place. In general, the writer of history would intend to document, reflect, and organize the past in relation to a particular subject or time period in order to understand, legitimate, or define in some way the institutional and social reality of the author's own time.

I Kings

CHAPTER 1
INTRODUCTION TO 1 KINGS

BIBLIOGRAPHY

P. R. Ackroyd, "Kings, I and II," *IDBSup;* R. Bach, "Deuteronomistisches Geschichtswerk," *RGG*³; G. A. Barton, "Kings, Books of," *Jewish Encyclopedia* VII (New York: Funk & Wagnalls, 1904) 503-7; I. Benzinger, *Jahwist und Elohist in den Königsbüchern* (BWANT 27; Berlin: Kohlhammer, 1921); U. Bergmann, "Rettung und Befreiung—Erzählungen und Berichte aus Exodus bis 2. Könige" (Diss., Heidelberg, 1969); A. van der Born, *Koningen* (De Boeken van het Oude Testament; Roermond en Maaseik: Romen, 1958); C. F. Burney, *Notes on the Hebrew Text of the Book of Kings* (Oxford: Oxford University, 1903; repr. New York: KTAV, 1970); B. S. Childs, *Introduction to the Old Testament as Scripture* (Philadelphia: Fortress, 1979) 281-301; F. M. Cross, Jr., "The Structure of the Deuteronomic History," in *Perspectives in Jewish Learning* III (Chicago: Spertus College, 1967) 9-24; idem, "The Themes of the Book of Kings and the Structure of the Deuteronomistic History," in *Canaanite Myth and Hebrew Epic* (Cambridge: Harvard, 1973) 274-89; W. Dietrich, *Prophetie und Geschichte. Eine redaktionsgeschichtliche Untersuchung zum deuteronomistischen Geschichtswerk* (FRLANT 108; Göttingen: Vandenhoeck & Ruprecht, 1972); O. Eissfeldt, *Geschichtsschreibung im Alten Testament* (Berlin: Evangelische Verlagsanstalt, 1948); idem, *The Old Testament: An Introduction* (tr. P. R. Ackroyd; New York: Harper & Row, 1965) 281-301; idem, "Die Bücher der Könige," *HSAT* I (Tübingen: Mohr, 1922) 492-585; J. Fichtner, *Das Erste Buch von den Königen* (Botschaft des Alten Testaments 12/1; Stuttgart: Calwer, 1964); G. Fohrer, *Introduction to the Old Testament* (tr. D. Green; Nashville: Abingdon, 1965) 227-37; K. D. Fricke, *Das zweite Buch von den Königen* (Botschaft des Alten Testaments 12/2; Stuttgart: Calwer, 1972); D. N. Freedman, "Deuteronomic History," *IDBSup;* R. E. Friedman, *The Exile and Biblical Narrative: The Formation of the Deuteronomistic and Priestly Works* (HSM 22; Chico: Scholars Press, 1981); idem, "From Egypt to Egypt: Dtr¹ and Dtr²," in *Traditions in Transformation* (*Fest.* F. M. Cross; ed. B. A. Halpern and J. D. Levenson; Winona Lake, Ind.: Eisenbrauns, 1981) 167-92; C. van Gelderen, *De Boeken der Koningen* (4 vols.; Korteverklaring der Heilige Schrift; Kampen: Kok, 1936-47); J. Gray, *I & II Kings. A Commentary* (2nd rev. ed.; OTL; Philadelphia: Westminster, 1970); A. K. Grayson, "Histories and Historians of the Ancient Near East: Assyria and Babylonia," *Or* 49 (1980) 140-94; H. Gressmann, *Die älteste Geschichtsschreibung und Prophetie Israels* (Göttingen: Vandenhoeck & Ruprecht, 1921); H.-D. Hoffmann, *Reform und Reformen: Untersuchungen zu einem Grundthema der deuteronomistischen Geschichtsschreibung* (ATANT 66; Zurich: Theologischer Verlag, 1980); H. A. Hoffner, Jr., "Histories and Historians of the Ancient Near East: The Hittites," *Or* 49 (1980) 283-332; G. Hölscher, "Das Buch der Könige, seine Quellen und seine Redaktion," in *Eucharisterion* I (*Fest.*

H. Gunkel; ed. H. Schmidt; FRLANT NF 19; Göttingen: Vandenhoeck & Ruprecht, 1923) 158-213; idem, *Die Anfänge der Hebräischen Geschichtsschreibung* (Sitzungsberichte der Heidelberger Akademie der Wissenschaften; Heidelberg, 1942); J. Hoppe, "The Book of Kings and the Future," *The Bible Today* 18 (1980) 311-15; E. Jenni, "Zwei Jahrzehnte Forschung an den Büchern Josua bis Könige," *TRu* 27 (1961) 1-34, 97-146; A. Jepsen, *Die Quellen des Königsbuches* (2nd ed.; Halle: Niemeyer, 1956); Z. Kallai, "Judah and Israel—A Study in Israelite Historiography," *IEJ* 28 (1978) 251-61; D. A. Kister, "Prophetic Forms in Samuel and Kings," *Science et Esprit* 22 (1970) 341-60; R. Kittel, *Die Bücher der Könige* (HKAT I/5; Göttingen: Vandenhoeck & Ruprecht, 1900); R. W. Klein, *Israel in Exile: A Theological Interpretation* (Philadelphia: Fortress, 1979) 23-43; K. Koch, "Das Profetenschweigen des deuteronomistischen Geschichtswerks," in *Die Botschaft und die Boten* (*Fest.* H. W. Wolff; ed. J. Jeremias and L. Perlitt; Neukirchen: Neukirchener, 1981) 115-28; A. Kuenen, *Historisch-kritische Einleitung in die Bücher des Alten Testaments* (3 vols.; 2nd ed.; Leipzig: Schulze, 1887-94); S. Landersdorfer, *Die Bücher der Könige* (Die Heilige Schrift des Alten Testaments [ed. F. Feldmann] III/2; Bonn: Hanstein, 1927); W. S. LaSor, "1 and 2 Kings," in *New Bible Commentary* (ed. D. Guthrie et al.; 3rd rev. ed.; Grand Rapids: Eerdmans, 1970) 320-68; J. Liver, "The Book of the Acts of Solomon," *Bib* 48 (1967) 75-101; N. Lohfink, "Bilanz nach der Katastrophe: Das deuteronomistische Geschichtswerk," in *Wort und Botschaft* (ed. J. Schreiner; Würzburg: 1967) 196-208; idem, "Kerygmata des deuteronomistischen Geschichtswerks," *Die Botschaft und die Boten* (*Fest.* H. W. Wolff; ed. J. Jeremias and L. Perlitt; Neukirchen: Neukirchener, 1981) 87-100; E. M. Maly, "1 and 2 Kings," *The Bible Today* 18 (1980) 295-302; J. Mauchline, "I and II Kings," in *Peake's Commentary on the Bible* (ed. M. Black and H. H. Rowley; New York: T. Nelson, 1962) 338-56; D. J. McCarthy, "*Běrît* and Covenant in the Deuteronomistic History," in *Studies in the Religion of Ancient Israel* (VTSup 23; Leiden: Brill, 1972) 65-85; idem, "The Wrath of Yahweh and the Structural Unity of the Deuteronomistic History," in *Essays in Old Testament Ethics* (*Fest.* J. P. Hyatt; ed. J. L. Crenshaw and J. T. Willis; New York: KTAV, 1974) 99-107; I. Meyer, *Gedeutete Vergangenheit. Die Bücher der Könige. Die Bücher der Chronik* (Stuttgarter Kleiner Kommentar, AT 7; Stuttgart: KBW, 1976); J. A. Montgomery, "Archival Data in the Book of Kings," *JBL* 53 (1934) 46-52; idem, *A Critical and Exegetical Commentary on the Books of Kings* (ICC; Edinburgh: T. & T. Clark, 1951); G. Morawe, "Studien zum Aufbau der Neubabylonischen Chroniken in ihrer Beziehung zu den chronologischen Notizen der Königsbücher," *EvT* 26 (1966) 308-20; R. D. Nelson, *The Double Redaction of the Deuteronomistic History* (JSOTSup 18; Sheffield: University of Sheffield, 1981); M. Noth, *The Deuteronomistic History* (tr. J. Douall et al.; JSOTSup 15; Sheffield: University of Sheffield, 1981); idem, *Könige* I (BKAT 9/1; Neukirchen-Vluyn: Neukirchener, 1964-68); O. Plöger, "Die Prophetengeschichten der Samuel- und Königsbücher" (Diss., Greifswald, 1937); idem, "Reden und Gebete im deuteronomistischen und chronistischen Geschichtswerk," in *Festschrift für Günther Dehn* (ed. W. Schneemelcher; Neukirchen: Erziehungsverein, 1957) 35-49; G. von Rad, "The Deuteronomic Theology of History in I and II Kings," in *The Problem of the Hexateuch and other Essays* (tr. E. W. Trueman Dicken; New York: McGraw-Hill, 1966) 205-21; T. Radday, "Chiasm in Kings," *Linguistica Biblica* 31 (1974) 52-67; A. N. Radjawane, "Das deuteronomistische Geschichtswerk. Ein Forschungsbericht," *TRu* 38 (1974) 177-216; M. Rehm, *Das erste Buch der Könige. Ein Kommentar* (Würzburg: Echter, 1979); J. Robinson, *The First Book of Kings* (Cambridge Bible Commentary; Cambridge: Cambridge University, 1972); A. Šanda, *Die Bücher der Könige* (2 vols.; Exegetisches Handbuch zum Alten Testament; Münster: Aschendorff, 1911-12); G. Sauer, "Die chronologischen Angaben in den Büchern Deut.

bis 2 Könige," *TZ* 24 (1968) 1-14; T. P. Schehr, "The Book of Kings: A Lesson to be Learned," *The Bible Today* 18 (1980) 303-9; H. Schulte, *Die Entstehung der Geschichtsschreibung im Alten Israel* (BZAW 128; Berlin: W. de Gruyter, 1972); J. Schüpphaus, "Richter- und Prophetengeschichten als Glieder der Geschichtsdarstellung der Richter- und Königszeit" (Diss., Bonn, 1967); John Van Seters, *In Search of History: Historiography in the Ancient World and the Origins of Biblical History* (New Haven: Yale, 1983); idem, "Histories and Historians of the Ancient Near East: The Israelites," *Or* 50 (1981) 137-85; I. W. Slotki, *Kings* (Soncino Books of the Bible; London: Soncino, 1950); R. Smend, *Die Entstehung des Alten Testaments* (Stuttgart: Kohlhammer, 1978) 110-25; idem, "Das Gesetz und die Völker. Ein Beitrag zur deuteronomistischen Redaktionsgeschichte," in *Probleme Biblischer Theologie* (*Fest.* G. von Rad; ed. H. Wolff; Munich: Kaiser, 1971) 494-509; N. H. Snaith, "The First and Second Books of Kings," *IB*; J. A. Soggin, "Deuteronomistische Geschichtsauslegung während des babylonischen Exils," *Oikonomia* (*Fest.* O. Cullmann; ed. F. Christ; Hamburg: Herbert Reich, 1966) 11-17; idem, "Der Entstehungsort des deuteronomistischen Geschichtswerkes," *TLZ* 99 (1975) 3-8; S. Szikszai, "Kings, I and II," *IDB;* T. Veijola, *Das Königtum in der Beurteilung der deuteronomistischen Historiographie* (Helsinki: Suomalainen Tiedeakatemia, 1977); M. Weinfeld, *Deuteronomy and the Deuteronomic School* (Oxford: Clarendon, 1972); H. Weippert, "Die 'deuteronomistischen' Beurteilungen der Könige von Israel und Juda und das Problem der Redaktion der Königsbücher," *Bib* 53 (1972) 301-39; J. Wellhausen, *Die Composition des Hexateuchs und der historischen Bücher des Alten Testaments* (3rd ed.; Berlin, 1899) 263-301; H. W. Wolff, "The Kerygma of the Deuteronomic Historical Work," in W. Brueggemann and H. W. Wolff, *The Vitality of Old Testament Traditions* (Atlanta: John Knox, 1975) 83-100; E. Würthwein, *Die Bücher der Könige. 1 Könige 1–16* (ATD 11; Göttingen: Vandenhoeck & Ruprecht, 1977).

Structure

I. The end of David's reign and the beginning of the Solomonic era	1:1–2:46
II. The reign of Solomon	3:1–11:43
A. Account of the kingdom (internal)	3:1–9:25
B. Account of the kingdom (external)	9:26–10:29
C. The end of Solomon's reign: judgment	11:1-43
III. Synchronistic account of a divided kingdom	12:1–22:54 (*RSV* 53)
A. The reign of Jeroboam	12:1–14:20
1. Jeroboam becomes king	12:1-24
2. Building activities	12:25-32
3. Judgment against Jeroboam	12:33–14:18
4. End of Jeroboam's reign	14:19-20
B. The reign of Rehoboam	14:21-31
C. The northern kingdom from the end of Jeroboam to the rise of Omri	15:1–16:28
1. Dissolution of the house of Jeroboam	15:1–16:7
a. Reign of Abijam (war)	15:1-8
b. Reign of Asa (war)	9-24

c. Reign of Nadab (Baasha destroys Jeroboam's house)	25-32
d. Reign of Baasha (judgment against Baasha)	15:33–16:7
2. Turmoil in the northern kingdom	16:8-28
a. Reign of Elah (throne conspiracy)	8-14
b. Reign of Zimri (civil war)	15-20
c. Note on civil war and the rise of Omri	21-22
d. Reign of Omri	23-28
D. The reign of Ahab	16:29–22:40
1. Introductory summary	16:29-33
2. Incidents in the reign	16:34–22:38
a. Building of Jericho	16:34
b. Triumph of Elijah against Ahab	17:1–19:21
c. Judgment on Ahab	20:1–21:29
1) Concerning wars with Syria	20:1-43
2) Concerning the murder of Naboth	21:1-29
d. The death of Ahab	22:1-38
3. Concluding summary	22:39-40
E. The reign of Jehoshaphat	22:41-51 (*RSV* 41-50)
F. The reign of Ahaziah: introduction	22:52-54 (*RSV* 51-53)

As a matter of convenience and custom this commentary separates the books of Kings into two divisions and considers both apart from 1–2 Samuel. Obviously the coverage of Ahaziah's reign (1 Kgs 22:52–2 Kgs 1:18) is artificially broken by such a division. Just as clearly, the books of Kings continue the account of David begun in 2 Samuel. The Talmud recognized a distinction of some sort between Samuel and Kings but implied no sharp division in the text (*b. B. Bat.* 14b-15a). The split into four of what may have been originally read as one (Samuel + Kings) may be seen in its earliest form in the Greek translators (followed by the Latin), who nonetheless implied a conceptual unity by referring to Samuel and Kings as 1–4 *Basileiai,* the four "kingdoms" or "reigns." Thus, any discussion of 1–2 Kings alone, and 1 Kings apart from 2 Kings, is bound to be incomplete and inadequate. We must have in mind at all times the larger context.

Turning away from this traditional sense of canonical unity, a long procession of modern scholars has understood the present books of Kings as a preexilic history of the monarchy revised in the light of the Judean exile, after 587 B.C. Beginning with Abraham Kuenen (I, 88-100), and reflected in standard works (e.g., Wellhausen; Barton), this "double redaction" hypothesis in various forms appeared in early twentieth-century commentaries (e.g., Kittel; Burney; Šanda) and survives in recent reference works (Fohrer, 235-36; Pfeiffer, 377-95).

Martin Noth (*Deuteronomistic History;* cf. *Könige* I) decisively altered modern discussions by emphasizing the essential unity not only of Kings, but of a larger body of material with which it is connected in style and theme. He argued that a single exilic author, using diverse older traditions, created a work of theological "history" from Deuteronomy through 2 Kings and unified it under the aspect of ideas reflected in, and derived from, the book of Deuteronomy. This "Deuteronomistic Historian" (DtrH) repeatedly emphasized the central Jerusalem cultus, saw prophecy fulfilled in human events, and illustrated divine justice: reward for the faithful and punishment for the miscreant. He unflinchingly condemned idolatry and the failure of Israel's kings to rule faithfully in God's stead. He forged a literary unity with the help of epitomizing digressions in the narrative (e.g., Joshua 12; Judg 2:11–3:6; 2 Kgs 17:7-23), grand speeches by leaders at pivotal moments (e.g., Josh 1:2-9; 23:2-16; 1 Samuel 12; 2 Samuel 7; 1 Kgs 8:14-61), and a schematic chronology of 480 years running from Moses to the building of Solomon's temple (1 Kgs 6:1). For Noth, the book of Joshua presented the occupation of the land as a success story following *obedience* to Yahweh, or, in short, receiving the blessings outlined in Deut 28:1-14. The books of Judges, Samuel, and Kings in turn showed the disastrous consequences of *disobedience,* the curses set forth in Deut 28:15-68. The DtrH made the books of Kings focus on a God-given vice-regency (cf. 2 Samuel 7; 23:1-7; 1 Kgs 2:1-4) and traced its decline from the heights of David-Solomon to the disgraceful exile of the last remaining scion of David's house (cf. 1 Kgs 7:13-50 with 2 Kgs 25:8-17). The tragedy was rooted in the kings' infidelity to Yahweh. All northern kings (Israelite) the deuteronomic author condemned for mimicking Jeroboam's non-Jerusalemite ways (cf. 1 Kgs 12:25-32); the kings of Judah, save for David, Josiah, and Hezekiah, are castigated for their tolerance of idolatry and forms of Yahwism not centered at Jerusalem (see Noth, *Deuteronomistic History,* 4-25).

Since the work of Noth, modern scholars fall roughly into three camps: those who reject his hypothesis, or take no note of it, and persist in a double-redaction theory for 1–2 Kings (e.g., Szikszai); those who basically accept Noth's argument but refine its literary and theological insights (e.g., Plöger; von Rad; Wolff); those who accept the notion of a Dtr history work but see evidence of double (e.g., Gray; Friedman; Freedman; Cross; Nelson) or even multiple redactions before and after the exile (e.g., Weippert; Dietrich; Smend, *Entstehung;* Würthwein). Van Seters ("Histories and Historians") offers an innovative initiative by postulating an exilic DtrH (as does Noth) who, for the first time, composed a history of the reigns, including the first connected portrayal of Saul's and David's rise to power (unlike Noth and most others, who supposed that these materials were composed during the days of David or Solomon). A postexilic writer supplemented the Dtr history with a "Court History of David" (2 Samuel 9–20 + 1 Kings 1–2), again contrary to recent scholarly consensus which dates this material to the early monarchy. The view of Jepsen that 1–2 Kings resulted mainly from the expansion of a synchronistic chronicle during the exile has not found much following.

The ambiguous evidence, not to mention the problems associated with the Greek versions of Kings, seems to prohibit certainty in these matters. Decisions essentially turn on a subjective judgment: the degree to which one is satisfied that a given hypothesis explains the literary facts. Are the differences in the books of Joshua through Kings best explained by differences in the sources utilized by an author-editor(s)? Or are these differences best accounted for by envisioning a series of independent editions? Ackroyd (p. 517) is appropriately cautious.

Yet, there are good reasons to doubt those who argue for multiple redactions, either of the books of Kings or of the entire Dtr history work. First, there are some inherent weaknesses in their arguments. The evidential base is often very narrow. For example, Weippert argues for several redactions on the basis of minor variations in the formulas used to evaluate the kings (e.g., 1 Kgs 14:22-24; 15:3-4; 15:26). Dietrich constructs hypotheses of several Dtr editors on little more than stylistic preferences and presumed differences of emphasis (cf. Veijola; Lohfink, "Bilanz"). Moreover, so equivocal is some of the evidence that scholars have drawn contradictory, but in themselves plausible, inferences. Nelson (pp. 23-27) exposes this problem very thoroughly. Following Cross ("Structure" and "Themes"; cf. Freedman; Friedman), Nelson tries to establish a double-redaction theory on what he takes to be stronger structural and thematic grounds. The result, however, is the sort of intricate criticism of sources and redaction that has led in the past to little or no consensus among scholars. It proves difficult to avoid circularity of argument and speculations about what an author or editor would or would not have done. One hardly nullifies the lack of consensus on disputed passages, such as 1 Kgs 8:14-61 or 2 Kings 17, by offering yet another analysis (see Nelson, 69-73, 55-65). Indeed, Nelson's work illustrates a more general problem: even while agreeing in principle, the advocates of multiple redactions have not achieved consensus on how to apportion the materials of 1–2 Kings among the various redactors. The literary facts prove intractable to the usual methods which deny redundancy, digression, or multiple viewpoints to an ancient author.

Nor do these scholars agree upon a date for the preexilic edition, and consequently they are unable to agree where it ended. The choices remain rather different—Josiah (some say before, some after, his death), Jehoiakim, or Zedekiah. As if all this disagreement were not unsettling enough, early in the debates, Šanda (pp. xxxvi-xlii) argued cogently—if one grants his starting point—that the primary edition of 1–2 Kings was written in exile shortly after 587 B.C., and that the second redaction really amounted to little more than minor supplements and comments here and there. There are hardly two "editions," and in any case, nothing preexilic except the sources used by the exilic author. In the face of such disagreements among the defenders of multiple redactions, one may be forgiven the suggestion that fine-tuning the approach is an unpromising venture.

A fundamental misunderstanding adds to the inherent weaknesses in arguments for multiple redactions. Often one reads that a preexilic DtrH's belief in the eternal dynasty of David (2 Sam 7:11b-16; cf. 1 Kgs 11:34-36; 15:3-4) had to be softened, made conditional upon obedience, by a second hand under the press of Judah's historical demise. One assumes therefore that Nathan's promise to David was actually understood as something absolute, to be eternally realized in every historical moment (see Friedman, *Exile,* 3-5; Nelson, 105-18; Cross, "Themes"). Yet, the very same passage which initially sets forth this paradigm of Davidic legitimacy has David understand this promise of a throne "forever" (*'ad 'ôlām*) considerably less grandly: Yahweh is simply speaking of David's house (= dynasty) "for a long time to come" (*lĕmērāḥôq,* 2 Sam 7:19). This language of royal legitimation is traditional, stereotyped, and rooted in the literary styles of ancient Near Eastern monarchies: royal grants, decrees, and treaties (Weinfeld, 74-81). Such documents all have to do with establishing temporal authority—often denied and contested of course, despite exalted claims. Deut 18:5 attempts to legitimate the Levites' priestly authority in perpetuity by claiming divine appointment "forever," literally for "all the days" (*kol-hayyāmîm,* a phrase which is parallel to *'ad 'ôlām* in respect to the Davidic promise in 1 Kgs 9:3). 1 Sam 2:30-36 is similar. It purports to supplant an earlier oracle which legitimated the Elides "forever" (*'ad 'ôlām,* v. 30) by a later divine word appointing a rival priestly dynasty to serve before Yahweh "forever" (*kol-hayyāmîm*, v. 35). Exactly the same hyperbole accompanies a person's appointment to position in the royal entourage (*kol-hayyāmîm,* 1 Sam 28:2; 2 Sam 19:14 [*RSV* 13]; cf. Jer 35:18-19). Clearly this manner of speaking was not and should not be taken literally. The language of legitimation presupposes a social reality in which legitimacy was arguable and ideology both adjustable and transferable. It is a mistake to take the promise to David as having been understood in its world as literally "eternal," for this assumes a denotive meaning for the language that is inappropriate to the social context in which it functioned.

Besides these problems inherent in the arguments for multiple redactions of the Dtr history, there are troubling assumptions which need to be challenged. First, a work by an ancient author will be rounded and unified by a climactic conclusion. Friedman states most clearly what others simply take for granted: "This first edition of the Deuteronomistic history (Dtr[1]) *properly* climaxed in its conclusion the reform of the Davidic Josiah according to the instruction of Moses" (Friedman, *Exile,* 10; emphasis mine). In a similar spirit, Noel Freedman wrote that 2 Kings 22–23 made a "happy climax" to the first edition of the Dtr history. The original ending is to be found in 2 Kgs 23:25 + 28 since v. 26 (assuming two redactions) is a "pathetic attempt at reinterpretation" (Freedman, *IDB* 3, 716-17).

Underlying this expectation of ending climax is a second assumption: an ancient author will relate all his materials to that climactic point. Again, Friedman states forthrightly what others leave unspoken: "Josiah is the figure to whom the Deuteronomistic presentation of history is *building*" (Friedman, *Exile,* 7; emphasis mine). He looks for a dramatic sweep toward a thematic height, as one finds in a short story. One understands parts of a narrative in relation to its climax. *Subordination* is the key word and seems to indicate unified authorial vision.

A third assumption commonly made is that a prose work will end with a density of content and theme as befits a richly developed beginning or midpoint. Thus, Cross ("Structure," 17-18) suspects that the vagueness in prophetic fulfillment reported after Josiah's death (2 Kgs 21:10-15 and 24:2) indicates a second editor at work. Similarly, Nelson (pp. 37-38) observes that the post-Josiah theological appraisals of the kings are "strikingly shorter" than earlier notes and show a "rubber-stamp" adherence to formula suggestive of "the woodenly imitative work of some supplementary editor, not the creative and free variation of the original author." Friedman (*Exile,* 6) notes that the last four Judean kings are not connected with the continuation of high places (*bāmôt*). The explanation? A second editor's simplified writing.

Finally, those who argue for multiple redactions of the Dtr history work share a commonly assumed model for recensional development: additions, interpolations, supplements at the end, are operations performed on what is essentially a fixed document, not subject to much, if any, rewriting. The result of these operations, of course, is to produce a *longer* document, and one that is *less consistent* internally, thereby one which retains the clues of multiple redactions that biblical scholars seek.

All these assumptions are based on little more than modern cultural preferences and literary tastes. Nowhere does one find examples of ancient historiographical writings being used to support these points of view. In fact, what we are able to see in the Near East suggests something quite different. Take recension making. There are examples of certain ancient Near Eastern texts having been transmitted over many centuries with extreme fidelity to a received tradition (W. H. Hallo, "Genesis and Ancient Near Eastern Literature," in *The Torah: A Modern Commentary* [New York: Union of American Hebrew Congregations, 1981] 8-9). There are also cases of "adaptation and reediting on a scale which defies prediction" (Hallo, ibid., 9; see J. Tigay, "The Stylistic Criteria of Source Criticism in the Light of Ancient Near Eastern Literature," forthcoming in *Fest. I. L. Seeligmann*). For example, the original "after the flood" Sumerian King List was apparently supplemented at some point with an antediluvian prologue which carried the ideological basis of kingship back into primordial times (*ANET,* 265-66; T. Jacobsen, *The Sumerian King List* [Chicago: University of Chicago, 1939] 55-64; J. J. Finkelstein, "The Antediluvian Kings," *JCS* 17 [1963] 39-51). Of specific relevance to Israelite historiography, however, is the evidence that Assyrian scribes periodically rewrote royal inscriptions, a primary type of history writing, to update the accomplishments of the king. The few available studies suggest a variety of techniques: abbreviation, paraphrase, deletion, interpolation, harmonization, often complete rewriting (H. Tadmor, "Observations on Assyrian Historiography," in *Ancient Near Eastern Studies in Memory of J. J. Finkelstein* [ed. Maria de Jong Ellis; Memoirs of the Conn. Academy of Arts and Sciences 19; Hamden, Ct.: Archon, 1977] 209-10). Study of one case in which this sort of activity could be directly observed in texts spanning a quarter-century showed just such complexity. The scribe(s) who wrote the final edition even abbreviated earlier material in the desire to update the king's accomplishments with more recent events (M. Cogan and H. Tadmor, "Gyges and Ashurbanipal: A Study in Literary Transmission," *Or* 46 [1977] 65-85; see also L. D. Levine, "The Second Campaign of Sennacherib," *JNES* 32 [1973] 312-17). Nothing here implies minor additions and adjustments to a "text" or tradition treated in principle as unalterable. In a very short span of time, the Assyrian scribes created entirely new or thoroughly reworked old editions mainly to update the royal inscriptions, all the better to glorify the monarch. And yet, the defenders of multiple redactions of the Dtr history ask us to assume that in the space of one short generation or less, *Israelite* scribes fussed over a version of their own history which was already revered and piously protected from extensive rewriting or abbreviation. (The study of Jeffrey Tigay, "An Empirical Basis for the Documentary Hypothesis," *JBL* 94 [1975] 329-42, uncovers conflation and harmonization, along with the attempt at maximal preservation of received documents. But this picture involves documents from the very late period [Sam Pent and the proto-Samaritan Qumran fragments of the Torah] when presumably Torah was just what the Dtr history work was not: a religious document revered over many centuries.) In fact, a contrary example already exists in the OT itself: the work of the Chronicler, widely held to be a later version of the "history" of Israel, that is, essentially a recension of Samuel and Kings with additional material, some of which comes from the restoration period. In this history work one sees the time from Adam through Samuel drastically abbreviated into genealogical material (1 Chronicles 1–9), along with an account of statist Israel based on Samuel and Kings, but compressed into roughly half the space and completely ignoring most traditions of Saul and the northern kingdom. Clearly, new material is both interpolated and added, even without taking Ezra-Nehemiah as part of the composition. (See J. M. Myers, *I Chronicles* [AB 12; Garden City, N.Y.: Doubleday, 1965] XLV-LXIII.) Whether there were multiple redactions of the Chronicler's work is irrelevant. Even a postulated original version implies models of recension making more like those used by the Assyrian scribes than anything else: free rewriting, abbreviation, supplementation of Genesis–Kings in the interest of updating the earlier version, and of course serving a particular aim, the glorification of Judean David and his Yahwistic cult for the restoration period.

When considering assumptions about ancient techniques of composition, such as ending with climax or dramatic subordination of narrative elements, one stands on less firm ground. We can only reconstruct how an ancient author used sources no longer extant to create a coherent text. So far, Assyriologists have been able to discover very little good information (see H. Tadmor, "The Historical Inscriptions of Adad-Nirari III," *Iraq* 35 [1973] 141-50; Grayson, "Histories and Historians," 164-70). Of more consequence for us are recent studies of classical Greek historians, especially Herodotus and Thucydides.

Many modern classicists have moved beyond source and redaction analysis of Herodotus, *Histories,* and since perhaps mid-century have been freshening the image of Herodotus as a genuine *author* as distinct from a compiler who randomly assembled his materials.* (See the thorough critique of the older fashion by William P. Henry, *Greek Historical Writing: A Historiographical Essay based on Xenophon's Hellenica* [Chicago: Argonaut, 1967]; and the cautions toward those who see unity in Herodotus by K. von Fritz, *Die Griechische Geschichtsschreibung* I [Berlin: de Gruyter, 1967] 104-21.) The most accessible statements of the case have come from H. R. Immerwahr (*Form and Thought in Herodotus* [American Philological Association Monographs 23; Cleveland: Western Reserve University, 1966]) and Henry Wood (*The Histories of Herodotus: An Analysis of Formal Structure* [The Hague, Paris: Mouton, 1972]). Herodotus was not a clumsy compiler of tales, but an author with clarity of purpose and a literary plan. His work is above all an example of archaic *parataxis,* that is, a composition built up with individual items of varied lengths placed in series. The technique is evident at the level of sentence composition (E. Lamberts, *Studien zur Parataxe bei Herodot* [Wien: Notring, 1970]) as well as for the whole composition (Immerwahr). It is rooted in older styles of Greek composition (B. A. van Groningen, *La Composition litteraire archaïque grecque* [Amsterdam: Noord-Hollandsche Uitgevers Maatschappij, 1958] 387-91). Paratactic style helps explain the ending of *Histories,* commonly felt as abrupt and unexpectedly thin, giving rise to questions of whether Herodotus even finished the work. Yet, according to Immerwahr and others, Herodotus carefully connected traditions with one another, preserved the multiplicity of factors in each account while stressing one point or another, and suggested connections to other portions of his work. Sometimes, for example, he

*I owe John van Seters the credit for first alerting me to this situation in conversations and through kind permission to look at some of his unpublished materials.

used a simple connective particle, or repeated a word or phrase to summarize certain aspects of the preceding item; or he bridged the end of one tradition to the beginning of the next with a repeated motif. Frequently, Herodotus shaped his material similarly to Homeric "ring" composition: introductory and concluding words or phrases form an integrative bracket while lifting up themes of importance for understanding larger units (see also Ingrid Beck, *Die Ringkomposition bei Herodot und ihre Bedeutung für die Beweistechnik* [Hildesheim/New York: Olms, 1971]). Moreover, Herodotus often filled the spaces between individual items in his "chain" with short remarks, a brief story, or even long digressions containing matters of great theoretical importance to the work (Immerwahr, 1-15, 46-72; see J. Cobet, *Herodots Exkurse und die Frage nach der Einheit seines Werkes* [Steiner: Wiesbaden, 1971]). Yet these elements of external connection were matched by regular emphasis upon repetition, anticipation, and summary, all of which add up to a system of cross references that ties the work together (Immerwahr, 67). Herodotus also schematized events into literary patterns: how a ruler rose to power, ruled, and fell, or how military campaigns were fought (Immerwahr, 68, 72-78).

Since these structural devices characterize a paratactic document, the fundamental principle of organization is neither chronological nor dramatic (rising toward a climax). It is analogical. Herodotus brings together what may seem to be disparate materials, arranges them in ways which are not necessarily pleasing to modern tastes, but thereby forces the reader to see analogous connections between events. Which is to say, Herodotus gives us his idea of the main theme of a historical period (Wood, 17-19).

Besides these techniques for building structural unity, Herodotus also established thematic patterns to unify his work. He analyzed human events into thought and action (the full literary pattern is counsel, decision, and action), or sometimes, nonreflective passion and action. Related is the correspondence he saw between warning and event. Prophecies, omens, and warnings point to necessary actions, and when ignored, disaster inevitably follows.

What finally makes Herodotus a historian and author rather than compiler is that he stretched to see a movement with sense and direction, if not purpose, in the events he described. For him, history was finally theodicy. Herodotus did not burden his work with morals and theological judgments—in this he differs from the OT—but he nevertheless looked to a larger context in which the tragic fate of individuals and nations were mechanisms for perpetuating world order, something guaranteed and jealously protected by the gods (Immerwahr, 313).

It is not difficult to see that these studies of Herodotus and other Greek historians legitimate a mode of composition which on first sight strikes a modern reader as distastefully unfinished. The key is to allow parataxis its due as a conscious literary technique in the ancient world—a way of stringing together materials of diverse age, origin, length, literary genre, and sophistication. Parataxis is clearly an alternative to source-critical and redaction-historical explanations for the literary phenomena before us. At the very least, the example of Herodotus, even though from the 5th century B.C., ought to give biblical scholars pause before they emphasize *dis*unity in the OT historiographical works (see Van Seters, *In Search of History*). Indeed, as will be apparent from the discussion which follows, there is much in Herodotus which seems similar to the biblical styles of composition. This being the case, there is no *necessary* reason to accept the multiple-redaction approaches to 1–2 Kings (and the Dtr history), and some additional justification for doubting them. An archaic work need not end with a flourish or an epilogue, just as the original books of Kings and the postulated conclusion to the Dtr history need not have ended other than they do—simply, abruptly, at the close of the chain of events. An ancient author need not arrange his materials according to dramatic models, a story sweeping to thematic climax, especially at its end, just as a DtrH need not have originally gathered his account into a blaze of encomium for King Josiah. An archaic work may by custom have begun richly and ended simply, just as the Dtr history may have opened with the complexities of Deuteronomy and the foreshadowings of kings but then have become increasingly abbreviated toward the conclusion.

It will come as no surprise to the reader, then, that we incline toward the assumption that 1–2 Kings, and the Dtr history, were composed by one person and remain essentially a unified work. Admittedly, this way of speaking presents a mental construct of "author" and a postulate—like its opposite—which can be convincing only as far as it is consistent with what we know of ancient modes of composition and with the literary facts of the Bible. Of course, we do not know who the "author" was, or where he wrote. And one may not rule out a few interpolations here and there from a time when the biblical text would have been more fixed than it is likely to have been early on (e.g., 2 Kgs 17:34-41). The imaginary "author," however, helps us focus on these books of Kings in their present form, a sensible procedure given the doubts expressed above and the lack of agreement among those who advocate multiple redactions.

At the very least 1–2 Kings must be seen as part of a fivefold recounting of the monarchy in ancient Israel:

1. Saul and David	1 Sam 7:15–2 Sam 4:12
2. David (Solomon)	2 Sam 5:1–1 Kgs 2:12a
3. Solomon	1 Kgs 2:12b–11:43
4. Divided kingdom to the destruction of Israel in the north	1 Kings 12–2 Kings 17
5. Judah in the south to its destruction	2 Kings 18–25

More specifically, 1 Kings shows us the transition from David to Solomon (I, 1:1–2:46), the glorious reign of Solomon (II, 3:1–11:43), and a large portion of synchronistically reckoned history in the divided kingdom, but with the principal focus on the north (III, 12:1–22:54). If one looks for narrative plot, one might say that the rather actionless picture of Solomon's grandeur (chs. 3–10) gains contrast by the headlong rush to destruction precipitated in his private failings (ch. 11), and carried forward in the perfidy of his successors, especially in the north (chs. 12–22). It remains for 2 Kings to carry the line to its end: the demise of the north and the soon-to-follow destruction of the south. The north perished because of Jeroboam (2 Kgs 17:21-22, 16; 1 Kgs 12:26-32; 14:10-11; 2 Kgs 10:28-31); the south because of Manasseh, a descendant of David who took on Jeroboam's guilt (2 Kgs 21:3; 1 Kgs 16:31) and so became, for the south, the patriarch of infamy (2 Kgs 21:20; 23:26, 37; 24:9, 19).

The distinctive literary feature of 1–2 Kings is the regular use of a stereotyped framework (→ regnal resumé) to introduce and conclude the material presented for a particular king's reign. Typically, we see:

A. *Introductory framework*
   1. Royal name and accession date (synchronistic when divided kingdom is in view)
   2. King's age at accession (Judah only)
   3. Length and place of reign
   4. Name of queen mother (Judah only)
   5. Theological appraisal

B. *Events during the reign*
   (materials of diverse source, length, and literary type)

C. *Concluding framework*
   1. Formula citing other sources for regnal information
   2. Notices of death and burial
   3. Notice of a successor

For examples, see 1 Kgs 14:21-31 (Rehoboam); 15:1-8 (Abijam); 16:29–22:40 (Ahab); and full discussion at 14:21-31.

The pattern extends even to David's reign (2 Sam 5:4-5; 1 Kgs 2:10-12a). It breaks down somewhat in a few cases, where the author-editor allows unusual circumstances at accession or death to override convention (e.g., no introductory framework for Jeroboam, whose accession is prophesied [1 Kgs 11:30-39] and described [1 Kgs 12:1-20]; cf. the rise of Solomon [1 Kgs 1:1-39] and the confused king making at 2 Kgs 9:30–11:20). The result is regular coverage of the reigns in serial fashion. Where the divided monarchy is in view, each ruler at accession is synchronistically related to his counterpart in the opposite kingdom. The author thus shaped monarchical history into enclosed blocks of tradition. Our eyes move through one regnal period to the next, shuttling back and forth between north and south. The impression is clear from the chart on p. 23.

In this system, chronology is linear only in a very general sense. Actually, the author starts and finishes one reign before beginning another, regardless of how far ahead of some absolute chronology this procedure takes the reader. Consequently, the reigns overlap where a king who is as yet unknown in the onward progression of time suddenly appears as a figure in the reign of his counterpart in the north or south (e.g., Baasha in Nadab's reign, 1 Kgs 15:25-30). Time flows ahead, then back, then far ahead again, until finally the reader faces the exilic situation, presumably the period in which the author-editor wrote. Monarchical history in fact consists of discrete time periods—or under the aspect of literary content, enclosed blocks of tradition, none clearly subordinate to another, all linked with the barest of connective tissue: a repeated name (1 Kgs 11:43 + 12:1; 15:32b + 33), or the simple conjunction "and" (1 Kgs 14:21; 15:1). Sometimes the author-editor simply juxtaposes two regnal periods without an explicit bridge (2 Kgs 12:1; 14:1). The work is an extended parataxis, regnal periods arranged like links of a chain, the "story" told without a strictly linear flow of time.

Parataxis is deeply rooted in the syntax of Hebrew poetic and narrative styles (G. B. Caird, *The Language and Imagery of the Bible* [Philadelphia: West-

END OF DAVID — SOLOMON'S REIGN
1 KGS 1:1 – 11:43

Israel	**Judah**
Reign of Jeroboam 1 Kgs 12:1–14:20	*in the time of Jeroboam* 1 Kgs 14:21–15:24 Rehoboam Abijam Asa
in the time of Asa 1 Kgs 15:25–22:40 Nadab Baasha Elah Zimri Omri Ahab	*in the time of Ahab* 1 Kgs 22:41-51 (*RSV* 50) Jehoshaphat
in the time of Jehoshaphat 1 Kgs 22:52 (*RSV* 51)–2 Kgs 8:15 Ahaziah Je(ho)ram	*in the time of Je(ho)ram* 2 Kgs 8:16–9:28 Jehoram of Judah
Jehu 2 Kgs 9:30–10:36	*in the time of Jehu* 2 Kgs 11:1–12:22 (*RSV* 21) Athaliah Joash
in the time of Joash 2 Kgs 13:1-25 Jehoahaz Jehoash	*in the time of Jehoash* 2 Kgs 14:1-22 Amaziah
in the time of Amaziah 2 Kgs 14:23-29 Jeroboam II	*in the time of Jeroboam II* 2 Kgs 15:1-7 Azariah
in the time of Azariah 2 Kgs 15:8-31 Zechariah Shallum Menahem Pekahiah Pekah	*in the time of Pekah* 2 Kgs 15:32–16:20 Jotham Ahaz
in the time of Ahaz 2 Kgs 17:1-41 Hoshea	*in and after the time of Hoshea* 2 Kgs 18:1–25:30 Hezekiah Manasseh Josiah Jehoahaz Jehoiakim Jehoiachin Zedekiah
Fall of Israel	

minster, 1980]; also, Cancik, 185-91 [see listing at "Introduction to Historical Literature"]). It is evident in the way in which the author has joined independent traditions together within these regnal frameworks. Clearly some materials used by the Dtr author-editor to create an account of a particular reign flow in high dramatic style, with grand narrative climaxes (e.g., the [→] story, 1 Kgs 1:1-53, or the [→] prophetic legends, 1 Kings 17; 22; 2 Kgs 6:8–7:16). Most sources, however, appear to have been brought together, chainlike, with minimal connections.

(1) The simple particle "and" (*wĕ*), a favorite link. Examples may be selected almost at random: 1 Kgs 17:1, joining the first of the Elijah materials with the preceding notice of Jericho's rebuilding (16:34); 1 Kgs 12:1, joining the beginning of Rehoboam's reign to the stereotyped closing formulas of Solomon's reign (11:41-43); 1 Kgs 12:25, affixing the notices of Jeroboam's building projects to a preceding report of prophecy (12:21-24); cf. 2 Kgs 3:4; 8:4; 11:1; 13:22.

(2) A simple connective word, "and it happened that . . ." (*wayĕhî*); e.g., 1 Kgs 11:15, where a titlelike statement of theme (v. 14) is joined by the Dtr author to a brief report of rebellious activity (1 Kgs 11:15-22; note also the transitional repetition of a catchword, "Edom," in vv. 14 and 15); 1 Kgs 14:25; 2 Kgs 14:5, joining brief reports to the preceding (→) introductory regnal resumé, or regnal framework; 2 Kgs 2:1, which connects an independent "interlude" about Elijah and Elisha to the closing of Ahaziah's reign (2 Kgs 1:18).

(3) A simple connective phrase, "and this is the matter about . . ." (*wĕzeh haddābār* or *wĕzeh dĕbar* . . .): 1 Kgs 9:15, linking listlike materials to the preceding independent tradition about Hiram's dealings with Solomon (9:10-14); 1 Kgs 11:27, which joins a brief report of building activities to a titlelike thematic statement used by the Dtr writer to create a three-part narrative package, 11:14-22, 23-25, 26-40.

(4) Temporal particles used to create vague links:

(a) "Then" (*'āz*). Whether or not this word indicates that the author quoted directly from his sources, as Tadmor and Cogan maintain ("Ahaz and Tiglath-Pileser in the Book of Kings," *Bib* 60 [1979] 491-508; cf. Montgomery, "Archival Data"), it is clearly used to join originally independent materials in a nontemporal way, despite its usual temporal translation. For example, 2 Kgs 15:16 and 16:5 each link a report of battle to the generalized regnal framework, 2 Kgs 15:15 and 16:4. So also 1 Kgs 16:21; 2 Kgs 12:18 (*RSV* 17); 14:8. The particle also seems to be an artificial linking device in 1 Kgs 3:16; 8:1; 9:24.

(b) Adverbial phrases such as "in those (his) days" (*bayyāmîm hāhēm*), "at that time" (*bā'ēt hahî'*). Common in Assyrian royal inscriptions (Montgomery, "Archival Data"; cf. Mowinckel, "Fürsteninschriften" [see listing at "Introduction to Historical Literature"]), these phrases do not always indicate real chronological sequence. They sometimes were used by the scribe to join, and perhaps quote in so doing, two items from separate sources (Tadmor and Cogan, "Ahaz and Tiglath-Pileser," 493-97). This is probably the case at 2 Kgs 16:6 as well (cf. 1 Kgs 14:1). Elsewhere, "in those days" simply links disparate summaries of events, as in 2 Kgs 10:32. In 2 Kgs 15:37 the author simply joins a brief report to his concluding framework.

(c) A phrase such as "after this (these) matters" (*'aḥar haddĕbārîm hā'ēlleh*). This phrase joins independent traditions in 1 Kgs 17:17 and 21:1; the latter connection was further anticipated in a repeated phrase, "to his house, sullen and resentful," 20:43 and 21:4. 1 Kgs 13:33 leads into the narrator's reflecting on preceding material (see 1 Kgs 12:30, 31) and provides a link to the following independent story, the prophecy against Jeroboam (1 Kgs 14:1-18).

(5) The use of repetition. Words and phrases may be repeated almost identically in two literary pieces, apparently as a deliberate authorial association of independent accounts. One example was mentioned above: the words "to his house, sullen and resentful" (1 Kgs 20:43) anticipate the same motif in the following narrative, 1 Kgs 21:4. The reader cannot help but see the author's analogy drawn between Ahab's dealings with Syria (ch. 20) and Naboth (ch. 21). Similarly, 1 Kgs 12:33b joins to 13:1b with the anticipatory phrase "to the altar to burn incense" and thereby links two items in the chain: the Dtr author's description of Jeroboam's "sin" (1 Kgs 12:26-32) and an old legend about prophets at Bethel (1 Kgs 13:1-32).

Repetition also appears as a framework around material, like "ring composition" in the Greek literature. The phenomenon has long been noticed (C. Kuhl, "Die Wiederaufnahme—ein literarkritisches Prinzip?" *ZAW* 64 [1952] 1-11; I. L. Seeligmann, "Hebräische Erzählung und biblische Geschichtsschreibung," *TZ* 18 [1962] esp. 314-24). But it has not been properly seen as a technique of parataxis. For example, 2 Kgs 8:29 and 9:14, 16 surround a digression in which the author incorporates explanatory material into his narrative. Similarly, 1 Kgs 2:12b and 46b mark a unified account hung into the space between the formulaic death notice of David (1 Kgs 2:10-12a) and the full reign of Solomon (1 Kgs 3:1ff.). The Dtr author appends a long reflection on the fate of the northern kingdom to his standard summary of a reign (2 Kgs 17:1-6) and marks that appendage by an enveloping repetition of motifs (2 Kgs 17:6b and 23b): "and he carried Israel . . . to Assyria."

This is not the place to carry out an exhaustive analysis of these and other techniques of paratactic composition. We note many other details in the pages which follow. Suffice it to suggest that the parataxis reflected in the larger composition of 1–2 Kings is also evident in the way the Dtr author assembled the individual traditions now associated with a particular reign.

One may fairly ask, then, what conceptual unity if any was brought to parataxis? Looking at the regnal frameworks again, we observe that they emphasize *particularity*. Relative to her neighbors, Israel is distinct from the other kingdoms, for only rarely are chronological bearings taken by "Babylonian time" (e.g., 2 Kgs 24:12; 25:8, 27). Within, synchronistic reckonings come only for a king's accession year; otherwise one moves in the time of Asa, or Solomon, or Ahab, and so on, with hardly a glance elsewhere. On the other hand, the frameworks mark out analogy, and thereby introduce a level of *generality* transcending particular regnal time. One recognizes striking similarities between Israel's parade of kings and the Assyrian and Neo-Babylonian chronicles and king lists (see full discussion at 1 Kgs 14:21-31). Within, the author draws a line between Mosaic exodus and Solomonic temple (1 Kgs 6:1) and defines its length as 480 years, as though to schematize in collective memory a liminal space between Egypt and Jerusalem (see Noth, *Deuteronomistic History,* 18-25). Regnal time periods merge into a metaphor of place: the suprahistorical "Yahwistic time" flows from Egypt (Moses) to Jerusalem (Solomon's temple) to Babylon (exile).

Thus, the literary frameworks imply a hermeneutic of time, or of history, both particular and general. It is already to be found in the Dtr writer's treatment of monarchical origins in 1 Samuel 8. The desire for a king was born in impulse: to be "like the nations" (1 Sam 8:5). Yet this same envy for those outside touched Israel's inward sense of origins too, because it stirred specifically Israelite memories. Lusting for kingship meant spurning the God-king who gave the love token of exodus-freedom (1 Sam 8:7-8). In the books of Kings, the similar case is Solomon's temple—obviously like those round about, built with the help of foreigners (1 Kgs 5:16-26), but with its foundation laid in relation to that inwardly Israelite "Yahwistic time" between Moses and Solomon (1 Kgs 6:1). The dissonance is unsettling in the Dtr history work, this making of common song with ancient Near Eastern peoples, as though the soul of Israel would be lost to the charms of the alien, or particularity lost in the general. With their faces turned inward and outward, the frameworks and their litanies of native and foreign temptations give the theme a certain kind of flesh.

One may observe this same interplay between particularity and generality in other motifs associated with the regnal frameworks. Concrete information always binds a king to a time, place, and people. We learn of the place of rule which in the north shifts from time to time; the queen mother, who on occasion becomes quite important to events (e.g., 2 Kgs 11:1-20); death and place of burial; or occasionally some peculiarity (e.g., King Asa's diseased feet, 1 Kgs 15:23). On the other hand, the stereotyped theological appraisals measure every king by one rule: how well he observed and supported the primacy of Yahweh and his temple in Jerusalem—or more usually, how a king failed to live up to this trust. It is in this leveling that the specific details of a reign are obscured and nearly overridden in analogy with others. Most of the kings are typed as being like or unlike another. The writer condemns northerners for their mimicking Jeroboam and his "sin" (refusing the centrality and primacy of the Jerusalem cult), and southerners for not following the pious ways of David. Even Solomon, so lavishly, albeit indirectly, praised for his glorious offerings to God, falls short in the end (1 Kgs 11:4). And in the very latest times, the author writes off Judean kings because they did as Manasseh had done (2 Kgs 21:2-15, 20; 23:26). The effect is not simply a hiding of individuality in collective judgments. It is also a system of intricate cross references which transcend the barriers between regnal periods. The appraisals of the kings are not randomly or unthinkingly assembled in these frameworks nor are their variations symptomatic of complicated redactional history. Together with long passages which focus on the cultic actions of the various kings, these framework appraisals weave a metahistorical pattern of analogies and repetitions, a system of echoes and anticipations which unify the work at a conceptual level apart from the constraints of time and space (Hoffmann, *Reform*).

The Dtr writer has done more than make limited motival connections, however. He has treated the points in the chain at which one expects another regnal period to begin as opportunities for inserting special material—pausal moments to be filled with matters of thematic importance. Immerwahr (pp. 61-62) observed that Herodotus added short remarks, digressions, even stories in these pauses between larger units or *logoi*. In the books of Kings, most cracks between regnal frameworks are passed over silently. The author, however, fills a few: 1 Kgs 2:12b-46; 12:1-20; 15:32; 16:7, 21-22; 2 Kgs 2:1-25; 11:1-21; 13:14-25; 15:12; 17:7-41; 24:7. One sees immediately the importance of at least some of these pausal moments. In lieu of a concluding framework for Hoshea, and before opening the reign of Hezekiah, the Dtr author-editor presents a theological commentary on the fate of Israel (2 Kgs 17:7-33 [+34-41]). Carefully framed by the repeated mention of exile (2 Kgs 17:6, 23b), one part of this digression justifies the exile of Israel and sees it as a culmination of that sin of Jeroboam which courses like some systemic poison throughout the life of the northern kingdom (vv. 21-23; cf. 1 Kgs 12:26-32; 13:33-34; 14:1-18; 15:29; 16:7; 2 Kgs 9:6b-10). At the same time, the comment extends our thoughts to the not-as-yet-narrated destruction of Judah (vv. 13, 19-20). A second part reveals the persistence of just those "sins" washed away by the Assyrian invasion (vv. 24-33 [+34-41]). Whether this text is an original literary unit is unsettled. Its parts make up a well-balanced literary composition (see details in the FOTL volume on 2 Kings). Yet the important point is that each of the parts, even those which are often seen as disrupting the flow (e.g., vv. 19-20, 21-23), clearly touch larger themes in the books of Kings. The pausal moment takes us out of regnal time and drops us, omniscient, into a reflective eternity.

Another example of a filled pause between reigns is 1 Kgs 2:12b-46. Following the concluding framework for David (1 Kgs 2:10-12a) and before Solomon's essential activity begins (3:1ff.), the author provides an excursus on Solomon's "establishing the kingdom." Here there is no question of literary disunity because of the carefully framed outer limits of the whole (2:12b and 46b) and the tight internal structure which binds three episodes together (see details at 2:12b-46). Anticipating Solomon's talent for decisive achievement while recalling incidents from David's reign, the pausal moment provides transition from David to Solomon, and at the same time allows Solomon more definition as a character in the larger drama. As transition the materials stir memories of a conflict driving much of the drama in the books of Samuel: the rivalry between the Saulides and David (compare the murders of Joab and Shimei, 1 Kgs 2:28-46, with the accounts associating Joab with the Saul-David conflict, 2 Sam 3:6-30, and Shimei with the "house of Saul," 2 Sam 16:5-10). As a definition of Solomon, who after all is only slightly known to the reader from ch. 1, the Dtr writer shows us a king acting decisively, even ruthlessly, in the interest of strong rule. This image contrasts with the still-life tableau which emerges later on like a photograph materializing from its developing solution, in colors of glory, wisdom, riches, and honor (cf. 3:12-13; 10:23-25).

Two other pausal moments, 2 Kgs 2:1-25 and 13:14-25, seem closely related. First, they both involve Elisha to a great extent. Second, they form a framework around *all* the Elisha traditions in 2 Kings (only one brief report, 1 Kgs 19:19-21, stands outside these boundaries). In the first passage, Elisha receives prophetic power; in the second, we read of his last deed of power and his death. In between, the narrator variously includes Elisha at the center or on the boundaries of the decisive action. In the final pause between reigns, we move away from Elisha to hear ominous tones sounded in the midst of divine protection: the inevitable end of the kingdoms is forestalled for a time, but in the full knowledge of what that end amounted to: "and he [Yahweh] did not destroy them, until now" (2 Kgs 13:23).

One should not claim that all material "between the reigns" is of similar consequence to the whole Dtr composition. Yet, about half of the pauses suggest an author who uses these moments to express the *logos* of events, those inner relationships among happenings which characterize a monarch, regnal period, dynasty, and by extension epitomize a whole monarchical history.

The Dtr author has created other lines of conceptual unity as well. Some of the most important may be glimpsed in the reigns of three monarchs: Solomon, Jeroboam, and Ahab, the three who account for nearly all the material in 1 Kings. As we shall see, David, who hardly appears in 1–2 Kings, is also crucial.

Jeroboam stands in a mediating position. With his rule, we move through a sequence reminiscent of Solomon, whom we have just left behind: (1) circumstances of his unusual rise to power (12:1-20; cf. 1:1–2:46); (2) building of cities and cultic centers (12:26-32; cf. 5:15–9:25); (3) condemnation for his infidelity to Yahweh (12:33–13:34; 14:1-18; cf. 11:1-13, 31-33). Also, Jeroboam's rise is linked to Solomon's fall, foretold by a prophet's oracle (11:29-39) and noted as divine word fulfilled (1 Kgs 12:15). On the other hand, the author-editor unvaryingly ties Jeroboam to all those who come after him. For it is Jeroboam's "sin" set forth in a Dtr creation (1 Kgs 12:26-32; so Hoffmann, 73; Van Seters, "Histories and Historians," 170-74) that becomes the author-editor's benchmark for judging each successive northern king. In Jeroboam was set loose a thought and a deed whose shock wave ran quite counter to Solomon's achievements. It was a disturbance which was not to be stilled until the body politic itself was laid to rest in the dissolution of the northern kingdom (2 Kings 17). Even then the apostasy lived on at Bethel in the hearts and actions of those settlers who took the place of deported Israelites (2 Kgs 17:24-41).

Thus, Jeroboam is paradigmatic for the Dtr author-editor: the history of the dynasties in the north radiate from this core of infamy. In him we may see the main themes governing the selection and shaping of this telling of royal history. The author insists on a kind of cultic orthodoxy for his kings. That is, a "good" king adheres to the religious principles enunciated in the book of Deuteronomy, chiefly: (1) the centrality and exclusivity of *one* cultic center, and (2) the temple in Jerusalem as the place of proper worship. Though faulted in the end, Solomon is effusively praised for his role in bringing injunction (Deut 12:5-7) to action (1 Kings 6–9). And Josiah stands tall above all others (2 Kgs 23:25) as defender of Yahwism and purifier of cult. With equal enthusiasm, the author condemns Jeroboam and all his successors for turning away from Jerusalem (1 Kgs 12:29-30). It was a "baneful legacy" (Gray, *Kings,* 11) indeed. Jeroboam's transgression is the crucial event in the history of the northern kingdom, rendering the succession of monarchs into a cursed procession of apostates.

Ahab is a worthy successor in this parade of sinners. Judged worse in degree but not in kind than his predecessor, Ahab is an adversary of Yahweh when he should have been a solicitor of God's word. Specific transgressions draw forth, therefore, prophecies of ignoble end (20:42; 21:19; 22:17), which are of course fulfilled (22:38). The corresponding culprit in the south was Manasseh, who did as Ahab had done (2 Kgs 21:3). Interestingly enough, Jeroboam's guilt, through Ahab, is transferred to the south, through Manasseh. Thus, Jeroboam's defection from Jerusalem-centered Yahwism carries within itself the seeds of destruction for both the northern and southern dynasties.

This shift of the burden of guilt onto Jeroboam must be understood within a Dtr principle: the intrinsic merit of David, associated with a promise of dynasty

(2 Samuel 7). David could do no wrong it seems, and the faithfulness of the dynastic founder was more important in principle than the disobedience of the successors (cf. Van Seters, "Histories and Historians," 167-68). David was the ultimate standard of righteousness for *all* of them (cf. 1 Kgs 15:9ff.; 2 Kgs 18:1-3; 22:2), including Jeroboam, who began the slide to destruction by departing from *David's* ways, and hence lost whatever claims to merit he or his northern kingdom may have had (1 Kgs 11:38; 14:8). The same principle was operative in the Dtr writer's view of the Saul-David period. David was accepted, Saul rejected, and this foregone conclusion essentially defined the tragedy. Saul could do nothing, despite his best efforts, to dislodge the principled favoritism (see David Gunn, *The Fate of King Saul* [JSOTSup 14; Sheffield: University of Sheffield, 1980]). It is not surprising, then, that in the view of the Dtr writer, the north *could* not succeed because the basic code of acceptance by God—the meritorious standard set in David—was violated. In this way, Jeroboam becomes a symbol of divine rejection, north and south, just as David symbolized God's acceptance. When the fall of the Judean kingdom was associated with Jeroboam through Ahab (cf. 2 Kgs 21:3), the demise of the south was assimilated to that basic paradigm: divine acceptance of David and rejection of those who walk apart.

Of course, the principle requires that David's merit continue in the exile, and that the claims of a Davidic kingdom remain uncompromised. It is understandable, then, that the Dtr author ends his paratactic telling of the monarchical history with a report that the Babylonian king elevated Jehoiachin, the last descendant of David, and "established his throne higher than the thrones of all the kings who were with him in Babylon" (2 Kgs 25:28). David's merit stands, effective in exile, as before.

Besides paradigmatic kings, other themes unify the work. At least a century earlier than Herodotus, the Dtr author involves the various monarchs continually with prophets. Hence, the arching line from prophecy to fulfillment is never far from view. In formulas (e.g., 12:15; 16:1-4, 12; 22:38), in dramatic patterns inherent in stories (e.g., 17:8-16), within reigns (21:19; 22:38), across regnal periods (11:11, 31-37; 12:15; cf. 13:2 with 2 Kings 22–23, or 19:18 with 2 Kgs 10:28), the divine word not only comes true, it seems to push and motivate the actors in the drama, announce the turns, and shape the tale (e.g., 17:1-6; 18:1-2). Prophecy is a history-creating force (von Rad, 221). The divine word, like water seeking its lowest point, will not be denied its egress. Indeed, prophets are ciphers at dramatic turning points, harbingers of crisis; they "warn" Israel and issue a summons to "turn back" to Yahweh (2 Kgs 17:13; 1 Kgs 11:11-13, 38-39; 18:21). When warnings go unheeded, destruction follows, and disaster thereby has its rationale for author and reader (see Weinfeld, 15-32).

Hanging onto this proleptic vision of things and based upon Deuteronomy 27–28 is a principle of retributive justice. Rewards (blessings) of obedience are offered as life, and disaster (curses) follow upon disobedience to those divine commands enshrined in the covenant between Yahweh and his people. These two consequences of covenant find flesh in 1–2 Kings. In the end, the monarchs and the nation they ruled are heirs to the curse (Deuteronomy 28) rather than the blessing (Deuteronomy 27), to death rather than life (Noth, *Deuteronomistic History*). Yet, for the author-editor, the irrevocable end is slow in coming. Yahweh's long-suffering mercy and his promise to David forestall disaster (11:34-36; 21:29;

2 Kgs 17:13; 22:18-20; cf. 2 Samuel 7). Even when Judah is no more, and the last link in the chain has given out, one wonders if for the Dtr writer the rehabilitation of Jehoiachin (2 Kgs 25:27-29) is not yet another opportunity for exilic readers to respond affirmatively to Yahweh's anger (Wolff; von Rad).

Genre

The genre of 1–2 Kings has never been specified with much precision. Within the body of the work are some similarities to Egyptian and Mesopotamian ROYAL INSCRIPTIONS which commemorate the military and building activities of the kings. Also, parts of 1–2 Kings resemble chronographic genres: KING LISTS and CHRONICLES, types of historical writing which record with extremely limited interpretation selected reigns, and events within reigns, in chronological order. At least one of these, the Neo-Babylonian "Weidner Chronicle," shares with the Dtr history a theological bias and penchant toward moralizing about good and bad kings (Grayson, *Chronicles*, 145-51). Yet nothing we know in the ancient Near Eastern documents rivals the scope and literary flow of 1–2 Kings (and the Dtr history work) and the "authorial" vision standing behind it.

Many scholars affirm the basic historical character and intent of the books of Kings but carefully distinguish the work from a modern "history" written by a critical historian. Hence, Gray (*Kings,* 5; cf. pp. 36-43) describes Kings as "philosophy, or theological interpretation, of history." Similarly, Montgomery (*Kings,* 27) speaks of "Historical Story" in the sense of Latin *historia*. 1 (with 2) Kings is HISTORY. We speak of a complete prose narrative whose basic structure and style suggests a "telling" of events in chronological sequence (whether or not the chronology is accurate or even clearly spelled out). History takes its form not so much from aesthetic interests, such as dramatic plot and artistic expression, as from the intent to narrate and interpret events as they were presumed to have occurred, and with awareness of cause-effect relations among them. Naturally the definition neither excludes fiction, or fictionalized "telling," nor rules out an author's biased interpretation of events. Indeed, we expect such. History appears in a variety of literary forms, may contain diverse content, and often reveals its author's varied selection, evaluation, and treatment of sources.

If one accepts Noth's hypothesis of a Dtr History extending from Deuteronomy through 2 Kings, then one might say that the history of the monarchy is one example of history within a larger history. One might also think of 1–2 Chronicles (perhaps with Ezra-Nehemiah) as another example of the genre in the OT. The name "Chronicles" is not a proper generic designation; it is simply a customary title rooted in early Latin Christian interpretation. The Hebrew title is (*sēper*) *dibrê hayyāmîm,* which refers to the book's content: (book) of daily events, literally, "things of the days," meaning something like "events of (past) time." Thus what we see in 1–2 Chronicles is a complex but chronologically ordered "telling" of Israel's past from the birth of Adam to the edict of Cyrus in the 5th century B.C. Like the Dtr author-editor of Kings, the Chronicler apparently freely rewrote, edited, and shaped his work with materials of diverse age, origin, and literary type, and unified his essentially paratactic recounting of the reigns with certain themes. So, for example, the kings tend to be archetypes of good or evil, and even to be arranged in schematic fashion such that a faithful king is followed by a faithless one. The Chronicler stresses the continuity of God's favor toward

Israel chiefly by retaining throughout the religious sense of "Israel" and understanding Israel's "history" as an outworking of an eternal covenant with David. It is a genuine effort at intellectual synthesis. (See Childs, 643-53; S. Japhet, "Chronicles," *Encyclopedia Judaica* V [Jerusalem and New York: Keter; Macmillan, 1971]; idem, *The Ideology of the Book of Chronicles and its Place in Biblical Thought* [Jerusalem: Bialik, 1977] [Hebrew]; S. De Vries in the FOTL volume on Chronicles.)

Within the history that is 1–2 Kings, we must recognize diversity of content and literary form in the individual traditions. The author-editor frequently used REPORTS, that is, prose narrations in third person, straightforward, matter-of-fact style, short and long, of events as they were presumed to have happened. There is little or no interest in aesthetic features or literary development. Reports cover a wide range of subject matter and appear in many different contexts in the larger work. See, for example, the death of a leader (2:1-12a), or royal building activities (7:1-12; 12:25; 6:2-36), or throne conspiracy (15:27-30; 16:9-11), or battles (14:25-26). Reports may tell of religious events, such as prophetic revelations (16:1-4), commissioning (12:22-24; 21:17-19), symbolic actions (11:29-31; 22:11), or dream epiphanies (3:4-15; 9:1-9; cf. 19:4-8) and oracles (6:11-12). In almost none of these examples does the report occur as an isolated fact, but as part of a larger context to which it relates.

A second major genre used in the books of Kings is STORY, that is, prose narration of diverse content, whose main organizing principles are dramatic and aesthetic. Story develops a dramatic tension and narrates its resolution. The plot, which may be simple or very complex, unfolds as an arc running from this tension to its resolution. Most of the examples in 1 (and 2) Kings deal centrally with prophets (e.g., 20:1-34; 21:1-29; 22:1-38) or kings (2:13-25; 3:16-28), and sometimes both together (e.g., 22:1-38). Frequently represented is a special type of edifying story, the LEGEND, the chief characteristic of which is its lessened interest in aesthetic elements and its augmented concern with miraculous power and exemplary conduct of the main character. In 1 Kings, legends deal mostly with prophets (e.g., 13:1-32; 17:17-24; 18:1-46), but at least once with the king (Solomon; 10:1-10, 13).

Besides report, story (and legend), most of which were in the author-editor's oral and written sources already, we may note the chief literary devices and literary genres used to create unity in parataxis. There are the frameworks, divided into introductory and concluding REGNAL RESUMÉ. There are pious speeches spoken by an important leader, as for example the PETITION of Solomon upon dedicating the temple (1 Kgs 8:14-53), or David's FAREWELL SPEECH (2:2-4), or pivotal PROPHETIC JUDGMENT SPEECHES (e.g., 11:31-39) and PROPHECY OF PUNISHMENT (e.g., 1 Kgs 13:21-22; 14:7-11), and divine address in DREAM EPIPHANY (1 Kgs 9:3-9). Finally, we hear the author-editor's voice clearly in THEOLOGICAL REVIEW (1 Kgs 11:1-13; cf. 2 Kgs 10:29-31; 17:7-23; 21:9-15).

Setting

History as a written composition must have been related in some way to the affairs of the royal court in ancient Israel, for there one would expect to find the economic and social support for a class of writers whose work involved keeping various kinds of records (→ annals, chronicles, kings lists, registers; see "Introduction to Historical Literature"). We may suppose that these same people would have on occasion composed history, that longer work of historical recollection and interpretation.

Whatever their theories about the redaction and compositional history, most scholars agree that in its present form the books of Kings (and the Dtr History of which they are a part) originated in the exile, probably in Babylon (some say Palestine, but see Soggin). Its author was a scribe (Weinfeld) who was closely aligned with deuteronomic ideology and committed to a "prophetic" vision of reality. At the same time, these people would have had access to a wide variety of source material, including records of the then extinct Judean royal court and Babylonian literary conventions (see, e.g., the discussion of Mesopotamian parallels at 1 Kgs 14:21-31). It is perhaps not too farfetched to connect these scribes, or the author-editor of 1–2 Kings, with those exiled, highly placed courtesans of Judah's last few kings who seemed to have had a vested interest in transmitting the traditions of Jeremiah with a pro-Yahweh and pro-Babylonian slant (see Burke O. Long, "Social Dimensions of Prophetic Conflict," *Semeia* 21 [1982] 31-53). Written history seems to have arisen among some such upper-class people in Israel, and clearly flowered in the 6th-5th centuries B.C., as seen in 1–2 Kings and 1–2 Chronicles.

Intention

From what has been said, it follows that the intention of the author-editor had much to do with social conditions during the exilic period of Israel's history. The point must have been to narrate the story of the Hebrew monarchy in such a way as to explain the disaster that was exile, and at the same time to speak to dispossessed royalists, courtesans of the Judahite monarchy now in need of a revised sense of self-understanding. It is a comprehensive story of failure—of the kings and of the people through the kings—and a tale of retribution (see Noth, *Deuteronomistic History*; Wyatt, "Historiography," 61 [see listing at "Introduction to Historical Literature"]). But it is also a story of God's consistent and persistent dealings with his covenant people through the steady press of his creative word—the word which controls, enlivens, warns, and condemns, and which decrees the merit of David (2 Samuel 7; 1 Kgs 11:13, 32, 36; 15:4; 2 Kgs 8:19). So the point was not so much to record *events* as to record the *point* of events.

Probably the author also wanted to moralize from historical examples (cf. the "admonitory anecdotes" among the Hittite royal inscriptions; Hoffner, 332, and 310-13). The final disaster comes by the hand of a long-suffering God who sometimes mitigated punishment. The chain comes to an end in the destruction of Jerusalem and temple, and the rehabilitation of Jehoiachin in Babylon, not Jerusalem. He was presumably the last Judean king to remain alive (2 Kings 25). In this way, the dissonance in the song of faith could be overcome through redoubled belief and exhortation: God and the merit of David can still work for this people even when homeland and royal capital are lost. From history comes a summons to renew one's efforts at obedience (see von Rad; Wolff), and *perhaps*, hope for political restoration.

Chapter 2
The Individual Units

THE END OF DAVID'S AND THE BEGINNING OF SOLOMON'S REIGN: THE CANONICAL FRAMEWORK, 1:1–2:46

Structure

I. Account of the end of David's reign	1:1–2:12a
A. Story of Solomon's accession	1:1-53
B. Report of the death of David	2:1-12a
1. Report of farewell speech	1-9
2. Concluding regnal resumé	10-12a
II. Account of transition: establishing the kingdom	2:12b-46
A. Introductory summary: the kingdom established	12b
B. Episode: the killing of Adonijah	13-25
C. Report: the expulsion of Abiathar	26-27
D. Episode: the killing of Joab	28-35
E. Episode: the killing of Shimei	36-46a
F. Concluding summary: the kingdom established	46b

It is easy to see signs of disunity in this complex of traditions: (1) the evidence of a Dtr hand in 2:2a, 3-4, and probably 2:10-12a, the latter being the usual concluding summary for each of the kings in the books of Kings; (2) the awkwardness of 2:1-9, 10-12a, coming as they do between 1:53 and 2:13-25; (3) while seeming to presuppose events narrated in ch. 1, 2:13-25 are firmly enclosed by a formulaic framework, vv. 12a and 46b, and, moreover, share stylistic and thematic features with 2:26-46a, which have little or nothing to do with ch. 1; (4) the two motives given for the death of Joab in 2:28-29, 32 connect this particular episode at once to the story in ch. 1 and the wider canonical vision reflected in 2:5-6. Add to all these points the fact that the LXX carries a miscellany of material at 2:35 that appears elsewhere in the MT, and one gets the impression that this block of traditions indeed has come through complicated stages of development.

Whatever their origins may have been, and in whatever order the various pieces may have come to their present position, this material has been shaped according to at least three redactional patterns. The easiest to see is the concluding summary, which simultaneously closes out one regnal period and introduces the next by naming the succeeding king (I.B.2, 2:10-12a). This is a nearly invariable technique by which the author-editor of Kings arranged his material. On the other hand, the concluding summary functions also as a death notice on the analogy of a clearly established canonical model—the death report of a hero positioned at critical junctures in the continuous story of God's people and including a farewell speech (cf. Gen 47:29–49:33; Josh 23:1–24:30; Deut 33:1–34:8; see full discussion below). Finally, the canonical shape of the Davidic traditions seems to have served as a rough organizing principle for these two chapters. For David, one reads of his becoming king (2 Sam 2:1-4a, 4b–5:5; note the summarizing 5:4-5), then how he consolidated his power and rule (2 Sam 5:6–8:14; again note the summarizing 8:13a, 14b), and finally one hears of his administrative apparatus (2 Sam 8:15-18; note the summarizing 8:15a). For Solomon, a similar progression is evident: the end of David's rule is also the story of how Solomon came to power (1 Kgs 1:1–2:12a), and this account, like David's, is followed by materials which show the rule being consolidated (II.A-F, 2:12b-46; note the refrain, vv. 12b and 46b); then in due course, one will read of Solomon's administrative organization (1 Kgs 4:1–5:14; note the summarizing 4:1 and cf. 2 Sam 8:15a). Even the form of 1:1 indicates continuity rather than difference: "Now David was old, advanced in age. . .," suggesting a quite unself-conscious, narrative continuation of something that has gone before. It is not the usual opening for a separate book, as may be seen in contrasting the conscious efforts at making connections between Exodus and Genesis in Exod 1:1-7, or the superscriptions to Deuteronomy and the prophetic books (Deut 1:1; Amos 1:1; Mic 1:1; Hos 1:1; etc.). In many ways, therefore, the canonical framework has molded a unity of diverse materials along traditional lines. It makes of this stuff an end and a beginning: the end of David's and the beginning of Solomon's reign. Exclusive focus on Solomon comes only in ch. 3.

Genre

Since it is a question of a redactional composition, one cannot specify with precision any particular genre. The text shows us an editorial framework which supports various traditions and many distinct genres of literature.

Setting

The setting, therefore, must be understood in a literary way, that is, in the canonical context of 1 Kings, following upon 2 Samuel. The unit is set at the end of David's reign and at the beginning of Solomon's. Viewing matters from the exilic time, the editor gives us the old age of David and the youth of Solomon—in the undiminished memory of David's prime and bittersweet glory, and in the adolescent glow of Solomon's future as yet uncreated.

Intention

Hence, the editorial composition marks the passing of one epoch to another. The author-editor wishes to narrate the end of David's rule—with all its greatness of rule and meanness of sibling turmoil—and the beginning of another. One suspects that the new may replicate what has gone before, like a curse from which one is never quite free.

STORY OF SOLOMON'S ACCESSION, 1:1-53

Structure

I. Exposition: account of circumstances	1-10
A. David's advanced age (Abishag)	1-4
B. Adonijah's conspiracy	5-10
1. Adonijah's self-aggrandizement	5
2. Narrator's comment: justification	6
3. Formation of conspiracy	7
4. Narrator's comment: those excluded	8
5. Confirmatory ceremonies	9
6. Narrator's comment: those excluded	10
II. Complication: account of counterconspiracy	11-27
A. Nathan and Bathsheba: the plan	11-14
B. Execution of plan	15-27
1. Bathsheba's appeal to the king	15-21
a. Formal meeting: David and Bathsheba	15-16
b. Statement of appeal	17-21
1) Basis for appeal	17-19
2) Appeal proper	20-21
2. Nathan's appeal to the king	22-27
a. Formal meeting: David and Nathan	22-23
b. Statement of appeal	24-27
1) Basis for appeal	24-25
2) Appeal proper	26-27
III. Climax: Nathan's plan results in royal oath	28-37
A. David's decision	28-31
1. Formal meeting: David and Bathsheba	28
2. Statement of oath	29-30
3. Bathsheba's response: blessing	31
B. David's orders	32-37
1. Formal meeting: David and aids	32
2. Statement of orders	33-35
3. Benaiah's response: blessing	36-37
IV. Denouement: Solomon's rise, Adonijah's fall	38-53
A. Account of Solomon's Coronation	38-40
1. Procession: down to Gihon	38
2. The Coronation	39
3. Procession: up to the palace	40
B. Account of Flight and Reconciliation	41-53
1. Conspirators' flight	41-50
a. Situation of conspirators	41
b. Report of coronation events	42-48
c. Response: conspirators' flight	49-50
2. Reconciliation: Adonijah and Solomon	51-53
a. Adonijah's terms reported	51
b. Solomon's reponse	52
c. Reconciliation	53

Since Leonhard Rost forthrightly articulated the hypothesis, most critics have viewed 1 Kings 1 as part of the ending to an originally separate narrative now deposited in its canonical dress in 2 Samuel 9–20; 1 Kings 1–2. Rost argued that the basic theme of this "Succession Narrative" was given by its ending, and in the words of Bathsheba: "the eyes of all Israel are upon you, to tell them who shall sit on the throne of my lord the king after him" (1 Kgs 1:20). Despite disputes over the exact configuration of its beginning and end and recent tendencies to discredit its unity, Rost's essentially theologico-political way of reading this whole narrative has held. The perspective, if not the notion of textual unity, has been reinforced by recent redaction-critical analyses which reconstruct a complicated history of pro- and anti-Solomonic versions (Würthwein, *Könige,* 2-9; Veijola; Langlamet).

Among the more recent critics, however, no genuine consensus has been achieved on a view of some earlier stage of this story which opens 1 Kings. Many also persist, as did Rost, in seeing 1:53 as demanding a continuation, and thereby link 2:13-25 directly to ch. 1. But there are difficulties with this move, since 2:13-25 is firmly rooted in the context of 2:26-46 (see discussion below). At the same time, attempts to delineate an earlier version of 1 Kings 1 untouched by editorial hands tend to overlook signs of real authorial unity: stylistic congruities, literary shaping, and structural patterns. A number of scholars have lately devoted special attention to these matters and have gained new appreciation, beyond what Rost was able to accomplish, for the literary skill reflected in the whole "Succession Narrative" as well as its ending (Fokkelman; Gunn; Long).

Indeed, the structure of 1 Kings 1 seems less determined by some political point than by the requirements of good narrative. The writer sets up the combined circumstances of David's advanced age and his son Adonijah's seizing of royal prerogative (I.A, B), and creates narrative tension when Nathan and Bathsheba devise a counterconspiracy to challenge Adonijah (II.A, B, C). The resolution of this tension constitutes the remainder of the story. It moves quickly to its climactic turning point, the royal oath to elevate Solomon to the throne (III.A, vv. 29-30), then through coronation and the flight of the conspirators in utter disarray (IV.A, B; vv. 38-50). The narrative finally comes to rest in reserved reconciliation between Solomon—now king—and his brother Adonijah, who would be king (IV.B.2, vv. 51-53).

By subtle characterization and allusion, repetition with minor variation, a good sense of narrative pace, and vivid imagery, the author has created a satisfying and imaginative narrative out of this skeletal plot. Only the most important details of his artistry may be mentioned here.

The *exposition* (I.A, vv. 1-4) simply and directly states a first background circumstance: the king is very old (v. 1). The narrator gives us a vivid image by describing the physical, even sensuous, efforts made to comfort the king with a comely young maiden, who does not arouse the aged king's sexual desire. Who can miss allusive contrasts? The lusty, robust David of 2 Samuel, and the shivering, impotent David of this story (see vv. 1, 4, 6, 11, 18, 27, and with special emphasis, v. 15b); the weak, aged king and his markedly handsome, preemptively assertive son just beyond the palace door (vv. 5-6b; the image recalls Absalom, 2 Sam 15:1). We meet here a biblical convention that links new impulses in the human drama with failure or dissolution, the old passing into the new (cf. Gen 6:1; Exod 1:8; 1 Sam 3:1; 8:3; etc.).

These suggestions of decay and new life also point to a second circumstance necessary for the dramatic action: Adonijah's feast near En-rogel (v. 9). With mention of this event, the narrator plants us in the center of his narrational time, at the moment of Adonijah's premature celebration of kingship (see v. 41). But this present is hedged about with a provocative past, actions which, as described in the Hebrew, carry a durative, pluperfect, or circumstantial sense (see Fokkelman, 348). "Adonijah was (had been) exalting himself [participle of circumstance, *mitnaśśē'*] saying, 'I alone will rule!' [Hebrew uses emphatic personal pronoun], and he (had) prepared chariots for himself [v. 5] . . . and he (had) conferred with Joab . . . and they followed after him [v. 7]." The narrator also weaves into this fabric some comments (vv. 6, 8, 10) to suggest the essential problem of the whole affair. For Adonijah's actions have a certain justification. Yet they also carry the prospect of arousing opponents. Thus while sketching relevant background for this one short period in the life of Adonijah, the narrator also gives portentous shape to divided loyalties. He twice mentions those "not with Adonijah" (vv. 8, 10) and both times uses an emphatic ordering of words. Perhaps we are meant to wonder if a counterconspiracy, stronger than Adonijah, will grow in these days of David's impotence.

This opposition to Adonijah is in fact the *complication* which propels the action forward (II, vv. 11-37). The pace moves more quickly now, with characteristic narrative tenses in contrast to vv. 1-10, which, because they sketched the background, carried a large number of circumstantial statements. Nathan proposes a way to manipulate the situation to his and Bathsheba's own advantage, Bathsheba agrees, and they both appeal to the king (II.A, B; vv. 11-27).

Typically, the narrator creates the event and his characters through direct speech (Alter; Fokkelman). Nathan's polite, crafty proposal consists of rhetorical questions to be put to the king; Bathsheba turns his words into a forceful, perhaps more harsh, confrontation with David: ". . . you swore" (not "did you not swear?" v. 13); "Adonijah is king and you . . . do not know it!" (not, "have you not heard . . . Adonijah . . . has become king and David our lord does not know it?" v. 11; cf. v. 13). Bathsheba goes further, however. The evidence for her conclusion is for all to see in Adonijah's feast, which must have come as news to the king. Pointedly noting Solomon's absence from this ceremony (the Hebrew word order is emphatic, v. 19b, and is aptly caught in the *RSV*), she takes David's thoughts back to her own opening gambit, the oath concerning Solomon (v. 19). Finally, Bathsheba voices the main petition (v. 20), which is indirect in form (it is a statement, not a request) but characteristically direct in its psychological force (the king must decide who is to succeed to the throne). In the event all these considerations are not persuasive enough, she raises the matter of her and her son's personal safety in Adonijah's effrontery (v. 21). Clearly Bathsheba, though acting on Nathan's words, shows herself no slave to them.

For his part, Nathan brings essentially the same information to the king. The author, however, suggests something of his character in the slight variations. Nathan speaks as though he knows nothing of an oath regarding Solomon (it is, so the inference would go, a private matter between Queen and King). He cleverly asks a question which indirectly implies a conclusion drawn from the news of Adonijah's feasting: "Have you said, 'Adonijah shall reign after me?' . . . For he has sacrificed . . . and they are eating and drinking . . ." (vv. 24-25). Nathan adds one last goad: ". . . they are saying, 'Long live King Adonijah' " (v. 25b). He complains about being left out of the celebration (still assumed, politely, as possibly sanctioned by the king), and finally returns to his starting point: "if this thing [*RSV* misleads slightly] has been brought about . . . by the king, you have not told your servant . . ." (v. 27). Nathan's posture is remarkable. In contrast to the more confrontational Bathsheba, who retains nonetheless a certain deportment, Nathan is the observant, almost dispassionate servant who speaks carefully and politely (note the author's extra descriptive touch, "he bowed . . . *face to the ground,*" v. 23; cf. v. 16). But he makes no accusations save the mild one that *perhaps* (it is really left only as a possibility) the king has neglected to inform him of a succession to the throne.

These three speeches—Nathan's proposal, Bathsheba's and Nathan's appeals to David—all seem well calculated to use rhetorical structure, repetition, and variation as instruments of literary characterization (cf. Fokkelman, 351-63, for a more detailed analysis and a somewhat different conclusion). Besides this, their cumulative effect in the story's movement is to prompt at last a decisive response from the infirm David. Not only is the king persuaded that he gave an earlier oath regarding his successor—he must be certain now of the gravity of Adonijah's challenge. David realizes the personal dangers to wife and son who hold a special place in court (cf. 2 Samuel 11–12; 12:24-25), and he also knows the identity of both loyalists and rebels.

We have reached the narrator's climactic turning point (III, vv. 28-37). As though stirred suddenly from dull-witted inattention, David moves decisively (he abruptly summons Bathsheba, v. 28) and deliberately (he pronounces a solemnly elaborate oath, vv. 29-30). Framed by a formal audience (v. 28) and courtly response/blessing (v. 31), his words form the essential center of the scene. They also stand at the thematic middle of the whole narrative. Nathan's and Bathsheba's appeals had aimed at just this result, and all events flow from it. We might visualize the author's work as a concentric arrangement of narrative elements leading into this center and out from it (cf. Fokkelman, 365).

A Adonijah's aggrandizement/David's impotence
B Appeals to David ("Let Solomon be king!")
C David's oath (David regains power)
B' Actions leading to coronation (Solomon *is* king)
A' Adonijah's fall

From this vantage point we see that the oath-leading-to-coronation really is the pinnacle of Solomon's ascendancy and simultaneously the peak from which Adonijah begins his slide downward. On the one side, Adonijah is aggressive, self-assured, handsome, powerful, successful. On the other side, he is terrified, fleeing, doing loyal obeisance to his brother Solomon (IV, vv. 38-53). In between is an unspoken partner to his rise and fall: the Solomon who is something of a shadow, pictured only in what people do for and to him. He is the beneficiary of Nathan's and Bathsheba's plot, the object of David's special attention, the passive recipient of monarchical royal standing ("made king," v. 43b; "made to ride"

David's own mount, v. 44b; anointed and acclaimed by others; enthroned finally by God's action, not by his own, v. 48). Thus the narrator depicts Adonijah's personal power, but does not create a similar vitality for Solomon. Instead, he invokes the report of massive royal and religious support to tell of a new king's elevation—and he creates for *us* a shadow character. Jonathan's words tumble out and pile up (note the series of addenda, all beginning with "and besides" [*wĕgam*], vv. 46a, 47a, 48a; a series like this gives us no good reason to suspect later editorial expansion of content; see 1 Sam 4:17; 2 Sam 1:4; 11:24; Long, 80-81). The images cluster around the decisive blow to Adonijah's self-presumed power (vv. 43b, 46, 48) and simply confirm, even elaborate with new information (vv. 47-48), the extent to which Solomon's dim shape in the narrative is lit up by others. Even if one may speak of Solomon's rise and Adonijah's fall, we must also see that the author has portrayed the real antagonists as David (Nathan-Bathsheba) and Adonijah (Joab-Abiathar), or a father and his unruly son, or something almost like David-Absalom *redivivus*.

In the end, however, Solomon emerges as a presence in his own right. He is decisive, aloof, somewhat noncommittal, very cautious. Having been reduced to ignoble clutching at life in a protected sanctuary (vv. 50-51), Adonijah meets this new king under a powerful constraint. "If he [Adonijah] proves to be loyal [*RSV* "worthy man," but see 2 Sam 2:7; 1 Sam 18:17], not one of his hairs shall fall to the earth; but if wickedness is found in him [says Solomon], he shall die" (v. 52). Adonijah "does obeisance" (as did Nathan and Bathsheba to King David), but is simply sent to his house. The narrator offers no comment, as though we are meant to suppose the reconciliation were less than total, or the wound between brothers not quite, or perhaps never to be, healed. In this moment of understatement, one feels that the narrative finds a resting point, but the matter not its end.

Genre

This unit has traditionally been classified as "historical narrative" with novelistic, epic, and legendary features (Gressmann; Montgomery; Noth; Gray). Its generic character, however, is determined neither by these more ephemeral characteristics, nor by its rootage in, or allusion to, historical events. Rather, the genre should be defined primarily by the text's artistically developed structure and its clear interest in plot and characterization. The unit is a STORY; in fact, it is one of the best examples of this genre in the OT. The narrative stages of exposition, complication, climax, and denouement are clearly visible, and the dramatic tension created at the beginning is resolved at the end. Of course, within the story are numerous examples of formulaic speech, e.g., (→) oath (1:29-30), wish for divine (→) blessing (1:37; cf. Gen 24:60; 1 Kgs 8:57), (→) praise speech, related to blessing formulas (→ blessing; 1:48; cf. Gen 14:20; 24:27; 1 Kgs 8:15, 56; see discussion at 1 Kgs 5:15-26). There is also what may be called a stock scene, wherein a petitioner pleads his case before the king (1:15-21, 22-27; cf. 1 Kgs 3:17-21; 2 Sam 14:4-11). Note also that the theme of fratricidal struggle for the throne finds a parallel in Esarhaddon's (ca. 680-669 B.C.) commemorative inscription for the royal palace in Nineveh (*ANET,* 289-90). Whatever their backgrounds may have been, these formulas and stereotyped scenes and motifs now sound important theological tones within the canonical story of David and Solomon.

Setting

The setting of the genre (→) story is not as specific as, for example, that of (→) funeral dirge. Moreover, one cannot with very much assurance guess at this story's particular literary origin, although some scholars have speculated that it derived from the royal court (Gray, *Kings*; Noth, *Könige*), or among partisans in the court who were less than fully supportive of Solomon's coming to power (Würthwein, *Erzählung*; Langlamet). No clear consensus exists on these matters. Given the uncertainty, the more important question has to do with the literary setting of this story, that is, its present position in the wider context which deals with the rule of David and the succession of Solomon to the throne.

The story narrates the penultimate events of David's reign, and thus opens on to the conclusion of that epoch (2:1-12) as well as the unfinished business of Solomon's "establishing the kingdom" (2:12b, 46b). Thus, 1 Kings 1 is a story within a larger "story" (the end of David's reign), set within a still larger "story" (the events in the royal court during David's years). In this context, an important pair of contrasting images find their greatest power. On the one hand, we are made to contrast the shivering, impotent David with a David of recollection—the powerful, lusting, weeping, grasping king of 2 Samuel. On the other hand, we see the aggressive, handsome Adonijah in contrast to both an aged David and a sort of David *redivivus*, that is, Solomon, who is neither character nor king until near the end of the story, but who will quickly come to dominate events. The personal and political drama lies in the fact that, as Adonijah ignores the specter of what David *used* to be, he is forced to deal with the prospect of what *will* be. The story is about Solomon becoming king, but also about a darkness between brothers we have heard before (2 Samuel 13–14), and about a grasping for the throne we have known before (2 Samuel 15–18) (Long; cf. Gunn; Blenkinsopp).

Intention

The intention of the story, therefore, cannot and should not be limited unnecessarily. Like any good story, this one functions on several levels. Obviously, in both its original and its present context, the story intends to tell how Solomon came to sit on his father's throne. But this point can hardly cover everything and has surely been overemphasized by those captivated by the notion of "Succession Narrative." Read in its present canonical context, the story, in deeply evocative images, describes another in a series of deadly serious disruptions in David's family, all of which are embodiments and reduplications of David's own personal and private violence (2 Samuel 11–12). Adonijah's grasping and his curiously restrained reconciliation with Solomon are part of a constantly unfolding cycle moving from harmony to disruption, then into unstable restoration, as though chaos lingers just around the edges of cosmos (cf. 2 Samuel 11–12; 13–14; 15–18; 19). Seen another way, the story evokes a biblical archetype—from destruction comes creation (Genesis 6–9). As with Israel, which was defined folkloristically as having "striven with God and men and prevailed" (Gen 32:28), so too the royal house (Long).

There are other theological overtones as well. After all, the events took place according to divine will—even if this is somewhat hidden from view—and they support the claims made about a special covenant drawn between God and the Davidic house (1 Kgs 1:47-48). Yet theological motifs need not blind us to the fact that the story means also to entertain. The plot is cleverly conceived, put together with a satisfying conclusion, and is finally neutral toward many moral judgments that might be made on the course of events (against critics who stress politically propagandistic purposes for the story, e.g., Würthwein, *Erzählung*; Langlamet; Thornton).

Finally, in its present literary setting, this story introduces Solomon for the first time since his birth and special name were mentioned in 2 Sam 12:24-25. Largely a passive figure, Solomon's character is merely hinted at in the decisive reserve with which he treats his rivalrous brother. There is clearly more suggested and more to be shown in subsequent materials.

Bibliography

R. Alter, "Biblical Narrative," *Commentary* 61/5 (1976) 61-67; J. Blenkinsopp, "Theme and Motif in the Succession History (2 Sam. xi 2ff) and the Yahwist Corpus," in *Volume du Congres: Genève* (VTSup 15; Leiden: Brill, 1966) 44-57; Lienhard Delekat, "Tendenz und Theologie der David-Salomo Erzählung," in *Das ferne und nahe Wort* (*Fest.* L. Rost; ed. F. Maass; BZAW 105; Berlin: W. de Gruyter, 1967) 26-36; J.W. Flannagan, "Court History or Succession Document? A Study in 2 Samuel 9–20 and 1 Kings 1–2," *JBL* 91 (1972) 172-81; J. Fokkelman, *Narrative Art and Poetry in the Books of Samuel: King David* I (Studia Semitica Neerlandica 20; Assen: Van Gorcum, 1981) 345-83; David Gunn, *The Story of King David: Genre and Interpretation* (JSOTSup 6; Sheffield: University of Sheffield, 1978); F. Langlamet, "Pour ou Contre Salomon?" *RB* 48 (1976) 321-79, 481-528; B. O. Long, "A Darkness Between Brothers: Solomon and Adonijah," *JSOT* 19 (1981) 79-94; L. Rost, *The Succession to the Throne of David* (Historic Texts and Interpreters in Biblical Scholarship 1; Sheffield: Almond, 1981); W. Thiel, "Die David-Geschichten im Alten Testament," *Zeichen der Zeit* 31 (1977) 161-71; T. C. G. Thornton, "Solomonic Apologetics in Samuel and Kings," *The Church Quarterly Review* 169 (1968) 159-66; T. Veijola, *Die Ewige Dynastie. David und die Entstehung seiner Dynastie nach der deuteronomistischen Darstellung* (Helsinki: Suomalainen Tiedeakatemia, 1975); E. Würthwein, *Die Erzählung von der Thronfolge Davids—theologische oder politische Geschichtsschreibung?* (ThSt[B] 115; Zurich: Theologischer Verlag, 1974); S. Zalewski, "The Character of Adonijah," *BethM* 19/2 (57) [1973] 229-55, 301 (Hebrew); idem, "The Struggle between Adonijah and Solomon over the Kingdom," *BethM* 20/4 (1974) 490-510 (Hebrew).

REPORT OF THE DEATH OF DAVID: CANONICAL FRAMEWORK, 2:1-12a

Structure

I. Report of farewell speech	1-9
A. Introductory setting	1
B. Farewell speech	2-9
II. Report of death: concluding regnal resumé	10-12a

Obviously an editorial composite, this unit has been built up of material reflecting Dtr theology (esp. in vv. 3-4), a wide view of the entire Davidic corpus (vv. 5-9), and an interest in closing out David's reign with the typical concluding summary (vv. 10-12a). The material is clearly separate from 1 Kings 1. It lacks the latter's narrative and dramatic style and deals with entirely different subject matter—while, in context, presupposing the outcome of Adonijah's abortive attempt at rule. Furthermore, the unit is to be distinguished clearly from 2:12b-46, which shows a well-formed thematic and structural unity within formulaic brackets, vv. 12b and 46b, and which can only with difficulty be related in all aspects to the content of David's final charge to Solomon (vv. 5-9).

The structure of this unit follows the conventional Hebraic schema for reporting the final acts and death of an important person. Such accounts typically contain the following elements: (1) introductory framework which alludes to advanced age and impending death; (2) a farewell speech containing admonitions and/or prophecies; (3) a concluding framework which reports the death and sometimes burial of the speaker (Gen 49:1–50:13; Josh 23:1–24:30; *T. 12 Patr.*; *T. Job*; 1 Macc 2:49-70; Tob 14:3-11; etc.; von Nordheim). Such skeletal elements, however, ought not to be construed as rigid constraints on authors or editors. The schema serves in practice as a motival framework within which diverse contents, cast in various literary genres, may be transmitted. Thus, for example, the recounting of Jacob's death has attracted to it several farewell speeches, a series of old tribal sayings, now cited as blessings, a story about the giving and disputing of patriarchal blessing, and a rather detailed account of Jacob's burial (Gen 47:28–50:14), all connected together with repeated references to the deathbed situation (Gen 47:29; 48:12b, 21-22; 49:29, 33; see Coats). So, in 1 Kgs 2:1-12a one finds a similar patterned diversity of elements.

Genre

The unit as a whole is cast as a REPORT of death (see Gen 47:29–50:14; Joshua 23–24; Deuteronomy 33–34; 1 Macc 2:49-70). At its center is the FAREWELL SPEECH, which contains thematic material important for interpreting the life and significance of the speaker whose death is being reported. Such accounts of death may have been a characteristic form of oral literature (cf. 2 Sam 17:23), but the important examples in the OT are already elaborate editorial compositions and thus are to be seen as literary constructs more important for extrinsic rather than intrinsic reasons. That is, these reports of death for particular heroes or famous persons serve as framework narratives for a variety of traditions and, generally speaking, reflect a canonical perspective not so evident in its smaller components or in other less extensive compositions.

Setting

From what has been said, it is plain that the setting for reports of death is primarily a literary one. In every case, one has to look at relationships to material coming before and after and to view the report as a redactional device by which a number of independent points of view or traditions have been brought together for a particular literary purpose. In 1 Kings, the report of David's death follows the selection of his successor and looks ahead to the first acts of the new king. It is placed as both a final act of the dying David and an initial background sketching of the opening acts of King Solomon.

Intention

Naturally the intention of this report is to narrate the last acts and death of King David. But since so much importance attaches to the farewell speech, we must see that the author-editor intends this element to carry the major theological perspectives for understanding these kings—their prescribed limits and potentialities. The report as literary construct pointedly looks ahead to those transitional episodes in which Solomon will solidify his control of the kingdom, while closing out the epoch of David (see detailed discussion below).

Bibliography

G.W. Coats, *Genesis* (FOTL; Grand Rapids: Eerdmans, 1983); E. von Nordheim, "Die Lehre der Alten: Das Testament als Literaturgattung in Israel und im alten Vorderen Orient" (Diss., Munich, 1973) (bibliography); idem, *Die Lehre der Alten. I. Das Testament als Literaturgattung im Judentum der hellenistisch-römischen Zeit* (Arbeiten zur Literatur und Geschichte des Hellenistischen Judentums 13; Leiden: Brill, 1980).

REPORT OF FAREWELL SPEECH, 2:1-9

Structure

I. Introductory setting	1
II. Farewell speech	2-9
A. Reference to advanced age	2a
B. Formula of encouragement: "Be strong . . ."	2b
C. Admonition	3-4
D. Directives	5-9
1. Concerning Joab	5-6
2. Concerning sons of Barzillai	7
3. Concerning Shimei	8-9

The traditio-historical shaping of this unit and the relationship to the rest of ch. 2 is a matter of some debate. The influence of a Deuteronomistic redactor appears to have been decisive in vv. 3-4, and perhaps v. 2a (cf. Josh 23:14; Deut 4:40; 2 Sam 7:12-16), but this influence is hardly evident, if at all, in vv. 5-9. Yet, a completely satisfactory earlier form of the material cannot be reconstructed. It seems best to consider that vv. 1-9 were put together by DtrH, using some older traditions about David's last testament (Noth, *Könige*; Würthwein, *Könige*; Gray, *Kings*). The structure of the unit is now largely determined by the traditional form of farewell speech, which typically has the speaker refer to his advanced age or approaching death, voice admonitions (in religious contexts, often exhorting pious behavior), and enjoin directives upon his audience (cf. Josh 23:2b-16; Gen 49:29-32; 1 Macc 2:49-70; Acts 20:18-35; *T. 12 Patr.*). In the OT, reports of farewell speeches are generally part of a larger editorial composition which reports the final acts and death of an important person (→ 2:1-12a). Often the accounts use the word *ṣāwâ*, "command," in the sense of giving final testamentary orders (cf. Gen 49:29; 1 Kgs 2:1; 2 Sam 17:23; 2 Kgs 20:1). 1 Kgs 2:1-9, however, is also similar in structure to Deut 31:23; Josh 1:2-9; and 2 Chr 32:6-8, three speeches which mark the transfer of, or installation into, some clearly defined leadership role or office. The formula of encouragement (II.B, v. 2b: "Be strong and show yourself a man" [*ḥāzaqtā wĕhāyîtā lĕ'îš*]) is typical of these speeches, as is an assurance of divine aid forthcoming to the officeholder (Lohfink, "Darstellung"; McCarthy, "Installation"). It is likely, therefore, that the unit in 1 Kgs 2:1-9 owes some of its structural features to the typical "installation speech" (McCarthy), but it is unsatisfactory to press the similarities with Josh 1:2-9 too far (against Veijola, *Dynastie*). It is preferable to speak of a certain natural overlap in structure owing to similar societal occasions which must have often come together: the approaching death of a leader and the transfer of his office to a successor.

The directives (II.D, vv. 5-9) usually reflect particular situations in the wider narrative context and thus contain no special formulas. Nevertheless, in this unit one may observe a striking literary pattern. Each directive includes brief background allusions as a kind of justification, and the first and third directives (II.D.1, 3; vv. 5-6, 8-9) contain parallel expressions. Moreover, the entire section is built out of reversing series: background-directive (vv. 5-6); directive-background (v. 7); background-directive (vv. 8-9). The impression is one of order and planning, consistent with the narrator's reflective allusions to incidents narrated elsewhere in Davidic materials (Joab—2 Sam 3:22-27; 20:4-10; sons of Barzillai—2 Sam 17:27-29; Shimei—2 Sam 16:5-13).

Genre

From what has already been said, it is clear that the genre of this unit is REPORT of FAREWELL SPEECH. The narrative elements are minimal, and the chief emphasis falls on the content of the speech, which in this unit follows a typical sequence: (1) reference to advanced age on impending death, (2) admonition, (3) directives. Distant parallels to farewell speech may be seen in the Egyptian genre of INSTRUCTION, a well-attested literary form stylized as a compendium of advice, wisdom, and exhortation that a dying father leaves his son. For royal figures, where notions of the ideal kingly rule play a role, see the Instruction of Amenemhet I, ca. 2000 B.C. (*ANET,* 418-19; M. Lichtheim, *Ancient Egyptian Literature* I, 135-39) and the slightly earlier Merikare, ca. 2100 B.C. (*ANET,* 414-18; Lichtheim, I, 97-107; [von Nordheim, "Die Lehre," 459-504]). The closest biblical parallels are Gen 49:29-30, now greatly elaborated in 47:29–49:33; Josh 23:1-16 (an elaborate, highly theological example); 1 Macc 2:49-70; *T. 12 Patr.* (later, fully developed examples); cf. Acts 20:18-35; John 13:1–16:28. In all these cases, the biblical authors have depicted the passing of special figures as momentous events, weighted with religious, social, and historical significance.

Setting

Originally, farewell speeches must have been commonly delivered when a national leader, or a family or tribal head, conscious of impending death, would pass on his final words and bequeath his last possessions to heirs and successors. The *report* of such farewell speeches naturally would belong to accounts of the death of such figures. In the OT examples we have, however, it is already a question of *famous* individuals and their last days. This fact suggests the importance of an established *literary* setting, a vehicle by which incidents in the lives of various figures who were important to national consciousness could be recounted in a public way. Actually we possess reports of farewell speeches only in such well-developed literary contexts: in the (→) sagas of the patriarchs, the book of Deuteronomy, which is entirely structured as Moses' farewell speech, and at the end of Joshua's "story." In Kings, the report of farewell speech draws to a close the account of David's reign. Hence, these texts are pivotal in longer accounts of theologically and historically demarcated epochs in the collective memory of those in ancient Israel who shaped the canonical traditions, in this case probably the exilic Dtr author of Kings. It is no accident, therefore, that many of these speeches include religious admonitions and evoke themes of major importance to the religious consciousness of ancient Israel (e.g., Genesis 49, the relationship among the twelve tribes; Joshua 23, the giving of the land; 1 Kings 2, the theological underpinnings of David's dynasty; 1 Maccabees 2, the blessings accruing to those who strictly observe the law).

Intention

Originally, in social affairs of ancient Israel, the intention of a farewell speech would have been to convey the last wishes and directives of a person nearing death. As we now have them, the literary *reports* of such speeches are most important for their thematic connections to larger literary contexts. They mean to bring to a close an epoch, a life, a period of history, and to cite a definitive theological perspective on such an era; usually they also look ahead to further episodes in the canon. Specifically, the intention of 1 Kgs 2:1-9 is to bring to a close the era of David's rule. The material immediately following constitutes the standard concluding (→) regnal resumé used for most of the monarchs in the books of Kings. But the report also looks ahead to Solomon's deeds to come, the unfinished business regarding Joab and Shimei. Finally, the report lifts up once again the theme of the dynastic promise and the religious conditions for legitimate theocracy, offered first in 2 Samuel 7 and reiterated at crucial transitional moments, especially in 1 Kgs 1:48. In this backward- and forward-glancing way, the report intends to view both David and Solomon theologically, setting forth the conditions under which Solomon's prosperity is to be realized, namely, by continuity with David's house, last wishes, and exemplary obedience to God's demands.

Bibliography

E. Cortès, *Los discursos de Adiós de Gn 49 a Jn 13–17* (Colectánea San Paciano 23; Barcelona: Herder, 1976); J. Fokkelman, *King David,* 384-90 (see listing at 1:1-53); N. Lohfink, "Die deuteronomistische Darstellung des 'Übergangs der Führung Israels von Moses auf Josue'," *Scholastik* 37 (1962) 32-44; D. McCarthy, "An Installation Genre?" *JBL* 90 (1971) 31-41; E. von Nordheim, "Die Lehre" (see listing at 2:1-12a); T. Veijola, *Dynastie* (see listing at 1:1-53).

CONCLUDING REGNAL RESUMÉ, 2:10-12a

Structure

I. Notice of death and burial	10
II. Regnal information: length of reign	11
III. Notice of succession	12a

The structure of this unit generally follows the standard summaries which appear at the end of most regnal periods in the books of Kings (→ 14:19-20, 29-31; 15:23-24; and the full discussion at 14:21-31). Here some features are atypical: (1) the summary appears isolated because the Davidic materials lack the usual introductory statement normally found at the beginning of a regnal period, the two summaries together forming a framework around diverse materials (but see 2 Sam 5:4-5); (2) the information on the length of reign (II, v. 11) would normally be contained in such introductory material and not in a concluding summary; (3) the report of succession, "And Solomon sat upon the throne of David his father" (*ûšlōmōh yāšab 'al-kiss'ē dāwîd 'ābîw* [Q], v. 12a) differs from the more usual "And so-and-so, his son, reigned in his stead" (*wayyimlōk* PN *bĕnô taḥtāyw*; see 14:31; 15:8, etc.). Nevertheless, the variations seem minor, and the unit moves simply and quickly through a series of short reports about the very last events of importance to the reign of David.

Genre

The genre of this unit is concluding REGNAL RESUMÉ, which in its classic form cites (1) other sources for regnal information, (2) a final bit of regnal information, (3) the death and burial of the king, and (4) the king's successor. Elements one, three, and four are typically expressed as formulas. (See the full discussion at 14:21-31.) The slight variations noted above may be due to the fact that the traditions regarding David and Solomon are in themselves somewhat atypical relative to much of 1–2 Kings and therefore were treated differently by the editors. Or in the interest of literary continuity, the normally formulaic notice of succession may have been altered to refer once again to the contested throne of David, one of the central dramatic images throughout the account of David and his contentious, rivalrous sons (2 Samuel 11–20; 1 Kgs 1:1-53). Certainly v. 12b, "and his kingdom was firmly established," does not belong to the genre, and is to be considered as a transitional introduction to subsequent material in the chapter (see the discussion at 2:12b-46).

Setting

Concluding regnal resumés clearly have their setting in literary accounts of the reigns of kings. They probably stem from the efforts of the redactor to create a selective portrayal of all the regnal periods in Israel and Judah, arranged in chronological order and clearly separated from one another. Since the books of Kings regularly cite other works recording activities of the rulers, one may speculate that the editor may have drawn upon a formulaic pattern indigenous to one or all of his sources. Somewhat similar regnal summaries are known from Mesopotamian, particularly Neo-Babylonian, king lists and chronicles (Morawe), but we do not possess comparable sources for ancient Israel. See full discussion at 14:21-31. The most important fact is that the concluding regnal resumé now has a strictly literary setting and function in 1–2 Kings. It is, moreover, usually part of a typical framework which both introduces and concludes a particular regnal period.

Intention

Enough has been said to suggest that the fundamental intention of this genre is to draw to a close in a final and definitive way the account of selected events during the reign of a particular king, in the case of 1 Kgs 2:10-12a, King David. Also, it completes the composite report of David's death. At the same time, the regular mention of the succeeding monarch looks ahead to new events in the kingdom. Thus, the epoch of David is over, and that of Solomon his son begins.

Bibliography

See the bibliography at 14:21-31. G. Morawe, "Studien" (see listing at "Introduction to 1 Kings").

ACCOUNT OF TRANSITION: ESTABLISHING THE KINGDOM, 2:12b-46

Structure

I. Introductory summary: the kingdom established	12b
II. Episode: the killing of Adonijah	13-25
A. Account of death oath	13-24
B. Report of oath carried out	25
III. Report: the expulsion of Abiathar	26-27
A. Report of royal command: banishment from court	26
B. Report of oracle fulfilled: expulsion from priesthood	27
IV. Episode: the killing of Joab	28-35
A. Exposition: Joab's flight (law of asylum invoked)	28
B. Resolution: Joab's execution (law of asylum ignored and overridden)	29-34
C. Conclusion: notice of replacements	35
V. Episode: the killing of Shimei	36-46a
A. Agreement with Shimei	36-38
B. Violation and consequences	39-46a
VI. Concluding summary: the kingdom established	46b

One expects that the text, following hard upon the concluding regnal resumé of vv. 10-12a, will focus on David's successor. However, the material that follows gives the contrary impression that David's story is not yet finished. The accounts of Adonijah, Abiathar, and Joab (II-IV, vv. 13-35) appear to answer rather smoothly any lingering questions that may have remained about the fate of these coconspirators known from ch. 1. Most scholars have viewed this material, along with 2:1-12, as supplementary to an original "Succession Narrative." Just what was supplemental, and in what order the supplements came into their present context, is debatable, and competing theories have been proposed. Undoubtedly there are problems of internal consistency, as can be immediately seen when one attempts to understand how the material relates, on the one hand, to David's farewell speech, and on the other, to the story of Solomon's becoming king. Some have supposed earlier secular material to have been given theological emphasis by adding vv. 24, 32-33, 44-45 (Würthwein, *Könige*). Moreover, the LXX at v. 35

includes a miscellany of information which appears elsewhere in the Masoretic version of Solomon's reign.

These observations suggest that a complex development lies behind the MT. But reconstructions have not reached any consensus. Furthermore, the material in its present form has a certain structural unity. First, the unit is set off from surrounding materials by nearly identical phrases which refer to Solomon's establishing the kingdom (I and VI; v. 12b: "And his kingdom was firmly established"; v. 46b: "And the kingdom was established in the hand of Solomon"). The first phrase (v. 12b) has often been taken as part of the conclusion to David's reign. But it is not a generic element in the concluding regnal resumé (→ discussion at 2:10-12a), and in the light of its virtual repetition in v. 46b, the two phrases together might better be seen as part of a framework which introduces and concludes a block of material now understood as a whole. Moreover, as framework these phrases set the main interpretation to be given the events, picking up a theme sounded in one of the four episodes, v. 24, as well as in the Greek text at v. 35. Thus, in context, the Niphal of *kûn,* "to be established," has the sense of making secure, solidifying control, getting rid of threats to central royal authority. This is exactly the meaning of the word when Saul tells his son Jonathan in 1 Sam 20:31, "as long as the son of Jesse lives upon the earth, neither you nor your kingdom shall be established [or secure, *tikkôn*]." A second indication of structural unity in this material is that three of the four incidents (II, IV, V; vv. 13-25, 28-35, 36-46a) follow a similar scenario and conclude with what amounts to a literary refrain—Solomon's grim orders to his aid Benaiah and the latter's striking the intended victim, an adversary of the king (II.B, IV.B, V.B; vv. 25, 34, 46a). Third, the killing of Joab (IV, vv. 28-35) naturally follows Adonijah's murder; in fact, this execution is set in motion by the report of Adonijah's death (v. 28). And this episode is now linked explicitly, though perhaps secondarily, to the immediately preceding traditions of Abiathar's expulsion by a note recording the appointment of both a new commander to replace Joab and a new priest to replace Abiathar (v. 35). Finally, we may observe that the given order of events—Adonijah, Abiathar, and Joab—is already foreshadowed in v. 22, and, moreover, follows a certain logical sequence: the elimination of a rival from the immediate family, then his chief cohort, then remaining opposition (Kegler, 197-98).

Thus, whatever its prior history may have been, the unit as it now stands presents four incidents in series, bound together by similarity of content and purpose, by a refrain appearing three times (vv. 25, 34, 46a), and by an administrative notice (v. 35); and, most importantly, the unit is set off by an introductory and concluding framework (vv. 12b, 46b), which provides an interpretative key for the whole.

Genre

The genre of this unit cannot be specified with precision. It seems to be an editorial composite of traditions and genres, some of which may have existed independently of their present context. Something of a structural parallel occurs in the account of David's reign. After being given the promise that the kingdom would be made sure and everlasting (2 Sam 7:16, 26; *nākôn,* Niphal participle from *kûn,* as in 1 Kgs 2:12b-46), the text immediately moves to a series of short reports, citing a string of military victories (2 Samuel 8). It is as though "defeat" of the enemy (Hiphil of *yākâ,* "defeat," as in 1 Kgs 2:12b-46, in the sense of "kill") illustrates the first steps taken toward realizing that prophetic promise of a kingdom made sure forever (2 Sam 7:16, 26).

Setting

Since it is a matter of an editorial composite, the setting of the unit must be seen strictly in literary terms. The unit probably stems from the exilic redactor of Kings—who likely used older materials—and is set as a bridge between the end of David's reign and those events during Solomon's rule that are clearly and wholly related to the latter's own initiative and fame (chs. 3–10). At the same time, the unit is secondarily set forth in the wake of the conspiracy and counterconspiracy of ch. 1, showing Solomon carrying out reprisals against the conspirators, while in a general way following up some of David's final directives and settling old scores deriving from David's reign (2 Sam 3:28-29, 38-39 [Joab]; 2 Sam 16:5-14; 19:17-23 [*RSV* 19:16-23; Shimei]).

Intention

The main intention of this composite series is to show how the kingdom "was established in Solomon's hand," that is, made secure after its uncertain beginnings in the waning days of David. In the process, some old grudges can be settled, an oracle fulfilled, and something of David's last wishes carried out. In the context of the larger Dtr history work, this unit is a filled "pausal moment" between reigns (see above, pp. 26-28), a bridge between David and Solomon. It makes a direct connection not only with the David-Solomon-Adonijah story (1 Kgs 1:1-53), but with a leitmotif important to the books of Samuel: the rivalry between Saul (and the Saulides) and David (cf. 2 Sam 3:6-30; 16:5-14). Belonging among Solomon's first deeds, the unit portrays a major aspect of Solomon's character—his decisive, ruthless action in the interest of strong, unquestioned rule (for David, cf. 2 Samuel 8). This image of Solomon will be set beside other images in subsequent material. It may not have been in itself an unsympathetic or derogatory characterization (we have little basis on which to judge such matters), but the episodes nevertheless give careful justification for each of Solomon's actions, as though to remove any doubt as to the legitimacy of his attempts to consolidate authority.

Bibliography

J. Fokkelman, *King David,* 390-410 (see listing at 1:1-53); J. Kegler, *Politisches Geschehen und Theologisches Verstehen* (Calwer Theologische Monographien 8; Stuttgart: Calwer, 1977) 196-213.

II. EPISODE: THE KILLING OF ADONIJAH, 2:13-25

Structure

A. Account: the oath of death	13-24
1. Adonijah and Bathsheba: a request	13-18
a. Audience with Bathsheba	13-14
b. Request by Adonijah	15-17

1) Basis for request	15-16
2) Request proper	17
c. Bathsheba's response	18
2. Bathsheba and Solomon: a request conveyed	19-24
a. Audience with Solomon	19-20
b. Request by Bathsheba	21
c. Solomon's response: oath of death	22-24
1) Basis for oath	22
2) Oath proper	23-24
B. Report of death oath carried out	25

The key to the structure of this unit lies in its carefully crafted dramatic movement. Adonijah, stung from his ignoble defeat, moves circumspectly and deviously to gain as his wife the comely maiden who comforted King David in his aged infirmity. The request implies more than meets our eye: it is a claim to the throne itself (2 Sam 3:6-11; 16:20-22; M. Tsevat, "Marriage and Monarchical Legitimacy in Ugarit and Israel," *JSS* 3 [1958] 241). And Solomon immediately perceives the implication. He moves decisively to eliminate Adonijah and rid himself once and for all of this rivalrous brother.

The account neatly balances two main scenes (A.1 and A.2; vv. 13-18, 19-24), which typically focus on two characters and concentrate the action in two conversations. The words of scene one travel back and forth, forming a repeated structure of eight members in four rounds (see Fokkelman, 391):

Bathsheba-Adonijah Adonijah-Bathsheba	greetings, v. 13
Adonijah-Bathsheba Bathsheba-Adonijah	introductory words, v. 14
Adonijah-Bathsheba Bathsheba-Adonijah	basis for request, vv. 15-16
Adonijah-Bathsheba Bathsheba-Adonijah	request proper, v. 17

Scene two (A.2, vv. 19-24) extends this dialogic symmetry:

Bathsheba-Solomon Solomon-Bathsheba	introductory words, v. 20
Bathsheba-Solomon Solomon-Bathsheba	request and response, vv. 21-24

It is obvious, however, that with scene two the narrator created a disequilibrium in the pattern. He begins (vv. 19-20) in the manner of vv. 16-17 (note the close similarity of wording), conveying a sense of absolute reciprocity between mother and son (v. 19). As the words flow back and forth, he suddenly lets Solomon's response burst forth like some dark eruption of animus spilling into polite conversation. The king's words are many and harsh, and they admit of no reply. Our expectations set up by the repeated dialogues are completely shattered. A Solomon who before remained rather indistinct appears now as a suspicious, quick-tempered, dominating, derisive monarch. What high contrast to Bathsheba's measured, polite words that cloak her motivations from our sight!

This quick turn of events suggests that our sense of Solomon and these motival contrasts may be more important than balanced verbal repetition to our grasping the formal artistry of the unit. The kingdom has "turned about" (v. 15b), and Adonijah seeks by his own manipulation to turn it back to his own. But ironically, the request, thought to appear innocent if transmitted to the king by Bathsheba, is itself "turned about" by Solomon's hostile reaction. King Solomon views the request for Abishag not as a kindness offered by Bathsheba, but as a deceptive ploy by Adonijah, and a proven sign of his brother's disloyalty to the crown (cf. 1:52). The ease with which the narrator has Solomon see through the situation suggests that Bathsheba all along may have anticipated this outcome. She is still the mother we remember from ch. 1: an eager and willing manipulator of events. Adonijah prevails upon the queen mother not to refuse his request, and she complies—but that works against him, since she knows what her son's reaction is likely to be. Instead of furthering Adonijah's cause, she undermines it. So, in the second scene, when Bathsheba—like Adonijah before—prevails upon the king not to refuse her request, Solomon *does* refuse, and this, too, undermines Adonijah's position, ultimately costing him his life. The fate of the rival is sealed both by acceptance (by the queen) and refusal (by the king) of his request. It is as though nothing Adonijah could have done in the situation would have changed the outcome.

Genre

This unit is a brief STORY. It shows a clear dramatic structure and movement from a tension or complication (the normalcy of the Solomonic rule is upset by a devious roundabout claim to the throne) to its resolution in the execution of the claimant. Alternatively, one might view it as an (→) episode within the larger story of Solomon becoming king (→ 1:1-53), since the events fit so well and presuppose much of what went on there.

Setting

Whether or not it originated among partisans loyal to David and Solomon, this story can hardly have existed apart from that told in ch. 1. V. 15 makes the connection clear, alluding to the "turnabout" (see 12:15; Gen 50:20) in the kingdom as Yahweh's doing (see 1 Kgs 1:48). Nor can Adonijah's execution be fully understood apart from 1:52-53, the scene in which the brothers came to a reserved reconciliation. In seeking to gain some claim on the throne, even if only through marrying into the dead king's harem (see 2 Sam 16:20-22), Adonijah now has broken the condition set for his life: that he be a loyal subject (*ben ḥayil,* 1:52; *RSV* translates "worthy man," but see 1 Sam 18:17; 2 Sam 2:7; 13:28). Hence, that instability in the final resting point of ch. 1 leads to further decisive action here in this story narrating the end of Adonijah. At the same time, the story is firmly set as the first action taken by Solomon in "establishing" his rule (2:12b, 46b). Just here, one catches sight of this new king's quick, self-serving discernment. It is as though he obliquely carried out David's final charge to be wise (2:6) and anticipates with some irony a major theme in the chapters to come: he is a king wise in *all* manner of things.

Intention

The main intention of this story is to record the final demise of Adonijah, an event which is the first of a series of accounts detailing Solomon's actions in making his rule secure, thus finally having the kingdom "established" in his hand. In relation to the curves of fortune for these two brothers (see the discussion at 1:1-53), this episode represents the nadir of Adonijah: from his self-propelled rise to his precipitous fall, not only from the throne, but now fallen dead, struck by royal assassins. At the same time, this episode brings Solomon to a climax of political and personal dominance over his brother. Save for brief references to Yahweh's aims and his covenant with the Davidic house (2:15, 24; see 2 Samuel 7), the story breathes a secular spirit, intending to portray the actions of Solomon according to the economy of human strivings. Theological claims are not boldly made, as though to say only that the deepest rift between brothers (fratricide) and the harshest of penalties exacted of a political rival without power (assassination)—like the turnabout in favor of Solomon's gaining the crown—are mysteriously, somehow, from the Lord.

Bibliography

J. Fokkelman, *King David,* 390-98 (see listing at 1:1-53).

III. REPORT: THE EXPULSION OF ABIATHAR, 2:26-27

Structure

A. Report of command: banishment from court	26
1. Introduction	26aα
2. Command	26aβ-b
a. Concerning banishment	26aβ
b. Concerning death and reprieve	26b
B. Report of oracle fulfillment: expulsion from priesthood	27
1. Report of expulsion	27a
2. Formula of oracle fulfillment	27b

The structure of this unit is determined by the juxtaposition of two reports, each of which could have existed independently of one another (III.A, B; vv. 26, 27). They are linked now by their common subject matter—the fate of Abiathar, the priest. The first simply reports and directly quotes the command of Solomon that presumably sends Abiathar to his own home, but spares him a deserved death. The second statement comments on and interprets the foregoing, reporting the "defrocking" of Abiathar as the fulfillment of an earlier prophetic word. Together, these two statements speak of the physical, legal, and theological aspects of banishment from court.

Genre

Both statements are reports, and both together constitute REPORT. Reports of a command are very common, and typically carry a very brief introduction naming the speaker and situation and/or subject matter. Then follows the main body of the report, the speaker's orders (cf. 2 Sam 9:9-10, part of a larger narrative). REPORTS of ORACLE FULFILLMENT are very common in the books of Kings. They sometimes are indigenous to narrative materials (e.g., 1 Kgs 13:26) and sometimes are associated with various levels of the redaction. Typically, these reports briefly cite a situation or event and then conclude with a formulaic expression that the circumstances have occurred "according to the word of Yahweh which he spoke by PN." Events actualize a word spoken by one of Yahweh's prophets (see the full discussion at 13:26). The slightly variant wording of v. 27b is not a significant alteration in the pattern.

Setting

The original settings for these reports, now put together, may have been different. The report of command may be a fragment from a narrative no longer extant. But, in general, just as spoken orders would have been given out in varied circumstances, so reports of such orders would find various settings, oral and written, in the life of Israel. Reports of oracle fulfillment seem to have had at least two important literary settings: in stories about prophets and in longer accounts of kings and heroes where the author or editor states his theological view that events are moved by Yahweh's word. The perspective is wide, the scope of traditions very broad. God speaks to the prophets, and the word is actualized in history (see the full discussion at 13:26). In this particular passage, the report in v. 27 likely stems from the exilic DtrH and along with v. 26 forms part of the longer account of Solomon's establishing the kingdom, but retrospectively ties the banishment of Abiathar into the traditions of Eli (1 Sam 2:31-35).

Intention

It is clear from what has been said that the intention of this report, or combined reports, is to record the fate of Abiathar, a coconspirator named both in ch. 1 and in the episode "The Killing of Adonijah" (2:13-25). Abiathar is spared execution, but exiled from life in court and cult—a position perhaps not unambiguously preferable to death. The report conveys the information that the priest was ordered from Jerusalem. From a religio-legal point of view, he was relieved of his official priestly duties. Both the physical and legal aspects are further intended to be seen summarily under a theological veneer: the events actualize a word spoken by the prophets against the priestly house of Eli (see 1 Sam 2:27-36, probably a Dtr passage as well). The report in this final composite form thus conforms to the intention of other parts of 1 Kgs 2:12b-46. It grounds the events in earlier traditions, as though the better to establish continuity between the reigns of David and Solomon and to forge a unity via normative interpretation of the diverse materials relating to the beginning and flowering of the monarchy.

IV. EPISODE: THE KILLING OF JOAB, 2:28-35

Structure

A. Exposition and complication: report to reader of Joab's flight (law of asylum invoked) 28

B. The execution of Joab	29-34
1. Solomon's order	29
a. Report to Solomon of Joab's flight	29a
b. Solomon's order of execution (law of asylum ignored)	29b
2. Joab's death	30-34
a. Benaiah's hesitation (law of asylum observed)	30
1) Narrative introduction	30aα
2) Dialogue (Joab and Benaiah)	30aβ
a) Order to Joab	$30a\beta_1$
b) Joab's reply	$30a\beta_2$
3) Benaiah's report to Solomon	30b
b. Solomon's new order	31-33
1) Order of execution (asylum ignored)	31a
2) Speech of justification	31b-33
c. Consequences: Joab's death (law of asylum overridden)	34
C. Conclusion: notice of replacements	35
1. Concerning Joab	35a
2. Concerning Abiathar	35b

As it was integrated into its present context this unit may have undergone some expansion, mainly in vv. 31-33, but also v. 35b. To assume, however, that *nothing* of Solomon's self-justification as given in vv. 31-33 would have belonged to an original story is to imagine a tale without dramatic power. Indeed, the key to the thematic and formal structure of the whole may be seen in just this section, a climactic point at which Solomon overcomes the strength of the law of asylum—a law which Joab invokes (IV.A, v. 28), Solomon ignores (IV.B.1, v. 29), Benaiah at first observes (IV.B.2.a, v. 30), and Solomon finally overrides (IV.B.2.b, vv. 31-33).

A concentric motival structure reinforces this sense of narrative development. We move from Solomon's first order (v. 29) in toward a little dialogue which centers on Joab's defiant statement (v. 30a), and back out to Solomon's issuing of his execution order again. We may visualize the structure as follows (cf. Fokkelman, 401):

A Solomon's order, v. 29
  B Benaiah comes to Joab, v. 30aα
    C Dialogue, v. 30aβ
  B' Benaiah reports back to Solomon, v. 30b
A' Solomon's order re-issued, v. 31a

In this way, the narrator puts the underlying confrontation between Joab and Solomon at the apex of a structural triangle. Joab's defiance, his challenge to Benaiah that he overlook the law of asylum and slay him in the sanctuary, really forces the issue and turns us back toward Solomon, who must now decide what action to take in response. The order which he gives is the climax in the narrative.

With great flourish, and with an elevated, well-crafted speech (see Fokkelman, 402), the king invokes a counter-principle of divine revenge, thus turning the action to his own advantage and determining its outcome. Joab will finally be murdered. Yet almost as a gesture in deference to the notion of asylum, he is to be buried (vv. 31a, 34), not cast out as an enemy of God (so Jezebel, 1 Kgs 21:23). The narrative tension falls away in the conclusion or denouement with a simple notice of Joab's replacement. (The note about Abiathar, v. 35b, may be a gloss which lacks clear integration into the structure of the account.)

Thus the fugitive can be killed, the Lord avenged (law of asylum overridden), and Solomon remain guiltless. In sum, the narrator has structured his effects on two levels: the one telling how Joab came to his end, the other—which takes up most of the space—dealing with the problem that Joab's invoking the law of asylum made for Solomon, and the justification for his finally breaking it. At the same time, the narrator has linked this episode with its wider canonical context (vv. 32-33; cf. vv. 5-6).

Genre

Although very compressed, this unit shows all the basic features of STORY. The *exposition,* or situational background, with its *complication* in Joab's clinging to the horns of the altar (IV.A, v. 28), comes to a *climax* (IV.B.2.b, vv. 31-33) when Solomon surmounts the problem, overcoming both his lieutenant's hesitation and the law of asylum. The action then falls away in a brief *conclusion* (IV.C, v. 35) that simply reports the execution, burial, and replacement of Joab (and Abiathar). As with many Hebrew stories, the descriptive prose is minimal, and direct speech maximal. Noteworthy is Solomon's ORDER given in vv. 31-33 (IV.B.2.c). The rather elaborate justification for the order is reminiscent of the (→) announcement of judgment insofar as this genre announces coming retributive disaster and speaks of its moral justification.

Setting

Perhaps originating among Solomonic partisans, this story's most important setting is now the larger literary context in which it appears. Its opening lines allude to the preceding episode, and its refrainlike conclusion in v. 34 ties it to other accounts detailing the fate of the conspirators against Solomon.

Intention

In this context, the tale intends to provide another example of how the kingdom came to be firmly established in Solomon's hand (see vv. 12b, 46b), while naturally providing justification for Solomon's actions. Like the preceding and the following episodes, the story makes clear the continuity between the rule of David and Solomon's first actions. It is continuity established in carrying out one of David's last directives (see 2:5-6) and rooted in the traditions of David's reign (2 Sam 3:6-30). All is seen somewhat superficially as the working out of the Lord's retributive justice (vv. 32-33), as though to suggest that revenge against coconspirators, like the coronation of Solomon, finally rests upon God's special covenant with David and the chosen heir.

Bibliography

J. Fokkelman, *King David,* 398-404 (see listing at 1:1-53).

V. EPISODE: THE KILLING OF SHIMEI, 2:36-46a

Structure

- A. Account of agreement with Shimei — 36-38
  - 1. Shimei summoned before Solomon — 36a
  - 2. Agreement — 36b-38a
    - a. Command and warning: conditions for life — 36b-37
    - b. Oath (agreement) by Shimei — 38a
  - 3. Report of agreement kept — 38b
- B. Account of violation and consequences — 39-46a
  - 1. Shimei's violation of oath — 39-40
  - 2. Violation reported to Solomon — 41
  - 3. Consequences — 42-46a
    - a. Shimei summoned before Solomon — 42a
    - b. Speech of accusation and punishment — 42b-45
      - 1) Concerning the situation — 42b
      - 2) Concerning the violation — 43
      - 3) Concerning the punishment — 44-45
        - a) Retribution on Shimei — 44
        - b) Blessing on Solomon — 45
    - c. Report of Shimei's execution — 46a

The structure of this unit is built on a simple plot: a sworn agreement, its violation, and the subsequent execution of the violator. The beginning and the end (A, B.3; vv. 36-38, 42-46a) form a balanced pair, each opening with identical phrases reporting a summons to the king (vv. 36, 42) and each dominated by speech. In between, the narrator tells simply and directly how Shimei violated the terms of his own oath. The unit closes with a brief report of Shimei's execution.

Quite possibly, vv. 44-45 (B.3.b.3) are late additions to an otherwise self-contained unit. Only here in this story does one find allusions to a wider context—David's farewell speech and Shimei's earlier offense cited therein (2:8-9; cf. 2 Sam 16:5-14) and the dynastic promise, a feature of the preceding episodes. In themselves, these two verses do not seem crucial to the structural logic of the story, and so one can imagine their being absent from some earlier version of the material. On the other hand, the verses have a clear literary function in their present position: they announce retributive punishment, following naturally after Solomon's charge of a violated oath. And the punishment is made all the more poignant for its contrast with the blessing resting upon Solomon's house.

Genre

This unit belongs to the genre of STORY. Its structure shows all the necessary form-critical elements: an *exposition* at the beginning sets the situation (an oath taken by Shimei), which is then *complicated* by Shimei's violation of the oath. The *climax* comes in the confrontation between Solomon and Shimei, in which the latter is accused and his punishment announced (if we accept the full text; see above). The *denouement* reports Shimei's execution, a coming to rest of the essential dramatic movement. Several elements of speech are worth mentioning. (1) The phrase in Solomon's mouth, "Your blood shall be upon your own head"

(v. 37), imputes liability to the addressee while declaring the speaker guiltless. Close parallels are in the Davidic traditions: 2 Sam 1:16, where David orders the murder of the Amalekite who has slain Saul; 2 Sam 3:28-29, where David declares Joab guilty of the murder of Abner and simultaneously absolves himself of any liability in the matter. There seems to be some (as yet not entirely clear) relationship between this pattern of speech and more formal declaration of liability associated with legal situations (Boecker; Koch; Reventlow). (2) Solomon's words in vv. 42-43 resemble an INDICTMENT SPEECH associated with formal trials. In such circumstances, the speaker would cite a state of affairs that had in some way been violated and then go on to accuse directly (→ imputation speech: Gen 31:26-30; Judg 8:1; 1 Sam 22:13). Accepting the present MT, one may observe that Solomon's speech also seems akin to (→) prophecy of punishment over an individual, with elements similar to a (→) prophecy of salvation added as a concluding contrast to the fate of Shimei (v. 45). In context, however, this climactic speech serves mainly to confront Shimei with his violation and to announce thereby his punishment. In the narratives about Israel's kings, this sort of confrontation and ensuing speech is most often associated with prophets (cf. 1 Sam 15:17-19; 1 Kgs 21:19-24; and contrast Yaron, 433).

Setting

An original setting for this story remains hidden from view. In its present literary context, however, the story completes the cycle begun in 2:12b, the way the kingdom was "established in Solomon's hand" (v. 46b), and plays out the theme—note vv. 44-45—of Solomon's carrying out David's farewell directives.

Intention

This unit intends to narrate the last of Solomon's unfinished business: settling up old scores for David (Joab, Shimei) and gaining reprisals for himself against the coconspirators for the throne (Adonijah, Abiathar, Joab). At the same time, this final story in the cycle begun in 2:13 asserts once again the strong continuity between David's reign and the epoch of Solomon—a continuity obvious in the acts of men and covertly in the design of God. Thus the dynastic promise and blessing (v. 45) is asserted plainly and in a form clearly derivative from 2 Sam 7:16, 26 one last time before the overall conclusion (v. 46b) and before moving on to new incidents in the Solomonic period.

Bibliography

H. J. Boecker, *Redeformen des Rechtslebens im Alten Testament* (WMANT 14; Neukirchen: Neukirchener, 1964) 138-39; J. Fokkelman, *King David,* 404-9 (see listing at 1:1-53); K. Koch, "Der Spruch 'Sein Blut bleibe auf seinem Haupt'," *VT* 12 (1962) 398-416; F. Langlamet, "David et la Maison de Saül," *RB* 86 (1979) 194-243, 481-513; H. Graf Reventlow, "Sein Blut komme über sein Haupt," *VT* 10 (1960) 311-27; R. Yaron, "A Rammesid Parallel to I K ii 33, 44-45," *VT* 8 (1958) 432-33.

THE REIGN OF SOLOMON: CANONICAL FRAMEWORK, 3:1–11:43

Structure

I. Account of the kingdom (internal): administration and building 3:1–9:25

A. Foreword to the account of the kingdom	3:1-3
B. Solomon's wisdom, administration, wealth	3:4–5:8
1. Account of Solomon's wisdom	3:4-28
a. Report of dream epiphany (promise of wisdom)	4-15
b. Story of wise judgment	16-28
2. Account of Solomon's administration	4:1–5:8 (*RSV* 4:28)
a. Register of royal officials	4:1-6
b. Organization for daily provisions	4:7–5:8
C. Solomon's building activities	5:9 (*RSV* 4:29)–9:23
1. Preparations (wisdom, labor, materials)	5:9-32
2. Temple-palace construction	6:1–7:51
3. Temple dedication	8:1-66
4. Report of dream epiphany (confirmation)	9:1-9
5. Supplemental accounts of construction activities	9:10-23
D. Conclusion	9:24-25
II. Account of kingdom (external): dealings, fame, wealth	9:26–10:29
A. Miscellany on imported wealth, fame, prosperity	9:26–10:25
B. Supplemental reports and statements: horses, imports, exports	10:26-29
III. Account of the end of Solomon's reign	11:1-43
A. A theological review	1-13
B. Account of adversaries	14-40
C. Concluding regnal resumé	41-43

Despite evidence of extensive editorial history, the final form of the Solomonic material has a fairly clear structure. First, along content lines one can see three major divisions: the kingdom in its internal aspect, in its external dealings, and in its ominous end. Everything from 3:1 to 9:25 has its main reference point in the internal affairs, organization, and activities of Solomon and his kingdom (I.A-D). Even the ostensibly international horizon of 5:9-32 (I.C.1) points by context to the necessary preparations for the great internal achievement of Solomon, the construction of the temple-palace complex, the section which takes most space in the text. On the other hand, everything in 9:26–10:29 has in common its reference to international dealings of King Solomon, all redounding to his prestige and power (II.A, B). Section III alone turns to the question of disruption, transgression, and appraisal from a theological point of view. The reign closes with the usual concluding regnal resumé.

This division of content is marked by a system of thematic bracketing. The smaller units, 3:1-3 and 9:24-25, enclose the somewhat disparate material gathered in 3:1–9:25. The mention of Solomon's taking the daughter of Pharaoh as his wife, which to many critics has seemed ill fitting in its present location (including the translators of the Greek VS), in fact reappears at 9:24 in an equally abrupt and puzzling manner (the syntax is rough, too). Yet, here the context agrees precisely with the temporal sequence indicated in 3:1, "he brought her into the city of David until he had finished building. . . ." So it is that after the various building activities have been reported, the text mentions "Pharaoh's daughter went up from the city of David to her own house . . ." (9:24). Furthermore, the mention of the peoples' and Solomon's sacrificing at high places outside Jerusalem before the temple had been built (3:2) is matched by the reference to Solomon's offering of sacrifices on the newly built and dedicated altar at 9:25. It seems no accident, therefore, that with this motivic bracketing, 9:25b can round off the whole complex with what amounts to a colophon: "and he completed the house" (*wĕšillam 'et-habbāyit*; cf. 7:51 = 2 Chr 5:1; Neh 6:15); this solidifies the grouping of traditions in 3:1–9:25 under the rubric of building the house of Yahweh. Similarly, the account of the *external* kingdom in large measure is gathered together and framed with the mention of Hiram and the fleet of ships that bring gold to the king (9:26-28; 10:22). This perspective finds its neat summary in 10:23-25. Lastly, section III has Dtr language in 11:1-13 that is picked up and elaborated as an oracle to Jeroboam (vv. 29-39), as though to cement a framework around the two inner pieces of tradition (vv. 14-22, 23-25), themselves linked in the final text by means of the thematic statement given almost identically in each: "the Lord raised up an adversary . . ." (vv. 14, 23).

From the point of view of motifs, one can see certain unifying tendencies as well. The wisdom of Solomon (*ḥokmâ*), which is asked of God in an opening scene (3:4-15), is then illustrated in Solomon's clever determination of truth in the dispute between two women (3:16-28) and in his superior intellectual wisdom (5:9-14); his wisdom is recognized—and given new nuance—by Hiram, who applauds the statecraft shown by this monarch (5:22, 27); it is recognized by the queen of Sheba as well, but in Solomon's building activities and wealthy royal retinue (10:4-5, 7); *ḥokmâ* is highlighted by the Judahite and exilic Dtr editor, who cites, or adds interpretation to, his sources (11:41). We are never far from a concrete example of Solomon's wisdom; it is an image which is elastic and encompassing enough to serve as a leitmotif through the material. And clearly, from the moment when wisdom is first mentioned as a gift of God (3:12, 13), it is linked with the pomp and substance of the kingdom, Solomon's "riches and honor," expressed with emphasis in the Hebrew (*gam 'ōšer gam kābôd*). We have at least a loosely unified composition hanging on this notion of wisdom, rooted in Solomon's kingdom.

Divine address occurs four times during the Solomonic reign: 3:11-14; 6:11-13; 9:3-9; 11:11-13 (cf. 11:31-49). All these literary moments likely stem from the DtrH, and they consistently stress—like a *cantus firmus*—the conditional basis on which Solomon holds the reign. The motif is sounded in its most positive form three times: at the beginning and twice in connection with the climactic centerpiece, the building and dedication of the temple. Thus, the editor-author(s) forged a kind of unity of exhortation out of the material, which then can be turned on end to become a deadly serious, twice-repeated message of conditions violated, promise lost, glory tarnished (ch. 11).

In summary, many signs point to substantial unity in the MT: a neat division of content, marked by techniques of bracketing and brought together under the aspect of Solomon's glory in wisdom, power, wealth, building activities, international influence, and fame. The total presentation carries a tone of exhortation, all the better to emphasize the conditional trust on which the kingdom depends.

Nothing is to be gained by forcing more artistry and plan to the material than the case warrants (against Porten and Radday).

Genre

Since this material is an editorial composition, one may not specify with precision a single genre. It functions as an overall editorial framework, into which diverse materials of varying content and genre have been placed. The designation as (→) biography is so ill-fitted to the material as to be of little help (against Baltzer). A distant parallel may be in the Egyptian "royal novel" (*Königsnovelle,* a designation for a type of narrative material common in royal inscriptions found on temple and tomb walls), which tells of the benefactions of the pharaoh for his gods. The Egyptian conventions, which do not constitute in the proper sense a literary genre, may account in part for the sequence of subject matter in the Hebrew composition (dream, temple-palace construction, dedication) and perhaps a few internal details as well (A. Hermann; S. Herrmann). Mesopotamian royal inscriptions offer equally impressive motivic parallels as well (→ 6:1–7:51).

Setting

The canonical framework undoubtedly owes most of its final shaping to the Dtr editor. This supposition is important for understanding the late perspective from which the kingdom of Solomon has been viewed. The material follows on the transition from David's reign and holds a major position in the account of all the kings. Only David is treated more extensively, but Solomon alone with such royal aggrandizement and public praise. The unit stands as a kind of centerpiece, an implicit measure for the reigns to follow and a reservoir of theological images for later generations.

Intention

The purpose of this editorial composition finds expression most clearly in the broad links to the wider canonical context. Of course, the account describes the reign of Solomon. But it really looks to, and creates, an epoch: the internal and external strength of the Solomonic era, gathered by images of wisdom, wealth, and power—simply put, "glory." It is an epoch given by God, increased in godly splendor and diminished in personal transgression. The author-editor intends to remember Solomon with national pride in the accoutrements of royal power—here the Israelites are like their neighbors—and also with theological critique, as though to interweave achievement with downfall, and humanly fashioned permanence with God-induced change.

Bibliography

K. Baltzer, *Biographie*, 88-93 (see listing at "Introduction to Historical Literature"); J. C. Trebolle Barrera, *Salomón y Jeroboán: Historia de la recensión y redacción de I Reyes 2–12:14* (Salamanca: Universidad Pontificia, 1980); A. Hermann, *Die ägyptische Königsnovelle* (Leipziger Ägyptologische Studien 10; Glükstadt/Hamburg/New York: Augustin, 1938); S. Herrmann, "Die Königsnovelle in Ägypten und Israel," *Wissenschaftliche Zeitschrift der Karl-Marx Universität* 3 (1953-54) 51-62; J. Kegler, *Geschehen* (see listing at 2:12b-46); J. King, "The Role of Solomon in the Deuteronomistic History" (Diss., Southern Baptist Theological Seminary, 1978); B. Porten, "The Structure and Theme of the Solomon Narrative (1 Kings 3–11)," *HUCA* 38 (1967) 93-128; Y. Radday, "Chiasm" (see listing at "Introduction to 1 Kings").

FOREWORD TO THE ACCOUNT OF THE KINGDOM, 3:1-3

Structure

I.	Report: concerning Solomon's marriage	1
II.	Statement of incidental circumstances: the religious situation	2
III.	Statement of theological appraisal	3

A complex history of redaction stands behind the present text. The LXX omits v. 1a and carries the rest of v. 1 in a supplement at 2:35. V. 2 seems ill fitted to the context and may be a gloss occasioned by v. 3, or a remnant of something more extensive which appraised the king (Weippert). V. 3 is typical of those theological appraisals which form an important part of introductory summaries to each reign. The occurrence of similar motifs again at 9:24-25 should give us pause in wanting to rearrange or eliminate certain elements in the text.

This unit is a composite of three rather independent items, now loosely related to one another. The first reports an action and is consequently cast in standard narrative form. In contrast, v. 2 offers a circumstantial participial clause, and v. 3 simply states an author-editor's evaluation of Solomon's rule. These three items seem to be related more by context than by form. The first sets up a temporal framework by mentioning Solomon's building activities. Thus the first seems to suggest the second, those incidental circumstances for the period of time prior to these activities. The third item ties a theological appraisal of Solomon to this same period and situation and to Solomon's sacrificing at the high places (*bāmôt*) when there was no temple in Jerusalem.

Genre

The first item belongs to the genre of REPORT and, owing to its brevity, one may speak of NOTICE. The second two items are simply STATEMENTS. Because of their contextual associations, however, all three constitute an editorial composite and, together with 9:24-25, seem to function as part of a compositional framework. They serve as a foreword to the material which follows in 3:4–11:43 (Noth, *Könige,* 45).

Setting

Naturally a report or notice may have many settings, depending upon its content and circumstances of use. This particular report of marriage, v. 1, may possibly have had its roots in archival records kept within the royal establishment. In fact, however, no examples of such records exist. In the cases of vv. 2 and 3, we must focus more intently on the present *literary* setting, for we probably see in these two verses fragmentary portions of theological appraisals common to the editing of the books of Kings (Weippert, 307-8). Such appraisals form an important part of the introductory (→) regnal resumé, and in style and purpose are far removed from the keeping of records, since they already presuppose sifting and evaluation of materials by an author (→ 22:43-44; full discussion at 14:21-31). These three verses form the first element of a bracket with 9:24-25 and thus delimit the first major portion of this account of Solomon's reign, the kingdom seen in its internal aspects, 3:4–9:23.

Intention

While each of the three items seeks to convey information deemed important to Solomon's reign, the most important fact for us is that the composite report is the functional equivalent of the introductory (→) regnal resumé. This foreword comes after the kingdom has been established and consolidated in Solomon's hand (2:12b-46) and introduces the fully Solomonic era with a clear emphasis upon theological appraisal. Moreover, these verses suggest interpretative parameters for the material to follow. It is a question of a "before" and an "after" time, that is, a period before the temple-palace was constructed, coextensive with those years when Solomon's wife remained in Jerusalem, and a period after the buildings had been completed and dedicated. It is thus a question of that time when sacrifices on the shrine hills, "high places," were matter-of-factly circumstantial, even understandable, and a time after which one's judgment on such matters would be considerably more harsh. It does not seem accidental, and it certainly is suggestive, that this "before" time is associated with the restriction of Pharaoh's daughter to Jerusalem (according to 9:10 this would amount to 20 years), and that the "after" time links all manner of transgression against God with this same woman and her coeval wives in the harem (ch. 11). The author-editor anticipates the tone of ch. 11, as though an evil influence were held in check while Solomon channeled his energies into his major achievement, the temple construction. By implication this selfsame force will be let loose once the rush of pious benefaction to Yahweh is spent.

Bibliography

H. Weippert, "Die 'deuteronomistischen' Beurteilungen" (see listing at "Introduction to 1 Kings").

ACCOUNT OF SOLOMON'S WISDOM: REPORT OF DREAM EPIPHANY, 3:4-15

Structure

I. Introduction: the situation	4
A. Travel (to Gibeon) to high place	4a
B. Sacrifices offered	4b
II. Report of dream epiphany	5-15a
A. Opening: location and epiphany formula	5a
B. Petitionary conversation	5b-14
1. Narrative introduction	5bα
2. God's request for Solomon's petition	5bβ
3. Solomon's petition	6-9
a. Distant background: concerning David	6
b. Immediate background: concerning Solomon	7-8
c. Petition proper	9
4. God's answer	10-14
a. Narrative background: concerning God's reaction	10

b. Divine address	11-14
1) Basis for response	11
2) Announcement of petition granted	12-13
3) Conditional promise	14
C. Closing: dream conclusion formula	15a
III. Conclusion	15b
A. Travel (away from Gibeon) to Jerusalem	15bα
B. Sacrifices offered	15bβ

On grounds of style and content, almost all scholars agree that this unit is separate from vv. 1-3 and 16-28. What is disputed is the identification and extent of old tradition and its later editorial shaping. The choices run from those who allow maximum space to original material (e.g., Montgomery, Šanda, Burney among the commentators; Görg and Zelevsky among the special studies) to those who shrink the recoverable original and give maximum space to the Dtr author-editor(s) (e.g., Noth, Würthwein among the commentators; Scott and Kenik among the special studies). There is no consensus; it seems best to view the present text as an essentially unified piece which has been heavily edited by the redactor(s) of the books of Kings (cf. esp. vv. 6-8, 12b, 13b, 14, 15 with 2:3-4; 5:3-5, 7; 6:12-13; 8:14-30; 9:3-9).

The impression of unity is strengthened by observing the careful arrangement of elements within the text. If one focuses on the aspect of dream and epiphany, the structural center falls on the meeting between Solomon and God: Yahweh appears and asks a question of Solomon, who requests that he be given discernment for his rule; Yahweh responds with an elaborate announcement that his petition is granted (II, vv. 5-15a). A travel-sacrifice motif stands as a framing motif at beginning and end (I.A, B and III.A, B, vv. 4 and 15b; note the repeated vocabulary "offered up burnt offerings" [*y'l 'ōlôt*; Porten, 99]). This structure is consistent with a widespread pattern for reporting dreams in the ancient Near East (Oppenheim).

If the structural center is the meeting between Yahweh and Solomon, then the climax surely comes in the divine address (II.B.4, vv. 10-14), the answer to Solomon's petition (see esp. Görg, 44-48; Porten, 99). The author has Yahweh cite the reasons for his response in a fivefold series of statements—three negative formulations framed by two positive assertions:

(a) positive statement: "Because you have asked . . ."
(b) negative statement (three times): "(you) have not asked . . ."
(c) positive statement: "(but) you have asked. . . ."

The *RSV* ignores the repetition of the verb "ask" (*š'l*), and so obscures the litanylike recitation that gives emphasis to the final statement in the series:

Because you have asked for this thing,
  and have not asked for yourself long life
    and have not asked for yourself riches
      and have not asked for the life of your enemies,
but have asked for yourself understanding to discern what is right. . . .

Then the main clause announces the climactic point: Yahweh has indeed granted Solomon's petition, and everything he did *not* ask for will redound to his person in incomparable ways. And just here, the text offers more artistic flair—a chiastic arrangement of superlatives in v. 12bβ:

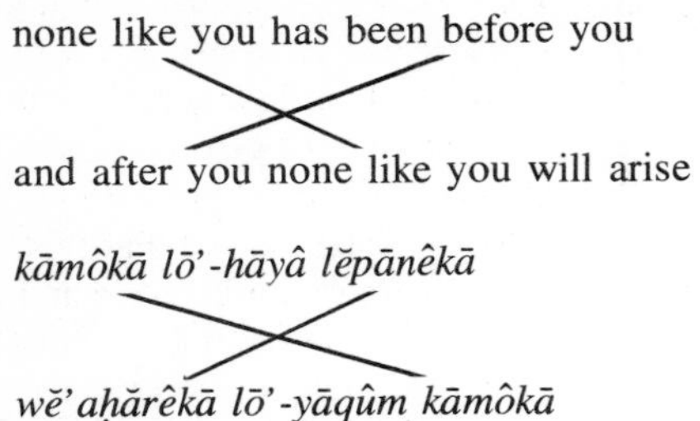

none like you has been before you
and after you none like you will arise
kāmôkā lō'-hāyâ lĕpānêkā
wĕ'aḥărêkā lō'-yāqûm kāmôkā

The overall effect is nearly lyrical; a patterned heaping up of similar expressions circling around what Solomon might have asked, but did not, coming to a climax in a chiastic parallelism expressing the promised incomparable substance of this king. Similar hyperbole is reserved in 1–2 Kings for Hezekiah (2 Kgs 18:5) and Josiah (2 Kgs 23:25). Cf. Neh 13:26, referring to Solomon; Gen 41:39, Pharaoh to Joseph; 1 Sam 10:24, referring to Saul, the king-designate. The climax is exquisite. Yet like an apparition's sudden shift, the text darts quickly away from its heady talk of this Solomon who will excel in wisdom, wealth, and honor, and jars us abruptly awake (cf. Gen 28:16), bringing us back with the dream recognition formula ("Behold, it was a dream," v. 15a; Oppenheim, 199a).

This text carries only brief narrative strokes, just enough to keep the movement clear. Everything seems weighted toward the conversation between God and Solomon. We are allowed to witness the event, hear the words, even for a moment to glimpse the interiority of God himself (v. 10). But the emphasis clearly falls on the properly pious petition, and the divine response in the form of promise.

Genre

The question of genre is complicated because a number of influential literary models may be discerned in the background. None seems to have worked a decisive or exclusive influence on this text.

The language clearly points to accounts of dreams known from the OT, but the style and vocabulary show a number of features atypical of many of these same accounts, e.g., Gen 37:5-11; Genesis 40 and 41; Judg 7:13-14 (Richter). On the other hand, this text in 1 Kings bears a strong resemblance to the schematic report of epiphany, which may or may not be described as dream (Gen 28:11-17; 48:3; Exod 3:2-6, 16; Judg 13:10; cf. the regular "P" usage in Exod 16:10; Lev 9:4; Num 14:10). Also the expression in v. 5, "appeared . . . in a dream of the night" (*nir'â . . . baḥălôm hallāyĕlâ*), is unparalleled in other OT accounts of dream and may suggest a more poetic rendering of the matter, more or less parallel with expressions such as "vision of the night" (*ḥezyôn lāyĕlâ,* Job 33:15) or "visions of the night" (*mar'ôt hallāyĕlâ*, Gen 46:2, with late Akkadian parallels; Oppenheim, 226). Perhaps the Hebrews made no firm distinctions among dream, epiphany, and vision.

More speculative is the attempt to see the Egyptian royal narrative (*Königs-*

novelle) as some kind of prototype for this text (S. Herrmann, followed for the most part by Görg, more cautiously by the commentaries, e.g., Noth and Gray). In fact, the main Egyptian text which S. Herrmann cited as evidence, the Sphinx Stele of Thutmose IV (*ANET,* 449), is fragmentary, and only by inference belongs in the company of the royal inscriptions first gathered by the Egyptologist A. Hermann. In any case, the Egyptian texts focus on the king's plans for, and making of, memorials for the gods, or they describe the king's military expeditions, the results of which are dedicated to the gods with the explicit expectation that such benefactions will accrue to the long reign and afterlife of the king. Hence these royal inscriptions seem remote from 1 Kings 3, both in content and general intention. Of course, one might make a case for general parallels between the royal novelette and the entire Solomonic account, but that is quite a different matter (→ discussion at 3:1–11:43).

Even less planted in firm evidence is the suggestion that the genre of this text reflects a royal ritual in which the king was granted his petitions (Würthwein, *Könige*).

We must come back to the point that the most direct formative influence on 1 Kgs 3:4-15 seems to be the OT REPORT of DREAM EPIPHANY. Typically, these reports are brief and schematic, merely mentioning that the deity appears (Niphal of *rā'â*) and presents a message or engages in dialogue with a human being. Such reports are found in the older and younger layers of the Pentateuch (Gen 12:7; 17:1-21; 18:1-33 [the last two reports include a closing formula, 17:22; 18:33]; 26:2-5, 24; 28:12-16; 48:3-4 [part of a longer farewell speech by Jacob]; Exod 3:2-12; Judg 13:10; 13:3-7; cf. Matt 2:19-20; etc.). The report of dream epiphany is different from the (→) dream report, which usually has more developed narrative features and emphasizes dream interpretation (see Genesis 37; 40–41; Richter).

An important generic element in 1 Kgs 3:4-15 is the PRAYER OF PETITION put into the mouth of Solomon (vv. 6-9). In its more or less everyday expression, a petition would almost always give (1) the basis for the petition, often including the objective to be gained; and (2) the petition proper, expressed directly or indirectly, negatively or positively (e.g., Gen 27:19; Num 22:16-17; Gerstenberger). The author-editor has put into Solomon's mouth a highly stylized version of such an ordinary petition. The language and tone are particularly religious, as though to emphasize the religious propriety of the petitioner. There are many parallels and the form is regular: (1) a statement of the situation forms the basis for the petition (in these pious contexts, the basis often involves citing transgressions or recalling Yahweh's past dealings with important persons, the petitioner, or the people of God); (2) a transition formula ("And now. . . ," *wĕ'attâ*), which leads into the substance of the petition proper, usually expressed with direct imperatives (see Exod 32:31-32; 33:12-13 [Moses]; 2 Sam 7:18-29 [David]; 1 Kgs 8:23-26 [Solomon]; 2 Kgs 19:15-19 =Isa 37:16-20 [Hezekiah]; Jonah 4:2-3; Neh 9:6-37; Ezra 9:6-15).

In the background may be a literary motif common in Mesopotamian (→) royal inscriptions: the petition for blessings, notably long life, lengthy rule, authority, riches, even death to enemies of the throne. See the examples from 10th-century Byblos, *ANET,* 653, 656 (*KAI,* nos. 4, 10); also *ANET,* 654, col. 1; fuller references in Malamat. If the author of the Kings text knew this ancient Near

Eastern convention (cf. Ps 21:5; 61:7; 2 Kgs 20:5-6), it is clear that he has shaped it according to an Israelite emphasis on Solomon's wisdom (*ḥokmâ*). Solomon asks only for an "understanding mind"; in v. 11 God responds by reciting in a negative way those conventional royal petitions and grants Solomon's more modest request. Then, as though custom is not to be denied, God goes on to give what Solomon did *not* ask for, and what his counterparts in Mesopotamia always request: riches and honor (*kābôd*), which in this case must be associated with long life (v. 14; cf. Prov 3:16; 9:11; 1 Chr 29:28; Malamat).

In the OT, all these religious petitions show a continuity of style and theme running through the Dtr literature into the Chronicler's postexilic work, and are mainly associated with important persons in the OT. Such prayers of petition form representative images of divine-human dialogue, and therefore tend to be vehicles for theological perspectives encompassing large sweeps of canonical literature. As such they demand, and are often given, a reply by God, as though to confirm, redirect, or give definitive understanding to the course of human history in the Israelite experience (see Exod 32:33-44; 33:14; 1 Kgs 9:1-9; 2 Kgs 19:20). The petition-answer pattern probably reflects genuine cultic experience (see Psalms 12; 60; 108), and thus points to yet another formative influence on the structure and genre of the text.

Setting

We do not know precisely what would have been a typical setting for a report of dream epiphany. Because such reports have occasional association with cultic sites, e.g., Gen 12:7 and 28:10-22, some have supposed that these reports would have been rooted in (→) legends circulating in and about a holy spot where epiphanies were frequent, and frequently remembered among people who visited such places. For the text in Kings, the prominence given to the location of the events at Gibeon (vv. 4a, 5a) and to the cultic activities carried on there (v. 4b) suggests something of this background. On the other hand, this particular literary text shows a great interest in Solomon and his monarchy, a fact that might point to an origin only as old as the royal court, among those courtesans who supported Solomon (Noth, *Könige,* 46) or were responsible for wisdom materials (Mettinger, 141). And the highly stereotyped prayer of petition suggests a still later setting for the whole unit, since it presupposes canonical models. More to the point, however, is to reflect on the present literary setting given the unit. It comes at the beginning of the Solomonic era—at least that part of the account of Solomon's reign which is exclusively focused on his achievements. The unit picks up the theological themes of ch. 1 (3:7; cf. 1:37, 47-48; 2:45), renews the religious basis of secular rule (3:14; cf. 2:3-4), and characterizes the epoch just beginning as a period of Solomon's wisdom and discerning governance (vv. 9, 12), a point to be reiterated in 3:28.

Intention

The intention of this unit in its present setting is to offer a general legitimation of Solomon before the fact, and before the selected details of his reign are highlighted (Görg, 113; Gray, *Kings,* 121). More specifically, however, the report adumbrates the theological theme that will be illustrated and elaborated in the material to follow. The authors claim that the wealth, wisdom, and honor redounding to this King Solomon correspond to divine initiative taken at the beginning of his reign. In this way, the report may counter any negative impressions left by the portrayal of the transitional period (2:12b-46). Indeed, Solomon's petition and Yahweh's promise are first illustrations of the theological appraisal of this man given in the foreword, v. 3a. We should expect more confirmation, as well as elaboration of the darker potential hinted at in v. 3b.

Bibliography

E. L. Ehrlich, *Der Traum im Alten Testament* (BZAW 73; Göttingen: W. de Gruyter, 1953); E. Gerstenberger, *Der Bittende Mensch* (WMANT 51; Neukirchen: Neukirchener, 1980); M. Görg, *Gott-König-Reden in Israel und Ägypten* (BWANT 105; Stuttgart: Kohlhammer, 1975) 16-115; A. Hermann, *Die ägyptische Königsnovelle* (see listing at 3:1–11:43); S. Herrmann, "Die Königsnovelle" (see listing at 3:1–11:43); A. Kenik, "The Design for Kingship in 1 Kings 3:4-15: A Study in the Dtr Narrative Technique and Theology of Kingship" (Diss., St. Louis, 1978); A. Malamat, "Longevity: Biblical Concepts and Some Ancient Near Eastern Parallels" (XXVIIIe Rencontre D'Assyriologique), *AfO Beihefte* 19 (1982) 215-24; T. N. D. Mettinger, *Solomonic State Officials: A Study of the Civil Government Officials of the Israelite Monarchy* (Coniectanea biblica 5; Lund: Gleerup, 1971); A.L. Oppenheim, *The Interpretation of Dreams in the Ancient Near East* (Transactions of the American Philosophical Society 46; Philadelphia, 1956); B. Porten, "Structure" (see listing at 3:1–11:43); W. Richter, "Der Traum und Traumdeutung im AT," *BZ* (1963) 202-20; R.B.Y. Scott, "Solomon and the Beginning of Wisdom in Israel," in *Wisdom in Israel and in the Ancient Near East* (*Fest.* H.H. Rowley; ed. M. Noth and D. Winton Thomas; VTSup 3; Leiden: Brill, 1955) 262-79; S. Zalevsky, "The Revelation of God to Solomon in Gibeon," *Tarbiz* 42 (1973) 214-58 (Hebrew).

ACCOUNT OF SOLOMON'S WISDOM: STORY OF WISE JUDGMENT, 3:16-28

Structure

I. The dispute	16-22
A. Narrative setting: audience with the king	16
B. The dispute proper	17-22a
1. First woman's speech: statement of complaint	17-21
a. Petitionary address	17aα
b. Circumstances	17aβ-19
c. Allegation	20-21
2. Second woman's speech: disputation	22aα
3. First woman's speech: reiteration of complaint	22aβ
C. Narrative summary	22b
II. Resolution of the dispute	23-27
A. The king's orders: toward establishing the truth	23-25
1. Restatement of the dispute	23
2. Order: concerning a sword	24

3. Order: concerning dividing the child	25
B. Consequences of the orders	26
1. First woman's speech: appeal to rescind order	26a
2. Second woman's speech: appeal to comply with order	26b
C. The king's judgment: truth established	27
1. Order: concerning the child	27a
2. Declaration: concerning the mother	27b
III. Narrative conclusion: Solomon's wisdom and fame	28

This unit is clearly distinguishable from that which comes before and after by its developed plot and its folkloristic style; there is nothing of the prolix theologizing of 3:4-15, or the archivelike succinctness of 4:1-6. The whole seems unified, almost all commentators agree, and apparently has not been subjected to extensive editing over the centuries.

The key to the structure of the unit is found in the predominance of direct speech over narrative prose, and in the situation which is portrayed by means of that direct speech, namely, a dispute to be settled on appeal to the king. Aside from the brief narrative statements, vv. 16, 22b, 28, and very brief introductions to speeches ("he said," etc.), the author portrays groups of speeches in series:

(1) three speeches by the two women (I.B, vv. 17-22a)
(2) the king's speech (II.A, vv. 23-25)
(3) two speeches by the women (II.B, v. 26)
(4) a final speech by the king (II.C, v. 27)

There is a fine balance here (contrast somewhat, Porten, 99). The action is verbal, not physical. The author sets forth the dispute in the women's speeches to one another before the king (I, vv. 16-22) and moves to its resolution in the judgment of Solomon (II, vv. 23-27). The whole drama illustrates for the narrator the famous wisdom of this King Solomon (III, v. 28). From the first and longest speech we learn the information necessary to understand the origin and nature of the conflict which powers the drama. Having heard this first testimony, a second woman denies the allegation the first has spoken (I.B.2, v. 22aα) and the king's dilemma rises up, sharply etched in the opposing claims: how shall the truth of these private moments be known? The king's response is pure folkloristic genius, and cleverly aimed at eliciting a more immediate *persona* from each woman (II.A, vv. 23-25). Still by means of speech, we discover the truth just as Solomon does—in the anguished cry of the first woman. She gives up any claims she may have had on the child—and this is the storyteller's art—because "her bowels grew warm for her son" (*RSV* "her heart yearned for her son"). It is then just a matter of saving the child and declaring what we, and Solomon, now know: "She is his mother" (II.C, v. 27).

One ought not to miss the artistry in this little incident. The issues and parties are simplified, the narration uncluttered. We have only the barest suggestion of character. Both women are nameless harlots (v. 16), but one is verbose, even courtly in her plea to the king, and the other is brusque, energized more for confrontation than explanation; the one is compassionate (v. 26a), the other chilling in her clipped speech (v. 22a and esp. 26b, which carries a singularly vindictive tone: "neither mine nor yours; divide it"). The author concentrates all his narrative power in the words spoken by his characters, with astonishingly economical and effective results. The words repeat, flying back and forth in artful chiasmus (v. 22a):

one woman says:	"No, *for my son is living,* and *your son is dead.*"
and this (one) says:	"No, *for your son is dead,* and *my son is living.*"
And Solomon repeats: this one says:	"This is *my son the living,* and *your son is dead.*'
and this (other) says:	"No, for *your son is dead,* and *my son is living.*"

bĕnî haḥay ûbnēk hammēt

lō' kî bĕnēk hammēt ûbnî heḥāy

zeh-bĕnî haḥay ûbnēk hammēt

lō' kî bĕnēk hammēt ûbnî heḥāy

The effect is wearisome, as though we are watching an intense struggle between children for a prized toy. The Hebrew at v. 22b captures it perfectly: "And they went on and on speaking" (*wattĕdabbērnâ*). Even the repetition of sounds contributes to this effect: in the chiastically arranged phrases above, but also in v. 18b, where the first woman begins to explain the circumstances: *'ittānû babbayit . . . šĕtayim-'ănaḥnû babbāyit,* "(no one) with us in the house . . . (only) we two in the house." The plays on sound continue in vv. 20b, 25b, 26-27. The sounds literally bounce back and forth between the characters, a mimicry of the two-sided dilemma posed for Solomon. In this context, the king's restating of the dispute (v. 23) amounts to a verbalized scratching of the head at the impossible conundrum.

In such ways, the drama emphasizes the problem to be solved; the author does not really portray a juridical proceeding (against Mabee), although the appeal to the king and some of the language used by the women might suggest a legal dispute. The real interest of the storyteller falls on the dilemma and Solomon's extraordinary cleverness in forcing the truth out of the women. For him, the event attests to Solomon's wisdom; and all Israel agreed, standing in awe of this king who showed such "preternatural wisdom" (Gray, *Kings*, 129 on *ḥokmâ 'ĕlōhîm; RSV* "wisdom of God").

Genre

This unit is a STORY, as all commentators have agreed, even if using slightly different terms. The essential elements of plot are clear: a situation—two women with two infants—is complicated when one child dies, one mother substitutes the dead for the living, and a dispute ensues. The climax to the story and the resolution to the dispute over whose child is living come through appeal to the king, who forces the truth into the open. The plot centers on verbal action among the characters, and we learn the important information only from what people say to one another. This technique, more than any other, gives the story its "modern" flavor.

Setting

Such a story probably originated in oral tales among the people. It has the flavor and appearance of such popularly held folk stories (Noth, *Könige*, 48; Gray, *Kings*, 116; Würthwein, *Könige*, I, 37), and many parallels are known in folktales from other cultures (Gressmann). Too speculative and without evidence is Mabee's opinion that the story stemmed from members of the royal court who were trying to overcome opposition to Solomon's rule (Mabee, 95 and n. 2). Because it is a question of folk story, we must be open to the obscurity of origin and a multiplicity of setting and occasions on which such a story might have been told. In any case, the present literary setting is of equal if not more importance. The story is now placed in a prominent position: immediately after Solomon has received God's promise of wisdom, wealth, and honor. V. 28 draws attention to this literary connection.

Intention

On the oral level this story's intention would have varied, depending on circumstances in the situations when it was repeated. But in its present literary context the story obviously is intended to illustrate and confirm the promise given to Solomon (Noth, *Könige*, 53; Würthwein, *Könige*, 38; et al.). The tale in a way sets the tone for all of Solomon's reign, providing one dominant image that will stick with us throughout and alongside others, and offering a first concrete definition of this "wisdom" which Solomon possesses as God's gift.

Bibliography

H. Gressmann, "Das Solomonische Urteil," *Deutsche Rundschau* 130 (1907) 212-28; C. Mabee, "The Problem of Setting in Hebrew Royal Judicial Narratives" (Diss., Claremont, 1977), 77-95; B. Porten, "Structure" (see listing at 3:1–11:43).

ACCOUNT OF SOLOMON'S ADMINISTRATION: REGISTER OF ROYAL OFFICIALS, 4:1-6

Structure

I. Introductory statement	1
II. Register of royal officials	2-6
A. Superscription	2a
B. List	2b-6

Most commentators take v. 1 as a redactional introduction functioning as a general heading to the administrative matters shortly to be discussed (for David's reign, cf. 2 Sam 8:15). The main material of the unit is contained in vv. 2-6, which carries its own superscription (v. 2a), of course now linked to v. 1 by means of the pronominal reference (*lô; RSV* "his") to Solomon. The text is clearly structured, despite a few glosses here and there that may have crept in. Furthermore, vv. (1)2-6 are clearly separate from v. 7 in subject matter, style, and overall form.

The structure depends upon a simple listing of items in series under a superscription. Grammatically these items are nominal phrases; sometimes they are linked by a conjunction, sometimes not. There are basically two styles: (1) PN_1 son of PN_2 plus a word or phrase indicating the office; (2) PN_1 son of PN_2 plus the preposition "over" (*'al*) followed by a noun which describes the area of responsibility. Both styles are evident in materials elsewhere, e.g., 2 Sam 8:16b, 17a; 20:24b (cf. 2 Sam 23:24b-29) for style one; 2 Sam 8:16a; 20:23a-24a; 1 Chr 27:2a, 4a for style two. The variations in style have something to do with what is recorded—whether an office or an area of responsibility. But they also seem to be variants which can be arranged indiscriminately or according to principles unclear to us (cf. the lists in 2 Sam 8:16-18a, parallel to the Kings text, with items and styles rearranged).

The superscription is similar to those frequently found at the head or end of lists of various kinds in the OT. In form, it is a nominal clause; in function, it briefly indicates the content of what follows. See 2 Sam 23:8a; 3:5b (at the end of a list of David's sons); Josh 12:7a (at the beginning of a king list); 1 Chr 27:1a (at the beginning of a list of officials; expanded greatly in v. 1b). Cf. the arithmetical tally given at the end of a list of mercenaries (2 Sam 23:39b), kings (Josh 12:24b), or cities (Josh 15:32b).

Genre

Almost all scholars speak of (→) list or (→) administrative list when referring to this unit. More precisely, one should identify the text as a REGISTER, i.e., an administrative list that records items or persons according to the ways they are subject to administration by an institution, corporate body, or as in this case, the king. Examples of register, or at least texts which are likely to be excerpts from a register, would be Joshua 15–19 (towns and boundaries); Ezra 10:18, 20-43 (men who married foreign women); Nehemiah 3 (builders); Nehemiah 7 (population census; cf. Ezra 2:1-58); Neh 10:2-27 (signers of the covenant). Thus, here in 1 Kgs 4:2-6, we may fairly suppose that we have something very close to a register of Solomonic officials and their respective responsibilities in the administration.

Setting

The original setting for register would naturally have been the record-keeping body and its archives within a governing organization. For this particular material we may look to the royal bureaucracy in Jerusalem. Similar registers have been found throughout the ancient Near East particularly associated with centers of civil and religious government (e.g., a Neo-Babylonian register of officials, *ANET,* 307-8; an Egyptian register of conquered countries from Thutmose III, ca. 1500

B.C., *ANET,* 242, excerpted for inscribing on a temple wall in praise of Amon [see Breasted, *ARE* II, § 402]; a register from Elephantine, ca. 400 B.C., of persons who had paid the temple tax, *ANET,* 491; census or property registers from the palace at Ugarit, Gordon, *UT,* 1080 and 2044). For Israel, events of registration are associated with kings (2 Sam 24:2-9; 1 Chr 23:3-6) and provincial governors in postexilic times (Neh 7:5-73; 12:22). Of course, 1 Kgs 4:1-6 is not an official register, and so an important question has to do with its present literary setting in the books of Kings. The text follows hard upon the statement that Solomon was king over all Israel, and leads off a collection of material having to do with Solomon's administrative districts.

Intention

An official register would have been designed to record persons, facts, information, etc. of importance to a governing body. The intention of this particular literary text is to record those officials deemed important for the author-editor in describing what was meant by Solomon's reigning over Israel (for David, cf. 2 Sam 8:15). Obviously not all officials appear here, and we may guess that those who do appear were important for different reasons in this selective presentation: the priests (emphasis falls on Solomon's religious "good deed" in building the temple, 6:1–9:9), the commander of the army (a standard interest in ancient Near Eastern historiography), the palace overseer (attention given to palace complex in 7:1-12), the captain of the "officers" (the same provincial governors who are listed in the immediately following unit, 4:7-19), the man in charge of the forced labor (an important aspect of Solomon's building activities, 5:27-32; 9:15-23). Why the other officials were named here—the "king's friend," v. 5; the "scribes" (*RSV* "secretaries"), v. 3a; and the uncertain *mazkîr* (*RSV* "recorder"), v. 3b—is more difficult to surmise. But on "scribe," see the important fiscal role such an officer plays in 2 Kgs 12:11 (*RSV* 10); and in 2 Kgs 18:18 both "scribe" and *mazkîr,* "recorder," negotiate on behalf of the king. The author-editor also shows us an administrative continuity between David and Solomon. If the religious continuity has been stressed in David's farewell speech (see discussion of 2:1-4) and in Solomon's prayer of petition (3:4-15), then the day-to-day continuity of royal office is given out here as a sort of counterpoint to these theological accents.

ACCOUNT OF SOLOMON'S ADMINISTRATION: ORGANIZATION FOR DAILY PROVISIONS, 4:7–5:8 (*RSV* 4:28)

Structure

I. Introductory framework: officers and provisions	4:7
II. Organization for daily provisions	4:8–5:6
A. Register of officers responsible for provisions	4:8-19
B. Miscellany: prosperity and provisions	4:20–5:6
III. Concluding framework: officers and provisions	5:7
IV. Supplemental report: provisions for horses	5:8

Critics have usually taken 4:7-19 as separate from 4:20–5:8, and have characterized the latter as supplemental, secondary expansions and the like, arranged in no particular order, or at least now presented in a disturbed order. They dispute what may have been original stages of tradition lying behind the present text. Undoubtedly, the material has a long history of redaction (against Porten, 100 [see listing at 3:1–11:43]).

What has been generally overlooked, however, is a certain ordering to the MT as it stands—not perfect by any means, but striking enough to warrant special comment. First of all, whatever the original relationship between 4:7 and 5:7-8 might have been, it is clear that these verses now form a bracketing framework. The "theme" in 4:7 (officers who are responsible for daily provisions) returns again in 5:7, as though the material in between somehow ought to be understood under this rubric. Enclosed by this motivic bracket is, first of all, a list of officers, 4:8-19, which by style and content is to be distinguished from 4:20–5:6 and connected with 4:2-6 only by means of the catchword *niṣṣābîm*. Second, the framework holds 4:20–5:6, a miscellany of brief statements and reports which provide information on and descriptions of conditions during Solomon's rule, along with some details of his enormous daily provisions. This miscellany, however, is not without its own ordering. The circumstances of Solomon's reign (4:20; 5:1, 4-5) form a chiastic pattern with its center in the statement regarding Solomon's daily provisions. In diagram:

a	Circumstances of plenty, happiness "all the days of his life"	4:20
b	Circumstances of Solomon's expansive rule	5:1
c	Statement of daily provisions	5:2-3
b'	Circumstances of Solomon's expansive rule	5:4
a'	Circumstances of peace, security, "all the days of Solomon"	5:5

V. 8 falls outside the material framed now by 4:7 and 5:7 and can be seen as supplemental, though not unrelated in terms of content—it clearly speaks of provisions for the horses (mentioned in 5:6) and has in view the *niṣṣābîm* ("officers") mentioned both in 5:7 and in the list of 4:8-19.

Genre

Since it is a question of a redactional composite here, no specific generic identification can be given. It is simply a redactional framework on which has been hung a number of diverse items, but not without some semblance of order. It is clearly not a random arrangement or simply a happenstance result of a long history of redaction.

Setting

One should understand the setting in strictly literary terms: part of the account of Solomon's reign, and specifically his administrative ordering of affairs in the kingdom.

Intention

The intention is clearly to account for the enormous amount of daily provisions provided this magnificent king (5:2-3) and to eulogize him with images of wealth and prosperity. Such wealth and daily provisions in support of the royal government required new organization, which in itself probably added further nuance to the introductory phrase, "ruled over all Israel" (4:1).

REGISTER OF OFFICERS RESPONSIBLE FOR PROVISIONS, 4:8-19

Structure

I. Superscription	8a
II. List of officers	8b-19
A. For districts north of Jerusalem	8b-19a+bα
B. For the district of Judah	19bβ

This unit begins with a superscription, which in the present context presupposes the introductory statement in v. 7. The main items flow in asyndetic series, and follow a similar stylistic pattern: PN_1 son of PN_2 plus locale of the officer's responsibility (mostly given with the preposition *bĕ,* e.g., vv. 12, 16, 17, 18, but once with the locative final *h,* v. 14). In other cases, the first name is missing, leaving only the second phrase in place, as in, e.g., v. 8: Ben-hur. Additions to this basic formula appear as information regarding possessions of these men, whether cities (e.g., v. 10) or wives (all daughters of Solomon, vv. 11 and 15), and further specifics as to the area for which the man was responsible. The variant style of v. 19bβ suggests textual or redactional problems, or both. But these problems, the solution to which also involves arriving at a sum of twelve districts in agreement with v. 7, have little effect on the basic structure of the unit.

Genre

Like 4:2-6, this unit is probably modeled after REGISTER. However, the more complex form and extra information, not all of which is necessarily secondary, moves us away from the probable structure of register toward the form of ANNAL, a selective recounting of events and facts pertinent to a particular reign. But the content, and the intention suggested by the content, belongs to the genre register. On generic parallels, see the discussion at 4:2-6.

Setting

For the background in official royal record keeping, see the discussion at 4:2-6. In its present literary setting, this text relates to the somewhat broader theme of Solomon's daily provisions (v. 7), and so is placed before the actual statements regarding the size of those provisions and the wealth and prosperity accompanying such.

Intention

For the intention of register in official record keeping, see the discussion at 4:2-6. In its present context, the unit explains how Solomon organized his affairs so as to produce the daily provisions of so grand a scale. Clearly, this material does not record the full range of Solomon's administrative apparatus, but selects that portion which contributes to the wider theme of wealth and honor redounding to this king.

MISCELLANY: PROSPERITY AND PROVISIONS, 4:20–5:6 (*RSV* 4:26)

Structure

I. Circumstantial statements: Solomon's reign	4:20–5:1
A. Plenty	4:20
B. Expansive hegemony	5:1
II. Statement: Solomon's daily provisions	5:2-3
III. Circumstantial statements: Solomon's reign	4-5
A. Expansive hegemony	4
B. Peace, security	5
IV. Statement: Solomon's horses and horsemen	6

As discussed above, this text forms the second unit now framed by 4:7 and 5:7. The first three parts of the unit (I, II, III; 4:20–5:5) have been arranged in a chiastic pattern (see discussion above). The circumstantial clauses (4:20; 5:1, 4) are all nominal phrases, giving the impression of a continuous present. The statements in 5:2-3, 6 (II, IV) use normal reportorial tenses and state information for the record.

The mix of these two kinds of prose in a special chiastic arrangement has a remarkable effect. The rather exaggerated figures for Solomon's daily provisions and equestrian retinue are enfolded in a collage of images which etch the lines of hegemony, peace, prosperity, and well-being. We hear the matter-of-fact statements of provisions through special filters: a numerous population, eating and drinking, taking of the bounty of Solomon's vast rule; a people living in peace, each man at home under his own fruit-giving boughs (5:5). The images evoke feelings of calm, as though utopian surcease from survival cares is what Solomon's being king over all Israel meant, and perhaps a part of his honor, weightiness, and glory (*kābôd*, 3:13).

Genre

Since this is a composite miscellany, one may not speak with precision of a genre. However, some of the important motifs, namely, the peace and prosperity of the reign and the fulsome requirements of the palace, find their parallels in ancient Near Eastern (→) royal inscriptions. For example, a statue of Sargon (we have only a copy of the text preserved in later times) offers a miscellaneous resumé of events during his reign, characterizing his (1) military exploits and building of large fleets of ships, (2) his piety and protection by the gods, (3) his vast hegemony, and this striking note near the end before the customary blessing-curse formulas: "5400 soldiers ate daily in his palace" (*ANET,* 268; H. Hirsch, "Die Inschriften der Könige von Agade," *AfO* 20 [1963] 37-39). Similar in interest are the propagandistic statements about exaggeratedly low market prices in Mesopotamian royal inscriptions, most of which commemorate a king's building activities (Grayson, *ARI* I, 20 n. 64). Also, numerous Egyptian building inscriptions extol the peace and prosperity due to a certain monarch, or recount the vast wealth accruing to the kingdom (and to the god's estate in the temple), as. e.g., Breasted, *ARE* II, § 288 [Queen Hatshepsut], §§ 554-62 [Thutmose III], both ca. 1500 B.C. A temple inscription of Ramses III, ca. 1200, after eulogistic recitation of triumphal events and royal attributes, concludes with a description of the land under his reign:

> "King Ramses III is kind-hearted toward Egypt, bearing the protection of the land on the height of his back without trouble; a wall casting a shadow for the people. . . . He has made hosts by his victories, filling the storehouses of the temples with the plunder of his sword, preparing the divine offerings from his excellent things. . . . Lo, the golden Horus, rich in years, divine water of Re . . . great in inundation bearing their sustenance for Egypt so that the people and the folk are possessed of good things; the sovereign, executing truth for the All-Lord, presenting it everyday before him. Egypt and the lands are at peace in his reign. . . . A woman goes about at her will, with her veil upon her head, her going extending as far as she pleases. The countries come, bowing down to the fame of his majesty, with their tribute and their children upon their backs. . . ." (Breasted, *ARE* IV, § 47)

See also the Azitawadda commemorative building inscription found in Karatepe, ca. 9th-8th century B.C.

> "In my days, the Danunites had everything good and plenty to eat and well-being. . . . I have made peace with every king. Yea, every king considered me his father because of my righteousness [*ṣdq*] and my wisdom [*ḥkmh*] and the kindness of my heart. . . . I have built strongholds in those places, so that the Danunites might dwell in peace of mind." (*ANET,* 653-54)

Setting

One might suppose with good reason, therefore, that this style of adulatory description of conditions around a kingdom and a monarch had its setting in the scribal classes whose profession it was to produce monuments suitable for extolling and memorializing the king and his gods. But this text in Kings is not a royal building inscription in itself, and so its present literary setting looms much more important than its possible background for our understanding. The unit is set in the final position of this larger complex grouped under the heading of Solomon's ruling over all Israel (4:7).

Intention

Therefore, the miscellany serves to point with concrete information and evocative images the result of Solomon's administrative organization—the peace and prosperity, and wonderful conditions concomitant with his reign.

In its way, the text seeks to glorify as much as describe Solomon (a main function of Mesopotamian royal inscriptions, too), and for this reason Kegler (p. 202; see listing at 2:12b-46) is right in characterizing the function of 5:1, 5 as *Herrscherpreis*. The author-editor continues to write in a double mode: at once describing the reign and praising Solomon, a gift held by the tenuous thread of his all too human response (3:13).

SOLOMON'S BUILDING ACTIVITIES, PREPARATIONS: ENUMERATION OF WISDOM, 5:9-14 (*RSV* 4:29-34)

Structure

I. Introductory summary: God's gift of immeasurable wisdom 9

II. Statements on Solomon's wisdom	10-14
A. Concerning its incomparability	10-11
B. Concerning its forms and content	12-13
C. Concerning Solomon's worldwide fame	14

Most critics have seen this unit as essentially unified in theme, although not tightly integrated in form. What is disputed is the question of its age and origin. In the books of Kings, the piece stands somewhat isolated and without obvious traces of literary dependence upon other portions of the OT. Separated from 5:1-8 by a shift in style and subject matter, and from 5:15-26, which is a clearly defined report of events, this text hangs on the theme of incomparability (vv. 9, 11b) and is thus loosely related in theme to wisdom (*ḥokmâ*) in 5:26; 10:7, 23-24.

The unit consists of a series of brief statements cast in typical reportorial verbal form, and strung together with sense, but not necessarily strict logic (Noth, *Könige*, 80); the *RSV* supplies connections between what in Hebrew are independent sentences joined by simple *waw* ("and"), i.e., v. 10, "so that," v. 11, "for," v. 12, "also." In fact, the arrangement of these statements is fairly loose, with a certain division by thematic nuance as the structural analysis indicates, but with no discernible integration or climax (against Porten, 101 [see listing at 3:1–11:43], who sees "climactic progression" too often and without careful definition). Thus, one moves from an introductory statement which speaks of God's gift, through statements on wisdom's incomparability and Solomon's fame, to a series of items that note the form of Solomon's wisdom (proverbs and songs) and the content (the natural order); finally, the unit concludes with a return to the image of Solomon's fame.

Genre

Although the style of individual parts may be termed reportorial, the effect of the whole is not that of (→) report; instead, the cumulative sum of this series of statements is rather more like a description somewhat similar to EULOGY, that is, to a speech which praises by citing praiseworthy deeds and characteristics (cf. Kegler, 202-3 [see listing at 2:12b-46]). It seems sensible to refuse a more precise generic identification. Distant parallels may be found in the language of ancient Near Eastern royal inscriptions as these texts seek to memorialize the memory and deeds of a certain king.

Setting

The literary setting in the books of Kings is the important consideration in light of the generic uncertainty. This unit is the third block of tradition in a thematic chain of "wisdom" images: 3:4-15, 16-28; 5:9-14, 15-26; 10:1-10; finally summarized by 10:23-24. Moreover, the unit comes at the head of the initial preparations that Solomon makes for his building of the temple, an achievement which is explicitly associated with "wisdom" by Hiram (5:21) and the queen of Sheba (10:4).

Intention

In context, then, this text gives a picture of Solomon's incomparable wisdom and its international importance such that "kings from all the earth" came to sit at his feet. And it is this wisdom which now frames our reading of the building activities (6:1–9:25), and so appears as the main ingredient in the characterization of Solomon—a code word for his qualities of leadership and for his most admirable achievement. One may also suppose that the author-editor intended to demonstrate Solomon's fame spreading from "all Israel" (3:28) to all the peoples of the earth (5:14), just as Solomon's administrative grip extends from "all Israel" (4:1-19) to the vast area from the Euphrates to Egypt (5:1-8). We see an ascendency in grandeur, from the center outward, aimed at glorifying both the king and the divine favor that makes it possible (cf. Luke 2:52; 1 Sam 2:26). The image is not unlike Isaiah's vision of *tôrâ* irradiating the earth from its center in Zion (Isa 2:3-4).

SOLOMON'S BUILDING ACTIVITIES, PREPARATIONS: REPORT OF SECURING RAW MATERIALS, 5:15-26 (*RSV* 5:1-12)

Structure

I. Opening initiative: Hiram's diplomatic overture	15
A. Diplomatic message	15a
B. Circumstances	15b
II. Counterinitiative: Solomon's proposal	16-20
A. Narrative introduction	16
B. The proposal for building materials	17-20
1. Basis for proposal	17-19
a. Concerning distant background	17
b. Concerning the immediate situation	18-19
2. Proposal proper	20
III. Response by Hiram	21-23
A. Rejoicing and praise	21
B. Hiram's message to Solomon	22-23
1. Narrative introduction	22aα
2. Message proper	22aβ-23
a. Speech of acceptance	22aβ-b
b. Statement of reciprocal terms	23
IV. Summarizing statements: results of agreement	24-26
A. Agreement executed	24-25
B. Gift of wisdom	26a
C. Peace	26bα
D. Treaty concluded	26bβ

Most critics view this unit as heavily edited by the DtrH (against Noth, *Könige*, 88, who attributed it entirely to the redactor). They cite in support the clearly Dtr language in vv. 17-19 (cf. 2 Samuel 7), 21 (cf. 1 Kgs 3:4-28), and 26a (cf. 1 Kgs 3:12-13). However, there is little agreement on what might have been the exact dimensions of the original tradition, and little reason to trust attempts at precise reconstruction. In fact, the MT is now essentially unified. Its structural logic depends upon a series of actions defined by initiative, response, and counter-response—diplomatic maneuvers which culminate in a treaty between sovereign states. Hiram's first overture (I, v. 15), which recalls the good relations between this same king and David (2 Sam 5:11-12), serves here as the occasion for Solomon to propose an arrangement whereby Hiram will supply the timber and the timber workers, and Solomon the wages (II, vv. 16-20). Hiram in turn responds with a diplomatic message declaring his acceptance of the proposal and stating the terms (III.A, B, vv. 21-23). This exchange of diplomatic messages is clearly marked out by the repetition of narrative introductions (vv. 15a, 16, 22aα). The unit ends quickly with a series of summary statements (IV, vv. 24-26) that adds no dramatic impetus, but ratifies the state of affairs reached by the two kings. They report the actions that carry out the agreement (vv. 24-25) and characterize the event as "peace" between nations, "covenant" between kings, and the result of God's gift of wisdom to Solomon.

By devoting so much space to the diplomatic messages, the author-editor centers the important action in the words of these monarchs, a technique already seen in 3:16-28. In the case of Solomon's counterinitiative, vv. 16-20, this device gives opportunity to set the whole incident in the context of the promises given to David (vv. 17-19; cf. 2 Samuel 7). Consistent with its emphasis on the diplomatic "conversations," the text maintains unobtrusive narrative flow (vv. 15a, 16, 21, 22aα) until v. 23. Participial clauses and a simple perfect verb then abruptly express simultaneous action, or rather a state of affairs: "while Hiram was providing . . . (then) Solomon provided" (*wayĕhî ḥîrôm nōtēn . . . ûšĕlōmōh nātan*) [vv. 24-25a]; then a frequentive imperfect: "thus Solomon [continuously] provided year by year" [*kōh-yittēn šĕlōmōh . . . šānâ bĕšānâ*; v. 25]). V. 26 brings forth the summarizing statements. Note especially the final clause, "and the two of them made a treaty," a way of characterizing the event and thus providing a final interpretative rubric. Cf. Gen 21:32; Josh 24:25; 1 Kgs 20:34.

Genre

This unit is a REPORT, typically cast in narrative prose, but unlike (→) story showing no artistic interest in dramatic plot. The text simply moves from one event to another with merely a hint of narrative interest, and then closes with a series of summarizing, characterizing statements. We may note Solomon's stylized PETITION attributable to the Dtr editor-author of Kings (vv. 17-20; see the full discussion at 3:6-9 and parallels cited there). Contrast the somewhat less elaborate, but still stylized, message sent by Hiram in vv. 22-23. Possibly the form of a (→) letter is in the background (2 Kgs 5:6; 10:2; Pardee; Montgomery, *Kings*, 408). In this text, however, we have no way of distinguishing between a letter and a message spoken by a diplomatic messenger (cf. Isa 36:13-20), and since there are abundant parallels to the style of Solomon's petition, we may safely conclude that the text was shaped primarily by OT literary styles without denying the substantive and stylistic connections with letter in the ancient Near East. Note also the PRAISE SPEECH with the blessing (*bārûk*) formula, v. 21. The basic formula has many parallels (cf. 1 Kgs 1:48; 8:15; 1 Sam 25:32, 39; 2 Sam 18:28; Ezra 7:27; etc.). Despite its connections with, and probable derivation from, (→) blessing, the utterance in this stereotyped form serves to give praise and thanks to God, who is perceived as having already given a concrete blessing. In 1 Kgs 5:21 we are drawn into a special sort of indirect comment by the author-editor: through the lips of a non-Israelite character, the Israelite author and audience may praise God and marvel at his power (cf. the similar literary technique in Exod 18:10; Num 24:3-9; Gen 14:20).

Setting

A report may have multiple settings; this particular report may have stemmed from a royal document we do not possess, the "Acts of Solomon" (Gray, *Kings*, 141; see 11:41). Noth (*Könige*, 88) thinks of a purely literary creation by the Dtr author-editor. It is more important for our understanding, however, to observe that the text takes its place in the preparatory stages of Solomon's building activities, and follows hard upon the summary of Solomon's great wisdom.

Intention

The most important intention, therefore, is to illustrate Solomon's wisdom, or rather to provide yet another nuance of that gift from Yahweh (see 3:12-13). This time we see a king wise in statecraft, gaining international agreements, establishing peaceful conditions in the kingdom, laying the groundwork for building activities. The unit in fact intends in this way to report the first important step in building activities—securing raw materials—but under the thematic aspect of wisdom (recognized by Hiram, v. 21, and remarked by the narrator, v. 26). In this regard, the report is consistent with Mesopotamian sources, which similarly view a king's building activities as illustrative of, or flowing from, the king's wisdom (see Isa 10:13; Luckenbill, *ARAB* I, § 804 for Tiglath-Pileser; see discussion at 6:1–7:51). The arrangements with Hiram explicitly forge a continuity with David's reign: God's promise that David's son would build a "house" for God, and that this same son would be the first sign of God's building a "house" for David. And from this wider perspective we see ironically as well. This king who seems ideally situated for success, notes for Hiram—and for us—his lack of adversary (*sāṭān*) and misfortune (*pegaʿ rāʿ*, v. 18). Yet we know that the peace and stability he enjoys stem from his ruthless actions in eliminating his opponents (the verb is *pāgaʿ*; 2:25, 29, 34, 46), and that the adversary Solomon misses (*sāṭān*) will not be long in appearing (11:14, 23).

Bibliography

D. Pardee, *Handbook of Ancient Hebrew Letters* (Sources for Biblical Studies 14; Missoula: Scholars Press, 1982).

SOLOMON'S BUILDING ACTIVITIES, PREPARATIONS: MISCELLANY ON SECURING A LABOR FORCE, 5:27-32 (*RSV* 5:13-18)

Structure

I. Statements concerning the workers	27-31
A. Timber workers	27-28
1. The levy of forced labor	27
2. Deployment	28a
3. Officer in charge	28b
B. Stoneworkers and supervisors	29-31
1. Workers	29-30
2. Deployment	31
II. Summary: timber and stoneworkers	32

The style of this material differs from vv. 15-26 chiefly in lack of narrative color. Instead, we find emphasis on statements of information and record. The redactional history is unclear. Critics dispute whether parts or all of vv. 29-30 were original to this text (the verses abruptly take up the subject of stoneworkers). And the LXX has vv. 31-32a after 6:1 of the MT. Yet the material reaches for unity: v. 32, as if to summarize, draws together both stone and timber workers, neatly linking what seems disparate in vv. 27-31.

Structure in this series of rather independent reports and statements is governed by an association of content. Essentially, we hear of two matters: the timber and stoneworkers, their numbers and their tasks. V. 32 provides a unifying perspective by relating both types of workers to Solomon's building activities, especially the temple. Each item shows typical reportorial verbal forms (*wyqṭl*, vv. 27, 28, 31, 32) or an information style for stating possession (*wayĕhî lĕ* + the person who possesses, vv. 29-30; cf. 5:6 in the midst of a similarly loosely joined series of items; 10:26αβ; 11:3; 1 Chr 2:22; 2 Chr 1:14αβ; also 1 Kgs 4:10b, 13b).

Genre

This text forms a miscellany, a term used less to designate a genre than to describe a conglomerate of material grouped together because of common subject matter (cf. 5:1-8; 10:26-29). Within the complex may be found brief REPORTS (vv. 27-28, 31) and informational STATEMENTS (vv. 29-30).

Setting

Some of the individual items in this miscellany may have had an independent origin in archival records within the royal establishment at Jerusalem. In their present literary context, however, the miscellany is placed as step two in Solomon's preparations for temple building, coming after his securing of cedar from Lebanon, and before the beginning of the actual construction work in ch. 6.

Intention

In its present context the miscellany means to report the second important step preparatory to Solomon's starting the work of building the temple: he must get the labor force in place. Its scale indicates, moreover, that the author-editor probably intended to comment on the grandeur of Solomon's preparatory efforts and indirectly on the splendor of this building activity devoted to Yahweh.

SOLOMON'S BUILDING ACTIVITIES; TEMPLE-PALACE CONSTRUCTION: CANONICAL FRAMEWORK, 6:1–7:51

Structure

I. Introductory setting	6:1
II. Report of building work	6:2–7:50
A. Concerning the temple	6:2-38
1. The exterior features	2-10
2. Report of prophetic word	11-13
3. The interior features	14-36

4. Concluding reports	37-38
B. Concerning the palace complex	7:1-12
1. Introduction	1
2. Concerning the palace	2-12
a. Buildings	2-8
b. Materials	9-12
C. Concerning the temple furnishings	7:13-50
1. The bronze work of Hiram	13-47
2. The gold work of Solomon	48-50
III. Conclusion	51

Internal tensions, duplications, other signs of disorder here and there, and the variant sequence in the Greek text (e.g., the major shift in placing MT 7:1-12 after 7:13-50) all indicate that the MT has had a long history of development. Beyond observing the more obvious redactional elements (6:1; 7:1, 51), including the emphatic position of a theological motif (6:11-13), we cannot see with much clarity the earlier stages of this material. Not surprisingly, critics have wrought no consensus. In any event, the final redaction has a certain ordered structure that should not be missed.

The keys to the structure of this redactional unit are found in the ways content and stylistic divisions correspond with one another. First, there are the larger divisions of content: (1) a description of the temple, its exterior features and its internal components, with a certain emphasis on the building materials (II.A, 6:2-38); (2) the palace complex, again looking first at the exterior features more or less, and secondly at the materials (II.B, 7:1-12); (3) the bronze and gold temple furnishings and cultic implements (II.C, 7:13-50). Second, some of the formal features signal beginnings and endings of blocks of subject matter. An introduction (I, 6:1) looks over the whole account, and a conclusion (III, 7:51a) declares the work to be finished. The first material on the temple (II.A, 6:2-38) carries its own conclusion in vv. 37-38, the palace section (II.B, 7:1-12) its own introduction in 7:1, and the section on the temple bronze work (II.C, 7:13-47) its own introduction and conclusion (vv. 13-14, 40b-44). Subsequent discussion will show that the various details appear in a regular pattern of reporting that also corresponds by and large to changes in content. Overall, the final order may not be perfect from our perspective, but it is certainly impressive.

The unit's reportorial character is never lost. There is no narrative to speak of, and aside from the rather vague *waw*-conversive verbs such as "he made" (*wy'śh*), "he built" (*wybn*), and "he overlaid" (*wyṣph*), the substance of the material is cast in nominal clauses with minimal connectives between them. The text enumerates in an inventory-like fashion. Because of its totally different style, the quoting of God's word to Solomon in 6:11-13 stands out sharply and resists easy integration into the whole (see discussion below).

Genre

Since it is a question of a redactional unit, we cannot identify a specific genre. However, one may speak generally of ACCOUNT, which includes, of course, a number of brief self-contained reports and statements now gathered together and unified thematically under the aspect of building the temple-palace complex. (See fuller discussion below.) The closest OT parallel would be the priestly report of building and outfitting the tabernacle, Exod 36:2–39:43, a passage which evidently has had some relationship to the history of redaction in 1 Kings 6–7.

A general parallel to the sequence of motifs, including dedicatory festivals, sacrifices, and prayers, may be found in portions of those ancient Near Eastern royal inscriptions which commemorate particular building activities of the king. From the very early period: Cylinder A of Gudea, ca. 2050 B.C., tells how the god inspired Gudea in a dream, and how he acted on his inspiration by building a temple for Enlil (Barton, *RISA*, 205-37; cf. also Statue "B," ibid., 181-89); Shamshi-Adad I, early 2nd millennium, recounts his building of a temple and provides a description of external architectural features, the fine materials for construction and ornamentation, and the precious substances laid in the foundation (Grayson, *ARI* I, § 126). For later times, see Shalmaneser I, ca. 1250 B.C. (Grayson, §§ 534-35), a text which adds a note about the festival to dedicate the building (see also Tiglath-Pileser I, *ARI* II, §§ 55-58); and from Sennacherib, ca. 705-681 B.C., a dedicatory foundation stela which describes in part the building activities of the king, the securing of artisans for the fine ornamentation, and the depositing of precious materials in the foundation stone (Luckenbill, *ARAB* II, §§ 440-41; cf. also §§ 452-55, which includes a number of symbolic names given to parts of buildings [cf. 1 Kgs 7:21]). Egyptian royal dedicatory inscriptions offer similar parallels in motifs. See, e.g., a temple inscription by Thutmose III, ca. 1468-1438 B.C., which reports the construction work, the finest materials, and then records the deposit of booty from military campaigns (cf. 1 Kgs 7:51b), as well as setting up annual offerings for the god Ptah (Breasted, *ARE* II, §§ 612-22; cf. §§ 131-66); and for Seti I, ca. 1300, a similar text, but emphasizing the acts of dedication more than construction (Lichtheim, *Ancient Egyptian Literature* II, 52-56).

The parallels could be multiplied. The point is not that 1 Kings 6–7 is directly dependent upon such royal inscriptions, or that the OT text is a royal inscription (cf. Mowinckel, "Fürsteninschriften"). Rather, the striking similarities suggest that the Hebrew writers owed something, perhaps a lot, to the style and ideology of these ancient Near Eastern monarchies. Or better said: the OT text is a Hebraic example of a royal and perhaps priestly literary document based on selective use of archival materials, just as a Mesopotamian royal inscription is a "public" extract from archival records of varied content no longer available to us. It is doubted that one should speak of a distinct literary genre, i.e., temple-building account (against Kapelrud; see Rummel). Finally, one may observe that this OT unit owes its importance and prominence in the Bible not to a peculiarly Hebraic notion, but to the general ancient Near Eastern ideology that the king *should* build temples for the gods, and *should* furnish them with all manner of finely wrought implements and decoration. These activities were evidently viewed as the king's chief religious act, and hence the act most worthy of memorializing in stone and parchment.

Setting

Since it is a matter of a redactional unit we should speak only of a literary setting in the books of Kings and the larger Dtr history (2 Samuel–2 Kings). Clearly, the author-editor set the temple construction as a kind of centerpiece for the reign of Solomon (see the discussion of 3:1–11:43). The report comes after Solomon has received and demonstrated "wisdom," when peace and stability are round about, and after Solomon recalls for us the promise of Yahweh for a "house." We are also witnessing a high point before Solomon's fall from favor in ch. 11.

Intention

Thus, the redactional unit intends much more than simply to recount the building activities of Solomon, although this is obviously an important aim. It is also a matter of picturing the fulfillment of divine promise in this grandly conceived and executed kingly act. The unit thereby glorifies Solomon—who after all is characterized by wisdom, wealth, and honor (3:12-13)—and in the process glorifies Yahweh, who stands behind the entire drama. More than a building is discussed here. The construction work finds its time-bound reckoning in that great rescue of the Israelites by Yahweh (6:1), as though the temple were a second mighty deed of God. And as usual in the Dtr history, the full reality of this event is hedged by a condition: Solomon must obey faithfully God's commands (the fullest meaning might allow us to think of divine plans for the temple, as well as commands of proper religious behavior) in order that the full blessing of Yahweh's presence to the people might be realized (6:11-13).

Bibliography

See bibliography at "Introduction to Historical Literature." A. S. Kapelrud, "Temple Building: A Task for Gods and Kings," *Or* 32 (1963) 56-62; S. Rummel, ed., *Ras Shamra Parallels* III (AnOr 51; Rome: Pontifical Biblical Institute, 1981) 277-84. Note an unpublished dissertation that reached me too late for incorporation here: A. Hurowitz, "Temple Building in the Bible in Light of Mesopotamian and North-West Semitic Writings" (Hebrew University, Jerusalem, 1983; Hebrew with English summary).

SOLOMON'S BUILDING ACTIVITIES: REPORT OF TEMPLE CONSTRUCTION, 6:1-38

Text

We retain the Hebrew reading in v. 20b: "And he overlaid (with gold) an altar of cedar," against the LXX and most critics. The Greek often appears in this section to be smoothing out a rough Hebrew text; and the context demands that the sentence relate to ornamental gilding, rather than introduce a report of construction (*RSV* "and he made an altar of cedar").

Structure

I. Introductory setting	1
II. Construction work	2-36
A. The exterior	2-14
1. Superscription	2aα
2. Description: exterior structures (stone)	2aβ-8
a. Dimensions	2aβ-3
b. Windows	4
c. Side wings	5-6, 8
1) Construction	5
2) Dimensions and features	6
[Statement: construction without iron tools]	[7]
3) Entrances and stairs	8

3. Colophon: work finished	9a
4. Description: exterior structures (wood)	9b-10
a. Cedar ceilings (main house)	9b
b. Cedar supports (side wings)	10
5. Report of oracle to Solomon	11-13
a. Prophetic word formula	11
b. Oracle: conditional promise	12-13
6. Colophon: work finished	14
B. The interior	15-28
1. Inside walls and floor coverings	15
2. Inner sanctuary (holy of holies)	16-28
a. Construction	16
b. Dimensions of nave before sanctuary	17
c. Cedar carvings; no stone work	18
d. Statement of purpose	19
e. Dimensions	20aα
f. Ornamentation	20aβ-28
1) Gold	20aβ-22
a) Overlay: inner sanctuary and altar	20aβ-b
b) Linings and chains	21
c) Overlay: whole house and inner altar	22
2) Cherubim	23-28
a) Construction	23
b) Dimensions	24-26
c) Installation	27
d) Gold overlay	28
C. Space exterior to inner sanctuary	29-36
1. Carvings on walls	29
2. Overlay on floor	30
3. Entryway to inner sanctuary	31-32
a. Doors	31
b. Ornamentation	32
4. Entryway to nave before inner sanctuary	33-35
a. Doors	33-34
b. Ornamentation	35
5. The inner court	36
III. Conclusion	37-38
A. Laying the foundation	37
B. Completion of construction	38a
C. Construction time	38b

This unit presents many special difficulties. Apart from the introductory statement, v. 1, and the prophetic oracle, vv. 11-13, both of which seem to nearly all critics to stem from the DtrH, the history of the redaction is unclear. The duplication of vv. 9a and 14 has led many to suppose one or the other, or both, may be glosses. The LXX offers a different order at points, and apparently "improved" texts at others; there are numerous textual problems, glosses, obscure words—all hindrances to our understanding. Evidently because of its subject matter, this text through the years has been subject to much editorial "fussing." Due to these complexities, and the many possibilities for explanation, few of which can be controlled very well, it is not surprising that scholars have achieved little consensus on the history of these traditions and their redaction (Rupprecht). Yet, attempts to find perfect symmetry in the final text (Porten [see listing at 3:1–11:43]), or the defense of textual integrity by simply reordering all its parts (Šanda, *Könige*), are not any more convincing. The text as it stands, however, is not without order, even if imperfect from our perspective. Thus, it seems best to deal seriously with this fact, to realize that compromises have to be made (already the number of footnotes in the *RSV* indicates this) and that no understanding is entirely satisfactory.

Looking at the large picture, one may easily see three content divisions: a description of the temple's exterior (II.A, vv. 2-14), its interior (II.B, vv. 15-28), and the space inside the temple compound but outside the inner sanctuary (II.C, vv. 29-36). These three large divisions are framed by an introduction (I, v. 1) and a conclusion (III, vv. 37-38). Within these boundaries, one moves visually and spatially from a survey of the stone and wood exterior of the temple to a tour of the inner reaches, dominated by wood and golden overlay, and back out again to the open spaces of the inner court to look at entryways and courtyards. The first movement carries a framing superscription (v. 2aα; the *RSV* obscures the nominal form, which more literally translated would be "and the house which King Solomon built for Yahweh"), then follow the dimensions, without verbs or qualifiers. A colophon closes out the section: "And Solomon built the temple, and he finished it" (v. 14). The identical phrase in v. 9a is a problem, and should perhaps be seen with v. 14 as a bracket around the more digressive material in vv. 9b-13 (see the "resumptive principle," Kuhl). Or v. 14 could have been a superscription for vv. 15ff. (cf. 7:1b). In any case, the first major movement in the text is now framed by vv. 2aα and 14, and is restricted in content to matters pertaining to the exterior of the temple—the stone work (vv. 2-8) and the cedar work (vv. 9b-10). At its center stands the statement that the stone was worked at the quarry, not at the temple site (v. 7). The verse seems to interrupt its surroundings, but nonetheless it emphasizes a perspective of ritual correctness on the construction (cf. Exod 20:25). Similarly, the second major movement dealing with the interior reaches of the temple (vv. 15-28) has a corresponding emphasis in v. 18b: ". . . all (was) cedar, no stone was seen," as though to emphasize for reasons obscure to us the propriety of the inner sanctuary constructed entirely of cedar.

Stylistic features of the text correspond rather well to these main divisions in content. In the first two sections (vv. 2-14, 15-28), major shifts in subject matter are marked by the use of *waw*-conversive reportorial style (*wyqṭl*): vv. 4 (windows), 5 (for vv. 5-8, side wings), 16 (for vv. 16-20aα, inner sanctuary, exclusive of decoration), 20aβ (for 20aβ-22, gold overlay), 23 (for vv. 23-28, the cherubim). Often, these narrative verbs govern a subject, as it were, which is filled out with descriptive nominal clauses. The chart on p. 87 shows graphically the clear distinctions in style. The point is that distinctive styles are used here, and never mixed up across natural subject matter divisions. Reportorial verbs always mark a new subject.

Another stylistic shift corresponds to the third major movement in the text,

Structural Element	Verses	Subject	Style
II.A	2-3	Exterior dimensions (stone)	D=descriptive (nominal)
	4	Windows	R=reportorial *(wyqṭl)*
	5-8	Side wings	
	5	Construction of wings	R
	6, 8	Dimensions and features of wings	D
	9-10	Exterior wood structures	R
II.B	15	Walls and floor coverings	R
	16-20aα	Inner sanctuary exclusive of decoration	
	16	Construction	R
	17, 18	Dimensions and features	D
	20aβ-22	Gold ornamentation	R
	23-28	Cherubim	
	23	Construction	R
	24-26	Dimensions	D
	27-28	Placing and decoration	R

II.C, vv. 29-36. As our visual sweep moves to the spaces outside the inner sanctuary, but still within the temple court, we suddenly encounter the use of perfect tense verbs (*qṭl*) in an inverted order (object + verb, vv. 29-32). The use of *qṭl* verb forms continues in vv. 33-35, but with normal word order. Only where we move entirely away from describing the building and its ornamentation to the concluding reports do we find a resumption of the narrative *wyqṭl* tenses (vv. 36-38).

Genre

As a whole, the unit belongs to the genre of REPORT, and of course, briefer reports and descriptive statements are contained within. We note especially vv. 11-13, the report of PROPHETIC REVELATION. Although no prophet is mentioned, this report follows the customary form for reporting a message from God to prophet in the midst of larger narrative contexts. (Cf. 2 Sam. 7:4-16; 1 Sam 15:10-11.) In later times, this type of report was no longer rooted in genuine narrative and was shaped chiefly by an intent to report and preserve the words of a particular prophet (cf. Jer 21:1-10; 32:1-44; Ezek 14:1-11). The absence of narrative context aligns 1 Kgs 6:11-13 more closely to these later examples than to the earlier ones. Furthermore, the various parts of the temple are described in what amounts to a standard reportorial form, as noted above: the *wyqṭl* verb which reports the construction, manufacture, or fabricating action, followed by description of features such as size, ornamentation, and the like, cast in nominal clauses (e.g., vv. 5-6, 8, 16-18, 20aα, 23-26). For these brief reports, we may speak of a distinctive priestly style and concern (→ discussion at 7:1-12 and 7:13-50).

Setting

The concern with details of temple construction and the close literary association with cultic furnishings (ch. 7) suggest that much of the material in this report stemmed from archival sources kept by priests (and/or scribes?) in the Jerusalemite royal establishment (→ fuller discussion at 7:1-50). Noth (*Könige*, 104) suggests that a written order for construction may have lain behind the form which the MT takes, but the idea is very speculative. In terms of literary setting, we may safely observe that the report is set as the first major accounting of Solomon's building activities and is really a part of the material to follow: the palace complex and the cultic implements for the buildings.

Intention

The intention, therefore, is to report selected details of this temple which Solomon built, and more specifically the materials and dimensions, and ornamentation of the buildings, from the exterior to the inner reaches, and including the courtyard around the sanctuary. Moreover, because of the strategic location of v. 7 (stressing the absence of iron tools), and vv. 11-13 (the report of Yahweh's conditional promises to Solomon), it seems clear that the author-editor meant to put the entire enterprise once again under (1) the rule of commandment (the prohibition against using iron in constructing the altar; see Exod 20:25; Deut 27:5; Josh 8:31) and (2) the shadow of conditional promise (that Yahweh would be present to his people, if Solomon remains faithful).

Bibliography

C. Kuhl, "Die Wiederaufnahme—ein literarkritisches Prinzip?" *ZAW* 64 (1952) 1-11; K. Rupprecht, "Nachrichten von Erweiterung und Renovierung des Tempels in 1 Kön 6," *ZDPV* 88 (1972) 38-52.

SOLOMON'S BUILDING ACTIVITIES: REPORT OF PALACE CONSTRUCTION, 7:1-12

Structure

I. Introduction	1
II. The construction activity	2-12
A. Reports concerning buildings	2-8
1. House of forest of Lebanon	2-5
a. Report of construction	2aα
b. Description	2aβ-5
2. Hall of pillars	6
a. Report of construction	6aα
b. Description	6aβ-b
3. Hall of judgment	7
a. Report of construction	7a
b. Description	7b
4. Private dwellings	8
a. Solomon's: description	8a
b. Wife's: report of construction	8b
B. Description of materials	9-12
1. The palace buildings	9-12a
2. Shrine: inner court and vestibule	12b

The structure of this unit is mainly determined by a twofold division of content: the buildings which Solomon constructed and the materials used (II.A, B, vv. 2-8 and 9-12). The first subject division is set forth in a series of rather stereotyped reports. Each begins with a brief reportorial statement, (1) cast with *waw*-conversive (*wyqṭl*) verb forms, as in v. 2aα; or (2) cast with a perfect verb form (*qṭl*) and inverted word order, as in vv. 6aα or 7a; slightly different is v. 8b. After each introductory reportorial sentence, a specific description follows, composed in nominal clauses with minimal connectives, as vv. 2aβ-5 and 7b. From this stylistic perspective, the text may be broken down into the following series reflected in the structural analysis: II.A.1 (vv. 2-5); II.A.2 (v. 6); II.A.3 (v. 7). The schema breaks down a bit in v. 8, and just here the content grows more vague as well. The second major subject division, II.B, vv. 9-12, is mostly descriptive, and hence the nominal clause predominates. There is no special conclusion to the unit.

Taken as a whole, the text moves through a series of reports detailing individual parts of Solomon's palace complex, and then highlights the fine stone and cedar which went into their construction. The account is tied explicitly to the larger context by the mention again of materials used in the courts of the temple (7:12b; cf. 6:36b). Clearly temple and palace buildings belong together in the presentation.

Genre

This unit is a REPORT, and, of course, it is made up of a series of brief reports dealing with specific details according to a clear schematic style. The form of the brief reports, and of the whole which is an aggregate of these parts, is clearly paralleled in priestly materials in the OT. Close at home would be 1 Kgs 6:5-6, 23-28; 7:15-40a. But so also would be the report of tabernacle building and outfitting (Exod 36:8-9, 14-15, 20-30; 37:1-9, 10-16, 17-24, etc.); the reports of census taking (Num 1:19b-46; 3:16-20); and reports of offerings presented at the tabernacle (Num 7:12-17, 19-23, 24-29, etc.). All these materials belong to the later stages of development in the OT priestly materials, and give evidence of careful shaping and systematizing. For parallels to the sequence of motifs in ancient Near Eastern royal inscriptions, see the discussion at 6:1–7:51.

Setting

It is quite possible that an archival style of record keeping stood behind these types of report, and specifically in the sources from which this particular text has been composed (Montgomery, *Kings*). It is also possible that this kind of schematic report would have been typical of royal inscriptions written for "public" memorial display, or of other kinds of record keeping. We can say with certainty only that this form of report has its setting among the priests (and/or scribes?) and their writings wherein the attempt is made to record, with rather a prescriptive tone, many matters pertaining to cult and state (see the full discussion at 7:13-47). The present literary setting of the text is easier to see. It comes as a part of the longer account of temple construction, and is set as the second major division of the material which focuses on Solomon's activity.

Intention

Whatever intention these types of report may have had apart from their present literary context, this unit means to record as part of Solomon's building of a temple his construction of a palace complex, which—like the temple courtyard—contains the finest of stones and cedar (7:10-12; 6:36). This must mean that in the overall evaluation given to Solomon, the work of palace construction is inseparable from the work of temple building.

SOLOMON'S BUILDING ACTIVITIES: REPORT OF TEMPLE FURNISHINGS, 7:13-50

Structure

I. The metal work of Hiram	13-47
A. Introductory setting	13-14
B. The work	15-40a
1. Pillars	15-22
a. Report of construction	15a
b. Description	15b-22a
c. Subscript	22b
2. The sea	23-26
a. Report of construction	23a
b. Description	23b-26
3. Stands	27-37
a. Report of construction	27a
b. Description	27b-36
c. Subscript	37
4. Lavers (ritual basins)	38
a. Report of construction	38a
b. Description	38b
5. Concerning placement of stands and sea	39
6. Concerning miscellaneous implements	40a
C. Concluding summary	40b-44
1. Superscription	40b
2. List of metal works	41-44
D. Supplementary reports	45-47
1. Concerning materials	45
2. Concerning location of casting operations	46
3. Concerning numbers and weight of implements	47
II. The gold work of Solomon	48-50
A. Superscription	48a
B. List of implements	48b-50

In terms of content, this unit is organized around two chief figures and two classes of metal work: Hiram and the bronze implements, Solomon and the gold articles (I.A, B, C, D; vv. 13-47; and II.A, B; vv. 48-50). The first subject division seems to have been rather clearly designed. Following a storylike introductory setting (I.A, vv. 13-14), a series of schematic reports, exactly parallel in form to those in 7:2-5, recounts Hiram's bronze work in some detail. For each bronze object(s), an introductory statement cast in *waw*-conversive style (*wyqṭl*) heads a description that usually mentions (1) the dimensions of the object and then (2) details about its design. The descriptive section is essentially an enumeration, and hence cast in nominal clauses, with no excess information and only implicit connectives between items. For example, vv. 23-26 (where the textual problems are minimal):

Formal Aspects	**Translation**	**Verses**
(1) Reportorial statement	"And he made the molten sea:	23a
(2) Description	Ten cubits from its brim to its brim; round;	23b
a. Dimensions	and five cubits its height, and a line thirty cubits measured all around;	
b. Design details	and gourds under its brim compassing about, thirty cubits; and two rows the gourds, cast when it was cast. Standing upon twelve oxen, three facing north, three facing west, three facing south and three facing east, and the sea upon them, and all their back (sides) inward..."	24-25

I have charted the text in this way with a rather literal translation to illustrate the form, which the *RSV* obscures by supplying connectives of various kinds. For each bronze object, the report follows essentially the same schema (vv. 15-22, 23-26, 27-37, 38; vv. 39-40a are different). A very full example appears in vv. 27-37, which includes a superscription for the design detail section (v. 28aα) and a colophon marking the end (v. 37).

This series of reports on the bronze work closes with a summary, vv. 40b-44, consisting of a superscription and listing of items. Though the correspondence to what has gone before is not perfect, the sequence of items is exactly the same and the placement of such a summary is precisely what one would expect from parallel texts (see below). Thus, even if the items in this concluding section originally belonged to another context, it is clear enough now that they are meant to close out in summary fashion a unit viewed as a whole. The supplementary reports (I.D, vv. 45-47) seem connected in theme only; they deal with Hiram and the bronze work, but in a decisively different literary style and with a different point.

The second subject division—the gold work of Solomon, vv. 48-50—is very close in structure to the concluding summary in the account of Hiram's bronze work (vv. 40b-44). But lacking any prior detailed report, the passage now serves to report new information, substituting, as it were, for a detailed account of the gold implements made by Solomon. The text seems associated with Hiram's work by the common use of *kēlîm,* "vessels," in vv. 45, 47 (Hiram), 48, 51 (Solomon), a word which appears nowhere else in the account of temple construction.

Thus, in the two large subject matter divisions, and in the schematic arrangements of its parts, especially the account of Hiram's metal work, we may see order in the MT, an order probably imposed in the redaction of these materials. We meet Hiram as a craftsman of the highest order. Then we hear of his manufacture of bronze furnishings and implements for the temple, along with supplementary notes on the site of their smelting and casting, and their vast weight. The unit closes with a summary of Solomon's golden implements made for this same temple.

Genre

The genre of the whole unit is REPORT, which in this case includes several priestly style reports, most of which appear in the stereotyped schematic form also found in 6:23-26; 7:2-7. In this regard, vv. 13-44, with introduction and concluding summary, represent a rather tightly organized unity. Outside the books of Kings, the closest parallels are in priestly materials: Exod 36:8-9, which contains all the elements and stylistic features important for the form, including a closing colophon; Exod 37:1-9, 10-16, 17-24; Num 1:19b-46; 3:16-20; 7:12-17, 19-23, 24-29, etc. For colophons, see Exod 36:13bβ (concluding 36:1-13a+bα); Lev 27:34 (concluding the entire book); Lev 26:46 (concluding 17:1–26:45); 14:57b (concluding the whole collection of laws on leprosy, and also a specific law, 14:54-57a). Note also that the concluding summary, 1 Kgs 7:40b-44, consisting of a superscription and list of items, is also well attested in these priestly traditions, e.g., Lev 7:37-38 (concluding 6:1 [*RSV* 6:8]–7:36, the *tôrâ* of offerings); Lev 11:46-47 (concluding 11:1-45); Lev 14:54-57 (concluding Lev 13:1–14:53); and finally, Exod 39:32-43, a somewhat variant concluding summary, but nonetheless one that enumerates the items included in the larger report of building and outfitting the tabernacle. These summaries suggest a scholastic, systematizing activity, and may in fact be based on, or drawn from, priestly (→) catalogues. See elsewhere Leviticus 11; Exod 25:3-7. From this formal perspective, we must also understand 1 Kgs 7:48-50. As to form, it is a concluding summary of the type found in these priestly traditions. In its present literary context, however, vv. 48-50 conclude no lengthy report, as do vv. 40b-44. Rather, they serve to introduce supplementary, but new material: the gold work of Solomon (see Structure above).

Setting

As with 7:1-12, much of the material which lay behind these reports may have been kept in archival records or royal documents of one kind or another. But more to the point is the overwhelming evidence that the particular form of this report on the temple furnishings had its setting among the priests (and/or scribes?) of Israel, probably in Jerusalem. The strongest evidence is that all the close parallels are found in the developed priestly traditions, that is, in those later elaborations of the basic "P" document in the Pentateuch (Noth, *Leviticus; Numbers;* Elliger). All these passages reflect attempts to standardize form and content and to portray events of the past in archetypal terms, that is, as paradigms having prescriptive force for later generations which seek to align word of God with human act. The report in 1 Kgs 7:13-50, both in its whole and its parts, with the exception of vv. 13-14, belongs to the same stylistic and formal class of writing, and hence probably to the same setting. There is every reason to think of this unit as perfectly congruent with the developed priestly traditions in the books of Exodus, Leviticus, and Numbers. In short, the final form of 1 Kgs 7:13-50 follows the forms of redaction customarily seen in priestly writings elsewhere in the OT. An even later example of a similar concern to write paradigmatically of cultic and temple matters may be seen in the Temple Scroll, fragments of which are known from Qumran (Yadin; Levine). Of course, there is still the matter of the literary setting in the books of Kings. And here, one may observe that the report is part of the larger account of Solomon's building activities, but particularly, it is set as the third stage of this activity: the first was the physical structure and materials; the second, the palace and its materials; the third, the furnishing of objects and implements for the establishment and maintenance of the cult.

Intention

The intention is clear, therefore. This report means to account for the bronze and gold objects in the temple, and to attribute them to Hiram the craftsman, and Solomon the king, respectively. What is actually described here centers on the cult: the pillars, which apparently have commemorative names (*yākîn,* "he establishes," and *bō'az,* "by him is he mighty," v. 21), although their exact significance is unknown; the sea, a great basin for ritual purification; the stands, and the basins which sit on them, for ritual use; the other implements, "vessels," and so on. So in its highly selective content and in its priestly form, the report surely must intend as much prescription as description, as though cultic space rightly reported and furnished is cultic space rightly observed and protected by later generations.

Bibliography

K. Elliger, *Leviticus* (Handbuch zum Alten Testament; Tübingen: Mohr, 1966); B. Levine, "The Temple Scroll: Aspects of its Historical Provenance and Literary Character," *BASOR* 232 (1978) 5-23; M. Noth, *Exodus. A Commentary* (tr. J. S. Bowden; OTL; Philadelphia: Westminster, 1962); idem, *Leviticus. A Commentary* (tr. J. E. Anderson; rev. ed.; OTL; Philadelphia: Westminster, 1977); idem, *Numbers. A Commentary* (tr. J. D. Martin; OTL; Philadelphia: Westminster, 1968); Y. Yadin, *Megillat Hammiqdāš (The Temple Scroll)* (3 vols.; Jerusalem: Israel Exploration Society, Hebrew University and Shrine of the Book, 1977).

SOLOMON'S BUILDING ACTIVITIES: REPORT OF TEMPLE DEDICATION, 8:1-66

Structure

I. Introductory setting: gathering of assembly	1-2
II. Installation of the ark in temple	3-13
III. Dedicatory ceremonies	14-64
A. Speeches	14-61
1. Before the assembly: address	14-21
2. Before the altar: prayer of petition	22-53
3. Before the assembly: parenesis	54-61
B. Sacrifices	62-64
IV. Conclusion	65-66
A. Summary	65
B. Dissolution of assembly	66

With good reason most scholars have sought a complicated history behind this unit, which is in fact the result of a redactional process. There appear to be at least two independent traditions joined together—the movement of the ark into the temple (vv. 1-13), and the dedication of that same temple by Solomon (vv. 15-61). The latter section reflects almost exclusively Dtr language and style, although it may not all have been composed at the same time (Levenson), and the former section is much more influenced by the style and vocabulary of the "P" writer and the Chronicler. Vv. 65-66, now a somewhat rough and probably secondary conclusion to the redacted whole, contain a dramatic shift in perspective in which the narrator (if the MT is correct) speaks in his own voice, addressing his reading or hearing audience directly (v. 65, "our God"), a rarity in biblical literature. The evidence for a complicated history of redaction is clear, but a consensus on the lines of that history eludes us.

Nevertheless, we ought not to miss the kind of unity which the whole unit offers. There is a flow from beginning to end, marked by spatial imagery and verbs in the narrative tenses, reporting movements and events. The account begins with gathering the assembly (*qĕhal yiśrā'ēl*) and closes with dissolving the assembly (*qāhāl gādôl*). The primary action, so to speak, takes place between these two sweeping events of gathering and dispersal. Various stages of this action are marked by reportorial verbs (*wyqṭl*): vv. 1, 2, 3-4, 14, 22, 54-55, 63, 66, and these correspond to the discrete elements in the structural analysis. Moreover, most major movements in the text are marked by some form of the root *qhl*, "assemble" or "assembly" in the English versions: vv. 1-2 (for II, vv. 3-13); v. 14 (for III.A.1, vv. 14-21); v. 22 (for III.A.2, vv. 22-53); v. 55 (for III.A.3, vv. 54-61) (Porten, 107 [see listing at 3:1–11:43]; the rest of his attempts to press perfect symmetry on the MT are strained and artificial). Finally, one may note that each of the speeches spoken on this occasion has its own narrative introduction which provides a proper setting for the words. The longest speech, the prayer of petition (III.A.2, vv. 22-53), is flanked fore and aft with special addresses to the assembled community. This "sandwich" construction corresponds to a visual image explicitly given in the text: Solomon faces the assembly, turns toward the altar and offers prayers of petition, and then faces the assembly once again. The literary architecture suggests a centering on the prayers offered to Yahweh—and indeed they take the most space, and have received the most attention from the Dtr editor. It is as though one buffers the prayer with speeches all around, like the outer courts which surround the holy of holies (ch. 6), defining and protecting at once the sacred center. Finally, the conclusion (IV, vv. 65-66) relates the events to the Festival of Tabernacles (the word *ḥāg* is abruptly introduced), and with its shift in perspective just as abruptly brings the reader into the proceedings, closing the whole on this singular note of participative joy for "all Israel," a "great assembly."

Genre

Since it is a question of a redactional unit here, we cannot specify the genre with much more precision than REPORT, and of course this covers a number of smaller units which have their own generic identity: e.g., PRAYER OF PETITION, vv. 22-53; PARENESIS, vv. 54-61; PRAYER OF DEDICATION, vv. 12-13. These and other lesser generic elements will be discussed in more detail below. The closest parallel to this report is Exod 40:16-33, the priestly account of Moses' erecting the tabernacle, and the epiphanic response by Yahweh that announces the beginning of a period of cultic propriety. Cf. also the briefer notes in Ezra 6:16-18 and 1 Esdr 5:47ff. None of these texts offers a direct, substantive parallel, however. The report in 1 Kings 8 is unique in the Bible, and uniquely placed in the recounting of the reigns. For motif parallels in Mesopotamian monumental inscriptions, many of which mention dedication ceremonies for a temple, see the discussion at 6:1–7:51. An Egyptian building inscription of Seti I, ca. 1300 B.C., is most interesting because it not only reports the building and dedication of a desert temple where Seti found water for his mining expeditions, but also includes a dedicatory prayer of petition (Lichtheim, *Ancient Egyptian Literature* II, 52-56). See full discussion below at 8:1-13, 22-53.

Setting

Since it is a question of a redactional unit making up this report, we must think primarily of its literary setting in the books of Kings, and more broadly in the Dtr history work. For the social setting, one would look to the history-writing activity of an author-editor in Babylonian exile (→ "Introduction to 1 Kings," pp. 31-32). The dedication of the temple is the centerpiece of Solomon's reign—in terms of space allotted, and in terms of the amount of Dtr-shaped language poured into its final form. It is both climax and paradigmatic center.

Intention

From the standpoint of this author-editor, therefore, the intention must have been to report what to him was the most important act of this King Solomon, the culmination, as it were, of the building projects, the chief act of kingly piety. Here also, the report could be a vehicle for demonstrating the importance of the temple for the religious meaning of the people of God. (See detailed discussion below.)

Bibliography

G. Braulik, "Spuren einer Neubearbeitung des deuteronomistischen Geschichtswerks in 1 Kön 8:52-53, 59-60," *Bib* 52 (1971) 20-23; A. Gamper, "Die heilsgeschichtliche Bedeutung des salomonischen Tempelweihgebets," *ZKTh* 85 (1963) 55-61; A. S. Wheeler, "Prayer and Temple in the Dedication Speech of Solomon, 1 Kings 8:14-61" (Diss., Columbia, 1977); J. D. Levenson, "From Temple to Synagogue: 1 Kings 8," in *Traditions in Transformation* (*Fest.* F. M. Cross; ed. B. A. Halpern & J. D. Levenson; Winona Lake, IN: Eisenbrauns, 1981) 143-66.

SOLOMON'S BUILDING ACTIVITIES, TEMPLE DEDICATION: REPORT OF THE INSTALLATION OF THE ARK, 8:1-13

Structure

I. Introductory setting	1-3a
II. The procession	3b-5
A. Carrying the ark and implements	3b-4
B. Description of accompanying sacrifices	5
III. The installation	6-13
A. Placing the ark	6
B. Description of cherubim, tables of stone	7-9
C. Confirmatory epiphany	10-11
D. Prayer of dedication	12-13
1. Opening address	12a
2. Background	12b
3. Dedicatory declaration	13

Even while disagreeing in detailed reconstructions, scholars generally admit that the present form of this unit reflects a connection of a priestly "ark" tradition with the Dtr presentation of temple dedication. The opening vv. 1-2 sound the "assembly" motif which is central to the literary and dramatic structure of ch. 8 (note *qhl,* used in verbal and nominal forms, "assemble" and "assembly," in vv. 1, 2, 14, 22, 55, 65). Moreover, the language of Solomon's prayer in vv. 12-13, whatever its original sense may have been, now carries double reference: to the ark and its protective cherubim on the one hand, and the temple, the "house" which Solomon built, on the other.

The structure of the unit is defined by reportorial verbs (*waw*-conversive forms, *wyqṭl*) which narrate the steps in the drama: coming together (vv. 1-3a), taking up and processing (vv. 3b-4), placing the ark (v. 6), receiving the confirmatory show of Yahweh's glory (vv. 10-11), and finally Solomon's prayer, the first and only direct quotation in the whole unit (vv. 12-13). Along the way, circumstantial nominal clauses (II.B, v. 5; and III.B, vv. 7-9) fill out the two main events, procession and installation. The latter description is also important in linking this account to the details of the temple's interior (cf. 6:23-28) and to the theologically shaped recollection of Israel's beginnings at Horeb (v. 9; cf. Deut 9:9-11).

Genre

This unit is a REPORT since it clearly narrates action, but stops short of developing a storylike plot with tensions and complications to be resolved in the working out of events. The parallel in 2 Sam 6:1-19 is interesting and instructive. Although this bit of Davidic tradition is now linked in complex ways to 1 Samuel 4–6 (the so-called Ark Narrative), to David's establishment of Jerusalem as his capital, and to the matter of David's relation to the house of Saul (the incident with Michal, 2 Sam 6:16, 20-23), the text is basically ruled by the same dramatic movement as 1 Kgs 8:3b-13. That is to say: (1) a procession to bring up the ark to Jerusalem (the people gather, 2 Sam 6:1-2; they carry the ark with festive joymaking, 6:5, and sacrifices, 6:13); (2) they deposit the ark in its proper place, again with cultic sacrifices, 6:17; (3) David offers blessings on the people; and (4) the crowd of celebrants disperses, 6:18-19. A typical procedure for moving holy things into their sacred repository may have shaped both the Samuel and Kings texts. In any case, the two accounts seem remarkably similar in their structural components, even allowing for great differences in style and context.

The report about Solomon's actions contains two additional features worth noting: the motif of Yahweh's "glory" (*kābôd,* vv. 10-11) and the prayer of dedication (vv. 12-13). Yahweh's epiphany in his "glory," filling the temple, suggests that with this sign God shows his approval (cf. 2 Chr 5:14; 7:2). Precisely this use of the motif appears in Exod 40:34-35. After Moses had erected the tabernacle according to command, the cloud covered the tent of meeting, and "the glory of the Lord filled the tabernacle" (*ûkĕbôd yahweh mālē' 'et-hammiškān,* Exod 40:34), as though to inaugurate a period of cultic propriety. For Ezekiel, compare the note of disapproval when the "glory" departs Jerusalem because of the deep transgressions of the people (Ezek 11:23) and the tone of approbation when "glory" returns to the restored and sanctified temple (Ezek 43:2). Yahweh's appearing in "glory" is frequently associated with schematic reports of epiphany in the priestly materials. The glory manifests itself, and Yahweh delivers a message (e.g., Exod 16:10-12; 24:16-18 + 25:1-9; Num 17:7-10 [*RSV* 16:42-45]; Num 20:6-8; Ezek 44:4-5). Evidently, then, the author of 1 Kings 8, or the tradition at his disposal, has followed a priestly convention in noting Yahweh's confirmatory epiphany in terms of "glory" (*kābôd*) filling the sacred space.

An important generic element in this report is Solomon's PRAYER OF DEDICATION (vv. 12-13; see Weinfeld, 35-36). Close OT parallels may be found in Deut 26:5-10 and 1 Sam 1:26-28. Like Solomon's prayer, each of these other texts includes (1) background which provides context for the dedications in progress, and (2) a simple declaration, in Hebrew perfect tense: "And behold, I bring [*hēbē'tî*] the first of the fruit of the ground, which thou, O Lord, hast given me" (Deut 26:10); "I have lent him [*hiš'īltîhû*] to the Lord; as long as he lives, he is lent to the Lord" (1 Sam 1:28); "I have built [*bānōh bānîtî*] thee an exalted house, a place for thee to dwell forever" (1 Kgs 8:13).

Behind Solomon's prayer may be a Canaanite poetic tradition (Loretz) or even a song book in Israel (the LXX at v. 53 quotes a fuller version of the prayer [now transferred by *RSV* and most critics to MT v. 12] and adds a citation, "Book of the Song"). Or perhaps a typical household dedicatory speech form lay behind the text (Noth, *Könige,* 181), or even a type of praise song with analogues in Egyptian literature (Görg). Reconstruction aside, a closer analogy in both literary content and form appears as part of a Sumerian dedicatory inscription, a prayer on the lips of Gudea:

> "Oh, my king, Ningirsu, lord, who turnest back the raging water; lord, whose word goes forth on high; O son of Enlil, thou warrior who commandest, my right

> hand has wrought for thee; I have built thy temple for thee; with joy I would bring thee into it. I will place my goddess Bau on thy left (?) side into a good dwelling ye shall go." (Cylinder B, col. 2:16–3:1; Barton, *RISA*, 239)

Note these formal elements especially:

(1) Address to the deity;
(2) Dedicatory declaration ("My right hand has wrought for thee/I have built thy temple for thee . . .");
(3) Statement of intention: installation of the goddess.

The full inscription provides a wider context similar to the Solomonic materials: Gudea built this temple, brought a gift for the gods, offered the prayer quoted here, and all was accepted by the goddess.

Gudea's memorial inscription is a very early and elaborate example of a rather stable literary genre: the DEDICATORY INSCRIPTION. Examples are known throughout Mesopotamian history well before and beyond the Israelite period. Despite many variations, these inscriptions are built on three essential elements: (1) the address to a particular deity who is named and honored, (2) identification of the donor, and (3) a declaration that the donor has built, caused to be made, etc., the object being dedicated with this inscription (Sollberger, 24-27; Hallo). In form a dedicatory inscription is a "prayer"; in function, both prayer and memorial to the king and his god(s). For early examples, see Sollberger, text I.C.5; II.C.2a; IV.A.2b. Later examples from Assyria: Grayson, *ARI* I, § 535 (Shalmaneser, ca. 1280 B.C.) and Luckenbill, *ARAB* II, §§ 999-1006, 1007-9 (both inscriptions of Ashurbanipal, ca. 668-626 B.C.); *ARAB* II, § 224 (Sargon, ca. 721-705 B.C.). From Egypt, the picture is more complicated because the form of dedicatory inscriptions was not so fixed a literary tradition as in Mesopotamia. But a constant feature is the simple dedicatory declaration, stating that the king has built, made, or renovated the object or edifice being dedicated to the god(s). See Breasted, *ARE* II, §§ 176, 599-601, 611 (Thutmose III, ca. 1500 B.C.); *ARE* IV, §§ 3-16 (Ramses III, ca. 1200 B.C.). This last text is especially interesting because a retrospective "background" section (§ 9) precedes the simple dedicatory declaration, as in the OT example.

Setting

Of course, the genre report may have many settings. But a report with this particular content, the installation of a holy object in a holy place, with the attendant dedicatory prayer, is likely to have been more restricted in its setting. We cannot know much for certain. In Israel, such reports would seem consistent with both priestly and royal interests. The language and style of this particular example suggests as much, although the situation is more complicated for the main parallel in 2 Samuel 6. The prayer of dedication is another matter. The Mesopotamian and Egyptian royal inscriptions may reflect ceremonial words spoken when something was offered to the deity. Certainly Deuteronomy 26 and 1 Samuel 1 point in this same direction for Israel. In Mesopotamia, written forms of such prayers would have been included in dedicatory inscriptions, designed for foundation deposits or smaller dedicated objects. However, as yet no exactly comparable royal inscriptions have turned up in Israel. Perhaps the OT report of installation and dedication derives from such royal conventions or is the functional equivalent of these written memorials to a monarch and his gods (cf. Corvin, 225-28). More to the point, however, is the immediate literary setting of this particular report in the books of Kings. The installation of the ark, the symbol of Yahweh's presence as associated with the tent-dwelling place of god (2 Sam 6:2; 7:2), follows the preparation of its resting place (chs. 6–7) and is the first step in dedicating Solomon's temple.

Intention

The intention of this report, then, in its present literary context, is to recount the installation of that cultic object, the ark of the covenant, in the temple which Solomon built. The text means to set this as the first stage of the dedication ceremonies, and thereby to establish the presence of God in this sacred space. Already the analogous dedicatory inscriptions from Mesopotamia suggest the importance of bringing the gods into the newly built city, temple, or other edifice. The report explictly serves to merge two ideological streams for ancient Israel: the ark/tent as a central symbol of Yahweh's presence, and the temple in Jerusalem, which is seen as the fulfillment of a promise given to David and the new symbol for that same spiritual availability of God. One might say that this report was Israel's way of recording that Solomon brought the gods into the temple, as the epiphany of "glory" might make clear. Just as David before had moved the ark to Jerusalem as a politico-religious statement, so this report of Solomon's action means to consolidate and unify. The report asserts the common affinity of the god of Horeb, covenant, and tables of stone, with David and ark/tent, and now with this physical place in Jerusalem, and with this scion of David, sitting upon his throne.

Bibliography

See bibliography at "Introduction to Historical Literature." A. von den Born, "Zum Tempelweihespruch" (1 Kgs 8:12f)," *OTS* 14 (1965) 235-44; J. W. Corvin, "A Stylistic and Functional Study of the Prose Prayers in the Historical Narratives of the Old Testament" (Diss., Emory, 1972); M. Görg, *Gott-König-Reden* (see listing at 3:14-15); idem, "Die Gattung des sogenannten Tempelweihespruchs (1 Kgs 8:12f)," *UF* 6 (1974) 55-63; A. K. Grayson, "Histories and Historians" (see listing at "Introduction to 1 Kings"), esp. pp. 156-57; O. Loretz, "Der Torso eines kanaanäisch-israelitischen Tempelweihespruches in 1 Kön 8:12-13," *UF* 6 (1974) 478-80; M. Weinfeld, *Deuteronomy* (see listing at "Introduction to 1 Kings").

SOLOMON'S BUILDING ACTIVITIES, TEMPLE DEDICATION: DEDICATORY ADDRESS, 8:14-21

Structure

I. Narrative introduction	14-15aα
II. Address before the assembly	15aβ-21
A. Praise speech	15aβ-16
B. Recitation	17-21
1. Background	17-20a
2. Statements of dedication	20b-21

a. The temple 20b
b. The ark 21

This unit marks a new phase in the dedicatory ceremonies. It appropriately begins with a narrative introduction which notes that Solomon now faces the assembly, and which goes on to characterize his action as blessing the people. New action begins in v. 22, when Solomon turns back "before the altar." The text moves us from Solomon's praise speech, introduced with the "blessing" (*bārûk*) formula (II.A, vv. 15aβ-16; see discussion at 5:21), to the address to the people. This address retrospectively recites the dealings of Yahweh with David, focusing on the promise that a son of David would build the temple which David intended, and then announces that fulfillment has occurred: "I have built the house for the name of the Lord. . . . I have provided a place for the ark" (vv. 20b-21). In context, these statements are strictly analogous to the simple dedicatory declaration at the end of Solomon's prayer in v. 13. One may even extend the analogy to the whole. Just as the prayer in vv. 12-13 (and parallels) sketches contextual background and declares the "house" built, so in this public address Solomon offers his brief doxology, then a more extended summary of contextual background, and finally declares the benefaction done—all under the aegis of what the narrator calls "blessing" the people.

Genre

This unit is a Report of dedicatory address, and its substance is distinguished from prayer of dedication as seen in 8:12-13 because the words are addressed to the people and not to God. Since Solomon does not seek to persuade or exhort, his speech is not (→) parenesis (against Kegler, 203 [see listings at 2:12b-46]). The terms "liturgical oration" or "discourse on the function of prayer in Yahweh's chosen place" (Weinfeld, 37 [see listing at "Introduction to 1 Kings"]) seem hardly accurate as generic descriptions but correctly capture the rhetorical stylization so characteristic of Dtr compositions in 1–2 Kings. An important element within the report is the Praise Speech, an utterance of approbation directed toward God and introduced with the blessing formula, "Blessed be [*bārûk*] the Lord, the God of Israel . . ." (v. 15a). See the parallels cited at 1 Kgs 5:21 and full discussion.

Setting

We lack the evidence to decide whether public addresses would have been common on occasions of dedication. Judging from its extensive Dtr language (e.g., vv. 16-19) and close ties with 2 Samuel 7, this particular report was likely created especially for the literary account of the dedicatory ceremonies. The text comes as the second distinct phase in the proceedings, before the grand prayer of petition (vv. 22-53) and immediately after the ark of the covenant has been installed in the sanctuary (vv. 1-13).

Intention

The intention of the report should therefore be seen primarily in terms of its literary function. In this respect, the substance of the unit parallels the prayer of dedication, vv. 12-13. That is to say, Solomon's words to the assembly essentially aim at offering the temple, now finished and furnished, to the deity (vv. 20b-21). What was first done in the inner reaches of this temple (vv. 12-13) is now done in public, so to speak. Thus this report begins the public phase of the dedication, and sets the occasion for the petitions to follow. The intention is analogous to that of Deuteronomy 1–3, which introduces with historical recollection the *tôrâ* to be given to the people. Theologically, this report of dedicatory address defines a moment of fulfillment as well as dedication. And the conjoining of these two ideas is fundamental to the Dtr author-editor: this house of Yahweh is an appropriate royal offering to God in response to divine promises given and fulfilled.

SOLOMON'S BUILDING ACTIVITIES, TEMPLE DEDICATION: PRAYERS OF PETITION, 8:22-53

Structure

I. Narrative introduction	22-23aα
II. Prayers	23aβ-53
A. First prayer of petition (for the dynastic promise)	23aβ-26
1. Opening address	23aβ
2. Hymnic praise	23b-24
3. Petition	25-26
a. First petition	25
1) Address	25aα
2) Petition	25aβ-b
b. Second petition	26
1) Address	26a
2) Petition	26b
B. Second prayer of petition (for general divine response)	27-30
1. Rhetorical disclaimer	27
2. Petition: hear and forgive	28-30
a. Present	28-29
b. Future	30
C. Third prayer of petition (for seven future circumstances)	31-51
1. First petition (juridical oaths)	31-32
a. Circumstance	31
b. Petition	32
2. Second petition (defeat)	33-34
a. Circumstance	33
b. Petition	34
3. Third petition (drought)	35-36
a. Circumstance	35
b. Petition	36
4. Fourth petition (plagues, famine)	37-40
a. Circumstances	37-38
b. Petition	39-40

5. Fifth petition (foreigner)	41-43
a. Circumstances	41-42
b. Petition	43
6. Sixth petition (the people in battle)	44-45
a. Circumstances	44
b. Petition	45
7. Seventh petition (the people in captivity)	46-51
a. Circumstances	46-48
b. Petition	49-51
D. Fourth prayer of petition (for general divine response)	52-53
1. Petition	52
2. Statement of reason (motive clause)	53

This unit is marked off from the preceding and following sections by content and form and by two narrative introductions, which clearly define phases in these dedicatory ceremonies (vv. 22-23aα; 54-55). Possibly some of this material reflects various stages in the history of tradition. For example, vv. 44-51 are formulated differently from the petitions in vv. 31-43 (the *RSV* obscures the difference), and they duplicate somewhat the thought of vv. 33-34. Or again, vv. 52-53 repeat the substance of vv. 29-30. We cannot be sure about the earlier stages of redaction.

In any case, the final text shows remarkable balance (Gamper), despite a temporal perspective which extends far enough to envision the exile or reflect on it *ex vaticinu*. There are four main prayers of petition: II.A, vv. 23aβ-26; II.B, vv. 27-30; II.C, vv. 31-51 (a series of seven, with each item formulated very similarly); II.D, vv. 52-53. These main petitions reduce the thematic content of the unit to prayers for (1) dynastic promise, (2) general divine response to petition, (3) seven future situations demanding prayers of petition, and (4) general divine response. Moreover, each major petition shows a distinctive beginning which marks it from its surroundings. The first, vv. 23αβ-26, carries a typical opening address to God, with hymnic epithets for the deity; the second, vv. 27-30, begins with typically Dtr rhetorical questions; the third and longest prayer offers a conditional clause, the first in the entire unit, and the first in a series of such extending through v. 51; the fourth and last major petition begins directly, without opening address or rhetorical flourishes. This last petition, like v. 51, includes a reason that Yahweh should respond, as though to better persuade the deity.

The center of the unit comes in the long series of seven conditionally formulated petitions (vv. 31-51) now framed by the second and fourth prayers, vv. 27-30 and 52-53. Each of these framing pieces cites a general theme with very similar language, and hence stands apart from the central prayer. Notably, the seventh and last petition in this middle series has been given special rhetorical emphasis. It is about twice as long as the others in the chapter, and the conditionally formulated circumstances (vv. 46-48) heap against one another with intricate wordplay on the roots "repent" (*šwb*) and "carry into exile" (*šbh*). Statements of deportation and hence enmity with God alternate with those of repentance and return to Yahweh, as the following chart indicates (Levenson, 136):

Deportation		**Return**
šābûm šōbêhem, 46b	→	*hēšîbû*, 47a
nišbû, 47a	← →	*šābû*, 47b
šōbêhem, 47b	← →	*šā́bû*, 48a
šābû, 48a	←	

At the close of this oscillating series, the pun approaches high art: the verbs look and sound alike, except for accent (*šābû* and *šā́bû*). Petition, long delayed by these rhetorical flourishes, then follows (vv. 49-51), and this central prayer thus finds its conclusion. The entire unit coheres with a refrainlike plea: "Hear thou in heaven . . . and forgive" (vv. 32, 34, 36, 39, 43, 45, 49).

Noteworthy in the context of so much rhetorical language characteristic of the Dtr history work is that vv. 37 and 41 are formulated very similarly to statements of *tôrâ* in Leviticus. V. 37a begins (literally, for the *RSV* smooths the word order): "a famine, if there be in the land, a pestilence if there be, blight, mildew, locust, caterpillar if there be . . . [then follow further circumstances, and then the main petition in v. 39, "hear thou in heaven . . ."]." Cf. Lev 13:2, 18, 24, 29, 38, 47, where the form is: "xx: if there is Y with regard to xx, [then follows the torah ruling]." So Lev 13:47 reads: "A garment, if there is a leprous disease in it . . ." or Lev 13:9, "A leprous disease, if it is on a man. . . ." This formulation in Leviticus and its rather startling appearance in 1 Kgs 8:37-41 suggest that a priestly literary model lay behind at least part of the present text.

Genre

This unit is a REPORT of petition; the substance of what is reported are the various PRAYERS OF PETITION, which follow in large measure the form of stylized religious petitions familiar from other Dtr passages such as 1 Kgs 3:6-9; 2 Sam 7:18-29; 2 Kgs 19:15-19. See the full discussion at 3:4-13.

Setting

Petition has roots in many situations of ordinary life, among which would be those religious occasions when objects, persons, or buildings would be dedicated to the deity. In the OT, such texts as Deut 26:5-10 and 1 Sam 1:26-28 suggest the cultic occasions on which prayers of petition would be appropriate. From the ancient Near East, we have another sort of literary reflex: prayers of petition as part of dedicatory inscriptions associated with royal building projects or dedicated objects. Perhaps behind these prayers contained in "public" inscriptions lie ceremonies in which petitions would have been offered orally. But as far as we can tell, the *report* of such dedicatory prayers belongs to literary accounts of the benefactions of the king toward the gods inscribed on monuments, foundation stones, or temple walls and designed to memorialize both the gods and the king's good name (→ full discussion and parallels at 8:1-13; cf. especially for Tiglath-Pileser I, Grayson, *ARI* II, § 58). For Israel, we have only the present literary context for anything roughly comparable.

It is here that the question of setting must be raised in its most important sense. The prayers are obviously stylized, rhetorical creations, programmatic and idealizing in character—"stereotyped religious declaration in the language of deuteronomic religio-national ideology" (Weinfeld, 52). Solomon's words in all of 1 Kings 8 form one of those grand discourses so important to the structural unity of the Dtr history work (Noth; see "Introduction to 1 Kings," pp. 14-15). We must recognize the exilic viewpoint. In the Dtr author-editor's account of the Solomonic era and, one might add, of the benefactions of Solomon toward Yahweh, the report of Solomon's petitions comes as the central dramatic moment. Yet the rhetorical fullness imparts a quality of timelessness to these words imagined to have been spoken at only one point in time. They become an expression, or fixation, of exilic longings and paradigmatic modes of worship.

Intention

The intention of the report is to enumerate the prayers spoken by Solomon on this dedicatory occasion. Perhaps more important is the theological effect. The heaping up of future conditions to which Yahweh should respond raises the situation to infinity. Solomon petitions God in advance for all possible contingencies, all situations that may face this people, and so places the unlimited future under the aegis of this beginning moment, when the temple is first opened to sacred power, and Solomon the righteous king stands at the apex of his royal and priestly powers on behalf of the people. The sacrality of that moment seems captured in the remarkable use of the number seven (Levenson, 136). The central prayer contains seven petitions; the wordplays on "repent" and "carry into captivity" (*šwb, šbh*) involve seven shifts of perspective back and forth, from sin to repentance; Solomon offered his dedicatory prayer in the seventh month (1 Kgs 8:2), perhaps during the Festival of Booths (which lasts for seven days; see 8:65). Even the construction of the temple lasted seven years (1 Kgs 6:38). The exilic Dtr author-editor clearly offered a paradigmatic moment from which the past and future, especially that longed for by the temple-shorn and landless exiles, derived its value and significance.

Bibliography

A. Gamper, "Die heilsgeschichtliche Bedeutung" (see listing at 8:1-66); J. D. Levenson, "The Paronomasia of Solomon's Seventh Petition," *Hebrew Annual Review* 6 (1982) 135-38; M. Noth, *Deuteronomistic History* (see listing at "Introduction to 1 Kings"); M. Weinfeld, *Deuteronomy,* 51-58 (see listing at "Introduction to 1 Kings").

SOLOMON'S BUILDING ACTIVITIES, TEMPLE DEDICATION: PARENESIS, 8:54-61

Structure

I. Narrative introduction	54-55
II. Parenesis	56-61
A. Praise speech	56
B. Wishes	57-60
1. First wish	57-58
a. For Yahweh's presence	57
b. Result: obedience	58
2. Second Wish	59-60
a. For Yahweh's response and defense	59
b. Result: Yahweh is known in all the	

earth 60
C. Exhortation 61

Like other major sections of the chapter, this unit has its own narrative introduction which marks another phase in the proceedings. The petitions completed, Solomon rises and faces the assembly, an effective counterpart to vv. 14-21. The narrator characterizes the activity, as he does in 8:14, as the act of "blessing" the people. In fact, the verb "bless" covers only the speech of praise with its "blessing" (*bārûk*) formula in v. 56. In vv. 57-60 we hear Solomon's wishes, which indirectly express petition in two parts (vv. 57-58, 59-60). Each part begins with the verb "be" (v. 57: "The Lord . . . be with us," and v. 59: "Let these words of mine . . . be near to the Lord . . ."). Each wish, whose scope is wide enough to look back over the entire dedicatory prayer, includes an intended result (v. 58, the wish for God's presence so that he will engender obedience in the faithful; v. 60, the wish for Yahweh's response in order that he be known in all the earth; cf. Deut 4:35). The whole speech then closes with an exhortation to the people (v. 61) expressed with second-person suffixes—the first time in these dedicatory ceremonies. Solomon praises God, utters the wishes for God's presence and continuing influence, and exhorts the assembly in a kind of climactic flourish, that they might obey fully and seize this opportunity to realize the conditions for those wishes to materialize.

Genre

This unit is a REPORT of PARENESIS. Solomon's words, of course, contain many identifiable generic elements: PRAISE SPEECH (→ 5:21 and discussion there); wish (cf. 1 Sam 20:13; Ps 72:17; Ps 104:31, 34, 35; Exod 18:19; etc.); ADMONITION (see Amos 5:4-7, 14-15; Job 22:21-30). As PARENESIS, Solomon's speech is aimed at a group and seeks to persuade or exhort toward a definite goal (Tiffany, 20-21). For parallels, Zech 1:3-6; Ezek 33:10-16; Josh 24:2-15.

Setting

This unit depends upon its present Dtr-shaped context for its meaning, and is fully integrated into it by means of the narrative introduction. Its important setting, therefore, is the literary one; it comes as the final phase of the spoken activity on this occasion, the penultimate act in the dedicatory ceremonies. Thus, the report of parenesis is placed as a conclusion to the prayerful activity of Solomon.

Intention

This particular speech of parenesis is designed to persuade or encourage compliance with the norms implicit in the entire Dtr royal theology; it urges in this case that the people obey fully and thereby be in a position of fully reaping the benefits of Yahweh's availability in this sacred place, the temple. At the same time, the report of such a parenesis in context aims at rounding out these dedicatory ceremonies by giving a picture of the king officiating, while evoking an image of Moses, Joshua, Samuel, or one of the prophets, exhorters all, carrying the waters of obedience in the deserts of defection.

Bibliography

F. Tiffany, "Parenesis and Deuteronomy 5-11" (Diss., Claremont, 1978).

SOLOMON'S BUILDING ACTIVITIES, TEMPLE DEDICATION: SACRIFICES AND CONCLUSION, 8:62-66

Structure

I. Dedicatory sacrifices	62-64
A. Report of peace offerings	62-63
1. Introductory statement	62
2. Description of offerings	63a
3. Concluding statement: dedication of temple	63b
B. Descriptive elaboration	64
1. Sanctification of courtyard	64a
2. Statement of reasons	64b
II. Conclusion of dedicatory ceremonies	65-66
A. The feast	65
B. Dismissal of people	66

Depending on their theory of composition for the books of Kings, critics see these verses variously as products of the DtrH (Noth, *Könige*, 190-91; cf. Gray, *Kings*, 203-4: Šanda, *Könige*, I, 246) or of a number of postexillic redactors (e.g., Würthwein, *Könige*, 101-3; Hölscher, *Quellen*, 170). The text *does* show a certain incoherence. Vv. 62-63 speak of sacrifices offered at the conclusion of, or during, Solomon's speeches; on the other hand, vv. 65-66 have in view *all* of ch. 8. V. 64 with its concern for explanation and definition moves in yet another direction, and many critics believe it is a secondary late expansion.

Despite these inner tensions, the material seems fairly well integrated into its context. Events begun by assembling the people (8:1-2) find a natural conclusion in their return home (v. 66). Moreover, v. 62 strikingly recapitulates v. 5 in language and grammatical construction:

(v. 62) "and the king and all Israel with him were offering sacrifices [participle *zōbĕḥîm*] before Yahweh."

(v. 5) "and King Solomon and all the congregation...with him before the ark were sacrificing [Piel participle *mĕzabbĕḥîm*]...."

This resumptive repetition between v. 5 and v. 62 (see Kuhl, cited above on p. 25) suggests here as elsewhere a conscious editorial bracketing of the main events in 8:6-61. Possibly the idea was that the installation of the ark and Solomon's long speeches were accompanied all around by enormous numbers of sacrifices like unbroken festive drama.

In any case, we may distinguish three subdivisions in the text according to content and form. They are now loosely joined together with temporal phrases ("on that day," v. 64: "at that time," v. 65). The first section (I.A, vv. 62-63) is complete in itself. In view are the "peace offerings" (*šĕlāmîm*, i.e., those offered for well-being and whose flesh is to be shared by worshipers or priests [Milgrom, *IDBSup*, 769]). The writer puts this subject at the center, and introduces it with a nominal sentence of immediate, continuous activity (v. 62 *zōbĕḥîm zebaḥ*, "making sacrifice"; the *RSV* past tense obscures the sense). As though to set the proper meaning, this first brief report concludes with a simple explanatory and summary statement: the sacrifices dedicate the temple (v. 63b; *ḥnk*, "dedicate," as in Neh 12:27; Dan 3:2; Deut 20:5).

The second subsection (I.B, v. 64) changes verbal form (from *wqṭl* to simple *qṭl*) and subject. We read now of *consecration* (*qdš*), not dedication, and of the open courtyard before the altar, not the temple itself. We also hear explanation and definition: not one type of offering, but three (whole burnt, peace, and cereal) and in such numbers that the bronze altar (only mentioned here; cf. 7:15-46) was insufficient to handle them.

A third section (II, vv. 65-66) reverts to the usual reportorial style and raises a new point, or rather recapitulates a point from the opening scene of ch. 8. This occasion of dedication is also *the* feast (*heḥāg*), presumably the Feast of Booths (see 8:2 and Neh 8:14). Then, the ark having been installed, the prayers and sacrifices offered, and the feast kept for seven days, Solomon sends the people home. They are now a dissolved "assembly" as it were in contrast to *qhl* in vv. 14, 22, 55. Precisely as one senses the ritual antithesis to solemn gathering, the curtain of reportorial objectivity parts, just for a moment. The author-editor asserts common heritage with events and his audience by speaking in direct and inclusive voice; "Solomon held the feast...before the Lord *our* God..." (v. 65, emphasis mine). Thus the account of dedicatory ceremonies ends with a participative note, as though *all* rejoice in Yahweh's connection to the world through king, dynasty, temple, land, and holy people (cf. vv. 33-36, 51-53, 59-61).

Genre

This unit is an editorial composition consisting of two brief REPORTS (vv. 62-63, 65-66) and one explanatory STATEMENT (v. 64).

Setting

While some of this material may have stemmed from royal or priestly records, or at least old sources (so Šanda, *Könige* I, 246; Gray, *Kings*, 203), we cannot achieve a very clear notion of what these might have been. We know of similar reports in commemorative (→) royal inscriptions (see discussion at 6:1–7:51), which describe festival sacrifices on the occasion of dedicating buildings, usually palaces and temples, or smaller objects to the gods. Most important for our understanding, however, is the present literary context in the Dtr history work. From the author-editor's exilic perspective, this composition marked an appropriate and typical (if royal inscriptions are any guide) conclusion to Solomon's dedicatory ceremonies and building activities. What remains is for the deity to acknowledge this gift (see discussion at 9:1-9).

Intention

It follows that a main intention of the author-editor would have been simply to report the conclusion to the dedicatory ceremonies. With this final note, the account of Solomon's primary religious act is complete. Like the scribes who praised kings in stelae and building inscriptions, the DtrH means to glorify King Solomon by recounting his benefactions to God, in this case—looking back over the whole—the planning, construction, and outfitting of a temple-palace complex and its dedication to Yahweh with idealized ritual. The author, or perhaps a glossator too, if v. 64 be a later addition, delocalized his ending as well. Concluding events of such exaggerated scale and sacrifices defined according to standards of post-Solomonic times (Gray, *Kings*, 234) meld here with observance of *sukkôt*, or Feast of Booths (Tabernacles). Solomon's position is therefore paradigmatic and originative for all times. It seems that this king first brought together ark of God with temple of Yahweh (cf. 2 Sam 6:16-19), and temple service with *sukkôt*. Just as his petitions on this occasion placed an unlimited future under the aegis of the first temple prayers (see discussion at 8:22-53), so these concluding sacrifices in that ritually defined space during the Feast of Tabernacles set all subsequent celebrations in their debt. Solomon the king was also priest in the eyes of later generations, just as the patriarchs were rabbis in the eyes of midrashic commentators. The text thereby at once recounts a moment in the past and assimilates its image and meaning to a timeless reality of religious experience.

Bibliography

See bibliography at "Introduction to 1 Kings."

SOLOMON'S BUILDING ACTIVITIES: REPORT OF DREAM EPIPHANY, 9:1-9

Structure

I. Opening	1-2
A. Setting	1
B. Epiphany formula: appearance of deity	2
II. Divine address	3-9
A. Narrative introduction	3aα
B. Divine address (promise)	3aβ-9
1. Basis for promise	3aβ-γ
a. Declaration of favorable response	3aβ
b. Declaration of temple consecrated	3aγ
2. Promise proper: Yahweh's presence	3b
3. Parenetic elaboration	4-9
a. Conditional promise of reward (for dynasty)	4-5
1) Condition	4
2) Promise	5
b. Conditional promise of punishment (for Israel and temple)	6-9
1) Promise proper	6-7
a) Condition	6
b) Promise	7
2) Elaboration (question-answer schema)	8-9
a) Situation	8a
b) Question	8b
c) Answer	9

This unit is marked off from its surroundings by a shift in style and content. The dedication ceremonies have clearly been concluded (8:66) and a new narrative introduction sets another scene, presumably at a later time (9:1). Another abrupt shift in subject matter and style in vv. 10-14 defines the outer limits of the unit. The text is characteristic of the Dtr author-editor of Kings and—as is appropriate to a last redactor—scans a rather wide horizon, seeing this event as related to the dream epiphany of ch. 3. The general consensus is surely right in supposing that the unit stems from the Dtr author-editor (although the change in addressee from Solomon to all Israel in vv. 6-9 might suggest secondary expansion).

This passage is similar in structure to 3:4-15, as the reference in v. 2 might already suggest. We move quite simply through a narrative setting (I.A, B, vv. 1-2) which reports the beginning of a dream sequence, with the stereotyped dream epiphany formula "and so and so appeared" (Niphal of *r'h*) to the body of the dream itself, which in this and so many other cases is a divine message (→ discussion and parallels at 3:4-15). The text obviously emphasizes the tripartite, prolix, divine address. A first section (II.B.1, v. 3aβ-γ) announces the fact of, and reasons for, the divine response to Solomon's actions; a second section offers the basic promise from God (II.B.2, v. 3b); and a third section—the longest—contains a parenetic elaboration of the promise (II.B.3, vv. 4-9). The declaration "I have heard . . ." leads into the specific announcement that Yahweh has consecrated the "house" or temple. In context, of course, this is in response to Solomon's dedication ceremony, and the declaration entails promise, expressed in *waw* plus perfect verb form for a future sense: "My eyes and my heart will be there for all time" (v. 3b). This latter statement is in fact the only direct promise in the entire speech, for immediately we are thrust into the middle of conditional formulations which envision times and circumstances which may either sustain or undermine this basic promise of Yahweh's presence in the community. The address is clearly shaped so as to encourage obedience with its rewards, and to discourage with its punishments—for both Solomon, the symbol of the Davidic dynasty and royal upholder of Yahwism (v. 5), and the people, who live or die with the sanctity of the holy place in its holy city, Jerusalem (vv. 6-9). There is no narrative ending for the text; the unit simply ends with the final words of Yahweh, projecting in question-and-answer style the distant future conditions.

Genre

The unit is a REPORT of DREAM EPIPHANY. See the close parallel and the full discussion in 3:4-15. This particular report contains special generic features worth noting. We hear at the beginning of the divine address a declaration of favorable response: "I have heard your prayer and your supplication . . ." (v. 3aβ). Such a formula has many parallels in the OT, and usually signifies to the hearer that a petition of some kind has been favorably received (but see a negative response in Num 14:27). The formula declares a divine response to be favorable, and leads into announcements of salvation in 2 Kgs 19:20; 20:5 (both prophetic oracles to King Hezekiah); 2 Kgs 22:19 (more complex, but showing the essential elements of form and function). See also the reports of epiphany which carry a divine message, as in Exod 3:7; 6:5 (Yahweh responding to the oppression in Egypt); 16:12 (Yahweh responding to the grumbling in the wilderness). The formulaic declaration turns up in a narrative about David where the king opens his response to a petitioner with the words, "See, I have heard your voice." In this case, the formula seems virtually parallel to the following, "and I have granted your petition" (literally, "lifted up your face," as in Gen 19:21; 32:21 [*RSV* 20]). See also 1 Kgs 5:22; Jer 42:4; and the more distant 1 Sam 12:1.

The parenetic elaboration on the basic promise of v. 3b is interesting because of two stereotyped elements: the series of conditional promises, and the question-and-answer schema. The former has a close parallel in the conclusion to the Holiness Code, and thus in the later layers of developed priestly tradition. There, the text recites a series of conditional promises of reward (Lev 26:3-13) followed by a series of conditional promises of punishment (26:14-39), both of which, of course, aim at encouraging obedience to the terms of the Levitical legislation. In Zech 3:7 a visionary angel offers a conditional promise of royal rule in the manner of those promises to David and Solomon, and the text characterizes this speech as solemn admonishment (v. 6, *wayyāʿad*; on this verb, cf. Exod 19:23; 2 Kgs 17:13; Neh 9:29, 30). Other conditional promises, with intent to exhort, may be seen in 1 Kgs 3:14; 6:12, two texts important for the shape of the Solomonic materials, and Josh 23:15-16. The second element in this prolix elaboration in 1 Kgs 9:4-9 is the Question and Answer Schema, vv. 8-9. This is a literary device which in this context elaborates further the conditional promise of punishment. Elsewhere, the schema appears in Jer 22:8-9 and Deut 29:21-24. Along with 1 Kgs 9:8-9, these three passages are examples of a literary convention in the work of the Dtr author-editor, a convention which goes beyond simply reporting what might have occurred in the bygone days but reaches out to the contemporary reader in its instructional point. Even in disaster, Israel witnesses to its covenant God, and is thereby forewarned. There are parallels in portions of Ashurbanipal's monumental inscriptions, or what have been loosely called "annals," as well (Long, 130-34; Vogels).

Setting

Since this text is very likely a creation of the exilic Dtr author-editor, one may focus most aptly upon its literary setting in Kings. The epiphany comes at the end of the dedicatory ceremonies and is now explicitly understood as a divine response to Solomon's prayer of petition. (Görg's attempt, 120-25, to reconstruct an original relationship with only a small portion of ch. 8 is too speculative to be convincing.) At the same time, the divine address links up with 3:14 and 6:12-13, and by contrast, to the "fall" which will be narrated in ch. 11. The unit represents a sort of climactic point by giving for a third time the conditional basis for Yahweh's presence to this monarch. The dark side of this reality, of course, is the punishment and rejection held in check by the frail thread of human choice and will for obedience.

Intention

The intention, therefore, is not merely to report on epiphany with divine message. The Dtr author-editor also provides approbation for Solomon's actions in building and dedicating this temple, and recounts God's acceptance of this offering (cf. the note in Gudea's building inscription that Ningirsu accepted his prayers and offering of a temple, with all its fine construction and precious implements and ornamentation [Barton, *RISA*, 239]). In this sense, the dream epiphany provides a parallel approbation to that given in 8:10-11, as though approval is necessary after the first stage of dedication (the installation of ark) and after the second stage (prayers of petition), with accompanying sacrifices (8:27-53, 62-64). At the same time, the parenetic elaboration of this divine address portrays what *might* be, and hence implicitly exhorts and admonishes through conditional promises of reward and punishment. The author gives us again the theological basis for theocracy, and the foundation for the king's position. Possibly the concluding question and answer schema attempts an explanation for the experience of exile. But certainly, one should not restrict the intention of the passage to such narrow scope. In a way parallel to the prayers of petition, which envisioned all circumstances which might befall the people of Israel, including exile, this divine message envisions all situations of reward and punishment, the better to exhort, the better to remain elastic for generations of interpretation.

Bibliography

On dream and dream epiphany see bibliography at 3:4-15. Manfred Görg, *Gott-König-Reden*, 116-77 (see listing at 3:4-15); B. O. Long, "Two Question and Answer Schemata in the Prophets," *JBL* 90 (1971) 129-39; Walter Vogels, "The Literary Form of 'The Question of the Nations'," *Eglise et Théologie* 11 (1980) 159-76.

SOLOMON'S BUILDING ACTIVITIES, SUPPLEMENTARY REPORTS: NARRATIVE FRAGMENT ON HIRAM'S DISPLEASURE, 9:10-14

Structure

I. Narrative setting	10-12a
A. The situation	10-11
B. Hiram's visit to the cities	12a
II. Hiram's reaction	12b-13
A. Displeasure	12b
B. Speech (etymological etiology)	13
III. Hiram's payments to Solomon	14

Clearly separated from 9:1-9 and 9:15-23 by style and content, the text of this unit does not flow smoothly, and has occasioned many critical suggestions of glosses, especially in the overfull v. 11 and the rather digressive etiological etymology in v. 13. On the other hand, the unit is not impossible as it stands. A proper understanding of its structure depends upon rightly grasping the relationship among vv. 10, 11, and 12 on the one hand, and vv. 10-13 and 14 on the other. The problem in the former may be stated succinctly: where is the main clause which completes the subordinate temporal clause of v. 10? Grammatically, one would expect the resumption of narration after a temporal clause to begin with a *waw*-conversive imperfect verb (*wyqṭl*); this would appear to rule out v. 11b as the resumptive clause because it begins with *'āz*, "then" (against many commentators, e.g., Gray and Montgomery, who acknowledge the grammatical difficulty but accept v. 11b as the main clause anyway, attributing the problems to an overfull redaction in v. 11; *RSV* essentially agrees). An alternative is to take v. 12 as the main clause (it begins with the grammatically correct verb form) and to accept all of v. 11 as still subject to the temporal clause in v. 10 (so essentially *NEB*). This approach would mean that vv. 10b-11 are explanatory, filling out the temporal expression ("twenty years," v. 10a) with more information, that is, citing those events during the twenty-year period which are necessary to understand the action to follow. So, translate: "And (at) the end of twenty years (during) which Solomon built the two buildings, the temple of Yahweh and the palace, (during which time) Hiram king of Tyre had supplied Solomon with cedar and cypress timber, and gold, as much as he desired—(then it was that) King Solomon had given to Hiram twenty cities in Galilee—then Hiram came from Tyre to see the cities. . . ." Our understanding and structural analysis suggest that vv. 10-12a provide a rather compressed setting for the brief unit, giving information essential to understand the occasion and circumstances by which Hiram had come to possess those cities in Galilee.

The "main event," then, is Hiram's *reaction* to the cities (II.A, B,

vv. 12b-13). It is here that the narrator has focused his attention, and here we are to find the significance of the whole. Yet precisely at this point, the problem of understanding v. 14 arises, for the reference to Hiram's gold seems misplaced. However, following the convention of "dischronologized narrative" (Martin, 186), we may understand this verse as delayed climax. It exposes the grandness of Hiram's contribution to Solomon's building program (120 talents of gold is an enormous amount, for a "talent," depending on the historical period, ranged from 45 to 130 pounds; Gray, *Kings*, 241). By contrast, we see the meanness of Solomon's payment in kind: twenty cities which were mere villages in the Galilean region. The text is a little gem of sorts, if our understanding is correct. It focuses on Hiram's hostile reaction to what at first glance appears to be a generous payment for building materials, and at the last possible moment conveys with one stroke the dramatic point: Solomon gave a lot less than he got; or Hiram got a lot less than he gave.

Genre

We cannot specify a genre because the unit is too fragmentary. It is not a fully developed (→) story with clear plot, although aspects of the unit point in this direction; and it is more than simply a (→) report because there is a kind of artistic sophistication in its construction with delayed climax and ironic contrasts. We may perhaps speak of a fragmentary ANECDOTE or episode. Of note is the phrase "So they are called the land of Cabul to this day," v. 13b. It resembles widely attested examples of ETYMOLOGICAL ETIOLOGY, brief explanations of personal or place names which depend on folkloristic wordplay (cf. Exod 2:22; Gen 26:32-33; 29:33; 1 Sam 7:12; Long). In this case, however, the crux of the etiological meaning is missing, or unclear, and the typical elements of the literary form somewhat broken.

Setting

Such a fragment may have originally belonged to a longer story. We cannot know. In any case, it is presently set at the end of Solomon's twenty-year period of construction activity (a sum apparently derived from adding together the figures in 6:38 and 7:1), and at the head of a number of supplementary materials winding down the account of Solomon's construction work. The text also is the first of four to mention Hiram's dealings with Solomon (see 9:26-28; 10:11-12; 10:22).

Intention

Basically, the fragmentary anecdote intends to tell of a falling out between Solomon and Hiram. But why place the unit at this point? Possibly because it has to do with Hiram and building materials, and is associated in context with the question of forced labor (vv. 15-23), a sequence of motifs exactly parallel to the beginning of the major account of Solomon's construction work (5:15-32). In other words, just as the longer account of Solomon's building activities began with a piece about securing materials and labor with Hiram's help, so these supplementary reports (9:10-25) also begin with a piece related to Hiram and building materials.

Bibliography

B. O. Long, *The Problem of Etiological Narrative in the Old Testament* (BZAW 108; Berlin: W. de Gruyter, 1968); W. J. Martin, " 'Dischronologized' Narrative in the Old Testament," in *Congress Volume: Rome* (VTSup 17; Leiden: Brill, 1969) 179-86.

SOLOMON'S BUILDING ACTIVITIES, SUPPLEMENTARY REPORTS: FORCED LABOR AND MISCELLANEOUS ACTIVITIES, 9:15-25

Structure

I. Forced labor for construction	15-23
A. Superscription	15-19
1. Superscription proper	15aα
2. Elaborating purpose clauses	15aβ-19
a. Labor for: Jerusalem projects	15aβ
b. Labor for: cities through Gezer	15b
c. Explanatory statement: Solomon and Gezer	16-17a
d. Labor for: cities elsewhere	17b-18
e. Labor for: miscellaneous constructions	19
B. The laborers	20-22
1. Foreigners and their descendants	20-21
2. Israelites (not slave)	22
C. Tally of supervisors	23
1. Superscription	23aα
2. Tally	23aβ-b
II. Reports of miscellaneous construction	24-25
A. Wife's house	24a
B. The Millo	24b
C. Altar for sacrifices	25a
D. Colophon: house finished	25b

With good reason, this unit has appeared to most critics as a redactional composite of disparate materials. There are special problems of unity; note the wholesale redistribution of material in the LXX and the bewildering mix of style and form. Despite numerous attempts, however, there is not enough evidence for reconstructing the history of redaction. We are left with a final text of curious tensions and only an approximate order under the theme of building projects.

We may discern both logical and problematic relationships. First, at the beginning of the opening section (vv. 15-23), what appears to be a superscription for an enumeration of items (v. 15aα: "This is the matter [*RSV* "account"] of forced labor . . .") receives its expected continuation in vv. 20-22, where the actual makeup of the forced labor is described, but in a form and style closer to a report than to simple enumeration. In between, vv. 15aβ-19 appear to expand the superscription, in the direction of an elaborate clause of purpose (why Solomon needed forced labor). In fact, the text devolves here to an enumeration of various building projects undertaken by Solomon, with emphasis on cities. V. 23 turns yet another way: with its own superscription, it is a statement of numerical sums, similar in style to what one might find in lists of various kinds (cf. 2 Sam 23:39b; Josh 12:24b; 15:32b). In its context, however, this little unit seems to record a tally of supervisory personnel, in contrast to the category of slave peoples mentioned in the preceding verses. There may also be simple word association: *śārê* (officers or officials) in vv. 22 and 23.

The second major division in the unit (vv. 24-25) consists of separate, brief reports, cast not in enumerative style with superscriptions, but with *wqṭl* statements of completed action (v. 24a, "went up"; v. 24b, "built"; v. 25b, "finished") and habitual practice (v. 25a, "used to offer up"). The reports seem only loosely related to each other, and, even with the curious colophon of v. 25b, seem only superficially related to the wider context. Yet they all have to do with Solomon's construction work. The verb *bnh,* "build," appears in relation to the Millo, the altar, and the queen's house. V. 24a probably also connects to the parenthetical remarks on Gezer (v. 16). Besides such loose inner associations, it may be that these concluding supplemental reports form a motivic bracket with 3:1-3, enclosing the entire account of the Solomonic construction program (see discussion at 3:1–11:43).

Despite these difficulties, we may also observe a certain logical progression in this unit—it moves from a discussion of forced labor, expanded with a focus on the building projects which were the purpose of the labor, through a tally of the supervisors for the laborers, and finally finishes with a supplementary series of brief notices or reports on other building projects of Solomon. One should not press for symmetry, but accept the rather loose association and flow of ideas. All the parts relate independently to the general theme. Yet the colophon of v. 25b suggests a still wider horizon. The "main" account of construction activities (5:15–7:51) moves through the matter of materials and forced labor (5:15-32), then to the actual building work (6:1–7:50), and concludes with 7:51a, "Thus all the work . . . was finished [*šlm*]." The supplementary materials in ch. 9 take us from the matter of forced labor and its supervisors through separate building projects (the wife's house, the Millo, the altar), and end with a colophon reminiscent of 7:51, "so he finished [*šlm*] the temple." Hence the structure of the unit may depend on thematic concerns as well as a positioning in the Solomonic materials, in which case the cycle of building activities repeats, 5:15–7:51 and 9:15-25.

Genre

Since it is a matter of a composite account here, we may not specify the genre with precision. On the thematic skeleton of forced labor and building projects have been hung some diverse materials. We have a miscellany which consists of materials approaching the form of list, especially in vv. 15-22, and brief report, especially vv. 16-17a, 24-25. Perhaps v. 23 is a fragment of a list, or the subscription from such on the analogy of other numerical tallies which appear at the end of a list (as in, e.g., 2 Sam 23:39b).

Setting

Some of this material, especially the information contained in those portions of enumerative style, may have been drawn from archival records of various kinds. Perhaps something analogous to ancient Near Eastern royal inscriptions, which customarily report the construction work of the king, would have stood behind this miscellany. But, for Israel, brief summaries of building activities of various kings are known from 2 Chr 11:5-12; 14:5-6; 17:12-13; 26:9-10; 27:3-4; 32:5,

6a; 33:14; cf. also 1 Kgs 12:25; 15:22; 2 Kgs 12:1-17 (*RSV* 16); 16:10-18; etc. (Welten, 7-52). The present literary setting, however, is the important consideration. The unit appears as a kind of second account of construction work, after the first account which focused almost exclusively on the temple and palace. The text clearly looks thematically back to what precedes rather than forward to ch. 10.

Intention

The intention in context, therefore, would be to supplement the temple-palace emphasis of chs. 5–7, 8, and 9:1-9 with material relating to the rest of Solomon's building activities, here explicitly the cities from north to south, and anything else which Solomon desired to build. The aim was in some tension with its primary vehicle, the enumeration of forced labor. The miscellany thus concludes the longer account of building works, and, in the light of the bracketing effect of 3:1-3 and 9:24-25, was meant probably to tie together the first major redactional unit covering the Solomonic era, i.e., all the materials stretching from the promise of divine wisdom to Solomon's actual building projects.

Bibliography

Peter Welten, *Geschichte und Geschichtsdarstellung in den Chronikbüchern* (WMANT 42; Neukirchen: Neukirchener, 1973).

II. ACCOUNT OF THE KINGDOM (EXTERNAL): DEALINGS, FAME, AND WEALTH, 9:26–10:29

Structure

A. Miscellany: imported wealth, fame and prosperity	9:26–10:25
1. An expeditionary fleet with Hiram (for gold)	9:26-28
2. Solomon and the queen of Sheba	10:1-10,13
3. Fine wood imports	11-12
4. Income of gold	14-21
a. Amount	14-15
b. Use	16-21
1) For golden shields	16-17
2) For throne of ivory overlay	18-20
3) For drinking vessels in palace	21
5. An expeditionary fleet with Hiram (for gold and other wealth)	22
6. Concluding summary	23-25
B. Supplementary reports and statements	26-29
1. Chariots and horsemen	26
2. General statement on prosperity	27
3. Import-export dealings	28-29

This block of material clearly is not smoothly unified. The text is a fairly loose redactional composition made up of independent bits of tradition of varying form and style. It is relatively easy to identify smaller units within the whole mainly on the basis of abrupt changes in subject matter. Three small blocks deal with Hiram, but not in such similar ways that one could say the verses belonged tightly together (A.1, 3, 5, 9:26-28; 10:11-12, 22). The first Hiram tradition clearly has nothing to do with the rest of the preceding material in ch. 9; the second piece, 10:11-12, now appears to break into the queen of Sheba section, which in its own right, because of its subject and its more highly developed narrative style, forms a smaller unit within the whole (A.2, 10:1-10, 13). The third Hiram tradition, 10:22, reverts to the theme of a mercantile fleet, but has in view one different from the fleet used for gold expeditions to Ophir (9:26-28). Besides the Hiram pieces and the queen of Sheba tradition, one can recognize a grouping of statements about gold which accrued to Solomon as income (A.4, 10:14-21), the summary (vv. 23-25), and finally the extra material on horses, silver, and exports, separated from the main body of material in the chapter by this summary statement of vv. 23-25, but associated with the latter apparently on the basis of the word "horses." Many, if not all, of these smaller subject matter units were probably at one time independent of one another, but the history of redaction is singularly unclear. Due to a lack of evidence, attempts to reconstruct that history have achieved no agreement.

Can we discover any principles of organization for this diverse block of material? First, a motivic thread might hold it together: gold and other riches were brought to Solomon because of his great fame. Each smaller unit displays this motif and uses a common verb, "bring" (*bô'*), as in 9:28 (for 9:26-28); 10:10 (for 10:1-10, 13); 10:11 (for 10:11-12); 10:22 (for 10:21-22); and finally, v. 25 (for the summary verses, 23-25). Second, at the beginning and end of a first large block (9:26–10:22) stands tradition about Hiram's and Solomon's jointly maintained mercantile fleets—even though they are obviously different fleets. Third, the block of material in vv. 14-21 + 22 has been arranged with a visible logic: the income to Solomon, and its amounts; its uses in manufacturing golden objects; and finally, v. 22, its means of supply to Solomon. Finally, a last motif: the incomparability of Solomon's wealth occurs throughout, like a golden thread: 10:10, 12b, 20b; cf. vv. 21b and 27. Such a thread of incomparable wealth holds diverse materials together from a common perspective. And the summary in vv. 23-25 makes clear the interpretative rubric from which we are to understand this material: it has to do with peoples' seeking this king for his wisdom (10:1-10, 13) and bringing him tribute of the finest kind (9:26-28; 10:11-12, 14-22). Herein might be one point of association for the supplementary reports, vv. 26-29, for there it is emphasized that Solomon was so grand, and his wealth so enormous, that silver and expensive cedar were common household articles.

The style and structure of the various smaller units in this composite are varied. Reportorial verbs (*wyqṭl*) rule a good deal of the material. There are typical reports of action: 9:26-28 (reports an expedition for gold); 10:11-12 (wood and gold); 10:26-27 (horses and silver). There are forms of report familiar from chs. 6–7; 10:16-17, 18-20 (note esp. vv. 18-20a, a reportorial verb [*wyqṭl*] followed by descriptive details in nominal clauses [the *RSV* supplies verbs]; see the discussion at 7:1-12). Besides these typical reportorial styles, there are statements of recordlike quality, not reporting action, but stating information for the record, as in 10:14-15, 21-22, 29. With this style belongs 10:28, which shows a superscription (obscured by *RSV*) and simple enumerative style: "And the importing of horses belonging to Solomon: from Egypt and Kue, the king's traders took them from Kue at a price."

The only smaller unit which does not share these reportorial and informational forms is 10:1-10, 13, the tradition about Solomon and the queen of Sheba. Obviously a more highly developed narrative unit, it deserves special discussion. See below.

Genre

We cannot speak very precisely about genre for this whole unit. It is simply an editorial composite or miscellany. Of course, the text contains a number of smaller generic units, such as REPORT (9:26-28; 10:11-12, 26-27, 16-17, 18-20) and STATEMENTS of record (10:28-29, 14-15, 21-22; Montgomery, *Kings*, 227, on 10:28-29, "much like a business memorandum"). As we shall note in the next section, the queen of Sheba material is a LEGEND. Reports of supply expeditions similar to 9:26-28; 10:11-12 are found in Egyptian materials, e.g., for Ahmose I, ca. 1575 B.C. (Breasted, *ARE* I, § 27) cut on a quarry wall; and the same for Ramses III, ca. 1200 B.C. (Breasted, *ARE* IV, § 19). See numerous earlier examples in Breasted, *ARE* I, §§ 440-48, 606, 647, 708-23. Also, we may note again that those statements of exaggerated prosperity, as in 10:27, 29, find parallels in Assyrian and other Mesopotamian royal building inscriptions (→ discussion at 4:20–5:6).

Setting

Since it is a matter of a redactional miscellany, one should think first of its literary setting, while allowing that some of the material was preserved in, or derived from, archives kept by scribes who labored over records of the kingdom. The queen of Sheba tradition likely found its setting in popular folk circles (see below). In literary context, we can see that the miscellany closes out that part of the account of Solomon's reign which has emphasized his grandest activities and worldwide stature.

Intention

From this contextual observation and from the leitmotif running through this material, one can suppose that the miscellany was intended to set forth the wealth, fame, and wisdom of King Solomon and the riches brought him. The admiration given Solomon by the queen of Sheba (10:6-7) and the summary statements in 10:23-25 draw all these motifs together, and echo with one last miscellaneous grouping the promise given to Solomon at the beginning of his reign, that he would receive more than he asked—wisdom, and riches and honor— "so that no other king shall compare with you, all your days" (3:13; cf. 10:6-7, 12b, 21b, 23, 27). Thematically, this miscellany looks back over the whole Solomonic epoch, at least in the aspect of its glory, wealth, and wisdom, and draws one last portrait of the king who possessed all three.

ACCOUNT OF THE KINGDOM (EXTERNAL): DEALINGS, FAME, AND WEALTH; LEGEND OF THE QUEEN OF SHEBA, 10:1-10, 13

Structure

I. Narrative setting 1

II. The contest	2-3
A. The queen's arrival	2a
B. Contest with Solomon	2b-3
1. Putting of hard questions	2b
2. Solomon's answers	3
III. Result: the queen's capitulation	4-10
A. Description: loss of courage	4-5
B. Speech of concession	6-9
1. Narrative introduction	6aα
2. Speech proper	6aβ-9
a. Eulogy to Solomon	6aβ-7
b. Beatitude	8
c. Praise speech	9a
d. Eulogy to Solomon	9b
C. Description: presentation of gifts	10
IV. Narrative conclusion	13
A. Solomon's gifts to the queen	13a
B. The queen's departure for home	13b

This unit is clearly distinguished from its surroundings by style and subject matter. Vv. 11-12 are very likely intrusions into the original (see discussion preceding). The text has two verses serving as a framework, vv. 1 and 13, both of which are marked by inverse word order sentences with perfect verb forms (*qṭl*), in contrast to the predominance of narrative tenses (*wyqṭl*) in the body of the unit. V. 1 is a true narrative introduction or exposition. It sets up the motivation for the events to come, states the action which brings the characters together, and defines the nature of the encounter, while giving the parameters of our interpretation: the queen comes to "test" Solomon with "hard questions" (*ḥîdôt,* riddles, conundrums, etc.; see Prov 1:6; Ps 49:5 [*RSV* 4]; 78:2). Thus, we expect the action that follows to revolve around such "hard questions," or, in short, a competition between the characters (see the contest between Darius's guards, 1 Esdr 3:1–5:6). And this is exactly what happens. The queen comes, she puts those riddles, the king answers everything (the verb "answer" in v. 3 is related to *ḥîdôt* of v. 1) with the result that the queen of Sheba recognizes her defeat in the contest. She makes an elaborate speech praising Solomon and admitting that he has bested her at this game of wisdom display. There is an exchange of gifts (vv. 10 and 13) and the queen then departs for home.

The author has given extraordinary emphasis to the queen's words. Much of the available space in the unit is devoted to her speech. Relative to the brief remarks in vv. 2-3 and 10, the action slows dramatically, and we are made to linger and savor the courtly remarks. Moreover, her speech is elegantly balanced with eulogy for Solomon (vv. 6aβ-7 and 9b) enclosing praise of his God and his servants. It is no accident, then, that the thematic center of the text finds expression in her speech, too. The storyteller seems interested not so much in contest—this motif seems more a device than anything else—as in the notion of Solomon's "wisdom," which is connected here with his uncanny problem-solving ability (v. 3), his amassing of royal accoutrements (v. 4), his skills of rule (justice and righteousness, *mišpāṭ* and *ṣĕdāqâ*; cf. Isa 11:1-5), and his enormous wealth (vv. 10,

13a). Solomon does not possess ordinary "wisdom," however; his wisdom is superlative, unmatched, incomparable. The narrator goes beyond a simple telling of the contest, and evaluates it with a tone matched only by the encomiums of the queen herself: ". . . there was nothing hidden from the king which he could not find out," v. 3b; or this statement: ". . . never again came such an abundance of spices. . . ," v. 10b; or this in v. 13a: "And King Solomon gave to (her) . . . all that she desired, whatever she asked besides what was given her by the bounty of King Solomon." The narrator's voice is strong, a rare thing in biblical literature, and the tone is eulogistic.

Genre

This unit is a Legend, that is, a story which has rather more concern for the stupendous characteristics of its character than in developing the dramatic possibilities inherent in the plot. The text is not without drama, of course, or without a narrative plot which moves from tension (the contest) to its resolution (the queen is beaten at her own game) and results (gift giving). It is just that the emphasis falls upon this wonderful king who is without equal. Other OT legends may be seen in, e.g., 2 Kgs 6:1-7; 1 Sam 7:2-14. Just this legendary interest lives on in subsequent popular literature about Solomon and this queen (Ullendorf), including the NT (Matt 6:29; Luke 12:27).

The legend contains some noteworthy forms of speech. First, there is Eulogy, vv. 6-7, 9b, a speech designed to praise an individual whether living or dead by citing specifically praiseworthy attributes (cf. 2 Sam 1:19-27, a lament, with eulogy proper in v. 23; similar speeches are frequent in courtiers' approving responses to the pharaoh's plans in Egyptian "royal novelettes," e.g., Sesostris I, ca. 2000 B.C., Lichtheim, *Ancient Egyptian Literature* I, 117; for Thutmose III, ca. 1500-1450 B.C., Breasted, *ARE* II, § 151). Second, we may note the Praise Speech, v. 9a, cast with the "blessing" (*bārûk*) formula, "Blessed be Yahweh your God. . . ," a frequent formulaic speech in the books of Kings and elsewhere (see 5:21 and discussion there). Here, of course, the words indirectly praise Solomon, too, because of the way they are inseparably bound to the eulogy in v. 9b and indeed to the eulogistic tone of the entire section (vv. 6-9). Third, one may note the Beatitude, v. 8. The form is completely typical. The utterance begins with *'ašrê,* "blessed" or "happy" (sometimes with a suffix added), which is then followed immediately by the subject and any special qualifiers, often introduced as a relative clause with the particle *'ăšer.* Thus we translate: "Happy [are] your wives! Happy [are] these your servants, who continually stand before you . . ." (cf. Ps 2:12; Prov 8:34; 16:20b; Deut 33:29; Isa 30:18b; Job 5:17). Of course, the basic formulaic speech is hardly more than an exuberant exclamation (Cazelles; H.-J. Kraus, *Psalmen* I [BKAT XV/1; Neukirchen: Neukirchener, 1960]3), and can be expanded with more elaborate clauses (e.g., Ps 1:1-2; Prov 3:13-14). In the NT, beatitude developed into a literary collection of teachings attributed to Jesus (Matt 5:3-11). Beatitude is different from the *bārûk* praise speech because the latter always offers praise to God, while the former never does. Beatitude is addressed to a person, or to Israel, who is the recipient of blessings from God. Beatitude describes one who is happy by reason of upright behavior, or in receipt of that which blessings have to bestow (Janzen). Background influences and parallels from Egypt are especially clear (Dupont). In context this beatitude in the mouth of the queen of Sheba shades over into eulogy and does not carry the didactic flavor associated with more highly developed examples, e.g., Ps 1:1-2 or Matt 5:3-11.

Setting

Most critics suppose that a legend has its setting among the people, in the folkloristic ethos. This particular legend, which extols King Solomon as a folk hero, is no exception, as its flavor, style, and timeless characteristics (no name for the queen, no specific dates attached to her meeting with Solomon) suggest. Yet, the particular literary context in the books of Kings is important, too. The story marks the return to the folkloristic theme of Solomon's wisdom and wealth after a long report of building activities. So 10:1-10, 13, along with 3:4-28, now bracket a large block of material which goes in quite another direction, without, however, being very far from the theme of "wisdom" (5:9-14, 21). The legend also sits congruently in the midst of a miscellany that deals with Solomon's international fame and fortune (9:26–10:29).

Intention

In an oral situation where folktales would be performed, the intentions for legend would vary considerably, depending on the situation and wishes of the storyteller (Finnegan; Long). Content alone is not the the final determinant of intention in such surroundings. However, as a literary product, placed in a particular literary context, it is another matter. We can see that the legend here is intended not so much to tell of an encounter between foreign queen and native king, but to show just how far Solomon's fame had spread, just how fabulous his "wisdom" and wealth really were, and how his wisdom withstood every test. The legend naturally seeks to glorify the king, but also in the immediate context to provide a concrete example of Solomon's amassing wealth from admiring foreign visitors (see 10:25). Yet, to look to a further horizon, the legend brings us back to the leitmotif that ties much of the Solomonic material together: wisdom, wealth, and honor, succinctly stated in 3:13, and embodied here in this queen's effusive admiration for Solomon. In a way, this legend, coming where it does, is part of a gathering encomium for this king, this favored son of David, a climax of sorts, perhaps before the precipitous decline forecast in ch. 11 as a result of "foolish" actions.

Bibliography

H. Cazelles, " *'ašrê*," *TDOT* I, 445-48 (bibliography); J. Dupont, *Les Béatitudes* (2 vols.; 2nd ed.; Bruges-Louvain, 1958); idem, " 'Béatitudes' égyptiennes," *Bib* 47 (1966) 185-222; Ruth Finnegan, *Oral Literature in Africa* (Oxford: Clarendon, 1970); W. Janzen, " *'ašrê* in the Old Testament," *HTR* 58 (1965) 215-26; B. O. Long, "Recent Studies in Oral Literature and the Question of Sitz-im-Leben," *Semeia* 5 (1976) 35-49; Edward Ullendorf, "The Queen of Sheba," *BJRL* 45 (1963) 486-504.

III. ACCOUNT OF THE END OF SOLOMON'S REIGN: CANONICAL FRAMEWORK, 11:1-43

Structure

A. A theological review	1-13
B. Account of Solomon's adversaries	14-40

1. External	14-25
a. Concerning Hadad	14-22
b. Concerning Rezon	23-25
2. Internal: concerning Jeroboam	26-40
C. Concluding regnal resumé	41-43

The structural outline reflects the widespread agreement among critics regarding the essential content and formal divisions of the present MT. Vv. 1-13 (section A) are heavily influenced by the Dtr author-editor, although possibly some pre-Dtr tradition glimmers through, e.g., in vv. 3, 7 (but the details are disputed). Vv. 14-25 (B.1) apparently include two originally separate traditions, each now beginning with a similar introductory phrase, vv. 14 and 23; a textual problem in v. 25b has suggested to critics that either the verse belongs with vv. 14-22 or with vv. 23-25. Section B.2, vv. 26-40, is seen by most scholars as a section built of at least two earlier traditions, the remains of which are seen in vv. 26-28, 40, and 29-31; the whole has been heavily edited by the DtrR (vv. 32-39) to make links to the theme of vv. 1-13. Finally, section C (vv. 41-43) is clearly the regular concluding summary familiar for most of the reigns in 1–2 Kings.

Although there is little agreement on the details of the history of this material prior to its present arrangement, we can see that these various traditions now are welded into a thematic and formal unity. First of all, the obviously Dtr pieces in vv. 1-13, 32-39 strongly set an overall thematic framework for everything except the concluding summary. It seems certain that the editor has meant for us to make the identification between the unnamed servant in v. 11 and Jeroboam in vv. 32-39. In between is the material having to do with "adversaries," now clearly linked together by formulaic openings, vv. 14 and 23, and also, if we accept the present text, by the mention of *both* Hadad and Rezon in v. 25. Thus, the text comes together under the theme of the promised division of the kingdom, the responsibility for which is laid upon Solomon himself, vv. 1-13, 33. The final section closes out the reign formally with the usual concluding summaries.

Genre

This unit is a redactional composition which cannot be defined with precision. Contained within the composite, however, are numerous genres and generic elements, such as REPORT of SYMBOLIC ACTION, ORACLE, STORY, concluding REGNAL RESUMÉ, and REPORT. See discussion below for details.

Setting

The literary setting is naturally most important to see clearly. The material comes at the end of Solomon's reign, following upon images of Solomon the wise ruler, the beneficent and wealthy builder, the famous king who inspires a world of adulation.

Intention

The intention therefore is very clear. As a penultimate word, the author-editor means to expose the dark side of this glorious reign. This is an occasion for theological appraisal, and of stating the first of many prophecies which will subsequently divulge a hermeneutic of history moved by divine word spoken in prophecy. The unit provides a theological explanation for the troubles that will beset the house of Solomon: the division of the kingdom (because of Solomon's transgressions) but in the days *after* his death (because of David's righteousness and the chosen city, Jerusalem). Here, the potential disaster tucked away in Yahweh's demand for obedience (2:1-4; 3:14; 6:11-13; 9:4-5) is exposed as more of a threat than previously imagined when we were swept along by the pomp, glory, and success of this son of David.

ACCOUNT OF THE END OF SOLOMON'S REIGN: A THEOLOGICAL REVIEW, 11:1-13

Structure

I. Theological appraisal: Solomon's offenses	1-8
A. Concerning foreign wives	1-6
1. Statement of offense	1-2
2. Report of results	3-5
3. Statement of appraisal	6
B. Concerning the high places: statement of offense	7-8
II. Report of Yahweh's judgment on Solomon	9-13
A. Yahweh's anger and its reasons	9-10
B. Divine address: prophecy of punishment	11-13
1. Narrative introduction	11aα
2. Address proper	11aβ-13
a. Reason for punishment	11aβ
b. Announcement of punishment	11b
c. Statement of mitigation	12-13

We may see one main element in the structure of this text by noting the move from offense (I.A, B, vv. 1-8) to punishment (II.A, B, vv. 9-13). The summary of transgressions is met with elemental anger and simple judgment. Contained within this dynamic, however, is a more complex flow of linguistic styles and thought. The text offers a mix of reportorial statements and reflective comment.

At the beginning, vv. 1-2, we meet description more than action, a condition rather than movement—simple perfect verbs, "Solomon loved [*'āhab*] many foreign women. . . . to them Solomon clung [*dābaq*] in love." Though separated by elaborate explanatory clauses (vv. 1b-2a), these simple statements of love read like poetic bicola, as though the better to suggest the simple stubbornness of Solomon's attachments. The text then shifts to a more direct reportorial style (*wyqṭl*) to state the results of Solomon's loving: the women "turned away [*wayyaṭṭû*] his heart" (v. 3b) and "Solomon went after [*wayyēlek*] Ashtoreth . . ." (v. 5). Entwined with these reports are statements of theological appraisal (vv. 4b, 6) that characterize and measure rather than describe and report. The overall effect is one of reviewing, summarizing, and evaluating.

The text takes another turn in vv. 7-8, marked by a temporal connective, "then" (*'āz*), and new information about additional offenses: Solomon built shrines for the gods of his wives. And perhaps in a tone of scorn, the narrator reiterates, "So he did for all his wives" (v. 8), again reverting to simple perfect tense, as though to depict an ongoing condition, otherwise more generally described as having his heart "turned away" from God (vv. 2b, 3b, 4aβ, 9).

Now having reviewed and measured the actions and the man, the text moves quickly to divine reaction—Yahweh is angry—and divine address. The narrator's voice again comes through: he tells us *why* Yahweh is angry, and from the emphasis given the matter (Solomon spurned this God who had appeared to him *twice*), we gather that the divine anger is partly pique at the singular obtuseness of Solomon. Vengeance is swift: the kingdom will be ripped from Solomon's hand and given to another. Yahweh's speech suggests the familiar style of prophecy of punishment in the books of Kings: a subordinate clause (beginning with "Because . . ." [*ya'an 'ăšer*]) provides the reason for the judgment. The main clause that follows, emphatically phrased, announces the judgment: "Surely I will tear [*qārōa' 'eqra'*]) the kingdom from you" (v. 11). A restrictive clause ("yet" [*'ak*]) then offers the mitigation of this punishment, but does not let us forget its full force (vv. 12-13). For similar prophetic speeches, cf. 1 Kgs 13:21-22; 14:7-11; 20:28; 2 Kgs 1:16; see also 1 Kgs 16:2-4 (divine word comes directly to the king, without mention of a prophet, as in the case of Solomon; cf. 1 Kgs 6:11-13).

Genre

The proper definition of genre begins with the observation that the text does not narrate action as much as it characterizes and measures a king and his reign. Not only are evaluative statements explicit in vv. 4b, 6, 9-10, but the author has not the slightest narrative or descriptive interest in telling us how and in what circumstances Yahweh communicates to Solomon (is it through a prophet? or a dream epiphany? and when? under what circumstances?). The unit seems ruled by these evaluative tones and remarks, and decisively shaped by the attempt at summarizing offense and punishment. Much of the language is typical of the Dtr editor of Kings (Burney, *Notes,* 152-53), and the basic structure has close parallels in portions of the Dtr (→) regnal resumé. These summaries typically include a positive or negative appraisal of the monarch's religious orthodoxy, which is often elaborated by stating some general offenses (if the appraisal is negative) or specific meritorious acts (if the appraisal is positive). As introduction to a reign, see 2 Kgs 21:2-9; 16:2b-4; 1 Kgs 14:22-24 (all negative); 1 Kgs 15:11-15; 2 Kgs 14:3, 5-6; 18:3-6 (all positive). Most interesting for our purpose is 2 Kgs 21:1-18, the full regnal resumé for Manasseh with no intervening narrative traditions. This summary is all the author-editor provides on the era of this king. But part of the rather elaborate theological appraisal reports a prophetic judgment speech spoken by "God's servants, the prophets" because of Manasseh's failings (2 Kgs 21:10-15). As with Yahweh's word to Solomon, the style admits of no narrative or circumstantial detail; there is not even a definite audience, except by implication, for the oracle. All is ruled by this summarizing, appraising, stereotyped style. And in all these cases of regnal resumé, the language is familiar in Dtr materials. Many are the parallels to 1 Kgs 11:1-13 (e.g., on v. 4b, cf. 1 Kgs 15:3, 14; on v. 6, cf.

1 Kgs 14:22; 15:26, 34; 2 Kgs 8:27; 21:2, 20; 24:9; on vv. 7-8, cf. 1 Kgs 14:23-24; 22:43b; 2 Kgs 12:4 [*RSV* 3]; 14:4; 15:4, 35; on the quote from *tôrâ*, which amplifies the basis for an appraisal [v. 2], cf. 2 Kgs 14:5-6; 21:4, 9; more distant, 1 Kgs 14:24b).

Other more distant parallels may be found in the framework portions of the book of Judges, where the Dtr editor offers a theological appraisal of the people of Israel, states Yahweh's anger, and reports his punishment of the nation (e.g., Judg 2:11-15; 3:7-8; 10:6-9; see Richter).

The Solomonic passage, however, is not a regnal resumé, because the text develops a theme which is only a *part* of the typical resumé. We have here basically a text which reviews, states offenses, and evaluates—even announces punishment. A more genetically similar parallel, then, is 2 Kgs 10:28-31, a text which offers a theological appraisal of Jehu in Dtr language and style, but independent of the standard regnal resumé. In fact, Jehu's appraisal comes at the end of an accounting of the Judean Ahaziah's reign, during which Jehu murders his way to center stage. Following upon this story of treachery against both Joram of Israel and Ahaziah of Judah, the Dtr editor gives an appraisal: "And Jehu wiped out Baal from Israel" (v. 28), "And Jehu did not turn aside from the sins of Jeroboam . . ." (v. 29). As he addressed Solomon, Yahweh addresses this king: "because you have done well . . . your sons of the fourth generation shall sit on the throne of Israel" (v. 30). Then follows a negative evaluation, v. 30, returning to the theme sounded at the beginning of this little passage. Thus, within small scope, we have a review of Jehu the king, a measure of this man, a divine address—styled as prophetic oracle, though without narrative detail—and both positive and negative appraisals. Similarly, 2 Kgs 17:7-18 offers an extensive review of the offenses of Israel, but here as a separate elaboration and comment on the introductory regnal resumé of Hoshea, king of Israel (2 Kgs 17:1-6). In this text, again in Dtr style, we have paraded before our eyes the transgressions of Israel, with evaluative comments sprinkled liberally throughout; there is even a summarizing report of constant warnings through the words of the prophets (v. 13) and quotes from God's previously given commands (v. 12), as the basis for negative appraisals. Everything suggests the Solomonic text, in sequence and theme and style. See also Jer 3:6-10.

Thus, we may designate our unit as THEOLOGICAL REVIEW, that is, a summary of offenses against Yahweh, heavily laced with evaluative statements which measure the king according to his religious orthodoxy. A review will often incorporate oracles from the prophets as messengers of judgment, warning, or salvation. The theological review is connected in theme and style with Dtr regnal resumés, and to Dtr framework portions of the book of Judges. Cf. 2 Kgs 10:28-31; 17:7-18; Judg 2:11-15; 3:7-8.

Setting

As far as we can see from the predominantly Dtr language and style, the theological review is a literary device with its setting in the Dtr history work, in those portions which seek to review and characterize an epoch (Judges) or a reign (2 Kgs 10:28-31) or a misfortune, such as northern exile (2 Kgs 17:7-18; Jer 3:7-8). We know of no parallels in ancient Near Eastern sources. This theological review is set near the end of Solomon's rule, apparently after all the accomplishments important to the author-editor have been set forth.

Intention

In context, this particular theological review was intended to provide a darkened horizon for the disruptions to follow. By contrast, we are shocked that underneath the wealth, prosperity, and wisdom of this king, and the seeming peacefulness of unopposed and strong rule, there was transgression, a fatal weakness that for the Dtr editor-author signalled the kingdom's slide into division and turmoil. One thinks of David. In a way, that long, twisting account of his reign is governed by the fateful events set in motion in the liaison with Bathsheba. From that moment, David's kingdom is never without trouble (2 Sam 12:10). So with Solomon, amid the fatness of unrivaled power and fame, a tragic seed grows in Solomon's old age. It will return manifold upon itself. In this way the theological review is a programmatic text for the Dtr author-editor. Solomon's misdeed, principally caught in his backsliding weakness for foreign women, reverberates like a *cantus firmus* in the divided kingdoms to follow. See 1 Kgs 15:13; 16:31; 2 Kgs 8:18, 27; 11:1-20 (Hoffmann, 47, 55-56).

Bibliography

H.-D. Hoffmann, *Reform und Reformen*, 47-58 (see listing at "Introduction to 1 Kings"); Wolfgang Richter, *Die Bearbeitungen des "Retterbuches" in der Deuteronomistischen Epoche* (Bonner biblische Beiträge 21; Bonn: Hanstein, 1964).

ACCOUNT OF THE END OF SOLOMON'S REIGN: ADVERSARIES (EXTERNAL), 11:14-25

Structure

I. Concerning Hadad	14-22
A. Introduction	14
1. Thematic statement: adversary	14aα
2. Identification: Hadad	14aβ-b
B. The flight from Edom (to Egypt)	15-20
1. Occasion for flight: David-Joab slaughter of Edomites	15-16
2. Description of flight	17-18bα
3. Description: life in Egypt	18bβ-20
C. The return to Edom (from Egypt)	21-22
1. Occasion for return: David-Joab deaths	21a
2. Request to return (dialogue)	21b-22
a. Request	21b
b. Answer	22a
c. Reiteration of request	22b
II. Concerning Rezon	23-25
A. Introduction	23

1. Thematic statement: adversary 23aα
2. Identification: Rezon 23aβ-b

B. The making of an adversary 24-25
1. Coming to power 24
2. Summary of adversarial status 25

This unit consists of two rather independent pieces of tradition loosely tied together by (1) thematic statements, vv. 14aα and 23aα, which provide a common interpretative perspective and (2) by v. 25aβ-b, which, despite textual difficulties and the possibility that it may have originally been associated with v. 22, apparently now brings Hadad and Rezon together in some sort of comparison. The first division (I, vv. 14-22) is largely styled with *waw*-conversive narrative tenses (*wyqṭl*). But the sentences seem clumsy (the *RSV* faithfully reflects this lapse); note the parenthetical v. 16, the awkward v. 17, and the repetition in v. 18.

Nevertheless, the tradition about Hadad seems to be bound together under its thematic statement (I.A.1, v. 14aα). We meet the chief character, hear how he was thrown onto a side opposing the Israelite monarchy, witness his flight to Egypt and his request of Pharaoh to return to Edom. In the light of the thematic statement, we must read a fairly innocent anecdote as an account of the making of an adversary: a potential enemy of Israel on the eve of his return, like Joseph, swelled with success in Egypt.

The second tradition (II, vv. 23-25), compressed and without significant detail, begins with a nearly identical thematic statement. We are introduced to Rezon, and given to understand something of the situation in which he is pitted against the Israelite monarchy (v. 24); he too returns after flight, becomes king in Damascus, and a troubler of Israel. Finally, if the MT is correct, both adversaries come together in the view of v. 25aβ-b: one from Edom, the other from Syria, "doing mischief" (*rāʿâ*).

Genre

The unit is a composite literary redaction. Its components offer elements of some generic significance. The Hadad tradition is perhaps best described as a fragment of a STORY. The piece lacks the full development of plot which we associate with genuine story; yet it is clearly more than a simple (→) report, which typically reflects no interest in narrative development. The second tradition, dealing with Rezon, is a REPORT and is similar to brief, summarizing reports in Babylonian and Assyrian Chronicles (Grayson, *Chronicles*; see esp. "Weidner Chronicle," lines 51-64, ibid., 149-50).

Setting

These two fragmentary traditions joined into a redactional whole are placed as the first two concrete incidents following the announcement of Solomon's punishment in vv. 9-13. There is no firm evidence to suggest some original setting for this particular material. Gray (*Kings,* 280) speculated that the Hadad tradition was drawn from Edomite annals—but of course we do not possess any such documents so as to be in a position to judge; anyway, the fondness of the flight-and-prosperity-in-Egypt motif to Israelite storytellers (see Joseph and Moses) is enough to explain this as a fully Israelite creation. More to the point is the literary setting near the end of the Solomonic materials.

Intention

The particular context for this unit makes it likely that the author-editor of Kings intended that we understand, besides a promise of demise in the form of a divided kingdom, that there was also constant trouble for Solomon *during* his reign. It is not enough to suggest that things will fall apart after death. It is more complete to say, even indirectly, that there were dark clouds on the horizon even in life, like a shudder in the darkness of impending destruction. Is Hadad the servant who is to receive ten parts of the kingdom? Or Rezon? Or someone yet unnamed? How is this darkness to become visible? Such are the questions raised, heightening the dramatic moves toward ch. 12.

ACCOUNT OF THE END OF SOLOMON'S REIGN: ADVERSARIES (INTERNAL), 11:26-40

Structure

I. Introduction	26
A. Identification: Jeroboam	26a
B. Thematic statement: opposition to the king	26b
II. The making of an adversary	27-40
A. Superscription	27a
B. Background: Solomon and Jeroboam (amity)	27b-28
C. Report of symbolic action	29-39
1. Setting	29
2. Symbolic action	30
3. Explanatory oracle	31-39
a. Narrative introduction	31aα
b. Oracle	31aβ-39
1) Basic word for Solomon	31aβ-34
a) Main message: kingdom torn from Solomon	31aβ-32
b) Reason	33
c) Mitigation: not in Solomon's lifetime	34
2) Basic word for Solomon qualified	35-36
a) Main message	35
b) Reason	36
3) Basic word for Jeroboam	37-38
a) Promise: king over Israel	37
b) Conditional promise	38
4) Conclusion: affliction for dynasty	39
D. Consequences: Solomon and Jeroboam (enmity)	40

Whatever the earlier history of the traditions which now combine to make up the present text (see Dietrich; Plein; Schüpphaus; Seebass; and discussion at

11:1-43), it seems clear now that we are meant to see essentially an encounter between Ahijah the prophet and Jeroboam, in which the prophet performs a symbolic action and delivers its explanatory oracle to Jeroboam, even though much of the oracle's content has to do with Solomon. The oracle is indeed the heart of the unit and the portion that is given most space, if not the most expansion at the hands of the Dtr editors, vv. 32-39. The dramatic power of the story emerges during this symbolic action as we become aware that the relationship between Solomon and Jeroboam turns completely around. At first the story suggests amity, sketched in vv. 27b-28 (the king sees that this young man is "industrious" and puts him in charge of the slaves in the house of Joseph; the narrator tells us he is very able); then we feel the suspicious, murderous enmity in the laconic, cold v. 40: "Solomon sought to kill Jeroboam." The narrator gives us no word at all about how Solomon came to his change in attitude—we must presume he heard of the oracle which promised the kingdom to Jeroboam. But he gives us enough to see the action, and to hear the irony at the end, when this member of the sons of Israel flees for his life to the place from whence an Edomite adversary had already got his strength (v. 40b). This thematic movement receives a title of sorts in v. 27a, clearly putting the action under the general *topos* "adversary," as in vv. 14-22, though with different language. There is an odd tension left by this editorial procedure: the implication is that Jeroboam is an active participant in the drama of God raising adversaries against Solomon, and the reality of the events narrated is that he is strictly passive, the recipient of an unsolicited oracle which made him into a persona non grata at Solomon's court. His first active move, so to speak, is to flee the murderous intentions of this one-time friend. The working out of the oracle, and of Jeroboam's direct role in those events, must await another day and another story—ch. 12.

The oracle delivered to Jeroboam is worth a few comments. There are some problems of internal consistency (e.g., the pronominal suffixes in v. 33 are inconsistently applied), but overall it is remarkable for its careful intertwining of the fates of Solomon, his son, and Jeroboam. Yet in vv. 31-36, the clear emphasis falls upon the destiny of Solomon, as though to change the flavor but not the meat in the stew. However, v. 37 brings a distinct shift. Unequivocally and with emphasis ("and as for you" [*wĕ'ōtĕkā*]), the prophet says what is meant for Jeroboam. Like Solomon earlier, this unknown youth is addressed, or admonished, as a king. He receives a conditional promise of dynasty, that word heretofore reserved for David and his heir, now ironically resting like a proleptic crown on an unsuspecting head. At last the oracle returns to its focus on Solomon—this time to mark the descendants of David for affliction, but not forever. This must undoubtedly be an anticipatory reference to the rest of the books of Kings. How this oracle resonates to past, present, and future! It is clearly meant to announce judgment on Solomon, and thus it parallels and amplifies vv. 11-13. But also, we should not miss the exquisite irony. A promise reserved in so special a way for the house of David has become weak and diluted, and offered to Jeroboam on behalf of a redefined Israel.

Genre

While the possibilities of artistic development are rather more incipient than fully exploited, this unit certainly approaches the genre (→) story. By taking account of what is not said, or rather, the implication of what *is* said, we may glean a rudimentary plot. Harmony between king and good worker, vv. 27b-28, is disrupted by the unwelcome (to Solomon) word of the prophesied passing of the kingdom to this same able worker, who is, after all, a "youth" (*na'ar,* v. 28). The understated and implicit tension leads to murderous pursuit, and we are left wondering about the outcome. Thus the drama carries us along toward climax and dénouement, but drops us short of the station platform. It is appropriate that the whole unit, therefore, receives a reportorial introduction (vv. 26-27a), more a characterizing title than a narrative opening: "This is the matter of raising the hand against the king" (cf. Josh 5:4; 1 Kgs 9:15). In the light of these considerations it is best to characterize the unit as EPISODE, that is, as a segment of a larger story, a chapter in a larger whole, a chapter which has narrative qualities of its own and may on some occasions be a complete story in its own right (cf. the episodes of transition at 2:12b-46).

An important influence on the shape and content of this episode is the REPORT of SYMBOLIC ACTION, a narrative genre used to report incidents in which the prophets accompanied their pronouncements with actions understood as symbolic signs (Fohrer). The roots may extend far back into conceptions of magical actions, but it is clear from the prophetic traditions that the acts were primarily used to dramatize and underscore what the prophets were saying. In the case of this prophet Ahijah and Jeroboam, perhaps owing to loss in transmission, only some of the essential elements typically found in such reports are visible: (1) the act (tearing a garment), and (2) an oracle that explains the significance of that act (vv. 29-31, 32-39). See Isa 8:1-4; Jer 13:1-11; Hos 1:2-8. The oracle itself as it refers to Solomon (vv. 31a-36) is somewhat typical of the PROPHETIC JUDGMENT SPEECH (see 2 Kgs 21:10-13; 22:16-17; Mic 3:9-12; Isa 8:6-8). The prophet refers indirectly to the one judged (note the third-person pronouns; Solomon is not on the scene) and provides a succinct ANNOUNCEMENT OF JUDGMENT, usually a disaster of some kind (v. 31b, "Behold I am about to tear the kingdom from the hand of Solomon . . ."). The reason for Yahweh's action then follows (v. 33); in other examples of the genre the reason may precede the actual announcement (see Hos 5:3-7; Mic 3:9-12). Here in 1 Kgs 11:31-36, Solomon is to lose the kingdom, though not completely. Judgment is mitigated, a somewhat unusual feature for this type of prophecy. For Jeroboam, whose destiny is interwoven with that of Solomon, Ahijah simply offers a promise of kingship conditioned on obedience to God (vv. 37-38; see 1 Kgs 3:14; 6:12-13). See full discussion of the genre at 13:21-22.

Setting

As it now stands, this episode hardly would have existed alone; it demands a larger context. We cannot know what that may have been, other than the context which it now has: the recounting of how opposition rose for Solomon—both externally (Edomite and Syrian) and internally (Jeroboam, an Ephraimite over the slaves in the house of Joseph). The story is set as the last event laid out in this thematic context, surely as a kind of anticipation of Jeroboam's story to follow in ch. 12.

Intention

The intention in context, therefore, would have been to narrate the third in a series of traditions that introduce the adversaries into the account of Solomon's reign, even though only Jeroboam is to play a role in the materials to follow. Clearly, the Dtr author-editor meant to link this episode with the announcement of demise in vv. 9-13 (vv. 29-39 confirm this point). And so the mysterious servant who is to receive the ten parts of the kingdom is none other than this Jeroboam. He is introduced, as it were, and given a sort of divine charter, presaging what is to come in ch. 12, where he will become active against Solomon. The events are also proleptic of the whole subsequent history of monarchy. It will be a story of division and strife and adversarial relations between north and south, scion of David and the successors to Jeroboam to whom the dynastic promise was passed in this moment. It is a powerful legitimation both of Solomon's failures and Jeroboam's sudden success.

Bibliography

Walter Dietrich, *Prophetie und Geschichte*, 54-55 (see listing at "Introduction to 1 Kings"); Georg Fohrer, *Die Symbolischen Handlungen der Propheten* (ATANT 54; Zurich: Zwingli, 1968) 20-21; idem, *Prophetenerzählungen (Die Propheten des Alten Testaments* 7; Gütersloh: Gütersloher, 1977) 12-15; I. Plein, "Erwägungen zur Überlieferung von 1 Reg 11:26–14:20," *ZAW* 78 (1966) 8-24; Otto Plöger, "Die Prophetengeschichten der Samuel und Königsbücher" (Diss., Greifswald, 1937) 14; J. Schüpphaus, "Richter- und Prophetengeschichten" (see listing at "Introduction to 1 Kings") 13-19; H. Seebass, "Zur Teilung der Herrschaft Salomos nach 1 Reg 11:29-39," *ZAW* 88 (1976) 363-76.

ACCOUNT OF THE END OF SOLOMON'S REIGN: REGNAL SUMMARY, 11:41-43

Structure

I.	Citation of source	41
II.	Regnal information: length of reign, capital city	42
III.	Notice of death and burial	43a
IV.	Notice of succession	43b

This unit follows the schematic outline typical of the concluding sections of most of the reigns in the books of Kings. The author-editor cites a source for further information, "The Book of the Acts of Solomon," tallies the number of years the king ruled in his central ruling place, Jerusalem, and then notes his death and succession. The style and structure is thoroughly typical, save for the inclusion of the notice about the length of reign, a feature usually found in the introductory summaries for the various monarchs. See the full discussion at 14:21-31.

Genre

This unit is a concluding REGNAL RESUMÉ, a literary device of the Dtr author. See full discussion at 14:21-31.

Setting

The setting therefore is in the situation and editorial work of the author-editor for the books of Kings. For possible settings outside this particular school of writings, see the discussion at 14:21-31.

Intention

As a literary device of the author-editor, this regnal resumé is clearly intended to close out the Solomonic era. At the same time, the schematic regularity of the formulaic summary at this point has a curious effect. Solomon's ending is utterly normal, without notoriety of any kind, in contrast to the sense of unusual royal grandeur conveyed by the preceding chapters and the ominous hints and promises of disruption immediately preceding. Having felt the foreshock we await the tremor, amid the routineness of a royal passing.

THE REIGN OF JEROBOAM: CANONICAL FRAMEWORK, 12:1–14:20

Structure

I. Account of Jeroboam's becoming king in Israel	12:1-24
A. Story of rebellion against Rehoboam and accession of Jeroboam	1-20
B. Report of reprisal plans stayed	21-24
II. Reports of Jeroboam's building activities	25-32
A. Concerning two cities	25
B. Concerning two cultic centers	26-32
III. Prophetic legend: judgment against Bethel	12:33–13:34
IV. Prophetic legend: judgment against Jeroboam	14:1-18
V. Concluding regnal resumé	19-20

Save for 12:1-24, which brings Jeroboam together with his southern counterpart Rehoboam, the traditions in this unit focus exclusively on Jeroboam's building activities (12:25-32) and the divine judgment brought against him by God (12:33–14:18). Even though the text lacks a typical introductory summary for the king (cf. 14:21-24 for Rehoboam; 16:29-33 for Ahab), the concluding summary at 14:19-20 indicates clearly the perspective of the author-editor: this is the account of Jeroboam's reign. Despite their emphasis on King Rehoboam, 12:1-24 must therefore be viewed in the canonical framework as pointedly aimed at the accession of Jeroboam. More broadly considered, the author-editor deals with the emergence of two separate kingdoms in the wake of Solomon's death.

The structure of these diverse traditions runs parallel to the Solomonic materials. Like Solomon, Jeroboam came to power in unusual circumstances (I.A, vv. 1-20; cf. for Solomon, 1:1–2:46; Solomon also does not receive an introductory summary). Then follows a section on building two cities (II.A, v. 25) and two cultic centers (II.B, vv. 26-32; cf. for Solomon, 5:15–9:25). Finally, we read of a prophet's condemnation of this king who transgressed Yahweh's limits (III and IV, 12:33–13:34; 14:1-18; cf. for Solomon, 11:1-13, 31-33).

The relationship between the materials of Solomon's and Jeroboam's reigns in the history of tradition is uncertain, but clearly suggested by 11:26-40. Whatever one's judgment might be on these matters, and scholars differ, it is obvious that the canonical shaping has provided thematic continuity. As part of his description of Solomon's malaise and downfall, the Dtr author-editor announced Jeroboam's eventual rise to power. The new king was to be favored of Yahweh while despised of Solomon (11:26-40). It is with some irony, therefore, that Jeroboam appears out of exile to rival the house of Solomon, and yet precipitously declines before Yahweh, his failings etched like moralistic tracings against a tableau of accomplishments: "this thing became a sin . . ." (12:30; cf. 13:34; 14:16).

Genre

Like all coverage of particular reigns in 1–2 Kings, this unit is an editorial compilation, whose genre cannot be specified with precision; the unit is an editorial account composed of materials of different origins and ages, carried by various literary genres. One may observe a REPORT of royal building activity (12:25), perhaps drawn from official records of some kind, and more folkloristic rendering of a report dealing with Jeroboam's establishment of cult centers (12:26-32). PROPHETIC LEGENDS (12:33–13:34; 14:1-18) and a more highly developed STORY (12:1-20) fill out the account, which closes with the typical concluding REGNAL RESUMÉ (14:19-20). All these literary genres have now been welded together into a selective but continuous account of Jeroboam's reign and the beginning of a divided kingdom in the wake of Solomon's death.

Setting

Since this unit is an editorial compilation, we must look primarily to its *literary* setting in the books of Kings. From the death of Solomon on, the Dtr author-editor deals with a two-part Israelite kingdom, and so synchronizes each reign in relation to the counterpart in the north or south. This procedure has its parallels among Mesopotamian chronistic writings (Grayson, *Chronicles*, esp. pp. 70-87 and 157-70). Synchronism begins here in the reign of Jeroboam, although without special synchronistic note, and will provide the chronological structure of the books of Kings through the reign of Hoshea in the north, 2 Kgs 17:6. Then will follow a long statement on the reasons for, and religious lessons to be gleaned from, the north's destruction (2 Kgs 17:7-41). In this wider context, the account of Jeroboam's rule begins a major section on the monarchs in the north, but recounted with a religious point of view deriving from exile in Babylon (→ "Introduction to 1 Kings"). It is probably not accidental that the author-editor envisions kingship in the north to have begun in the midst of conflict and with a religious problem at its heart. In exactly this way, Israel's very first king burst upon the scene of history (1 Samuel 8). This new impulse in Israel's story doubles back and recalls the beginning.

Intention

From these comments, it follows that the main intention of this editorial composite is to measure the dissolution of the Solomonic era in the rise of Jeroboam. But the author-editor also puts this event ambiguously under both the direction (11:37-38; 12:24) and judgment of God (13:33; 14:10-16). The account explains at once the triumph and misadventure of the northern experiment. Like some powerful legacy from Solomon's transgressions, the divided kingdom emerges out of enmity between the house of Solomon and Jeroboam. But beyond the horrors of divided kin, of brother fighting brother, can be seen the miscalculation of Jeroboam in reckoning his religious duty to Yahweh. The road will end in destruction.

REBELLION AGAINST REHOBOAM AND ACCESSION OF JEROBOAM, 12:1-20

Text

Difficult textual problems which involve variants in the Hebrew MSS and Greek VS, particularly at vv. 2-3, resist easy solutions. Critics differ in their opinions. With the main Greek VSS we omit MT v. 3a ("and they sent and called him; and Jeroboam . . .") along with the reference to Jeroboam in v. 12 (Burney, *Notes*, 166-67; Gray, *Kings*, 301; Montgomery, *Kings*, 248-49). See now Julio Trebolle Barrera, "Jeroboán y la Asamblea de Siquén (1 Rey. TM 12:2-3a; LXX 11:43; 12:24d.f.p.)," *Est Bib* 38 (1979-80) 189-220.

Structure

I. Narrative setting	1-2
A. Rehoboam and all Israel at Shechem	1
B. Parenthetical note: Jeroboam returns	2
II. Account of king-making negotiations	3b-16
A. Rehoboam and people of Israel	3b-5
1. Israel's offer of loyalty	3b-4
a. Narrative introduction	3b
b. Proposal to Rehoboam	4
1) Background	4a
2) Conditional promise of loyalty	4b
2. Rehoboam's response	5a
a. Narrative introduction	$5a\alpha^1$
b. Order to depart	$5a\alpha^2$-β
3. Israel's departure	5b
B. Rehoboam and his advisers	6-11
1. Consulting the elders (*RSV* "old men")	6-7
a. Narrative introduction	6a
b. Question to elders	6b
c. Reply of elders: accept proposal	7
2. Consulting the young men	8-11
a. Narrative introduction	8-$9a\alpha^1$
b. Question to young men	$9a\alpha^2$-b
c. Reply of young men: reject proposal	10-11
C. Rehoboam and people of Israel	12-16a
1. Narrative introduction	12
2. Dialogue	13-16a
a. Rehoboam	13-15
1) Characterizing introduction	13-14a
2) Speech to Israel	14b

3) Characterizing conclusion (prophecy fulfilled)	15
b. People of Israel	16a
1) Narrative introduction	16aα
2) Speech: rebel cry	16aβ
D. Narrative conclusion: Israel's departure	16b
III. Epilogue	17-20
A. Rehoboam's rule in Judah	17
B. Report of rebellion	18-19
1. The king's man stoned to death	18a
2. Rehoboam's reaction: flight	18b
3. Epitomizing conclusion	19
C. Report of two kingdoms	20
1. Israel makes Jeroboam king	20a
2. Judah follows house of David (Rehoboam)	20b

The beginning of this unit stands out clearly from the formulaic summary in 11:41-43, which closes out the reign of Solomon. Its ending, however, is not as clear. Vv. 21-24 may have originally been separate from the main tradition of Jeroboam's rise to the throne (note the shift from "*tribe* of Judah," v. 20b, to "*house* of Judah," v. 21a). In any case, the verses open a new scene after the conclusive v. 20 that neatly encapsulates the meaning of the previous events. Scholars dispute what, if anything, in vv. 17-20 belonged originally with the main tradition. Quite apart from this question, opinions differ widely on the sources and literary relationships among vv. 17, 18-19, and 20. In the absence of scholarly consensus, it seems best to recognize the appendixlike character of vv. 17-20 (indeed, v. 17, with its odd formulation in the Hebrew, suggests the remains of an independent subject heading; cf. 2 Sam 8:15 and 1 Kgs 4:1). Yet in its present form, the material presupposes events in vv. 1-16. Thus, we are left with a main tradition in vv. 1-16, admirably rounded off by the narrative conclusion in v. 16b, and an epilogue to this main tradition, vv. 17-20. Throughout, but especially in the latter, one must admit to the likelihood of a process of redaction no longer very clear to us (Lipinski; Plein; Debus).

The unit opens typically, bringing the characters together and briefly sketching the situation of possible conflict. Rehoboam, the successor to Solomon, has journeyed to Shechem, where apparently the northerners have gathered with the aim of accepting his rule over them in the wake of Solomon's death. A possible rival, an enemy of the Judahite monarchy, Jeroboam surreptitiously returns from exile to his homeland—a cloud on the distant horizon, or an agent waiting for the moment to ripen. The ambiguity of Jeroboam's intentions convey mystery and arouse expectations, but the narrator gives nothing more at this point.

The heart of the narrative action, vv. 3b-16, is built "sandwich" or "ring" style (S. Bar-Efrat, "Some Observations on the Analysis of Structure in Biblical Narrative," *VT* 30 [1980] 154-73). Two scenes featuring Rehoboam and the people of the north (II.A, vv. 3b-5; II.C, vv. 12-16a) enclose a dramatic center: the king's consultations with his advisers (II.B, vv. 6-11). We face this new king as do the northerners. He is brash, arrogant, and politically insensitive—a captive of impetuous youth, the "young men [advisers] who had grown up with him" (v. 8). The movement of plot is clear and straightforward. At Shechem, kingmaking runs into a complication: the northerners demur slightly and offer their loyalty only if Rehoboam agrees to lighten the burdens of Solomon's previous rule. Tension builds around this question of loyalty and is finally resolved in the third scene (II.C, vv. 12-16a) when all Israel breaks away from Rehoboam, a cry of derisive rebellion ringing through the air (v. 16b; cf. 2 Sam 20:2). This scene closes with a brief note that Israel "departed to their tents."

The epilogue (III, vv. 17-20) reports a series of subsequent events: (1) a direct act of rebellion, stoning a Judahite royal official (III.B, vv. 18-19), undoubtedly illustrative for the narrator of the continuing problems between north and south: ". . . Israel has been in rebellion against the house of David to this day" (v. 19); (2) the accession of Jeroboam to kingship over these northern tribes, v. 20a; (3) a note that Rehoboam rules in the south, but formulated as conclusion to a report of rebellion: "There was none that followed the house of David, but the tribe of Judah only" (v. 20b; cf. 2 Sam 20:2b; 2 Sam 2:10b; 1 Kgs 16:21). With this last note, a circle is closed, but with ironic reversal. All Israel had come to Shechem to make Rehoboam king (*lĕhamlîk 'ōtô,* v. 1) and they went away to make a Solomonic rival, Jeroboam, their king instead (v. 20a, *wayyamlîkû 'ōtô*). Despite the somewhat problematic status of the epilogue in the flow of narrative action, it completes a thematic framework (vv. 1 and 20) around the main tradition, and brings the incident of Shechem to a satisfactory, definitive close.

This unit shows artistic completeness and high drama. It carries characteristic folkloristic features (cf. 1 Kgs 3:16-28). Whenever persons are mentioned in the drama, they are drawn as types rather than individuals. It is "all Israel," "the elders," and the "young men" (literally, "young boys," *yĕlādîm*). The king himself works rather indecisively, apparently swayed by others and reacting throughout to the firm initiative from the north. Partners to the drama use stylized speech. The "elders" (*RSV* "old men") counsel with wise words, advising moderation; the youngsters with impetuosity, foolishness, even cynicism. The reply of the Israelites to Rehoboam's harsh terms is a stylized cry found on the lips of earlier rebels (2 Sam 20:1). Corresponding to stylized characters and speech is a complete lack of interest in closer specification of the background circumstances. The narrative instead reveals an "inner" dimension to events. It dramatizes the motivations behind the decisions leading to the dissolution of Solomon's empire, and it fixes obsessively on the question of culpability for this division among kinsmen. Oddly enough, the answer is twofold: Rehoboam's obstinacy, dramatically contrasted as his despotism over against others' will to freedom; and, second, Yahweh's overriding will, enunciated in prophecy (v. 15). Although a favorite for the Dtr author-editor (cf. 15:29; 16:12; 22:38), the latter theme is formulated here in a style indigenous to popular narrative. See 2:15; 2 Sam 17:14b.

Repetition is important to the style, flavor, and impact of this narrative. It is not necessarily a sign of heavy editing (against Šanda, *Könige*, 346-417). The narrator repeats a phrase or a motif, but with significant additions as the action develops. V. 9 repeats the query addressed to the elders in v. 6, but adds a characterizing epithet that repeats language of v. 4. The young men's speech in v. 10, a repeated "Thus shall you speak," frames the advice. The advice itself takes up the northerners' remarks of v. 4. Repetition has a contrastive effect: the petitioners' solicitous courtesy etched against Rehoboam's possibly obscene, certainly derisive, dismissal, "My little finger is thicker than my father's loins." V. 11 again repeats images from v. 4, and adds a contrasting statement for Rehoboam, built of similar images, and formulated for emphasis: "I [emphatic *'ănî*] will add to your yoke." For good measure, the narrator adds another contrast with entirely new metaphors: "My father chastised you with whips, but I will chastise you with scorpions." The essence of this counsellor's speech is then taken up again in v. 14b.

The effect of all this repetition is to recapitulate continuously the very first scene. It is a constant presence in our hearing the deliberations within Rehoboam's camp. Repetition thus focuses and sharpens the characterization of Rehoboam as arrogant, brash, politically naive, and insensitive. The narrator assigns clear responsibility for the opposition of north and south, old and young, wise and foolish.

Genre

The unit is clearly a STORY, and has been so designated by many critics (e.g., Fichtner, *Könige*, 189; Gray, *Kings*, 299; Noth, *Könige*, 270; Würthwein, *Könige*, 150). Its folkloristic artistry suggests that Debus's designation "folktale" is essentially correct in its flavor. The unit is not a "historical work" (against Donner, 383; Plein, 15), but a story with typical marks of folkloristic or popular narration. The development of plot is clear. Action moves from a situation that implies tension, builds complications in the negotiations between people and Rehoboam, and reaches a resolution in the complete severance of ties between negotiating parties. The tension drains away in a reportorial epilogue which notes a reversal of the initial situation: the northern people (all Israel) came to make Rehoboam king, and went away having crowned Jeroboam instead.

There are no close parallels in the Hebrew Bible. But we should note the (→) report of rebellion in 2 Kgs 8:20-22, which offers a structure similar to 1 Kgs 12:18-19. A rival king is set up (Hiphil of *mlk*), characterized as a revolt (*pš'*), and the action to quash the rebellion follows immediately. Finally, the whole is closed with an epitomizing summary which refers to a state of continual rebellion. A similar structure appears in 2 Sam 20:1-2, and includes a rebel cry: "We have no portion in David, and we have no inheritance in the son of Jesse; every man to his tents, O Israel." Other more general motivic parallels may be found in Judg 9:1-6, a scene of rival kingmaking, and 2 Sam 2:8-10, 11—the followers of Saul splitting off from loyalists of David (cf. 2 Sam 5:1-5). Division of loyalties and establishment of rival claimants to rule are thus frequent motifs in the OT, and are frequently enshrined in similarly styled literary materials. From the ancient Near East, note the Sumerian poem "Gilgamesh and Aggada," which contains a scene of the impetuous young ruler (Gilgamesh) seeking and rejecting the moderate advice of the city elders in favor of the rash counsel of his young arms bearers (*ANET*, 45-46; Malamat).

Setting

It seems likely that folkloristic story would have had its primary setting among the general populace. This particular story could be Judahite in origin (Noth, *Könige*, 271-72). Plein (p. 13) more fancifully imagines a circle of old Solomonic advisers, shortly after the rise of Jeroboam. It is also possible that the story is northern Israelite (Debus; Šanda, *Könige*, 347; Würthwein, *Könige*, 150). In any case, the interest in Rehoboam's role in the dissolution of the Solomonic kingdom could have been shared equally by persons Israelite or Judahite, inside and outside official royal circles. More accessible to us is the present literary context of this story. It is a continuation of the tradition about Ahijah and Jeroboam (11:29-40; vv. 2 and 15 make the direct link). This is the Jeroboam who unwittingly became the enemy of Solomon and the recipient of a crown which would rival the Solomonic splendor in the south (see discussion at 1 Kgs 11:26-40). In context it is Jeroboam who is guided by Yahweh, girded with Yahweh's favor, and who will shortly be singled out as offensive to this same God—in short, as failing his prophetic "charter" (11:38).

Intention

From what has been said, it follows that the story in context was intended to narrate the rise of Jeroboam in fulfillment of prophecy (v. 15), and to do this in contrast to a near caricature of a Judahite king, Rehoboam. The latter bears responsibility for the dissolution of the Solomonic empire. Or rather it was this man's foolishness that led to such a momentous tear in Solomon's robe. The story reflects a Judahite perspective on God's role in the affair, without approving or defending Rehoboam. In the end it is Yahweh who directs events and accomplishes his purpose in both sensible and misguided human actions. The narrator interprets the experience of divided and warring kinsmen who compete for earthly power and the same divine favors. He also assigns a double cause: Rehoboam's actions and Yahweh's plans (v. 15; cf. v. 24; 11:29-40). At one stroke, the narrator ties the complicated events to a prophecy and a fool.

In contrast, Jeroboam stands as a fugitive from Solomon, recently returned from hiding, but nonetheless sketched with positive strokes. He received a promise reserved for kings of special favor (11:37-38) and accepted a kind of draft choice from the northern Israelites once they—like Yahweh—had turned away from the Solomonic house. While certainly reflecting a momentous event in Hebraic history, the story looks inward, to characterize the affair and to offer a newly positive interest in this man destined for high things. Like Solomon before him, Jeroboam has an opportunity for faithfulness. There is as yet no hint of his precipitous fall to come.

Bibliography

J. Debus, *Die Sünde Jerobeams* (FRLANT 93; Göttingen: Vandenhoeck & Ruprecht, 1967) 19-30, 34-39; H. Donner, "The Separate States of Israel and Judah," in *Israelite and Judaean History* (ed. J. Hayes and J. M. Miller; OTL; Philadelphia: Westminster, 1977) 386-89; E. Lipiński, "Le récit de 1 Rois xii 1-19 à la lumière de l'ancien usage de l'hébreu et de nouveaux textes de Mari," *VT* 24 (1974) 430-37; A. Malamat, "Kingship and Council in Israel and Sumer: A Parallel," *JNES* 22 (1963) 247-53 (rev. and expanded in "Organs of Statecraft in the Israelite Monarchy," *BA* 28 [1965] 34-65); E. Nielsen, *Shechem. A Traditio-Historical Investigation* (2nd ed.; Copenhagen: G. E. Gadd, 1959) 171-208; W. Plein, "Erwägungen zur Überlieferung von 1 Reg 11:26–14:20," *ZAW* 78 (1966) 8-24; M. Weinfeld, "King-People Relationship in the Light of 1 Kgs 12:7," *Lešonénu* 36 (1971) 3-13 (Hebrew).

REPORT OF REPRISAL PLANS STAYED, 12:21-24

Text

The Greek VSS show a long supplement at v. 24: a summary of Rehoboam's reign, and another version of the origin and rise of Jeroboam. The text contains elements from, and variants of, traditions in the MT of chs. 11–14, plus some materials not known from the Hebrew. Its tone is decidedly negative toward Jeroboam. The Greek seems to have drawn upon an independent variant tradition at this point. Since its relationship to the history of the MT is uncertain, it is best ignored in our analysis. (See Debus, 55-89; Gordon; Burney, *Notes*, 163-69.)

Structure

I. Narrative setting	21
A. Gathering of forces	21a
B. Statement of mission: reclaim north for Rehoboam	21b
II. Report of prophetic commission	22-24a
A. Prophetic word formula	22
B. Divine address to prophet	23-24a
1. Commission	23
2. Message for delivery	24a
a. Messenger formula	24aα^1
b. Tactical orders: make no war	24aα^2-β
III. Report of people's obedience: mission stayed	24b

Although this unit presupposes to an extent the subject matter in vv. 1-20, it develops a new theme after the rounded conclusion to the main Jeroboam tradition. In distinction from v. 20, this scene refers to the "house of Judah" (v. 21) and adds "tribe of Benjamin" (however, the Greek at v. 20b includes this phrase). These variants suggest that vv. 21-24 may take up an originally separate tradition. One may see its end in the shift to a more straightforward chronistic style with entirely different subject matter in v. 25.

The unit is simply structured. It builds the action with typical narrative tenses (*waw*-conversive, *wyqṭl* verbs) and includes little description and only minimal speech. The opening provides the setting—Rehoboam is gathering his forces together in preparation for a military campaign. In this situation, we hear a prophetic commission in which the "word of God" charges Shemaiah, a "man of God," to deliver an order to Rehoboam staying the reprisal attempt. The order is grounded by Yahweh's admission that "this thing is from me" (v. 24), presumably explaining that the departure of the northerners from Solomon's house was consistent with divine wish. We must infer that Shemaiah carried out his commission, for the narrator immediately adds that the king and his forces obey. They "went home again, according to the word of the Lord" (v. 24b).

The lack of narrative detail highlights the divine word. Even here, the narrator pays no attention to the circumstances of its reception beyond the formulaic "the word of God came to Shemaiah" (v. 22a). As readers, we simply overhear a private word from God to prophet. Everything leads up to this word-moment, and quickly leads away from it.

Genre

This unit is storylike, but has no developed plot. At best it might be a scene from a no longer extant (→) story, as Šanda (*Könige,* 347) suggested. It is clearly wrong to speak of a (→) legend (against Würthwein, *Könige,* 150), since the unit is too undeveloped to show even the minimal narrative features of dramatic tension and resolution. It seems best to designate the unit as a REPORT, while granting that its style and substance tend toward story. The main content, of course, lies in the REPORT of PROPHETIC COMMISSION set now in this brief account of Rehoboam's planned, and stayed, reprisal actions against the northern rebels. This prophetic genre is frequently found in narratives about prophets (see Exodus 3; Hosea 1; Amos 7:15-17) and often in the books of Kings (→ 1 Kgs 19:15-18; 21:17-19; 2 Kgs 9:1-3). The example here in 1 Kgs 12:22-24a is entirely typical. It opens with the PROPHETIC WORD FORMULA ("the word of God came to . . .") and moves to a COMMISSIONING FORMULA ("Go," or "Say to so-and-so," identifying the addressee). Then follows the message or oracle to be delivered in the name of God, introduced with the typical MESSENGER FORMULA, "Thus says the Lord." Sometimes a report of prophetic commission goes on to describe its execution. More often, such is assumed. Thus the *content* of the divine message stands at the center of interest. Prophetic speech has its roots in a direct charge from God and may imply, if not evoke, the image of the prophet-messenger who proclaims the decrees of a council of heavenly beings surrounding Yahweh (Mullen, 222-26; cf. 1 Kgs 22:19-22; Isa 6:1-10; Jer 23:18, 22). Reports of prophetic commission appear mostly in narrative contexts (1 Kgs 19:15-18; 21:17-19; 2 Kgs 2:3-4; 20:4-6; Isa 7:3-9).

A stylized motif perhaps stands in the background. Elsewhere, biblical narrators will describe a consultation before battle in which one asks for tactical guidance through the oracles managed by priests (2 Sam 2:1; 1 Sam 30:7-8; report of (→) oracular inquiry). Similar scenes involve a "prophet" (*nābîʾ*) or "man of God" (*ʾîš hāʾĕlōhîm*) who may be consulted (1 Kgs 22:5-6; cf. 20:14) or who may offer unsolicited oracles (20:13, 22, 28). With prophetic figures especially, such stock scenes usually stress the correspondence between prophetic oracle and subsequent events. In 12:24, however, the phrase "according to the word of the Lord" indicates obedience to a prophetic word rather than its fulfillment (cf. 1 Kgs 17:5, 15; Jer 13:2; Jonah 3:3 with 1 Kgs 14:18; 15:29; 16:12).

Setting

It is difficult to imagine an independent setting for this unit. It is possibly reworked from an older report of a military campaign (Grønbaek), or it may have originally been attached in some different way to the main tradition in vv. 1-20, or it may be simply a late insert (Schüpphaus, 19-21; Dietrich, 114 n. 6; Würthwein, *Könige,* 150; Noth, *Könige,* 279-80; Debus, 34; Gray, *Kings,* 299). In any case, it is doubtful that such reports of military events, even styled with emphasis on the prophetic word, would have been created and transmitted apart from some larger literary work, oral or written. The literary context in the books of Kings is now of most consequence anyway. The report follows on, and depends for its sense upon, the story of Jeroboam's rise and the kingdom's dissolution, vv. 1-20. It comes as a second response by Rehoboam to the refusal of the northern Israelites to submit to his rule (the first was reported in v. 18). The report also provides a second glimpse of Yahweh's role in the whole affair (the first was in v. 15).

Intention

From these considerations, it is clear that the report in context intends to explain the no doubt surprising absence of reprisals against the north as the result of a prophetic command from God. The report is clearly meant to be less historical than edifying. Even if a very late addition to Jeroboam's reign, the report reinforces a point already made in v. 15 and implicit in the horizon defined by 11:29-40. Yahweh himself ordained the split in the Solomonic kingdom. A surprising accent is that despite his brash and culpable actions in vv. 1-19, Rehoboam in the aftermath is quickened by a prophet's voice and obedient to an unsolicited oracle from Yahweh. This suggestion is consistent with the full summary of Rehoboam's reign in 14:21-31, where the man himself is not attacked, and responsibility for transgressions against God are laid at the feet of the people.

Bibliography

J. Debus, *Sünde Jerobeams* (see listing at 12:1-20); W. Dietrich, *Prophetie und Geschichte* (see listing at "Introduction to 1 Kings"); G. Fohrer, *Prophetenerzählungen*, 18-19 (see listing at 11:26-40); R. P. Gordon, "Source Study in 1 Kings 12:24a-n (LXX)," *Transactions, Glasglow University Oriental Society* 25 (1973 [ed. 1976]) 59-70; J. H. Grønbaek, "Benjamin und Juda, Erwägungen zu 1 Kön xii 21-24," *VT* 15 (1965) 421-36; E. T. Mullen, Jr., *The Assembly of the Gods: The Divine Council in Canaanite and Early Hebrew Literature* (HSM 24; Chico: Scholars Press, 1980); J. Schüpphaus, "Prophetengeschichten" (see listing at "Introduction to 1 Kings").

REPORTS OF JEROBOAM'S BUILDING ACTIVITIES, 12:25-32

Structure

I. Report of city building	25
A. Concerning Shechem	25a
B. Concerning Penuel	25b
II. Account of establishing shrines	26-30
A. The problem: Jeroboam's thoughts	26-27
1. Narrative introduction	26a
2. Jeroboam's thoughts	26b-27
a. Possible reversion of kingdom to Rehoboam	26b-27a
b. Consequences for Jeroboam	27b
B. The solution: Jeroboam's actions	28-29
1. Construction of golden calves	28a
2. Presentation speech	28b
3. Installation of golden calves	29
C. Results	30
1. Narrator's evaluative comment	30a
2. Description of pilgrimage to the shrines	30b
III. Report of further cultic establishments	31-32
A. Concerning high place (*bāmôt*) shrines	31

1. Construction of shrines	31a
2. Appointment of priests	31b
B. Concerning Bethel	32
1. Appointment of feast day	32aα[1]
2. Offering of sacrifice	32aα[2]
3. Epitomizing conclusion	32aβ-b
a. Sacrificing	32aβ
b. Priests from high places	32b

This unit stands apart from the previous one (vv. 21-24) because of a complete shift in subject matter and literary style. Without clear transition (the *RSV* "then" in v. 25a is an interpretation of the simple Hebrew conjunction *wĕ*), we plunge into the midst of a matter-of-fact chronistic statement about Jeroboam's building of fortified cities (v. 25; see 1 Kgs 9:15b, 17-19 and parallels cited there). What follows in vv. 26-30 is related only loosely to the theme of building, and in style seems more storylike. This material on shrine building, like vv. 1-20, portrays the king as "taking counsel" (v. 28). Then vv. 31-32 break the sense of narrative and revert to reportorial detail and a repeated, colorless use of the verb "make" (*'āśâ,* twice in v. 31, once in v. 32; the *RSV* disguises the repetition by translating with "appoint"). Finally, v. 33 repeats in large part the content of v. 32, while echoing in the phrase "devised of his own heart" the similar perspective of v. 26. Most commentators have taken the verse as a redactional transition to ch. 13 (otherwise, Montgomery, *Kings,* 259, without explanation).

All these considerations support the view that the basic unit is vv. 25-32, and that this section is a compilation of distinct units of tradition probably from various sources and ages. The author-editor has stamped the compilation with his Judean perspective and provided a general thematic rubric—Jeroboam's building activities (cities and cultic centers)—along with a theological appraisal.

The unit presents a series of topics, with no clear introduction or conclusion, and little internal shaping. We move from a note about Jeroboam's building (or fortifying) two cities (I, v. 25) to a double section dealing with his establishing cult centers at Dan and Bethel. The first of these sections (II, vv. 26-30) could be a fragment from a larger account. It offers a glimpse, relatively rare in the Bible, of a character's motivation. The scene hangs on a rudimentary plot line: Jeroboam fears the future, namely, that for religious reasons the people will in time revert to Rehoboam's leadership. His way of avoiding this political consequence is to establish cult centers to rival the one great Solomonic shrine in Jerusalem (→ 1 Kings 6–9). By implication the action moves from problem to resolution in three neat stages: Jeroboam's thoughts (II.A, vv. 26-27), his actions (II.B, vv. 28-29), and their results (II.C, v. 30). The theme has a double edge. Jeroboam's political problem clearly stems from an evaluation of *religious* sentiments, and his solution is a *religious* action which is to reap *political* dividends. From this perspective, the comment and description of pilgrimage (II.C, v. 30) narrow the focus. Singled out from a Jerusalemite perspective is a single religious motif—the shrines "became a sin." Evidently, to the author-editor the religious implications are more important than the political.

This simplification of focus continues in the second little section dealing with cult centers (III, vv. 31-32). V. 31 presents actions which can in context only be read as "sin" (*ḥaṭṭā'*). Jeroboam constructs shrines ("high places") and appoints non-Levitical officials to manage their activities. Our attention rivets on Bethel, Dan having been forgotten in v. 32a. Descriptive detail (shrine, priests, special festival) is followed by an epitomizing conclusion (v. 32aβ-b) marked by a shift from reportorial *wyqṭl* verbs to simple perfect forms, *qṭl* and *wqṭl*. Here we look back on the actions at Bethel (sacrifices) and draw together the motifs of "high places" and non-Levitical priests from v. 31. Jeroboam placed "priests of the high places" at Bethel.

Genre

This unit is a literary miscellany, a compilation of different traditions carried by various genres. Designating the unit as consisting in "extracts from annals" (Donner, 383) or as "official notices" heavily redacted by Judahite editors (Debus, 37) gives too much stress to hypothetical sources among royal archival materials. "Historical resumé" (Gray, *Kings*, 312) seems to ignore the quite self-contained, storylike qualities of vv. 26-30, and especially their dramatic and hardly "historical" interest in the inner thoughts of Jeroboam. It is best to look at the whole as miscellany, and to recognize within the whole two important genres: REPORT of building activities, v. 25, and of cultic establishments, vv. 31-32; fragment of a STORY, vv. 26-30.

Setting

Originally, reports of royal building activities might have been based on archival records of the monarchy (Montgomery, *Kings*, 254; cf. 6:2–7:51 and full discussion there). Perhaps they would have found a secondary literary setting in longer chronistic records, including commemorative inscriptions and chronicles of Judean and Israelite kings (see reference to "chronicles" in 14:19 and elsewhere in regnal summaries, e.g., 15:23; 22:39; full discussion at 6:1–7:51). There is little reason to doubt that the report in 12:25 stemmed from such records, probably kept in royal libraries. Vv. 31-32 may have had a similar background, although now the report stands in a heavily edited and tendentious form. Originally, the fragment of story in vv. 26-30 may have had its setting in popular tale-telling.

Hoffmann (p. 73) concludes that vv. 26-32 are a Dtr "fiction" created to define the "sin of Jeroboam" so often alluded to in the reigns of his successors and finally eliminated by Josiah (2 Kgs 23:15-20). Whether or not he is correct on the matter of literary origin, Hoffmann rightly highlights the crucial role which this miscellany, vv. 25-32, plays in the Dtr author-editor's treatment of Jeroboam's reign and the entire history of the northern kingdom. The establishment of rival shrines follows the fundamentally political telling of the dissolution of Solomon's monarchy, and precedes a prophetlike judgment brought against one of these royal shrines, the "altar" at Bethel (1 Kings 13). In context, then, we are led to see Jeroboam's kingly accomplishment as a pivotal problem in the eyes of the author-editor.

Intention

The original intentions of the smaller units that make up this miscellany are a matter of speculation. In its setting in the books of Kings, however, we may see two main purposes for the larger compilation. The miscellany recounts how Jeroboam consolidated his political strength in the north and projects Jeroboam as transgressor against Yahweh. From his exilic perspective, the author-editor points us toward ch. 13 and beyond, stringing evaluative comments like flawed pearls: 12:30; 13:33-34; 14:16. The king who began with Yahweh's favor now is creating the occasions for his disfavor.

Bibliography

See listing at 12:1-20. H.-D. Hoffmann, *Reform,* 59-73 (see listing at "Introduction to 1 Kings").

JUDGMENT AGAINST BETHEL, 12:33 – 13:34

Structure

I. Jeroboam and man of God: the oracle against Bethel	12:33–13:10
A. Narrative setting	12:33–13:1
1. Jeroboam at Bethel	12:33
2. Judahite man of God at Bethel	13:1
B. Prophetic announcements	2-3
1. First announcement	2
a. Narrative introduction	2aα
b. Prophecy against the altar	2aβ-b
1) Invocation of addressee (altar)	2aβ^1
2) Messenger formula	2aβ^2
3) Message: promise of desecration	2b
2. Second announcement	3
a. Narrative introduction	3aα
b. Announcement of sign	3aβ-b
1) Introduction	3aβ
2) Sign proper	3b
C. Confirmations	4-10
1. Miracles at Bethel (power of man of God; confirmation of oracle)	4-6
a. Withered hand	4
b. Actualization of sign	5
c. Restored hand	6
2. Aftermath (obedience of man of God)	7-10
1. King's invitation: temptation	7
b. Speech of refusal: resistance to temptation	8-9
1) Refusal	8
2) Reason: Yahweh's prohibitions	9
c. Man of God's departure in obedience	10
II. Judahite man of God and Bethelite prophet: oracle against Bethel confirmed	11-32
A. Bethelite prophet and sons: preparations to find man of God	11-13
1. Narrative setting	11a

2. Man of God's actions reported	11b
3. Preparations to find man of God	12-13
B. Bethelite prophet and man of God: the transgression	14-23
1. Scene at oak tree	14-18
a. Narrative introduction	14a
b. Identifying exchange	14b
c. Dialogue	15-18a
1) The Bethelite's invitation home	15
2) Man of God's reply	16-17
a) Narrative introduction	$16a\alpha^{1}$
b) Refusal	$16a\alpha^{2}$-b
c) Reason: divine prohibition	17
3) Bethelite prophet's response	18a
a) Narrative introduction	$18a\alpha^{1}$
b) Report of prophetic commission	$18a\alpha^{2}$-β
d. Narrator's comment: the prophet's lie	18b
2. Scene at Bethelite's table	19-23
a. Acceptance of invitation home (transgression of divine prohibition)	19
b. Results: prophetic judgment speech	20-22
1) Narrative setting (prophetic word formula)	20
2) Bethelite's prophecy of punishment against man of God	21-22
a) Narrative introduction	$21a\alpha$
b) Speech proper	$21a\beta$-22
(1) Messenger formula	$21a\beta$
(2) Announcement of punishment	21b-22
(a) Reason	21b-22a
(b) Punishment	22b
c. Aftermath: leavetaking	23
C. Prophecy fulfilled	24-26
1. Man of God's death	24
2. Death reported to Bethelite prophet	25
3. Speech of recognition	26
a. Narrative introduction	$26a\alpha$
b. Speech proper	$26a\beta$-b
1) Interpretative identification	$26a\beta$
2) Prophecy fulfillment formula	26b
D. Bethelite prophet and sons: preparations to bury man of God	27
E. Bethelite prophet and corpse of man of God: confirmation of power and oracle	28-32
1. Body found	28
2. Body buried and mourned	29-30

3. Bethelite prophet's instructions for own burial	31-32
a. Narrative introduction	31aα
b. Speech	31aβ-32
1) Instructions for burial	31aβ-b
2) Explanation: confirmation of oracle against Bethel	32
III. Concluding evaluative comments: consequences for King Jeroboam	33-34

The opening of this unit is uncertain. In v. 1, "and behold" can hardly have been the original beginning (Gross, 100); nor is 12:33 a likely beginning, since it repeats motifs from 12:26, 30-32 and seems rather more a redactional transition to ch. 13, as many have argued. At the other extreme, 13:33-34 strike an evaluative tone and reportorial style which contrast sharply with the folkloristic narrative in vv. 1-32. These verses also look back to 12:30-32, repeating some of the phrases found there, and have little direct connection with the main tradition in ch. 13 (Dietrich, 114ff.). Most critics thus distinguish older tradition in vv. 1-32, now bracketed and reworked a number of times.

The history of this supposedly pre-Dtr tradition is much in dispute. Scholars see tensions within vv. 1-7, and between these verses and the rest of the chapter. For example, vv. 3, 5 appear to interrupt the sequence of vv. 4 and 6, and subsequent events in vv. 11-32 completely ignore the themes of vv. 1-7, the Bethelite altar and the king's confrontation with the man of God. Moreover, v. 2 may be heavily influenced by 2 Kgs 23:15-18 and the Dtr author-editor. Beyond these considerations is the unresolved question of a possible relationship in the history of tradition to Amos 7:10-17.

Since the evidence is equivocal, critics differ widely on what to make of these problems and internal tensions. Würthwein has most recently suggested even more inconsistencies in the tradition. On the opposite side, Simon defends artistic unity in the text. The plain fact is that both the unity and antiquity of ch. 13 in various reconstructed forms have over the years been affirmed and denied (see summary of research in Gross, 100-6; Lemke, 303-4). It is fair to say that the evidence is ambiguous, and judgments have often been arbitrary. Certainly from the standpoint of style, vv. 1-32 stand closely linked together. The difficulty lies in understanding the sometimes confusing movements and developments in the narrative.

Whatever its prehistory may have been, earlier forms of this tradition are hidden. It seems best to accept the present text, look for continuity, allow for tensions, and recognize that even though 12:33 and 13:33-34 may stem from redactional activity, they contribute to a final and sensible shaping of the tradition. Our structural analysis has tried to capture a sense of wholeness in the final form of the text without denying its complex stages of growth.

Broadly seen, the structure of the unit is clear. A narrative setting (I.A, 12:33–13:1) brings Jeroboam to Bethel and up against an unnamed Judahite "man of God" who announces desecration for the shrine and a confirmatory "sign" (I.B, vv. 2-3). The prophet's words are apparently confirmed by a whole series of wondrous happenings at Bethel (I.C, vv. 4-10) and by the unhappy fate of this man of God in his strange dealings with an old Bethelite prophet (II, vv. 11-32). The Bethelite treacherously induces the Judahite oracle-giver to disobey part of his original commission (three times cited, vv. 9, 17, 22), and as a result he dies by Yahweh's death-dealing lion. But to the Bethelite who perpetrated such a bizarre chain of events, the outcome authenticates this Judahite man of God, his commission, and his oracle against Bethel (vv. 26, 32).

The main elements of structure seem to hang on these movements which confirm the original prophetic pronouncement, but not simply or without surprises. The man of God himself first arouses these expectations. He announces a "sign that the Lord has spoken" (v. 3). Together with its fulfillment in v. 5, the Judahite's words form a context of expectancy by which to understand the withering and restoration of the king's hand (vv. 4, 6). Not only a destroyed altar (v. 5), but a withered and restored hand, and perhaps the man of God himself, may be "signs" (Simon).

Yet our expectations are not directly met. Events move in puzzling ways (II, vv. 11-32) and their sense will not be clear until near the end of the narrative. When the old Bethelite prophet utters his speech of recognition ("It is the man of God. . . ," v. 26) attesting to the legitimacy of the Judahite, and when he bases his own burial instructions on the conviction that the oracle against Bethel will come true, we suddenly see with a prophet's eyes. The sense of ending gives point to beginning and middle, as it were. *Our* insight, gained with the Bethelite's, overrides what might otherwise seem to be a curious break between vv. 1-10 and 11-32. The dealings of prophet with prophet confirm the dealings of prophet with king (and royal shrine).

Yet this larger interpretative perspective ignores or bypasses the motivations given the characters. Indeed, difficulties in understanding the flow of the narrative mount up and to some extent confound this broad unity. The narrator seems to lodge his point in the ironic relation between his thematic structure and the reader's expectations for narrative events. We expect one thing and get another. We suspect one motivation, and then become unsure. The actions issue in one point: the word of Yahweh stands—unwittingly affirmed by a deceiver of a prophet (the Bethelite) and maintained by the man of God, the deceived one (the Judahite). Oracle, sign, disobedience, even punishment and death all attend to the divine word. It is as though God's word triumphs over all obstacles—over the king who naturally resisted its implications for the cult at Bethel; over the Judahite man of God who disobeyed his commission, and paid with his life; over the Bethelite prophet, who sought to deceive, and perhaps even to undermine the commission of the oracle-giver (Simon, 106).

We may glimpse the irony in the narrative details. At the beginning, the narrator uses a bracketing effect to set the stage for the main narration. He tells us that the king "went up to the altar to burn incense" (12:33b), and later, in a circumstantial participial clause, that "Jeroboam was standing by the altar to burn incense" (13:1b). In between, the man of God thrusts his bulk into this ceremonial calm, transforming the festive moment (note *ḥag*, "festival," in 12:33) into mystery. Like an apparition ("and behold . . ."; cf. Gen 15:17; 2 Kgs 2:11), a man of God darts out from Judah, impelled by divine command ("cried against the altar by the word of the Lord . . ."), nothing more. With a surrealistic obsession, the Judahite completely ignores the king and the circumstances. He narrows his gaze on the altar and sees not stone, but some impenitent miscreant. Still, his first words suggest hope and salvation: "O altar, altar . . . behold, a son shall be born to the house of David . . ." (cf. Isa 11:1-10; Jer 23:5-6; Isa 7:14-17). But the Judahite speaks parody. The words develop into polemical sarcasm. Instead of hope, we hear of desecration and violation. Burial sites will be desecrated—disinterred bones will be burned on this altar. And in this unholy sacrifice, the altar itself will be soiled, its sanctity violated with human remains. The man of God quickly follows his oracle with an announcement of a "sign" (*môpēt*), added as in other prophetic examples to confirm a word just spoken. *Môpēt* is an event which presages the fulfillment of an oracle. As though in proleptic vision, we see in the sign the events of oracle coming to pass. The "sign" dramatizes and makes urgent the proclamation. Thus, in the destruction of the altar and scattering of ashes is prefigured the final desecration when priests will be offered as sacrifice and men's bones burned instead of incense.

As expected, the "sign" materializes (v. 5; cf. Isa 38:7-8; 2 Kgs 20:8-11; 1 Sam 2:34; [4:11]). But in terms of narrative flow, the sign materializes awkwardly, pressed between the king's resistance and the withering-restoration of his hand (vv. 4, 6). Significant powers are at work, as though the king's withered hand is in itself another kind of sign—not so much confirming the oracle as attesting the power of the oracle-giver. With Jeroboam, we must recognize this man of God and his oracle as power to be dealt with respectfully, to be tapped for healing as well as for destruction. Ironically, *we* know this much about the situation, but the old Bethelite yet to come does not.

A stage has been set: oracle given, power of oracle-giver manifest, fulfillment presaged in signs, Jeroboam's resistance overcome. The king quickly moves to invite this man of God home (v. 7). A genuine transition, the scene looks backward, reflecting Jeroboam's changed attitude, and forward, revealing new information of import for subsequent events. The Judahite operates with a peculiar commission which alienates him from those things touched by desecration. He must not eat or drink, or return to Judah by the way he came, as though to do such would somehow violate his status as emissary and sign-giver. If the harbinger of destruction cannot tarry or retrace his own steps, how much less his tidings (Simon, 91)? So, we are given a picture of resolute obedience and the divine prohibitions on which it rests—and the hint of a word which is irrevocable. The scene closes with its mystery intact; the man of God wanders away by a different route, in obedience, and without intimacy of any sort. He bodies forth in his own action the impact of his alienating word against the altar (cf. Šanda, *Könige* I, 353; Rofé, 160). The mystery suggests that he has become a "sign" as well as a sign-giver.

The next major scenes (II, vv. 11-32) are clearly marked with a change in locale, new characters, and a new departure shown in narrative syntax: "Now there dwelt an old prophet in Bethel" (v. 11a; participial phrase, subject first; cf. Judg 13:2; 1 Sam 1:1). Yet the narrator recapitulates for us the events at Bethel. The prophet (always *nābî'*, "prophet," never *'îš hā'ĕlōhîm*, "man of God") learns of the situation and sets about to entice the man of God away from his strict path. So commission nurtures possible transgression. We do not yet know the Bethelite's motivation. But he takes a measure of some sort. He inquires of the man of God's whereabouts, goes and finds him, and issues an invitation exactly like that given by King Jeroboam. Of course, the man of God refuses, as he had done with Jeroboam. Yet deliberate deception sets aside the refusal, and with surprisingly little effort. The narrator's voice, intrusive, puts the matter succinctly: "But he lied to him" (v. 18b). The reader, however, is left to wonder again at the Bethelite prophet's motivation.

Falling for the fakery, the Judahite man of God returns home with the Bethelite, accepting in this case what he refused from the king. Suddenly, this same man of God—like the altar previously—is a miscreant. A prophecy of judgment, fully from Yahweh, spoken by the Bethelite prophet of Yahweh, and not a lie, tumbles him suddenly from his station of resolute obedience (II.B.2, vv. 19-23). If the Judahite somehow in obedience was a "sign," in disobedience he becomes merely ordinary. Even so, the attachments of wondrous power do not drop away. Though violent, his punishment of death is tucked inside a serene, nature-stopping miracle: the lion kills, but does not eat the corpse or tear at the ass standing near it. The two animals, the one an attacker, the other a mute reminder of the slain Judahite, stand beside the corpse like silent sentinels of some unspoken mystery (vv. 24-25, 28). It is a fitting climax to the narrative, for the man of God is as powerful in death as he is in life. But in what sense?

The old Bethelite prophet ignores the miracle and sees the meaning, apparently. In a surprising turnabout, the prophet recognizes the beginnings of the fulfillment of prophecy against the man of God (vv. 21-22, 26). With characteristically steady resolve, the Bethelite sets about to provide a proper burial for the slain man of God, thus completing the fulfillment of prophecy: the Judahite is buried at Bethel, away from his family land (cf. v. 22b), in the deceiver's own burial plot. It is not entirely a matter of giving honor, either. Seeing something else in this bizarre affair, the old Bethelite gives his sons instructions that he himself is to be laid out in the selfsame plot, next to the man of God, "my bones beside his bones." Why? Because the man of God is reckoned as legitimate and authoritative—and his oracle against Bethel is pregnant with its own fulfillment. With consummate irony, the strange alienation imposed upon the Judahite (vv. 1-10) turns to intimacy in the Bethelite grave. The prophet has seen that the Judahite in life was a harbinger and a portent of destruction. In death he is still that, and his power lingers. The old Bethelite prophet who had kept his counsel when first told of the man of God (v. 11) now becomes a spokesman for the dead man's prophecy (v. 32), as though it were confirmed in punishment and guarded by the lion and the ass. The bizarre chain of events has its point after all, the narrative its sense of ending which gives meaning to the whole.

Thus, the Judahite man of God has a double dramatic function. He announces the oracle of doom for the Bethel altar, and in his strange fate, confirms its irrevocability. Once spoken, judgment is necessary and sure, having been decided by Yahweh (Jepsen, 180). And the Bethelite prophet? Despite himself, he affirms the truth of that same oracle, and the legitimacy of the Judahite so quickly and wrathfully dismissed by God. Put another way, the fulfillment of the Bethelite's word of judgment in the death of the Judahite man of God is another "sign," the means to affirm the oracle against Bethel. The divine word will win out, whatever the wayward actions of men, even prophets, may be!

Of course, the concluding editorial and evaluative comments (III, vv. 33-34) make a slightly different point. They focus on the strange events as illustrative of

Jeroboam's continued sinful support of the Bethel cult. Despite the oracle and its confirmations in deed and death, the king goes on as before, making priests for Bethel, supporting its activities, such that "this thing became sin to the house of Jeroboam" (v. 34).

If the content of this tradition remains in many ways impenetrable, the narrator's scene-building techniques are plain. Each scene consists of two characters, or one character and a group which functions dramatically as one person. There are three main scenes:

(1)	I, 12:33–13:10:	man of God; Jeroboam the king
(2)	II.B, 13:14-23:	Bethelite prophet; Judahite man of God in life
(3)	II.E, 13:28-32:	Bethelite prophet and Judahite man of God in death

In between these main scenes we find two interim scenes, each portraying the Bethelite prophet with his sons (II.A, vv. 11-13; II.D, v. 27). In addition, scenes 2 and 3, which cover the path from life to death, frame a climactic centerpiece: the death of the man of God, its report to the Bethelite prophet, and the latter's cry of recognition (II.C, vv. 24-26). The striking balance is clear in the following outline:

First main scene:	man of God, Jeroboam, and the altar (I, vv. 1-10)
Interim scene:	prophet and his sons (II.A, vv. 11-13)
Second main scene:	prophet and man of God (II.B, vv. 14-23)
CLIMAX:	death of man of God (II.C, vv. 24-26)
Interim scene:	prophet and his sons (II.D, v. 27)
Third main scene:	prophet and man of God (II.E, vv. 28-32)

(Note a similar structural analysis by Simon, 104-5, who considers 2 Kgs 23:16-18 to be part of the original tradition, and who presses symmetry at the cost of reading into several of the events a portentous value. Sign and portent become integrative principles of interpretation, even where the text gives no explicit indication. While many of Simon's insights have found their way into my own interpretation, the tradition finally resists neat packaging. De Vries, 59-60, offers a different structural outline, without stating any justification. See also the outline by Gross, 107.)

In the latter sections, vv. 11-32, the dramatic movement from a tension to its resolution is fairly clear. But because of the context given by vv. 1-10, this plot movement cannot be simply conceived. Part of the action seems to turn on the question of whether the Judahite man of God will follow explicitly the terms of his commission from Yahweh (vv. 8-9). Repeated allusions to these prohibitions emphasize the matter (vv. 11, 16-17, 21-22, 26a). The question really is whether this man of God will remain as he was first presented: energized by the word of Yahweh alone, driven by commission, obligated by necessity. The answer comes in his disobedience, the prophecy of judgment on him, and his death, which is explicitly recognized as fulfillment. Yet, the material in vv. 28-30, 31-32 stands within another dramatic circle: confirmations of the oracle against Bethel and expectations aroused by vv. 1-10. In the latter portions of the unit, this opening theme emerges again in the fate of the man of God. Both dramatic movements, obedience to divine commission and the oracle against the altar, climax in vv. 24-26. It may not be inappropriate, therefore, that this scene stands out as the only one free of human interaction. We watch the moment from a distance, almost dispassionately; and the literary style is similar: descriptive, without dialogue, carrying only indirect allusion to a report given the Bethelite prophet (v. 26aα). Even the prophet's speech of recognition (v. 26aβ-b) could just as well be private thought.

Thus the narrative carries complex focus. The tradition cannot center simply in obedience/disobedience or "unconditional claim of God's command/prohibition" (Gross, 108, 124). Nor can it simply revolve around confirming the oracle given at Bethel. What emerges in the conjoining of these two themes is a point about the divine word itself: the oracle stands—inviolate, alien, and irrevocable, quite without the ambiguity and ambivalence which arise from intimacy with another. The man of God's actions in the first major scene are paradigmatic for this impersonality of divine word. His lapse from commission in the second and third scenes only confirms the paradigm.

Genre

Despite certain loose ends in the plot, it is clear that this unit is a PROPHETIC LEGEND, that is, a STORY centrally involving prophet(s), and is interested less in the artistic development of plot and character than in the wonderful, marvelous deeds of, and edifying example to be found in, its heroes (see Dietrich; Gray, *Kings*, 320; Noth, *Deuteronomistic History*, 68-69; Würthwein, *Könige*, 168). For other examples of prophetic legend, see 1 Kgs 14:1-18; 17:1–19:21; 2 Kgs 1:2-16; 2:1-25. Rofé (pp. 158-60) designates the unit as parable, a story which teaches a definite moral lesson: the man of God is God's messenger (= angel) and his behavior must conform to this role. Rofé's identification of a single moral for a complex narrative seems too restrictive, however, and ignores the import of v. 32, which goes in quite another direction. Other attempts at precise generic identification rest as a rule on competing reconstructions of a presumed original narrative. So Hossfeld (p. 26) speaks of "didactive narrative" for vv. 1-2, 4, 6-19, 23b-26a, 27-31. De Vries (pp. 59-61) reconstructs an original story not including vv. 3, 5, 18b ("he lied to him"), 32b, and argues for "prophet-authorization narrative," a type of legend that demonstrates the power of a prophet to prevail over institutional rivals. Both scholars reduce resonances in the legend too much.

This example of prophetic legend carries within itself other smaller generic units. Of structural and interpretative importance is the PROPHETIC ANNOUNCEMENT OF SIGN, v. 3, a type of prophetic speech normally consisting of three main elements: (1) a demonstrative phrase declaring the presence or future appearance of a "sign" from God: "This is the sign (for you) from Yahweh . . ." (Jer. 44:29a; Isa. 38:7a=2 Kgs 20:9a; Isa 37:30=2 Kgs 19:29); (2) a subordinate clause indicating the significance or purpose of the sign, e.g., "that the Lord has spoken," or "that the Lord will do this thing" (Isa 38:7b=2 Kgs 20:9b; Jer 44:29b); the immediate context may be enough to supply the meaning, however; (3) the description of a wondrous event or state of affairs which is to be taken as a "sign" (1 Sam 2:34; Isa 37:30b-32=2 Kgs 19:29b-31; Isa 38:8a=2 Kgs 20:9b; Jer 44:30). It is not unusual for the fulfillment of the "sign" to be noted as well (Isa 38:8b= 2 Kgs 20:10-11). Announcements of "signs" appear in the context of PROPHECIES

OF SALVATION or PUNISHMENT, and are always offered as confirmation of the prophecy. In this legend of 1 Kings 13, the announcement of sign and its fulfillment in effect confirms the oracle just spoken to the altar at Bethel. This announcement of sign sets a thematic focus that dominates the legend—even if the reader clearly learns of this only at the end of the bizarre series of events (v. 32).

In vv. 20-22, the legend carries a PROPHECY OF PUNISHMENT. The clearest examples show analogues to indictment and verdict of trial procedures. Thus the prophet states the accusation or declares a reason for judgment ("Because [*ya'an kî*] you have disobeyed . . ."), then follows with the actual announcement of punishment, formulated variously (". . . your body shall not come to the tomb of your fathers," v. 22b). In this case, the typical MESSENGER FORMULA heads up the whole speech (cf. 1 Sam 2:27-36; Amos 7:16-17). Note, too, that the prophetic speech is now part of a REPORT introduced by the PROPHETIC WORD FORMULA, v. 20, "The word of the Lord came to. . . ," which alludes to the experience of receiving the divine word and prepares the reader for hearing that divine communication (cf. 1 Kgs 16:1; 17:2; 18:1; 19:9). The language suggests, but does not require, the familiar image of prophet-messenger who proclaims judgments and decrees issued by Yahweh and his council of heavenly beings (→ 12:21-24 and bibliography there; 22:19-22; Isa 6:1-10; Jer 23:18, 22). Prophecies of punishment often appear in the books of Kings (e.g., 1 Kgs 14:7b-11; 20:36, 42; 21:19, 20b-22; 2 Kgs 22:16-17). They seem to have been a favorite literary genre for the final editors and collectors of the traditions in Kings as they told the "history" of the monarchy from a prophetic perspective, that is, as history moved, shaped, and guided by prophetic words and deeds (cf. 1 Kgs 11:9-13; 2 Kgs 17:13-18).

The prophecy of punishment in 1 Kings 13 finds its explicit notice of fulfillment in vv. 24-25, which brings out, in addition, a typical ORACLE FULFILLMENT FORMULA: "(so-and-so happened) according to the word which the Lord spoke to (so-and-so) him" (v. 26b). This formula often appears in Kings, as an original part of narrative traditions (e.g., 1 Kgs 16:34; 17:16; 2 Kgs 1:17), or as an editorial device of the Dtr author-editor(s), as in 1 Kgs 15:29; 16:12; 22:38 (Dietrich, 58-61).

Finally, in passing, we should mention the fragment of a DIRGE, "Alas, my brother!" (*hôy 'āḥî,* v. 30b). The cry is apparently a stylized representation of mourning cries and laments which could well have been longer and more highly developed in their actual situation of usage among the people.

Setting

In oral tradition, legend would have originated and flourished in many different societal settings and would have found numerous occasions for use depending on the circumstances and aim of the narrators. This particular example of prophetic legend may have arisen among prophets in the north (Noth, *Könige,* 295), perhaps at Bethel (De Vries, 59-60). But the folkloristic features (Hossfeld, 25-26) suggest a wider provenance among the people. Since origins are so obscure, we may emphasize the literary setting in the books of Kings. The legend follows directly on the evaluative summary of Jeroboam's building activities, particularly his establishment of the cult at Bethel—a point of view picked up immediately in 13:33-34. In a way, the legend serves as a centerpiece in the author-editor's telling about the reign of Jeroboam. As such, it reflects a late perspective on the continuing failure of the monarchy in general and the fate of the northern kingdom in particular.

Intention

From what has been said, the important intention still visible to us has to do with the positioning of the legend in the Dtr history work, or the books of Kings. Because of its uncertain origins, we cannot very easily evaluate those speculative views of intention which rest on a reconstructed original text, for example, the suppositions of Hossfeld (p. 26), that it illustrates prophetic teaching about disobedience and punishment, or De Vries (p. 55), that it enhances belief in prophetic authority to challenge usurpations of Yahweh's supremacy. Clearly, in final form and in context, the legend inveighs against the cult at Bethel and sees Jeroboam's support of this cult as "sin" (vv. 33-34). It dramatizes a flaw in this reign despite the assertion that Jeroboam had his beginnings in Rehoboam's obstinacy, and Yahweh's mysterious overarching plan (ch. 12). Already condemned (12:30-32), the practice of Yahwistic cultic life at Bethel is roundly judged here as irrevocably destined for desecration. For the Dtr editor of Kings or perhaps later, the connection with King Josiah must have been made (v. 2; cf. 2 Kgs 23:15-18). The oracle is clear enough. But the actions of prophet and the fate of oracle-giver, quite without personalistic moralizing, serve a greater destiny. They dramatize the finality of this prophetic condemnation of Bethel. From this perspective the issue is syncretism (Jepsen), precisely that "sign" which the author-editors never tire of assaulting. The legend edifies in this way—it draws a "lesson" from history, so to speak. It seems quite wide of the mark to read the legend historically, as a story originally told to establish the authority of this Judahite intruder in Bethel (against De Vries, 61).

Bibliography

S. J. De Vries, *Prophet Against Prophet* (Grand Rapids: Eerdmans, 1978); W. Dietrich, *Prophetie und Geschichte* (see listing at "Introduction to 1 Kings"); G. Fohrer, *Prophetenerzählungen*, 20-24 (see listing at 11:26-40); W. Gross, "Lying Prophet and Disobedient Man of God in 1 Kgs 13: Role Analysis as an Instrument of Theological Interpretation of an O.T. Narrative Text," *Semeia* 15 (1979) 97-135; F. Hossfeld and I. Meyer, *Prophet gegen Prophet* (Fribourg: Schweizerisches Katholisches Bibelwerk, 1973); A. Jepsen, "Gottesmann und Prophet: Anmerkungen zum Kapitel 1. Könige 13," in *Probleme Biblische Theologie* (*Fest.* G. von Rad; ed. H. W. Wolff; Munich: Kaiser, 1971) 171-82; M. A. Klopfenstein, "1 Könige 13," in *Parrhēsia* (*Fest.* Karl Barth; ed. E. Busch et al.; Zurich: EVZ, 1966) 639-72; W. E. Lemke, "The Way of Obedience: I Kings 13 and the Structure of the Deuteronomistic History," in *Magnalia Dei: The Mighty Acts of God* (*Fest.* G. E. Wright; ed. F. M. Cross et al.; Garden City: Doubleday, 1976) 301-26; A. Rofé, "Classes in the Prophetical Stories: Didactic Legenda and Parable," in *Studies on Prophecy* (VTSup 26; 1974) 143-64; J. Schüpphaus, "Prophetengeschichten," 21-26 (see listing at "Introduction to 1 Kings"); U. Simon, "1 Kings 13: A Prophetic Sign—Denial and Persistence," *HUCA* 47 (1976) 81-117; E. Würthwein, "Die Erzählung vom Gottesmann aus Juda in Bethel: zur Komposition von I Könige 13," in *Wort und Geschichte* (*Fest.* K. Elliger; ed. H. Gese et al.; Neukirchen-Vluyn: Neukirchener, 1973) 181-90.

JUDGMENT AGAINST JEROBOAM, 14:1-18

Structure

I. Narrative crisis: son of Jeroboam sick	1
II. Coping with crisis: seeking a prophetic oracle	2-18
A. Preparations for consultation	2-4a
1. Jeroboam's orders to wife	2-3
a. Narrative introduction	2aα^1
b. Orders proper	2aα^2-3
2. Execution of orders	4a
B. Consultation with prophet Ahijah	4b-16
1. Description of circumstances	4b-5
a. Ahijah's frailty	4b
b. Ahijah's prior prophetic commission	5a
c. Wife's disguise	5b
2. Audience with Ahijah	6-16
a. Narrative introduction	6aα
b. First prophetic speech	6aβ-11
1) Introductory announcement	6aβ-b
2) Commissioning of wife as messenger	7-11
a) Instructions	7aα^1
b) Message: prophecy of punishment	7aα^2-11a
(1) Messenger formula	7aα^2
(2) Reason for judgment	7aβ-9
(3) Announcement of punishment on Jeroboam's house	10-11a
c) Concluding oracle statement	11b
c. Second prophetic speech	12-16
1) Instruction to Jeroboam's wife	12a
2) Announcement of judgment	12b-16
a) Concerning the child	12b-13
(1) Death	12b
(2) Mourning and burial	13a
(3) Explanation: measure of Jeroboam's disfavor	13b
b) Concerning Jeroboam's dynasty	14
c) Concerning Israel	15-16
(1) End in dispersal	15
(a) Exile	15a
(b) Reason: apostasy	15b
(2) End in abandonment	16
(a) Yahweh gives up	16a
(b) Reason: Jeroboam's sins	16b
C. Aftermath of consultation	17-18
1. Wife's departure, return to Tirzah	17a

2. First fulfillments of prophecy	17b-18
a. Death of child	17b
b. Mourning and burial	18a
c. Oracle fulfillment formula	18b

The beginning of this unit makes an abrupt shift in subject matter and style from the moralizing comments of 13:33-34. The storylike prose is linked to the foregoing only by a vague connective, "At that time . . ." (v. 1a). The unit clearly ends with v. 18, for the following vv. 19-20 provide a formulaic closing to the entire reign of Jeroboam.

Critics seem to agree that an old tradition has been heavily edited by the Dtr editor of Kings, especially in vv. 7-11, 14-16. Of late some have envisioned complex, multileveled stages of redaction (Dietrich, 51-54; Würthwein, *Könige*, 174-75), without reaching agreement, however. Since most disputes of this sort center on the speeches in vv. 7-16, even if one reached a consensus on these matters, the form of the unit as a whole would not be substantially affected. Thus, in this case, one gains no particular form-critical advantage in knowing exactly what the original content of the prophetic speeches might have been. We may analyze the final form of the tradition, recognizing its probable development by the Dtr author-editor (Hoffmann, 59 n. 2) in the blending of foci on the son of Jeroboam, the dynasty as a whole (vv. 10-11, 14a), and all Israel (vv. 14-16).

The key to seeing the structure of this unit lies in recognizing a minimal narrative framework (vv. 1-6, 17-18) which encases a dominant prophetic speech (vv. 7-16). The narrator begins with storylike plot: a problem (the king's son is ill) and the king's quick action to deal with the crisis. This dramatic tension drains away, however, with the long and complex speech of Ahijah the prophet. The speech falls into two parts (II.B.2.b, vv. 6-11; II.B.2.c, vv. 12-16), and the minimal narration which follows (II.C, vv. 17-18) does less to answer Jeroboam's question (v. 3) than it does to suggest fulfillment of a portion of Ahijah's prophecy. The unit, then, is not a developed narrative, but prophetic speech framed by narrative.

At the beginning, the narrator quickly and directly conveys the main problem and provides us with important information. An oracle is to be sought from a prophet (*nābî'*), but in disguise, and from the same prophet who prophesied Jeroboam's rule (cf. 11:29-39). The purpose? To find out what will become of the child. In a quick stroke, then, we (1) know the problem which drives the action, (2) have embarked on a course which promises some resolution, and (3) have recalled Jeroboam's prophetically toned conditions of rule. In this, new expectations arise. For the tradition of 11:29-39 has its fulfillment in 12:1-20 and its deepening shadow in ch. 13. What now can one expect, save disaster?

The narrative pace, having so briskly begun, now slows and finally halts in the ensuing consultation with Ahijah (II.B, vv. 4b-16). A circumstantial aside in vv. 4b-5, marked by an inverted word order with suffix verb ("Now Ahijah could not see . . ." [*wa'ăḥîyāḥû lō'-yākōl lir'ōt*], v. 4b), offers ironic play. Ahijah is old and dim of eye—but no matter, for he has had a prior revelation concerning the queen's errand. Whatever the intent of her disguise (it is twice mentioned—vv. 2, 5b), it has no effect on a man privy to God's own plans and sighted with God's own eyes. The old prophet's speech is ironic: the queen, sent as the *king's* messenger, is faced about to become the *prophet's* messenger. She it is who is to be the bearer of "heavy tidings" for King Jeroboam.

Ahijah's main words to the queen are typically structured: a messenger's (→) commission and (→) messenger formula followed by a prolix statement of reasons for divine judgment (vv. 7aβ-9) that is in turn logically connected ("therefore," *lākēn*) to the declaration of judgment (vv. 10-11a). The first speech closes with a statement which identifies the word as coming from Yahweh, adding emphasis and authority: "for the Lord (has) spoken (it)," v. 11b (cf. Isa 21:17; 24:3; and the comparable "for the mouth of the Lord [has] spoken [it]" in Isa 1:20; 40:5; 58:14; Mic 4:4).

Immediately Ahijah begins a second speech. Although he still addresses the queen, she is no longer a messenger to her husband, but a witness to disaster. She is to go back to the royal palace, where she will encounter a sort of sign—the death of the son about whom she came to inquire. But this event, like speech, and unlike an expected reply to the king's question (v. 3), aims at prophetic declaration. The death of the boy and his proper burial is to be singular in Jeroboam's household. This boy alone of all of Jeroboam's house will come to his grave. Ahijah implies that Jeroboam and his other scions will not meet a similarly respectable end. Hence, this lad's favor in death is a grim mark of Jeroboam's disfavor in life. From this point, the narrator, through the prophet, paints a terrifying picture of Jeroboam's destiny. A newly chosen king will cut off his dynastic issue, like some latter-day avatar of the "destroying angel" at Yahweh's first "passing over" (Exodus 12–13). Even all Israel, Jeroboam's social offspring, so to speak, will languish, unnourished, like a plant uprooted violently and thrown on arid soil. Why so extensive a judgment beyond the king's house? Because the people, too ("they," v. 15), are apostate, but at Jeroboam's urgings (v. 16).

Minimal narration follows this prophetic blow. The pace is quick. Events seem designed to show fulfillment, actualizations of the prophet's judgment. As a proleptic glimpse into the ultimate working out of the divine word, the narrator cites the boy's death, burial, and mourning in quick succession. He seems to suggest that as part of the prophecy materializes, so the main point, the demise of Jeroboam's house, and the far-reaching consequences for the northern kingdom, will in its time come to pass. Partial fulfillment, a first "sign" of sorts, may have resulted from the history of redaction, which extended the tradition far beyond Jeroboam's immediate reign. A similar partial fulfillment of prophetic word will be seen in 1 Kgs 19:19-21. From the perspective of the last editors, complete fruition of divinely ordained judgment is simply a matter of the fullness of God's time.

Genre

It is difficult to specify with confidence the genre of this unit. We may recognize a rudimentary plot, at least at the beginning, and so think of STORY. The narrator also lingers a bit on the marvelous powers of Ahijah (vv. 4-6, 12, 17), and thus we may speak of PROPHETIC LEGEND. Yet, prophetic speech now dominates the whole, and the climax of the unit seems to lie more in prophetic declaration than in fulfillment. In this respect, the unit—except for its length—is similar to (→) apophthegm or pronouncement story found in the NT (Mark 12:13-17), brief narratives whose primary point lies in the saying of Jesus (Bultmann; Taylor). It seems best to speak of Prophetic Legend, therefore, but with certain qualifications (so Debus; cf. Dietrich, who prefers the general term story). See 1 Kgs 13:1-32; 2 Kings 1–2. De Vries (p. 54) speaks of "Succession Oracle Narrative," a subcategory of prophetic legend in which an oracle specifies the terms of royal succession. However, the structural analysis shows clearly the emphasis upon judgment rather than the question of succession.

A thematic pattern associated with narrative scenes of prophetic inquiry was important in shaping this prophetic legend. Typically, one would describe the preparations for inquiring for a divine word through a prophet, and then portray the prophet holding audience, responding to a request, and delivering God's word. Following this event, the narrator might often report that the fulfillment of a prophetic word came to pass (cf. 2 Kgs 3:4-25; 8:7-15; 1 Kgs 22:4-37; 2 Kgs 1:1-17; more distant, 1 Sam 9:1-14, 20). Such a Report of Oracular Inquiry may appear in larger narrative contexts or in formal units defined by the correspondence between prophetic word and human events (e.g., 2 Kgs 8:7-15; 3:4-25; Long; cf. Debus). In 1 Kgs 14:1-18, however, the echo of this literary pattern is overshadowed by the two prophetic speeches which retard and finally overwhelm the narrative flow begun in vv. 1-6. The fulfillment of prophetic word, or part of it, serves in this case to foreshadow the entire oracle's full actualization.

Finally, we note the typical Prophecy of Punishment, vv. 7aα^2-11a, cast here, of course, as the message portion of a Commission to a messenger, vv. 7-16. The style and vocabulary of this judgment speech are entirely typical of the Dtr editor(s) of Kings (→ 1 Kgs 13:21-22 and full discussion with parallels). The second speech, vv. 12-16, is an example of a Prophetic Announcement of Judgment, similar in theme to (→) prophecy of punishment, but lacking direct address and appearing usually in less fixed form. The announcement is equivalent to that element in the full prophetic judgment speech that declares divine punishment. Note, finally, the Oracle Fulfillment Formula in v. 18b, which refers us back to Ahijah's words and claims their actualization in human events (→ the full discussion at 13:26).

Setting

As a literary type, prophetic legend would have originated among prophets as well as with the popular "folk." Such legends may have been preserved and transmitted especially by prophetic groups, since the narratives often seem to serve so directly prophetic interests (→ 1 Kgs 13:1-32; 2 Kgs 8:4). Because of its concern with Jeroboam's condemnation and its association with Shiloh (v. 2), unusual in the traditions of Jeroboam, this particular example may have originated with prophets in the north, perhaps at Shiloh (Gray, *Kings*, 333). Certainly the point of view is prophetic, or rather, in the text's present form, the point of view is Dtr, as projected in the books of Kings through an ideology of prophetic activity and speech. Here we inevitably must deal with the literary setting given this legend: it is part of the account of Jeroboam's rise and fall, his troubles in this post-Solomonic period. The legend follows immediately the condemnation of Bethel, and of Jeroboam for building and supporting that place (12:26-32; 12:33–13:34). Thus the legend is the final incident chosen by the Dtr editor(s) of Kings to characterize Jeroboam's reign and to set the context for subsequent and untiring references to the "sin of Jeroboam."

Intention

The original intentions of prophetic legends, and probably even of this particular example, would likely have been varied, depending on circumstances of use and transmission, all of which remain obscure to us. Whatever our speculations on these matters, the legend in context now clearly serves a rather programmatic point: Jeroboam's dynasty is doomed, condemned by Yahweh's word because of Jeroboam's own transgressions. The late author-editor makes a theological judgment in narrative dress, and as such, he amplifies upon the thematic statement of 13:34. In this way, prophetic legend articulates the last of God's words on Jeroboam and his reign, beginning with selection (11:29-39), exile, and accession (11:40; 12:1-20)—events at Yahweh's initiative, no matter what human motivations were driving the characters (cf. 12:15, 21-24)—moving through building (12:25-32) into judgment and rejection (12:33–13:32; 14:1-18). In this canonical context (→ fuller discussion at 12:1–14:20), the legend brings to a climax the downhill slide of Jeroboam, who began with the same possibilities as Solomon and for a time seemed to be the object of Yahweh's special guidance and favor (12:1-20, 21-24). Yahweh pronounces through Ahijah the end of the brief experiment, and simultaneously the Dtr author-editor seals Jeroboam's fate as an example to all of failure and perdition (→ 15:26, 34; 16:19, 25-26, 30; 22:52-53; 2 Kgs 17:21-22). What more remains to be said than to note the death of this king? In short, at the core of Jeroboam's promise was decay, just as for the DtrH, the beginning of monarchy itself was flawed by rebellion and confusion (1 Samuel 8). From this perspective, and from this point forward, the rest of the accounting of Israelite monarchy is to be done in synchronistic fashion, weaving back and forth between overlapping reigns in north and south, always assigning religious responsibility for success and failure and condemning northern kings for their following of Jeroboam's ways.

Bibliography

R. Bultmann, *The History of the Synoptic Tradition* (tr. J. Marsh; rev. ed.; Oxford: Blackwell, 1968) 39-69; J. Debus, *Sünde Jerobeams* (see listing at 12:1-10); S. De Vries, *Prophet* (see listing at 12:33–13:34); W. Dietrich, *Prophetie und Geschichte* (see listing at "Introduction to 1 Kings"); G. Fohrer, *Prophetenerzählungen*, 15-18 (see listing at 11:26-40); B. O. Long, "2 Kings III and Genres of Prophetic Narrative," *VT* 23 (1973) 337-48; H. Seebass, "Die Verwerfung Jeroboams I. und Salomos durch die Prophetie des Ahia von Silo," *WO* 4 (1967/68) 163-82; idem, "Tradition und Interpretation bei Jehu ben Chanani und Ahia von Silo," *VT* 25 (1975) 175-90; V. Taylor, *The Formation of the Gospel Tradition* (2nd ed.; London: Macmillan, 1935).

CONCLUDING REGNAL RESUMÉ, 14:19-20

Structure

I. Citation of sources	19
II. Regnal notices	20
A. Length of reign	20a
B. Death of king	20bα
C. Successor	20bβ

This unit is easily separated from the surrounding tradition in style and subject matter. The structure is entirely typical of concluding summaries at the end of most reigns in the books of Kings (→ 11:41-43; 14:29-31; 15:7-8; etc.). The content is unusual only in that the notice about the length of reign normally comes in a regnal summary at the beginning of a reign (cf. 15:1-2, 9-10; 16:8; etc.). David's and Solomon's concluding summaries show a similar peculiarity. The variation in the pattern seems related to the unusual way in which Jeroboam, David, and Solomon came to power and the resulting absence of the normal introductory material. In this detail we see but a small part of the larger assimilation to the Solomonic materials (→ discussion at 12:1–14:20).

Genre

This unit is a concluding REGNAL RESUMÉ, an editorial device of the Dtr author-editor (→ full discussion at 14:21-31).

Setting

Since regnal resumé is a literary device, the important setting is in the work of the Dtr editor(s) of Kings, in their historical situation of early exile, as they put together an account of Israel's and Judah's monarchy.

Intention

Obviously, the editor intends to close the reign of Jeroboam and to cite a source for further information or for further confirmation of the editorial viewpoint. Like Solomon, Jeroboam's passing is noted with formulaic regularity, despite the violence intimated by the previous prophetic legend (→ 14:1-18) and the contradiction with 14:10, a part of the prophecy of punishment which suggested a quick end to Jeroboam's house. Jeroboam's son succeeds his father to the throne, albeit for a brief time, as subsequent events will show (cf. 15:25).

THE REIGN OF REHOBOAM, 14:21-31

Text

Already given in v. 21, the name of the queen mother appears again in MT v. 31. Elsewhere, such an item is always part of the introductory resumé. Thus, on form-critical grounds, and with the support of the principal VSS, the phrase (v. 31aβ) is omitted from the structural analysis.

Structure

I. Introductory regnal resumé	21-24
A. General information	21
1. Synchronistic accession date	21a
2. Accession age	21bα¹
3. Length and place of reign	21bα²
4. Name of queen mother	21bβ
B. Theological appraisal	22-24
1. General statement	22
2. Illustrative details	23-24a
3. General statement	24b

II. Report of incidents in the reign	25-28
A. Concerning plunder of temple	25-26
B. Concerning Rehoboam's shields	27-28
III. Concluding regnal resumé	29-31
A. Citation of sources	29
B. Additional information	30
C. Death and burial of king	31aα
D. Successor	31b

This unit stands apart from the conclusion to Jeroboam's reign, v. 20, and the formulaic beginning of Abijam's rule in 15:1. Its structure is clear enough. Two summary statements containing information pertinent to the reign of Rehoboam (I, vv. 21-24; III, vv. 29-31) now enclose a report of events dated to Rehoboam's fifth year (II, vv. 25-28). This two-part framework is a constant feature of 1–2 Kings after the reign of Solomon, and a fundamental key to the editor's organization of his materials. With very few exceptions, the Dtr author-editor introduced each monarch with a summary similar to that in vv. 21-24, told the "story" of a reign with selected materials of diverse age, origin, length, and literary type, and then closed out the regnal period with concluding remarks similar to those found in vv. 29-31. Wherever they occur, these introductory and concluding summaries take essentially the same schematic form and include set information cast in stereotyped, though not slavishly repetitious, language. According to whether it is a Judean or Israelite king in view, the summaries vary slightly, but hardly enough to support theories of multiple redaction (against Weippert). During the period of a divided kingdom, the frameworks carry synchronistic dates which reckon the years of one king against the years of his counterpart in north or south. The framework is occasionally omitted, or some of its formulas may appear elsewhere in traditions associated with a given monarch. Sometimes special historical circumstances dictate a change in the pattern. (For details, see discussion below, and Burney, *Notes,* ix-xiii; Cortese.)

Genre

This unit is a literary composition, an editorial construct very likely stemming from the Dtr author-editor. It contains two important genre elements: (1) a CHRONISTIC REPORT (vv. 25-28) and (2) the introductory and concluding REGNAL RESUMÉ (vv. 21-24, 29-31).

Cast in the usual *waw*-conversive style, the REPORT relates its subject matter, a military assault on Jerusalem, to a regnal year, as though the narration of events were ruled by an explicit and detailed chronological ordering (cf., e.g., Jer 52:4-11, 12-16 [reports]; 52:28-30 [list]; 2 Kings 25). Aside from its appearance in formulas which announce the year of a king's accession to the throne, such regnal dating of events is fairly rare in the OT. A comparable style and form, especially referring to military events, may be seen in an Assyrian (→) king list, ca. 8th century B.C. (Grayson, "Königslisten," 105-6): "In the eponym of Ātamar-Ištar, Šamšī-Adad came up from Ekallāti" (*ina lim-me* ^{m}*A-ta-mar-Ištar* ^{md}*Šam-šī-*^{d}*Adad ultu* ^{uru}*Ekallāti*^{meš} *e-la-a*). See further, Grayson, "Königslisten," 111, 113 for similar chronistic statements. Note the similarity to 1 Kgs 14:25, "In the fifth year of King Rehoboam, Shishak king of Egypt came up against Jerusalem" (*wayĕhî baššānâ haḥămîšît lammelek rĕḥab'ām 'ālâ šîšaq melek-miṣrayim 'al-yĕrûšālāyim*). Cf. the chronistic statements, sometimes part of a longer report, in 2 Kgs 17:6; 18:9, 13; Jer 39:1 (all of which refer to military events); 2 Kgs 12:7; 15:30.

The introductory Regnal Resumé for Judean monarchs typically includes the following elements:

(1) An accession date, given by a Synchronistic Accession Formula where the divided kingdom is in view: "in the nth year of RN_1, king of Israel, RN_2, king of Judah, began to reign" (*bĕ* + year *lĕ* + RN_1 *melek yiśrā'ēl mālak* RN_2 *melek yĕhûdâ*). See 1 Kgs 15:9; 2 Kgs 8:25; 14:1; 15:1; 15:32; 16:1; 18:1. Slightly variant wording will be found in 1 Kgs 14:21, under discussion here, and 15:1; 22:41; 2 Kgs 12:1.

(2) The king's age (not always given), expressed by an Accession Age Formula: "X years (was) RN when he began to reign" (X *šānâ* [*hāyâ*] *bĕmolkô*). See 1 Kgs 22:42; 2 Kgs 12:1. In the synchronistic reckoning, this formula is normally the second element in the introductory resumé. When no synchronism is given, the accession age formula suffices to introduce the reign, as in 2 Kgs 21:1, 19; 22:1; 23:31, 36; 24:8, 18.

(3) A statement, never omitted for these Judean kings, on the length and place of reign: "he (RN) ruled X years in Jerusalem" (X *šānâ mālak* [RN] *bîrûšālāyim*). See, e.g., 1 Kgs 15:10a; 2 Kgs 12:2.

(4) Name of the queen mother, omitted only for Jehoram (2 Kgs 8:16-17) and Ahaz (2 Kgs 16:1-4). See, e.g., 1 Kgs 15:2; 14:21; 2 Kgs 8:26.

(5) A theological appraisal, worded variously, but containing a limited number of stereotyped phrases, such as: "and RN did what was upright (or evil) in the eyes of Yahweh" (*wayya'aś* RN *hayyāšār* [*hārā'*] *bĕ'ênê yahweh*); see 1 Kgs 15:11; 2 Kgs 12:3; 14:3; or "he (RN_1) walked in all the ways (all the sins) of his father (RN_2)" (*wayyēlek* [RN_1] *bĕkol-ḥaṭṭō't* [*derek*] *'ābîw* [RN_2]). See 1 Kgs 15:3; 22:43; 2 Kgs 22:2. Often such vague appraisals will lead into somewhat more specific allegations of misconduct, or less often, illustrations of faithfulness, always expressed in stereotyped Dtr language and measured by the standards of Dtr piety. (For further details on style and variant language, see Burney, *Notes*, ix-xv; Weippert; Nelson.)

For the kings of Israel, the introductory resumé is more compressed. It typically contains the following elements:

(1) A notice which provides an accession date given by a synchronistic accession formula, together with length and place of reign. The age of the king is never given. For example, 1 Kgs 15:33: "In the third year of Asa, king of Judah, Baasha the son of Ahijah began to reign over all Israel at Tirzah" (*bĕ* + year X *lĕ* + RN_1 *melek yĕhûdâ mālak* RN_2 [*'al-yiśrā'ēl*] *bĕ* + place X years). See 1 Kgs 16:8, 15; 2 Kgs 13:1, 10.

An alternative notice treats the accession date and the length of reign as separate items. For example, 1 Kgs 15:25: "Nadab the son of Jeroboam reigned [*RSV* "began to reign"] over Israel in the second year of Asa, king of Judah; and he reigned over Israel two years" (RN_1 *mālak 'al-yiśrā'ēl bĕ* + year X *lĕ* + RN_2 *melek yĕhûdâ. wayyimlōk 'al-yiśrā'ēl* X years). See 1 Kgs 16:29; 2 Kgs 15:13. Sometimes the alternative forms of expression mix together, as in 1 Kgs 22:52; 2 Kgs 3:1.

(2) A theological appraisal, negative throughout, consisting usually of a general statement, "And he did evil in the eyes of the Lord," followed by a variously expressed but formulaic reference to the king's not turning from the sins of Jeroboam, the first king of the north. For example, 1 Kgs 15:26: "He did what was evil in the sight of the Lord, and walked in the way of his father, and in his sin which he made Israel to sin." Cf. 2 Kgs 3:2-3; 13:2, 11; 14:24. (For further details on the minor variations, see Burney, *Notes,* x.)

The concluding regnal resumé which completes the framework for the Dtr author-editor's treatment of a particular reign is much simpler, less varied, and identical for Judean and Israelite kings. It may be omitted altogether (e.g., Joram and Hoshea) or severely truncated (e.g., Ahaziah). Typically, the resumé includes:

(1) A CITATION FORMULA which alludes to other sources of information for the reign: "And the rest of the acts of RN and all which he did . . . (various briefly expressed details may be added), are they not written in the chronicles of the Kings of (Judah) Israel?" (*wĕyeter dibrê* RN *wĕkol-'ăšer 'āśâ . . . hălō'-hēmmâ kĕtûbîm 'al-sēper dibrê hayyāmîm lĕmalkê yĕhûdâ* [*yiśrā'ēl*]). See, e.g., 1 Kgs 14:29; 15:7; 16:14.

(2) Notices of death and burial. The regular DEATH AND BURIAL FORMULA is: "and RN slept with his fathers, and he was (and they) buried (him) in X (place)" (*wayyiškab* RN *'im-'ăbōtāyw wayyiqqābēr* [*wayyiqbĕrû*] *bĕ* + place). See, e.g., 1 Kgs 14:31a; 15:8; 2 Kgs 10:35a. Notices of death and burial are strongly influenced by peculiarities of a particular reign. Especially in cases of violent death, they may be omitted altogether (e.g., Nadab, Elah, Zimri, 1 Kgs 15:25–16:20), or they may be replaced by narratives covering the same ground (see 2 Kgs 12:21-22; 14:19-22).

(3) Notice of successor, given with a SUCCESSION FORMULA: "and RN his son reigned in his stead" (*wayyimlōk* RN *bĕnô taḥtāyw*). See, e.g., 1 Kgs 14:31b; 15:8b; 16:28b.

The introductory and concluding regnal resumé functions as a two-part framework for the author-editor's selective recounting of a particular reign. Clear examples may be seen in their entirety in the unit under discussion, 14:21-24, 29-31, and in 15:1-5, 7-8. For a wider scope of this framing device, see 16:29-33 and 22:39-40, resumés which enclose all the traditions associated with King Ahab, 16:34–22:38. In some cases, the regnal resumé suffices for the author-editor's entire coverage of a monarch, as in 1 Kgs 16:23-28; 2 Kgs 13:10-13; and possibly 1 Kgs 15:1-8 (if 15:6 is a scribal error repeating information from 14:30).

A broadly similar schema for handling whole reigns in chronological order may be found in one major group of Babylonian CHRONICLES, all of which share—among other things—a prominent and regular use of a regnal dating formula to demarcate events in their proper chronological order, for example, the following: "the fifth year: Shalmanezer (V) died in the month of Tebet" (Grayson, *Chronicles,* 1:i, 29). Each reign covered in this type of chronicle (Grayson's type A) follows a schematic sequence:

(1) Accession formula: "RN ascended the throne in Babylon."
(2) Narration of events dated by regnal year: "year nth," followed by one or a series of items, spanning one or more years, each dated, but not necessarily mentioning all years of a given reign.

(3) Concluding summary: "N (= total) years RN ruled in Babylon."

The schema repeats for each succeeding king. A brief example will make the pattern clear:

Chronicles, 1:i, 13-15:
13 (Nabu)-nadin-(zeri), his son, ascended the throne in Babylon

---

14 The second year: (Nabu)-nadin-(zeri) was killed in a rebellion.
15 For two years (Nabu)-nadin-(zeri) ruled Babylon.

See Grayson, *Chronicles,* 1:i, 32–ii, 4 (Merodach-baladan); ii, 30-43 (Ashur-nadin-shumi); 2:14–5:9 (Nabopolassar). Broken texts prevent us from seeing this complete schematic pattern in all reigns, but it persists in a significant number of texts, and even holds true when the Babylonian scribe treated foreign monarchs. We may compare the Dtr author-editor's schematic organization of the Israelite and Judean reigns:

(1) Introductory regnal resumé (which includes an accession formula)
(2) Narration of events during the reign (some of which occasionally receive regnal year dating, as in 1 Kgs 14:25)
(3) Concluding regnal resumé (occasionally noting total years of rule, as 2:11; 11:42; 14:20).

Besides this general similarity in organization of materials, some of the elements constitutive of the Hebrew genre find their close counterparts in Mesopotamian (→) king lists and (→) chronicles, two types of historiographic literature which cannot always be sharply separated (Grayson, "Histories and Historians," 171-72; *Chronicles,* passim; Morawe's article is both incomplete and inaccurate). Besides the accession formula, a functional rather than strict linguistic parallel, a Babylonian formula for expressing length of reign distinguishes a second type of chronicle (Grayson's type B): "RN ruled for N years" (*mu* X *in. aka* = in Akkadian, x *Mu*^{meš} *šarru-ta īpuš*^{uš}). The formula occurs in various schematic contexts, ranging from mere listing of kings to fuller prose narration in chronicle style, for example, the dynastic chronicle (Grayson, *Chronicles,* 18):

18:i, 1-3
1 [Enm]egalanna [ruled for] N years.
2 [Dum]uzi, the shepherd, [ruled for N years].
3 [Three] kings [of the dynasty of Badtibira ruled for N years].

18:v, 2-8
2 The knight, resident of the Sealand, Simbar-shihu, son of Eriba-Sin,
3 soldier of the dynasty of Damqi-ilishu, was slain with the sword. He ruled for seventeen years.
4 He was buried in the palace of Sargon.
5 Ea-mukin-zeri, the usurper, son of Hashmar, ruled for three months.
6 He was buried in the swamp of Bit-Hashmar.
7 Kashshu-nadin-ahi, son of SAPpaya, ruled for three years. In the palace <of...he was buried>.
8 Three kings of the dynasty of the Sealand ruled for twenty-three years.

Compare the similar length of reign formulas in king lists: Assyrian, ca. 8th century B.C. (Grayson, "Königslisten," 107-15, no. 9, §§ 13-77), and from Hellenistic times ("Königslisten," 98-99, no. 6). Cf. the Hebrew length of reign formula in the introductory resumé: "N years RN ruled in (place)," as in 1 Kgs 14:21b; 15:10a; 2 Kgs 12:2; "and he ruled over Israel for N years," 1 Kgs 15:25; 16:29; 2 Kgs 15:13. Note further the OT king list in Gen 36:31-39 and the list of "judges" (*šōpĕṭîm*) in Judg 12:7-15.

In addition to these OT accession and length of reign formulas, which seem rooted in the style of chronicles and king lists, one also finds in these same chronistic works notices of death and burial, though less frequently. Note the excerpt above from the dynastic chronicle (Grayson, *Chronicles,* 18:v, 2-8) and the stylized references to the royal death which closes out an era in a king list from Hellenistic times (Grayson, "Königslisten," 98-99, no. 6, lines 10-13; reverse 6-7, 9).

Synchronistic reckoning, so regular a feature of 1 Kgs 15–2 Kgs 17, is known in the Babylonian materials as well. It appears in its clearest form in the "Synchronistic History" (Grayson's Chronicle type D, *Chronicles,* 157-70), a document distinguished from other chronistic writings by its juxtaposition of two different reigns as a way of ordering its narrativelike material chronologically. The typical synchronistic formula in this text is: "(in the time of) RN_1 king of Assyria, RN_2 (was) king of X." Then follows a prose narration covering events during the reign of RN_1. With or without the temporal phrase "in the time of" (*ina tar-ṣi*), the formula serves as a subject heading (e.g., Grayson, *Chronicles,* 21:ii, 14') or as the immediate syntactical subject of the narration to follow (e.g., *Chronicles,* 21:i, 24; ii, 1-2, 3-4). One should note, too, a kind of synchronistic reckoning in Grayson's type A Chronicle, where the schematic pattern for the Babylonian kings (noted above) is often entwined with the same schematic summary of foreign reigns as these kings impinge on Babylonian affairs. Thus, in the midst of recounting events of a single Babylonian king, the standard elements (accession formula, dated events during reign, summary conclusion = length of reign formula) for a foreign king will appear, interwoven and split apart, but nonetheless in their proper sequence (see, e.g., *Chronicles,* 1:i, 9-10, 33-37, 38-39, which summarizes the reign of an Elamite king in the midst of the Babylonian monarch's years).

Finally, we may observe that whereas theological appraisals are regular and stereotyped in the Hebrew regnal resumé, similar devices are rare indeed in the existing Mesopotamian chronistic documents. An exception is the "Weidner Chronicle," a propagandistic work, perhaps of the 13th or 12th century B.C., that orders events in chronicle fashion, but otherwise is very unlike other chronistic texts. It is mainly prose narrative, a selective recounting of various rulers and regnal periods apparently with the aim of judging whether certain kings were supportive of Marduk's cult at Babylon. Typical is the following (Grayson, *Chronicles,* 19:48-55):

> [After the text tells how Sargon refused to offer wine to Marduk, but offered the ritually correct fish in the temple Esagil, it continues:]
>
> 48 Marduk, "son of the temple" of Apsu, looked with joy upon him and gave to him sovereignty over the Four Quarters.

[But this same Sargon later committed an offense against the god, and thus]:

52-52b Because of the wrong he (Sargon) had done, he (Marduk) became hostile towards him (Sargon). They (his subjects) rebelled against him from east to west. He was inflicted with insomnia.

[Several punishments follow, and reach a climax]:

55 He (Marduk) gave his sovereignty to the army of the Guti.

Cf. the "Chronicle of the Early Kings," in Grayson, *Chronicles,* 152-56, no. 20, which apparently drew upon the "Weidner Chronicle."

Setting

Most scholars agree that the entire unit originated with the exilic Dtr author-editor who organized a recounting of the Hebrew reigns, in this case, that of Rehoboam, by means of the introductory and concluding resumé. In the light of Mesopotamian parallels to the general organizational pattern and to particular formulas, however, it seems safe to conclude that the author-editor drew upon models already well established among Babylonian and Assyrian scribes who were responsible for chronicles, king lists, and other chronistic works. (Egypt never developed anything to rival the Babylonian chronicles.) Yet the Dtr resumé may rest upon indigenous conventions of Judean and Israelite king lists (Bin-Nun). The matter will not be settled without real examples, however (cf. Gen 36:31-39). Similarly, chronistic report seems at home in the chronistic literature of Mesopotamian royal scribes. The example in 1 Kgs 14:25-28 may have ultimately stemmed from the archives in Jerusalem (so Montgomery, *Kings,* 268; Gray, *Kings,* 344).

Actually, such vague allusions by scholars only suggest our ignorance of Hebrew literary history. Perhaps we should think of utilitarian texts and records of various kinds (e.g., lists, records, daybooks, annals, astronomical diaries, copies of commemorative inscriptions) from which an author might have abstracted and arranged a Babylonian-type chronological summary of the reigns (the *sēper dibrê hayyāmîm* or "chronicles" referred to in the concluding resumé). In turn, the Dtr author-editor, working in the exilic climate of Babylonian culture, might then have selected and arranged from these "chronicles" his own distinctly propagandistic summary of the reigns (see Montgomery, *Kings,* 31-37; Noth, *Könige,* 327; Van Seters, *In Search of History*).

Intention

It follows from what has been said that the author-editor's main intention in constructing such stylized treatments of particular reigns is to summarize and characterize a monarchical era. This particular example, of course, focuses on the reign of Rehoboam, and sees it as besmirched by apostasy (vv. 22-24), troubled by invasion (vv. 25-28), and plagued by internecine war (v. 30). Originally, the chronistic report (vv. 25-28) may have been part of chronicles or king lists and would have been used for a variety of purposes, from objective utilitarian record keeping to highly select, propagandistic recounting of past events. It is a mistake to routinely and uncritically assume historical objectivity on the part of scribes who authored or copied texts in the chronicle and king list style (against Montgomery, "Archival Data"; Gray, *Kings*; et al.). In this particular example of chronistic report, the Dtr author-editor may have had a special interest in selecting from his sources affairs which impinged on the Solomonic temple in some way (→ discussion of 6:1–9:25). This seems likely because of the extremely limited view of Shishak's campaign, which we know from other sources to have been very extensive indeed (cf. Breasted, *ARE* IV, §§ 709-17). For the Dtr author-editor, the campaign may have represented decline and lasting trouble, expressed in the durative sense of v. 28: fallen from the splendor of temple treasures and *golden* shields associated with Solomon, Rehoboam is forced to live out his kingly days guarded with *bronze*, reminded of his fate at the hands of Yahweh (cf. 12:15; 14:30; Robinson, *Kings*, 172).

Bibliography

See bibliographies at "Introduction to Historical Literature" and "Introduction to 1 Kings." E. Cortese, "Lo schema deuteronomistico per i re di Giuda e d'Israele," *Bib* 56 (1975) 37-52; R. D. Nelson, "Redactional Duality of the Deuteronomic History" (Diss., Union Theological Seminary: Richmond, 1973) 39-66; E. J. Smit, "Death and Burial Formulas in Kings and Chronicles Relating to the Kings of Judah," in *Biblical Essays* (Proceedings of Ninth Meeting, Die Ou-Testamentiese Werkgemeenskap in Suid-Afrika; Potchefstroom: Pro Rege Pers Beperk, 1966) 173-77.

THE NORTHERN KINGDOM FROM THE END OF JEROBOAM TO OMRI (During the Judahite Reigns of Abijam and Asa), 15:1–16:28

Structure

I. Dissolution of the house of Jeroboam	15:1–16:7
A. The reign of Abijam: regnal resumé	1-8
B. The reign of Asa	9-24
1. Introductory regnal resumé	9-15
2. Account of war with Baasha	16-22
3. Concluding regnal resumé	23-24
C. The reign of Nadab	25-32
1. Introductory regnal resumé	25-26
2. Report of throne conspiracy (Baasha destroys Jeroboam's house)	27-30
3. Regnal resumé citation formula	31
4. Concluding statement: war between Asa and Baasha	32
D. The reign of Baasha	15:33–16:7
1. Introductory regnal resumé	33-34
2. Report of prophetic revelation (judgment on Baasha for destroying Jeroboam's house)	16:1-4
3. Concluding regnal resumé	5-6
4. Explanatory comment	7
II. Aftermath: turmoil in the Northern Kingdom	16:8-28

A. The reign of Elah	8-14
1. Regnal resumé accession formula	8
2. Report of throne conspiracy (Zimri destroys house of Baasha)	9-11
3. Notice of prophecy fulfilled	12-13
4. Regnal resumé citation formula	14
B. The reign of Zimri	15-20
1. Regnal resumé accession formula	15a
2. Report of Zimri's death in civil war	15b-19
3. Regnal resumé citation formula	20
C. Report of civil war and the rise of Omri	21-22
D. The reign of Omri: regnal resumé	23-28

The material contained in this unit is easily distinguished from 14:31, which closes out the reign of Rehoboam, and from 16:29, the opening summary for a large block of tradition dealing with King Ahab (16:29–22:40). What remains are two biblical chapters which cover seven reigns (eight, if one counts Tibni, 16:21). Astonishingly, more than one-half the material included in chs. 15–16 consists of formulas characteristic of the Dtr regnal resumé (see full discussion at 14:21-31): 15:1-8; 15:9-15, 23-24; 15:25-26, 31; 15:33-34 + 16:5-6; 16:8, 14; 16:15a, 20; 16:23-28. In fact, regnal resumé suffices to cover the entire reigns of Abijam (15:1-8) and Omri (16:23-28). The author-editor has included only a few specific traditions relevant to particular reigns: 15:16-22, war; 15:27-30 and 16:15b-19, conspiracies against the crown; 16:1-4, a report of prophetic revelation; 16:21-22, civil war before the rise of Omri.

Although some traditions may predate the Dtr author-editor, it is clear that the unit now reflects this editor's dominant interest in quick summary and frequent theological appraisal. The latter, of course, is especially clear in those summaries which introduce each reign, but it also shows up in Dtr-styled evaluative comments integrated into the more specific description of events. For example, note the prophetic revelation of 16:1-4, referred to again in the notice of fulfilled prophecy, 16:12-13, and the explanatory statements of 16:19 and 15:29-30, alluded to again in 16:7, which is linked to the prophecy of 16:1-4.

The main structural device is evident in the chronologically arranged, synchronistically reckoned survey of the reigns—one by one, each one complete before beginning another. With the exception of the transitional report of civil war leading to the establishment of Omri (16:21-22), all material falls into discrete regnal periods demarcated by the usual introductory and concluding regnal summaries (I.A, B, C, D; II.A, B, D). Even in those cases where violence interrupted the normal succession of kings, formulaic elements from these typical summaries serve to open and close regnal periods, as in 15:31 (closing out the reign of Nadab); 16:8, 14; 16:15a, 20 (formulas which open and close the tempestuous periods of Elah and Zimri). In short, this unit presents seven (eight) monarchical periods in their proper order and as part of the terrace-like organization which is fundamental to the entire period of the divided kingdom. That is, the author-editor presents extensive chronological coverage of the *Israelite* reigns in blocks of material which have been related synchronistically to less extensive blocks covering the *Judean* kings. A chart will make clear this larger context for 15:1–16:28, which resembles in its essentials nothing so much as a king list (→ full discussion in "Introduction to 1 Kings," pp. 22-23).

Reign of Jeroboam (1 Kgs 12:1–14:20)	*Judah in the time of Jeroboam* (14:21–15:24) Rehoboam Abijam Asa
Israel in the time of Asa (15:25–22:40) Nadab Baasha Elah Zimri Omri Ahab	*Judah in the time of Ahab* (22:41-51) [*RSV* 50] Jehoshaphat
Israel in the time of Jehoshaphat (1 Kgs 22:52 [*RSV* 51]–2 Kgs 8:15) Ahaziah Jehoram	

(and so on until the downfall of the northern kingdom)

Yet, one may observe in 15:1–16:28 lines of structural and thematic continuity which transcend the reign-by-reign pattern. First, a simple regnal resumé at beginning and end suffices to cover two reigns in their entirety: Abijam (I.A, 15:1-8) and Omri (II.D, 16:23-28). Thus, stylized summary, normally a framework for a particular reign, serves here as a kind of frame for a *series* of regnal periods. Second, 15:1–16:7 emphasize the house of Jeroboam, even though the main traditions connected with this king have already appeared and his concluding summary has been given in 12:1–14:20. The author-editor mentions warfare between north and south, refrainlike, in 15:6 (which may be a scribal error, repeating 14:30), 15:7b, 15:16, and 15:32. There is, finally, a pointed reference to the end of Jeroboam's dynasty in 16:7. What emerges, then, is strife between kings of north and south: Jeroboam and Rehoboam (15:6; cf. 14:30), and the successors of Rehoboam, Abijam and Asa, pitted against Jeroboam and his successor by conspiracy, Baasha. Moreover, a rubric of prophecy-fulfillment ties the tradition together: an already uttered prediction of troublesome demise for Jeroboam's house (14:10) finds explicit fulfillment in 15:29 and a further extension in the punishment of the dynasty killer, Baasha, in 16:7b.

One should note further the inner linkage provided by the interweaving of the events and main figures. During the reign of Asa (15:9-24) Baasha (whose rule has not been introduced) plays a decisive role (15:16-22). In the reign of Nadab, and still before his rule is formally described, this same Baasha conspires to overthrow the Jeroboamic house (15:27-30). When the author at last presents the reign of Baasha (15:33–16:7), he makes an explicit retrospective link to this king's treacherous destruction of Jeroboam's entire house (16:7b). Despite the reign-by-reign organizational pattern, Baasha takes on the size of a main character in the understated drama telling of the dissolution of Jeroboam's rule and the end of his dynasty.

A kind of reprise of this first theme begins in 16:8. In the aftermath of Jeroboam's demise, circumstances repeat, and the victor becomes victim. Baasha's son, Elah, loses the throne to Zimri, a high-ranking commander. And as Baasha did, this Zimri wipes out the entire family line, leaving himself free to start a new royal succession. Then events reverse. Zimri is driven to suicide—without heir—by the strong opposition of another military man, Omri, who in time solidifies his control over the northern kingdom and creates a remarkably long-lived successor in his son Ahab. Thus, this section of the reign-by-reign summary of the kings has a "story" to tell also. The turmoil swirling around Jeroboam's house spawns another unstable and equally treacherous time of dissolution, as though to suggest something worse than Jeroboam's fate. And as in 1 Kgs 15:1–16:7, the king and the usurper entwine in a net of foreshadowing: during the reign of Elah (II.A, vv. 8-14), Zimri is introduced as conspirator (before his rule is formally presented); then when Zimri sits uneasily and briefly upon the throne (II.B, vv. 15-20), Omri rises as the rival claimant to the northern throne. The whole section concludes with full focus on Omri finally established as king without challenge (II.D, vv. 23-28).

In sum, as the structural outline suggests, the reign-by-reign skeletal recounting of the monarchs carries a "story" of sorts: the tale of Jeroboam's demise, and Omri's rise out of the confused lunges for royal power. The motif of prophecy fulfilled, 16:3 and 16:12, neatly bridges these two themes. A prophet Jehu marks Baasha's family for extinction, and the Dtr commentator observes the deed done (16:12). The sins of Jeroboam are visited even upon his illegal successor!

Genre

Most critics agree that this literary complex is an editorial composite made up of stereotyped summary material and a limited number of older traditions relevant to particular reigns. One may not therefore designate a precise genre for the whole. On the other hand, recognizable genres and generic elements make up this composite. The Regnal Resumé, which introduces and concludes a given reign with formulaic information, is the most obvious feature: 15:1-8 (Abijam); 15:9-15, 23-24 (Asa); 15:25-26, 31 (Nadab); 15:33-34 and 16:5-6 (Baasha); 16:23-28 (Omri). Note the generic elements from regnal resumé in 16:8, 14; 16:15a, 20 (Accession and Citation Formulas for Elah and Zimri). See the full discussion of regnal resumé at 1 Kgs 14:21-31.

Within this formulaic framework, one may observe various literary genres. Of importance is Report, for example, 15:16-21, the border war; 16:15b-19, the death of Zimri; or 16:21-22, the civil war between followers of Tibni and Omri. Two reports of Throne Conspiracy, 15:27-30 and 16:9-13, are representative of reports on a similar theme found elsewhere in the books of Kings. Typically, such reports are very brief and offer a conventional sequence of motifs:

(1) a conspiracy against the crown is noted (the verb *qāšar*)
(2) the king is "struck down" (the verb Hiphil *nākâ*)
(3) the murder is reported (the verb Hiphil *mût*)
(4) the conspirator assumes the throne (often expressed with a phrase very similar to the regnal resumé SUCCESSION FORMULA: "and X reigned in his stead").

See the series of reports in 2 Kgs 15:10, 14, 25, 30; 21:23.

This basic form is amplified in 1 Kgs 15:27-30 and 16:9-13 with circumstantial detail (15:27b; 16:9b) and a moralizing conclusion. Here the Dtr author-editor employed the typical ORACLE FULFILLMENT FORMULA (so-and-so happened "according to the word of the Lord which he spoke by his servant PN"; see full discussion with parallels at 13:26; Dietrich, 58-61). The reports end with explanatory comments (in line with remarks in 16:7 and 19) which link the murderous conspiracy to divine judgment upon kingly misdeeds (15:30; 16:13). In the context of 1 Kings 15–16, this matter-of-fact report of conspiracy flows into object lesson, the better to claim prophetic word actualized in events and to expose the moral flaw at the core of the Israelite confusion.

The author-editor has used report of PROPHETIC REVELATION in 16:1-4 to voice the same perspective. Of special interest is the PROPHETIC WORD FORMULA (16:1), which defines the situation as private communication from God to the prophet (→ full discussion of the form at 17:2-16). The content of that communication is simply narrated as a PROPHECY OF PUNISHMENT (16:2-4), styled as so many others in the Dtr portions of 1–2 Kings (cf. 1 Kgs 14:7b-11; 21:20b-22; 2 Kgs 22:15-20; see full discussion at 13:21-22). Of course, the author-editor does not rest with private communication. Because of its place in the coverage of Baasha's reign, the prophetic revelation explains to the reader the unseemly end of Baasha.

Finally, one should note the stereotyped diplomatic exchange in 15:18-19, part of the longer and well-developed account of a border war between Asa and Baasha, 15:16-21. Asa sends gifts to a potential ally against Israel (v. 18) along with a request for, or declaration of, a military alliance (the Hebrew is ambiguous): "A treaty [*bĕrît*] between me and you; between my father and between your father. . . . Go, break your league with Baasha . . . that he may withdraw from me" (v. 19). The narrative goes on to report that Ben-hadad "hearkened" (*šmʿ*) and responded with aid. A very similar report in 2 Kgs 16:7-9 notes that King Ahaz requested aid from the Assyrians, and similarly refers to, or requests, a treaty: "I am your servant and your son. Come up, and rescue me . . ." (2 Kgs 16:7). Note finally 1 Kgs 20:31-34 and full discussion there. In all cases the scenes reflect practices of making and breaking military alliances (D. J. McCarthy, *Treaty and Covenant* [AnBib 21A; 2nd rev. ed.; Rome: Pontifical Biblical Institute, 1978]).

Setting

Given the heavy use of regnal resumé and other evaluative elements throughout the chapters, one can hardly doubt that this unit as it stands originated with the exilic Dtr author-editor. Certain materials having to do with, for example, chronology, disturbed successions (15:27-29; 16:9-11, 15b-18), Jerusalem temple (15:17-22), and acquisition of Samaria (16:24) were probably drawn from selectively edited "chronicles" or archival records, the literary deposit of royal scribes. However, we can only speculate about these matters (→ fuller discussion at 14:21-31). Thus, the more important question has to do with the literary context in 1 Kings. The unit stands as a transition between the main tradition of Jeroboam (12:1–14:20) and the longer complex recounting the reign of Ahab (16:29–22:40). In other words, it is part of a larger block of material which covers the northern kingdom between its beginnings in Jeroboam and its center in Ahab. Both reigns are extraordinary points from which the Dtr author-editor will take his measure of kingship in the north.

Intention

In this light, the intention of the text and its author has to do with showing the malfunctioning of monarchy in the north. The unit finds its place in a larger context: the demise of Jeroboam and of his house, a king who began with such promise (11:37-38), disqualified himself in impious acts (12:30; 13:33-34; 14:9-11; 15:29-30), and came to an ignoble but fully prophesied end (15:27-30; cf. 16:7). Jeroboam really is a symbol of an experiment gone awry. His "sin" becomes the measure, or rather the standard, of decadence, which all successors in the north will exceed. At the same time, his reign is a kind of bridge mined with turmoil and strife, as though his life and its aftershocks were some kind of cursed legacy. Jeroboam is the father of a short-lived dynasty, and the sire of an affront against Yahweh that refuses to die, but lives on in the ways of successor kings, sons and usurpers alike. It will be Ahab—the king on the other side of this "bridge"—who will do him one better in becoming a Dtr symbol for the malfeasance that was at the core of northern kingship.

Bibliography

W. Dietrich, *Prophetie und Geschichte* (see listing at "Introduction to 1 Kings"); H. Seebass, "Tradition" (see listing at 14:1-18).

THE REIGN OF AHAB: CANONICAL FRAMEWORK, 16:29–22:40

Structure

I. Introductory regnal resumé	16:29-33
II. Incidents in Ahab's reign	16:34–22:38
A. Building notice: Jericho	16:34
B. Legends: Elijah, Ahab, and Baal (the triumph of Elijah over Ahab, Yahweh over Baal)	17:1–19:21
C. Wars with Syria and Ahab's violation of *ḥērem*	20:1-43
1. Victory over Ben-hadad	1-34
2. Prophet's confrontation with Ahab	35-43
D. Ahab and the murder of Naboth	21:1-29
E. Death of Ahab	22:1-38
III. Concluding regnal resumé	22:39-40

This large body of traditional material has been brought together by the Dtr editor. Divided into its usual introductory and concluding parts, a regnal summary (16:29-33 and 22:39-40) frames traditions of various ages, origin, and genres. The center holds together primarily because of a single theme: Ahab's offenses against Yahweh, justifying in full the initial condemnation of 16:30, ". . . (he) did evil in the sight of the Lord more than all that were before him." The narrator's voice comes through in four major confrontations involving Ahab: with Elijah (chs. 17–19); with an unknown prophet (ch. 20), with Elijah again (ch. 21), and finally with Micaiah ben Imlah (ch. 22). Thus, the twists and turns of the encounters with Elijah in chs. 17–18 all relate to the idea (perhaps an editorial rubric) that the drought sent by Yahweh because of Ahab's (and Jezebel's) ways was broken only when Yahweh was recognized and acknowledged as God. Yet, despite this climactic defeat of Baal and the Baalist prophets, the cancer in the body of the kingdom was not purged. On hearing Ahab's report of those events at Carmel, Jezebel redoubled her antipathy toward Elijah, and hence toward Yahwism (19:1-3), whose eventual triumph in the kingdom is foretold and presaged on Mount Horeb (19:4-21). Like a momentary sweetness, Ahab triumphed mightily over Syria, and with pious courting of Yahweh. But in a second confrontation we learn along with the king that he has nevertheless violated the divine taboo for spoils of war (*ḥērem*), and so merits punishment prophesied by an unknown, wandering prophet (ch. 20). As though not to be outdone, Jezebel plotted treachery (ch. 21), implicating Ahab in the murder of Naboth and the seizure of his choice vineyard for royal lands. This double offense called forth the declarations of punishment from Elijah in a third confrontation, generalized to touch the thematic condemnation of 16:30. Finally, after standing firm in his hatred for another Yahweh prophet, Micaiah ben Imlah, Ahab met his ignoble end. Events in and after confrontations fulfill generally the demise prophesied twice before (22:38; cf. 20:42; 21:19; further, 22:17); but it is Yahweh's power—implicated in all the human sparring and tested at Carmel, Samaria, Aphek, and Ramoth-gilead—which remains supreme.

In view of this thematic coherence to the Ahab material, the enigmatic and somewhat isolated notice at the beginning (16:34) probably should be taken as a first example of an offense against Yahweh. Clearly the man Hiel bore the brunt of the curse pronounced in Josh 6:26 and echoed here in identical language. But whatever it entailed, the Dtr editor must have viewed the event as somehow Ahab's responsibility as well, as indeed it may have been, since we would expect royal patronage for building projects of any magnitude. Thus, from the canonical perspective, the act of building a city, often a praiseworthy and pious action by a monarch, ironically quickens an old curse and starts the regime of this King Ahab within an ominous shadow (Gray, *Kings*, 369).

Genre

Even if certain portions of this unit coalesced before the final editor of Kings assembled his materials, the presentation of Ahab's reign is finally a matter of an editorial grouping of diverse material. Therefore a precise genre may not be specified. We are to look to the whole for an accounting of Ahab's rule, and to the parts for identifiable generic pieces with varying degrees of literary sophistication. On the general editorial plan for presenting a reign, see the full discussion at 14:21-31.

Setting

As expected for an editorial composition, we think of setting as a matter of literary context. The exilic author-editor brought together selected traditions having to do with the reign of Ahab and placed them at an appropriate point. The Ahab material is extensive, second only to Solomon. His reign stands forth as a first full-scale, almost entirely negative characterization of the Omride dynasty, which was introduced and evaluated in 16:22-28, and which will serve as a kind of literary and theological centerpiece for the editor's presentation of the northern kingdom (1 Kgs 12:1–2 Kgs 17:41).

Intention

Obviously, the intention of this editorial composition is to present the reign of Ahab, son of Omri, in such a way as to illustrate and make concrete the theological appraisal given this king in 16:30. Ahab finally has no redeeming features, as far as one can tell from the editor's presentation—and probably he was meant to have none for the reader. His real achievements are probably badly understated in this literary portrait because of his worship in Samaria and his association with foreign powers (Whitley). Finally Ahab represents an age to the Dtr editor—one of religious zeal and devilry characteristic of evangelical imagination. The reign focuses and typifies struggle: contest of power between Yahweh and Baal, struggle for the life of Yahweh's prophet Elijah. Ahab is a symbol for the misbegotten and misguided northern kingdom, the centerpiece of perversion, the epitome of Baalistic confusion (2 Kgs 17:7-18).

Bibliography

M. A. Cohen, "In all Fairness to Ahab: A Socio-political Consideration of the Ahab-Elijah Controversy," *Eretz Israel* 12 (1975) 87*-94*; T. Ishida, "The House of Ahab," *IEJ* 25 (1975) 135-37; C. F. Whitley, "The Deuteronomic Presentation of the House of Omri," *VT* 2 (1952) 137-52.

INTRODUCTORY REGNAL RESUMÉ, 16:29-33

Structure

I. Regnal information	29
A. Name and year of accession	29a
B. Length of reign and capital city	29b
II. Theological appraisal of king	30-33
A. General evaluation	30
B. Specific evils	31-33a
C. General evaluation	33b

This unit is typical of introductory summaries for particular reigns in 1–2 Kings. It is therefore easily distinguished from the concluding resumé for the reign of Omri (16:27-28) and the building notice in 16:34, which belongs more typically to the series of events reported in a given monarch's time (e.g., as in 14:25-28). The structure and language of the unit are entirely typical of these summaries (→ full discussion at 14:21-31). We move from synchronistic accession formula (v. 29a; cf. 14:21; 15:25; 22:52) through information about the length and place of reign, to a conventional theological evaluation. The text shows the normal pattern: (1) a general appraisal ("Ahab . . . did evil in the sight of the Lord . . .") followed by (2) a series of specific evils (e.g., "He erected an altar for Baal . . . ," v. 32), all given as short reportorial notices bereft of description, returning to (3) a statement of general evaluation (v. 33b). The latter element picks up language from the first appraisal in v. 30, neatly rounding off a compact, formulaic, and summarizing entity standing at the beginning of a reign.

Genre

This unit is an introductory REGNAL RESUMÉ and has many parallels in the books of Kings (→ discussion at 14:21-31).

Setting

Since the regnal resumé is a device of the Dtr author-editor of Kings, we do best to consider setting as a question of literary context (→ discussion at 14:21-31). Possibly some information about Ahab's marriage would have been drawn from royal archives (Noth, *Deuteronomistic History,* 134-35 n. 40), but the highly tendentious form for describing these specific actions certainly originated with the Dtr editor.

Intention

This unit introduces the reign of Ahab and sets forth the Dtr editor's appraisal of the king. He is found wanting, and he stands condemned from the start. Ahab's ties to a Phoenician woman stress the king's weakness: the queen's name suggests, perhaps in parody, *zĕbūl,* a title of the Canaanite Baal known from the Ras Shamra texts; her father's name may be an abbreviation for *'ittôba'al,* "with him (is) Baal" (Montgomery, *Kings,* 291; Gray, *Kings,* 368). There are pointed references to Ahab's devotion to Baal. Both the foreign queen and devotion to Baal will serve as leitmotifs in subsequent chapters.

BUILDING NOTICE: JERICHO, 16:34

Structure

I. Notice of building activity	34a-bα
II. Prophecy fulfillment formula	34bβ

Missing from the Lucianic Greek text, this brief tradition simply states that Jericho was built "in his (Ahab's) days" and affirms that this act fulfilled a curse spoken by Joshua (Josh 6:26). The style is reportorial and highly compressed: perfect verbs with a bare minimum of connectives between clauses; a simple Hebrew preposition *bĕ* concealing as much as revealing, now translated in the *RSV* as "at the cost of"; the minimal formula of fulfillment, "according to the word of Yahweh which he spoke through Joshua ben Nun." The temporal expression "in his days" may be modeled on Mesopotamian archival style (Montgomery, "Archival Data," 49). One may perhaps speak more appropriately of a commemorative style, since both stylistic and subject matter parallels are mostly to be found in royal building inscriptions and other public monuments eulogizing a particular monarch (Mowinckel, "Fürsteninschriften," 281-86). For example, Grayson, *ARI* I, § 409: "At that time the Step Gate of the temple of the god Ashur . . . had become dilapidated . . . I built (the new structure) with limestone and mortar from the city Ubase. I restored it and deposited my stele." See also Grayson, *ARI* I, §§ 423, 440 (Adad-Nirari I, ca. 1300), 691, 701 (Tukulti-Ninurta I, ca. 1240); Grayson, *ARI* II, § 576 (Ashur-Nasir-Apli II, ca. 875). Cf. the Moabite Mesha Inscription (*ANET*, 320-21) and 1 Kgs 12:25; 15:22; 2 Kgs 24:1; 2 Chr 11:5-12; 26:9-10. If much in the Kings material finds its parallel in the ancient Near East, the oracle fulfillment formula (v. 34b) has its roots in the biblical narrative traditions (1 Kgs 17:16; 2 Kgs 1:17; 2:22; → full discussion at 1 Kgs 13:26).

Genre

This unit is a brief REPORT or NOTICE of building activities.

Setting

Elements in this report suggest different, and even contradictory, backgrounds. The commemorative style and the subject matter, rebuilding a city, might suggest royal scribes and their archives as an original setting for this type of report (Noth, *Könige*, 355). On the other hand, the integration of this subject matter with an apparently folkloristic tradition of a curse on Jericho (Josh 6:26), but in the style of prophecy fulfillment (cf. 1 Kgs 13:26; 15:29), points in the direction of a more popular setting for this particular tradition and its literary form (Würthwein, *Könige*, 204). We cannot be certain of provenance. In context, however, the report is the first event mentioned in Ahab's reign—not as part of the introductory regnal resumé, and not belonging to the extensive Elijah traditions which follow. The report stands isolated in an almost overlooked, but nevertheless commanding, position.

Intention

Admittedly, the intention of this report remains unclear, owing to its brevity and relative isolation in the text. However, the notice reaches far back into canonical tradition (no doubt revealing the wide perspective of the Dtr editor) and links the beginning of Ahab's reign to an offense revealed when an old curse is actualized (Josh 6:26). It is as though the editor saw that the troubles that were to beset Ahab's reign were anticipated in this little event. With irony, perhaps, normally praiseworthy building activity revives a dormant curse as a sort of omen for the regime.

Bibliography

See bibliographies at "Introduction to Historical Literature" and "Introduction to 1 Kings."

AHAB, ELIJAH, AND BAAL: CANONICAL FRAMEWORK, 17:1 – 19:21

Structure

I. Triumph of Elijah and Yahweh (Mount Carmel) 17:1–18:46

A. Report of Elijah's word to Ahab	1
B. Legend: care and provisioning of Elijah	2-16
C. Legend: Elijah's benevolent powers	17-24
D. Legend: Elijah's (and Yahweh's) triumph (fulfillment of Elijah's word)	18:1-46
II. Triumph of Elijah and Yahweh (Mount Horeb)	19:1-21
A. Account of epiphanies in wilderness (predicted triumph)	1-18
B. Anecdote: Elisha's selection (beginning of triumph)	19-21

Despite voices to the contrary (e.g., Šanda, *Könige*; Burney, *Notes*; Montgomery, *Kings*; Radday), a persistent opinion since the ground-breaking work of Albrecht Alt has held that this block of material consists of a number of originally separate stories and fragments of tradition. In holding such views, critics have generally been interested in defining those original layers of tradition and reconstructing the history of composition and redaction. The finely tuned recent attempts along these lines (e.g., Steck; Hentschel) differ markedly and show the limitations of method and lack of consensus in results. For ch. 17, a majority of scholars isolate three smaller units: vv. 2-6, 7-16, 17-24 (Fohrer; Plöger; Rofé; Schüpphaus; Smend; Dietrich; Eissfeldt). More differences emerge for chs. 18 and 19. Except for perhaps the intensely studied 18:20-39, we can be less confident about recovering independent materials or deciding finally how the traditions in ch. 19 related in composition and redaction to chs. 17–18. (See Alt; Smend; Steck above all.)

The fact remains, however, that editing has made of this complex body of tradition some kind of thematic and structural unity, which has been illuminatingly explored as a literary whole (Bottini; Cohn; Childs), even with "structuralist" principles (Jobling). We may observe first that ch. 18, which focuses on the struggle between Yahweh and his *rival* (Baal), is framed on either side by material which highlights Yahweh and his *advocate* (Elijah). In these bracketing sections (17:2-16; 19:4-6, 7-8), it is clear that God favors and sustains his prophet in adversity (17:2-16, the famine and flight from Ahab; and 19:1-8, the flight from Jezebel's murderous intent). At the same time, events or words affirm Elijah (17:24; 19:15-18) despite questions and doubts about his position (17:17-23; 19:1-3, 4, 10). We may represent the bracketing in a diagram:

Elijah cared for:	17:3-6, 8-16
Elijah's position in doubt:	17:18 (17-23)
Elijah affirmed:	17:24
Mount Carmel Episode:	18:1-46
Elijah cared for:	19:4-6, 7-8
Elijah's position in doubt:	19:1-3, 4, 10, 14
Elijah affirmed:	19:15-18

Within this large motivic structure are two paired relationships: chs. 17–18 and 18–19, each pair held together by a shared center, and yet retaining a certain independence. The first pair (chs. 17–18) shows a clear thematic structure, the movement from divine word (17:1; 18:1) to its fulfillment in human events (18:41-46). Under this rubric a word announced in 17:1 finally comes to pass with the coming of rain in 18:41-46. Along the way the supreme power of Yahweh, implied in his provisioning for Elijah in ch. 17, is mightily and unforgettably confirmed (18:20-40). In the case of chs. 18–19, it is not thematic *movement* which unites, but thematic *repetition*. There are two mountains, one Baal-space (Carmel) and the other Yahweh-space (Horeb). In both places, someone challenges Yahweh and his prophet, and in both, the challenger loses. Against the background of enmity between Ahab and Elijah, the author-editor focuses the first challenge: a contest between Yahweh and Baal (or between Elijah and Baalistic prophets). In the second god-space, Horeb, the challenge seems in visionary retrospect to have been carried by Jezebel's death oath toward Elijah and Elijah's death wish for himself. For the prophet's renewal and survival is occasion for a proleptic glance into Yahweh's final triumph (19:17-18), as though narrative time were stopped to loop us back to the underlying struggle between Yahweh and Baal.

This outer bracketing and inner thematic linkage simultaneously emphasize a traditional portrait of Elijah and a god (Yahweh) triumphant over his rival(s). We are drawn to Elijah's "life": his appearance (ch. 17), his moment of high heroism (ch. 18), his flight, his fear for his life, and the indication of a successor (ch. 19). At the same time, this series of arranged vignettes serves as context for another drama: the struggle between Yahweh and Baal. The conflict becomes apparent to us in Elijah's early dealings with various people (ch. 17), is explicit in the public defeat of Baal and his prophets (ch. 18), is reasserted in Jezebel's oath toward Elijah (19:2), and finds resolution—a kind of thematic successor—in a final victory glimpsed by prophecy (19:16-18; cf. Cohn, 334).

As a last suggestion of unity in these redacted traditions, we may note an arrangement of narrative elements into parallel sequences, a sort of meta-unity cutting across the linear process of events (Cohn, 343-49). The following chart (modified from Cohn, 343) outlines the pattern:

A.	*Announcement*		
	by Elijah (17:1)	by God (18:1)	by Jezebel (19:2)
B.	*Journey* (by Elijah)		
	from Israel (17:2-5)	to Israel (18:2)	from Israel (19:3-4)
C.	*Two Encounters*		
	1) ravens (17:6-7)	Obadiah (18:7-16)	an angel (19:5-6)
	2) widow (17:8-16)	Ahab (18:17-20)	angel again (19:7)
D.	*Manifest power*		
	resuscitation (17:17-23)	fire (18:21-38)	theophany (19:9-18)
E.	*Transformation*		
	widow (17:24)	Israel (18:39-40)	Elijah renewed, and his successor tapped (19:15-21)

Even though the parallels are not always exact and their significance not always clear, the cumulative impact is impressive. Each major act in the present narrative sequence begins with an announcement which initiates action (A) and thereby precipitates a conflict or tension to be resolved. In each case, this spoken word connects with Elijah's move to a new locale (B). In this new setting, Elijah has two successive encounters (C), the second of which leads to divine manifestation of power (D). This results in transformation (E)—from disbeliever to believer (the widow; Israel); from despairing prophet to one with renewed commission and the first hint of future victory (19:15-21).

Moreover, certain repeated motifs create a system of cross references to reinforce coherence in the material (Cohn, 344-49). We have already noted the move from word (17:1) to its fulfillment (18:1, 41-46). Cohn observes further examples: the use of divinely commanded journeys (17:2; 18:1; 19:15), the importance of "feeding" throughout (17:4; 18:4, 19; 19:4), "voice" (17:22; 18:26, 29), "to know" (17:24; 18:36-37). All these repetitions mark out a contextual unity in support of the larger structural patterns.

Genre

This material is clearly a composite editorial unity welded of diverse, some originally independent, elements. Thus a genre cannot be specified with precision. It is perhaps too strong to call it an "artful prophetic tale" (Cohn, 350), since signs of unity do not entirely override the roughness of disparate origins. Baltzer's description of chs. 17–19 as "biography" carries some truth, but overlooks much that moves away from a biographical focus, especially the interest in describing a triumph by Yahweh over Baal.

Setting

Since it is a question of a composite literary work here, the idea of setting must be conceived in terms of literary place within the reign of Ahab, the books of Kings, and the social context in which the final Dtr author-editor worked. Looking back on the history of the northern kingdom as religious miscarriage (2 Kgs 17:7-18), this editor set the struggles between Ahab (Jezebel) and Elijah, writ large as between Baal and Yahweh, as the opening piece in the largest block of material telling the canonical "story" of the northern kingdom. Thus in chs. 17–19, this structured bypass of narrative time that captures the rivalry among the gods dominates the canonical characterization of both Ahab's reign and the entire series of northern monarchs.

Intention

The Dtr author-editor intends therefore to portray two struggles on two mountains: Yahweh and Baal, Ahab (Jezebel) and Yahweh's prophet Elijah; the one on Carmel, the other on Horeb. The aim must be to show the depth of the Baalism in the northern kingdom and at the same time to characterize the Omride dynasty in the person of Ahab. It is a pit from which one must and *can* be rescued, to judge from the proleptic reference to the eventual triumph of Yahweh's forces and Yahwism in the kingdom (19:17-18). In the widest canonical context this must refer to 2 Kings 9–10. The darkness is not without its light, the king not without his "troubler," and God lacks neither vanquished rival nor loyalist in Israel.

Bibliography

A. Alt, "Gottesurteil" (see listing at 18:1-46); K. Baltzer, 95-99 (see listing at "Introduction to Historical Literature"); G. Bottini, "Il racconto della siccita e della pioggia (1 Re

17–18)," *Liber Annus. Studii biblici franciscani* 29 (1979) 327-49; L. Bronner, *The Stories of Elijah and Elisha as Polemics Against Baal Worship* (Leiden: Brill, 1969); B. S. Childs, "On Reading the Elijah Narratives," *Int* 34 (1980) 128-37; R. Cohn, "The Literary Logic of 1 Kings 17–19," *JBL* 101 (1982) 333-50; G. del Olmo Lete, *La Vocación del Líder en El Antiquo Israel* (Salamanca: Pontifical University, 1973); S. J. De Vries, *Prophet Against Prophet* (Grand Rapids: Eerdmans, 1978); W. Dietrich, *Prophetie und Geschichte* (see listing at "Introduction to 1 Kings"); O. Eissfeldt, *Der Gott Karmel* (Berlin: Akademie, 1953); idem, "Die Komposition von I Reg. 16:29–II Reg. 13:25," in *Das ferne und nahe Wort* (*Fest.* L. Rost; ed. F. Maass; BZAW 105; Berlin: W. de Gruyter, 1967) 49-58; F. C. Fensham, "A Few Observations on the Polarisation Between Yahweh and Baal in 1 Kings 17–19," *ZAW* 92 (1980) 227-36; G. Fohrer, *Elia* (2nd ed.; Zurich: Zwingli, 1968); idem, *Prophetenerzählungen* (see listing at 11:26-40); H. Gunkel, *Elias, Jahve, und Baal* (Tübingen: Mohr, 1906); G. Hentschel, *Die Elijah-Erzählungen* (Erfurter Theologische Studien 33; Leipzig: St. Benno, 1977); D. Jobling, *The Sense of Biblical Narrative* (JSOTSup 7; Sheffield: University of Sheffield, 1978) 63-88; O. Plöger, "Prophetengeschichten" (see listing at "Introduction to 1 Kings"); Y. Radday, "Chiasm" (see listing at "Introduction to 1 Kings"); A. Rofé, "Didactic Legenda" (see listing at 12:33–13:34); J. Schüpphaus, "Prophetengeschichten," 41-49 (see listing at "Introduction to 1 Kings"); R. Smend, "Das Wort Jahwes an Elia," *VT* 25 (1975) 525-43; O. H. Steck, *Überlieferung und Zeitgeschichte in den Elia Erzählungen* (Neukirchen: Neukirchener, 1968); S. Timm, *Die Dynastie Omri* (FRLANT 124; Göttingen: Vandenhoeck & Ruprecht, 1982) 54-111.

REPORT OF ELIJAH'S WORD TO AHAB, 17:1

Structure

I. Narrative introduction	1aα
II. Word proper: oath	1aβ-b

This small unit stands out from its immediate context as a distinct scene in the larger dramatic movement. It follows on 16:34 without transition and explicitly concerns Elijah's word to Ahab. In contrast, vv. 2-3 report a word from Yahweh to Elijah. The style is reportorial and the structure simple: a brief narrative introduction with typical *waw*-conversive verb leads to a quote of Elijah's message for the king (v. 1aβ-b). Save for the enigmatic designation of Elijah's background, no circumstantial details are given. The emphasis clearly falls on the content of the word which is formulated in the style of an oath, "As the Lord the God of Israel lives. . . ."

Genre

This unit is a Report of Oath. The direct quotation is entirely typical and carries the main declaration sanctioned by invoking the deity. Cf. 1 Kgs 17:12; Gen 42:15; Ezek 33:11; Judg 8:19; 1 Sam 14:39, 45 (Blank; Lehmann; Pope).

Setting

Since it was an ancient means of impressing on parties their mutual obligations in agreements and investigations, oath would have had various social settings in the life of ancient Israel. In many circumstances, oaths would have been associated with shrines and their caretaker priests. Here, oaths might be sanctioned by the deity and uttered within the powerful environs of sacred places and holy objects (Pope). Oath taking found several literary reflexes. *Reports* of oath belong to narratives about people, places, or memorable events. These literary settings should be carefully distinguished from treaties, contracts, or other legal materials which often contain lists or records of oaths. An original setting for this word attributed to Elijah is of course not visible. We may with more profit focus on its present literary context in the reign of Ahab. It follows the mention of Joshua's curse (16:34) and opens the cycle of narratives which will have Elijah and King Ahab as main characters.

Intention

In this context, the report naturally introduces Elijah to the reader and into the Ahab "chronicle," while offering a divine sanction for the truth of what the prophet says, and what he *will* say. Like a prophecy, the oath announces to King Ahab an irrevocable state of affairs bound to weigh on his rule. In short, the report makes a large thematic statement. It suggests the necessary background for the events to follow: the rain bottles are corked and may be opened only at a prophet's insistent word. It is an ominous way to begin a narrative—as though Elijah's sudden appearance, fully described by a threatening oath, were analogous to the startling eruption of divine word in human affairs. As Elijah's lineage is only suggested mysteriously, so his power is only hinted at darkly. And yet, we see enough through the opaque glass to suspect conflict with royal prerogatives. It will be his or the king's word that will seek its fulfillment in events—not both.

Bibliography

S. H. Blank, "The Curse, the Spell and the Oath," *HUCA* 23 (1950/51) 73-95; M. R. Lehmann, "Biblical Oaths," *ZAW* 81 (1969) 74-92; M. H. Pope, "Oaths," *IDB*.

LEGEND: CARE AND PROVISIONING OF ELIJAH, 17:2-16

Structure

I. First miracle: water and food by ravens	2-6
A. Divine word: announcement of provision	2-4
1. Prophetic word formula	2
2. The divine word	3-4
a. Command: depart!	3
b. Announcement of provision	4
B. Actualization of word: miracle of water and food	5-6
1. Execution of command	5
2. The miracle: food and water	6
II. Second miracle: meal and oil	7-16
A. The situation: no water	7
B. The solution: miracle of meal and oil	8-16
1. Divine word: announcement of provision	8-9
a. Prophetic word formula	8
b. The divine word	9
1) Command: arise, go!	9a

2) Announcement of provision	9b
2. Actualization of word: miracle of meal and oil	10-16
a. Narrative setting	10a
1) Command executed	10aα
2) Meeting of Elijah and a widow	10aβ
b. Dialogue	10b-14
1) Elijah's requests for water and bread	10b-11
a) Narrative introduction	10bα
b) Requests	10bβ-11
(1) Water	10bβ
(2) Bread	11
2) Widow's statement (her objections)	12
a) Narrative introduction	12aα^1
b) Statement proper: oath	12aα^2-b
(1) Oath formula	12aα^2
(2) Declaration	12aβ-b
3) Elijah's rejoinder	13-14
a) Narrative introduction	13aα^1
b) Renewed request	13aα^2-b
c) Justification: prophetic oracle	14
(1) Messenger formula	14aα^1
(2) Oracle	14aα^2-b
c. Execution of Elijah's request	15a
d. Result: the miracle	15b-16
1) Unending food and supply of meal and oil	15b-16a
2) Oracle fulfillment formula	16b

Most critics agree that vv. 2-16 are to be distinguished from vv. 17-24 because of the latter's different subject matter and theme. The connective in v. 17a, "after this," appears to be a secondary linkage between separate traditions. Yet vv. 2-16 may themselves have not been originally a smooth literary unit. Vv. 2-6 are schematic, totally defined by divine word and its actualization in human events. On the other hand, vv. 8-16, while beginning in a way parallel to vv. 2-3, develop a more complex path to the fulfillment of God's private word to Elijah. Neither the prophet nor the widow of Zarephath are passive agents, in contrast to the Elijah of vv. 2-6. They discuss, Elijah makes demands, they argue, Elijah persists and finally persuades by citing an oracle of God. Only by this circuitous route is divine word, vv. 8-9, finally brought to fruition, vv. 15-16. Whatever their backgrounds might have been, the episodes in vv. 2-6 and 8-16 seem now to be linked together by the use of a duplicated thematic structure: both begin with a schematic rendering of Yahweh's word to the prophet (I.A, vv. 2-4; II.B.1, vv. 8-9). In this way, both present a promise of God to sustain Elijah, and both tell how that promise came to pass.

The first episode (I, vv. 2-6) is ruled by a schematic perspective which inhibits narrative richness. There are simple commands with an announcement that Yahweh has provided for Elijah (vv. 3-4). The resolution of whatever minor dramatic tension has been aroused comes in the ravens' obedient response to Yahweh's wishes. The text seems defined by the correspondence of divine command with its execution (vv. 2-4 and 5-6). Like the ravens, Elijah is passive, the mere recipient of command and blessing. Given no narrative flesh, he simply conforms to the important action—the guiding of events by Yahweh's command. In this light, the familiar formula, "according to the word of the Lord" (*kidbar yahweh,* v. 5a), does not allude to the fulfillment of prophecy (as it will in v. 16), but to simple obedience. V. 7 is a transition, an event impulsing the action into a second stage.

The second episode (II, vv. 7-16) builds somewhat on the schematic pattern of vv. 2-6, and also on a more general convention for narrating stories of miracle. A problem is stated and overcome by divine intervention (Culley). Yet this episode is richer than such comments might suggest. The characters have body, and they interact through dialogue, which indeed constitutes a good deal of the dramatic action. This poor, bereft widow suddenly encounters a prophet commanded and empowered by God who at first requests a little water, then adds, as an afterthought, some food as well. Considering her impoverished state, and that famine enwraps the scene like some kind of stifling blanket (vv. 7, 14 [v. 1]), one is not surprised by the woman's reaction. It is her last meager meal that Elijah requests with studied politeness (*qĕḥî-nāʾ lî/liqḥî-nāʾ lî,* "bring me, please"; cf. 2 Kgs 5:22; Gen 12:13; GKC, § 110d). But to her, the prophet's request must appear as cruel demand. She resists fervently, with (→) oath (note the oath formula, v. 12a) and resigned self-pity. Apparently the widow is won over by Elijah's assurances ("Fear not . . .") and his serene confidence. An oracle announces the real situation, which only the prophet can know and which is contrary to what the widow in her dejected state might imagine. Elijah simply points to an impending miracle, and at the same time he argues that the widow's perception of reality and thus her resistance to Elijah's requests should be suspended.

The miracle then is reported matter-of-factly, drained of all drama and suspense. It is not even clear that Elijah actively brings about the deed (cf. 17:21; 18:42-44; 2 Kgs. 1:10; against Cohn, 335). We hear the narrator's voice, as though to show us the point in the oracle fulfillment formula of v. 16 (cf. 2 Kgs 1:17; 2:22; 4:44). What is finally important is the correspondence between divine word as spoken by the prophet and events in human experience. Thematically, the point is similar to that of vv. 2-6, even though more complexly put and developed. Yet, in the wider scope provided by the context, this correspondence between word and event is subordinate to the theme of God's providing for Elijah during the famine, and, one must presume, in the aftermath of speaking an unpleasant word to King Ahab (17:1).

Genre

It is best to identify this unit as PROPHETIC LEGEND, that is, a STORY which focuses both the teller's and the reader's interest on wonderful attributes and miraculous action of God and his prophet (Fichtner, *Könige,* 257). One might specify the genre a bit more precisely, perhaps, by speaking of "miracle story" (Hentschel, 93-95) or "didactic legend" (Rofé, 148-50), but with limited gain (cf. Steck, 142-44; Hals). De Vries (pp. 54-55) divides legend according to a functional scheme and calls this unit a "supplicatory power story." The label rests on too restricted and rigid a view of narrative function, which after all varies according to the teller as well as the social situations in which legend might be used. Even less satisfactory, and hardly cited any longer, is Plöger's designation, "prophetic story that forms a part of an Israelite history" (Plöger, 57).

Because the two episodes show a certain independence of one another, Fohrer *(Prophetenerzählungen,* 52-53) speaks of distinct "anecdotes." But even viewed separately, the traditions conform to the basic type, legend. The first simply narrates the miracle that Yahweh cares for Elijah, quite without special merit or solicitation. For close parallels see Exod 15:22-25a; 16:1-21; 17:1-17; Mark 8:1-10; Matt 15:32-39, all legends involving miraculous feedings (see R. Bultmann, *History,* 209-44 [see listing at 14:1-18]). The second episode, vv. 10-16, connects the miracle of meal and oil with the spoken prophetic word, and thus is similar to other prophetic legends which take the actualization of divine word as their main point (e.g., 2 Kgs 2:19-22; 4:42-44; Long, 346-47). Yet in 1 Kgs 17:14, the prophet's oracle serves a more complex narrative function. It explains Elijah's persistent request for food and water, and reveals the irony between the prophet's and the widow's understanding of the situation. In its larger context, this episode focuses not only on word and its fulfillment, but also on God's provision for Elijah: indirect, mysterious, finally overcoming a widow's miscomprehending and misplaced opposition.

Smaller generic elements within this legend deserve special mention. The familiar PROPHETIC WORD FORMULA, "And the word of the Lord came to so-and-so. . . ," appears in vv. 2 and 8. In both cases, the formula introduces a REPORT OF PROPHETIC REVELATION, that is, a private communication from God to his prophet. This genre is to be distinguished from prophetic ORACLE(S) which quote directly various kinds of prophetic speech addressed to another person, and are typically introduced with a MESSENGER FORMULA, "Thus says the Lord" (see 17:14). The genre is also distinct from the later REPORT OF PROPHETIC WORD, which typically begins with the prophetic word formula, but stands rather free of any narrative concern with the deeds and experiences of the prophet (cf. Jer 21:1-10; Ezek 14:1-11). We may also note the OATH in v. 12a (→ the full discussion at 17:1), and the formulaic way of stating the fulfillment of prophecy given in v. 16 (→ ORACLE FULFILLMENT FORMULA and 2 Kgs 1:17; 2:22; 4:44; full discussion at 1 Kgs 13:26).

Setting

In situations of oral transmission, prophetic legend may have lived among prophets and in prophetic groups (De Vries, 54-55; Gray, *Kings,* 371; cf. 2 Kgs 8:4). Yet, we may not exclude other elements of Israelite society. Ethnographical studies where our knowledge is not so dependent on a literary tradition indicate that similar legends are rarely, if ever, the exclusive preserve of one social group. In a genuine sense, such stories are folk stories, belonging to the people (cf. Bascom). The particular legend in 17:2-16 receives an important *literary* setting, however, as part of the cycle of stories pitting Elijah and Ahab opposite one another, locked—like Yahweh and Baal—in moral and social combat. The legend offers a first glimpse of events in the reign of a king already roundly condemned

(16:30-33) and under the shadow of curse (16:34) and drought (17:1). The incidents fall between a word which barely hints at enmity, perhaps even the prophet's flight from royal reprisal (17:1, 2), and a coming confrontation with King Ahab in 18:17-18. It is this larger literary framework with its attachment to both Yahwism and the Israelite defender of Yahwism, King Jehu (19:17; cf. 2 Kgs 9:1–10:31), that S. De Vries (114-16) associates with a pre-Dtr editor or circles who were sympathetic to Jehu's efforts to eradicate Phoenician (Baalistic) elements from Israelite society. In any case, this legend now is part of the exilic author-editor's presentation of King Ahab's reign, and Elijah as the king's great "troubler" (cf. 18:17).

Intention

Since the background of this legend remains obscure, we must comment mainly on its intention in literary context. Certainly, the author(s) suggest that Yahweh cared for Elijah during this period of double adversity: the presumed hostility of Ahab (17:1, 2; cf. 18:9-12, 17) and the drought with its increasingly severe effects (vv. 7, 12, 14; cf. 18:5). The story illustrates how life was preserved for one who proclaimed death by famine (Plöger, 17-18), and indeed preserved by Yahweh's word. Surely in the wider context of a power struggle between Yahweh and Baal (ch. 18), the Israelite reader must have championed Yahweh's power over life to the detriment of Baal—the weather and rain god who does nothing to counteract drought and death (Bronner; Fensham). This picture prepares the reader for Elijah's confrontation with Ahab which looms in the near future. For the "troubler" of Ahab is under the care of Yahweh (vv. 2-6, 7-16) and has special knowledge (v. 14); it remains to be seen if he possesses unusual gifts of power (vv. 17-24).

One thinks of a similar folkloristic theme: the hero undergoes a period of private trials in preparation for extraordinary, public adventures. We meet the theme elsewhere in the Bible: the wilderness trek (Exodus 15–Joshua 1) as symbolic image of that liminal affliction and isolation leading to the promised land; Jesus sojourns in the wilderness, is tempted by Satan, and receives the spirit that empowers him to heroic mission (Luke 4:1-13). It is a typical literary reflex of widely observed shamanistic experiences, a sort of *rite de passage* (Eliade).

Thus, the legend of miraculous feeding of Elijah portrays a time apart, which also demarcates this prophet's peculiar providential preservation. We know him first as mysteriously moved by God and fed by God's creatures, even a victim of God's famine. And he survives by God's miracle. Here is a moment of strange power apart from the organized center that is Ahab; it balances the time of despair and powerlessness in ch. 19, again apart, in the wilderness of Beer-sheba and Horeb.

Bibliography

Note bibliography at 17:1–19:21. W. Bascom, "African Folklore and Literature," *The African World: A Survey of Social Research* (ed. Robert Lystad; New York: Praeger, 1965) 469-560; R. Culley, *Studies in the Structure of Hebrew Narrative* (Philadelphia: Fortress, 1976); M. Eliade, *Shamanism: Archaic Techniques of Ecstasy* (Princeton: Princeton University, 1964); B. O. Long, "2 Kings III and Genres of Prophetic Narrative," *VT* 23 (1973) 337-48.

LEGEND: ELIJAH'S BENEVOLENT POWERS, 17:17-24

Structure

I. The situation of crisis: a child's illness	17
II. Complication: mother's reproach of Elijah	18-19
A. Reproach (= denial of Elijah's benevolent power)	18
1. Rhetorical question	18a
2. Reproach proper	18b
B. Elijah's reaction	19
1. Command	19a
2. Action (withdrawal)	19b
a. Child taken from mother	$19b\alpha^1$
b. Move to upper chamber	$19b\alpha^2$-β
III. Resolution of crisis: revival of child	20-22
A. Elijah's petitionary actions	20-21
1. Lament	20
2. Petition	21
a. Ritual action	21aα
b. Petition proper	21aβ-b
B. God's response: child revived	22
IV. Conclusion	23-24
A. Elijah's actions	23
1. Return	23a
a. Move to lower chamber	23aα
b. Child delivered to mother	23aβ
2. Declaration: life	23b
B. Mother's reaction: confession (=affirmation of Elijah's benevolent power)	24

This unit opens a new theme—not Elijah's receiving God's special provisions (vv. 2-16), but Elijah actively dispensing the blessing of life. The unit seems only vaguely related to the chronology of vv. 7, 14-15, has no connection with the longer background motif of drought (vv. 1, 12, 14), and is now clearly set off from its surroundings by imprecise connectives: "after these things" (v. 17) and "after many days" (18:1). Possibly the material was originally independent of its present literary context, and even related in now obscure ways to a similar tradition about Elisha in 2 Kgs 4:18-37 (Fohrer; Kilian; Schmitt). At the least, we may deal with a well-defined and well-wrought unit.

Typical narrative style verbs (*wyqṭl*) and direct speech between major characters dominate the material. Even though descriptive passages are minimal (vv. 17, 19, 21a, 22b, 23), they sketch key actions (as in vv. 19, 21a, 23) or offer vivid descriptions (e.g., "no breath in him," v. 17b; "the soul [*nepeš*] of the boy returned to his corpse, and he lived," v. 22b; cf. Gen 2:7). The incident is told with restraint, but not without emotion. Important emphases come in speech which travels between Elijah and the woman and from Elijah to God.

The key to the structure of this unit lies in a double-faced thematic movement. First, there is a crisis, an illness to death which is resolved through Yahweh's intervention, mediated of course by Elijah, who is addressed here as "man of God." Second, the woman's perception of Elijah undergoes a complete turnabout by the end of the incident. Her rhetorical question (II.A.1, v. 18a) carries a tone of rejection (literally, "What do you and I have to do with one another?"; cf. 2 Kgs 3:13; Judg 11:12; 2 Sam 16:10; 19:23 [*RSV* 22]), and her reproach (II.A.2, v. 18b: "You have come to me to kill my son") suggests that she attributes both malevolent powers and evil intention to Elijah. The boy's revival, therefore, demonstrates to the woman Elijah's power for *good* and hence motivates her final confession, reversing all she implied at the beginning. Thus, the climax (III, vv. 20-22) has a double meaning, a balanced reversal of key elements: a movement from illness (death) to life and from denial to affirmation.

This double theme hangs on a carefully balanced narrative skeleton. There are three scenes: Elijah and the woman (II.A, B, vv. 18-19), Elijah and Yahweh (III.A, B, vv. 20-22), Elijah and the woman (IV.A, B, vv. 23-24). These are set in a kind of "sandwich" or "ring" (Bar-Efrat) construction, in which the first and third scenes (elements II and IV) balance one another and enclose the action between Elijah and Yahweh, withdrawn from public encounter (element III; cf. Schmitt, 460-61). The climactic revival of the child is thus isolated physically (it takes place in the upper chamber), socially (away from the mother), and thematically (it takes place between the woman's denial and her affirmation). Our eye moves from public (Elijah and the woman) to private (Elijah alone with the corpse) back to public (Elijah and the woman); from outward (the house) to inner (the upper chamber) back to outward (the downstairs room); or from community (prophet and his public) to withdrawal (Elijah alone with Yahweh) back to community (prophet and the woman). Throughout, the son is passive, an instrument of dramatic struggle, something to be taken from the mother, dead, and returned to the mother, living. The child is a curious prop as mystery takes place on stage. Only in that moment of withdrawal does the narrator focus on Elijah. A diagram may help to make the movement clear:

Structural Element	**Action**	**Verses**
II.A, B	Elijah, son, and woman together	vv. 18-19
III.A, B	Elijah and son withdrawn, separated from others; Elijah and Yahweh	vv. 20-22
IV.A, B	Elijah, son, and woman together	vv. 23-24

A similar structure appears in 2 Kgs 2:1-18, another Elijah tradition which sets the narrative climax in that liminal moment of physical and social separation:

Action	**Verses**
Elijah and Elisha with sons of prophets	2 Kgs 2:1-8
Elijah and Elisha withdrawn across Jordan	2 Kgs 2:9-14
Elisha with sons of prophets	2 Kgs 2:15-18

Cf. 1 Kgs 18:42, where Elijah withdraws to conjure a rainstorm; Exodus 19–20, where Moses shuttles between the people who stand, profane, at the base of Sinai and God whom Moses, specially chosen, meets on the heights, withdrawn and wrapped in cloud.

Besides in-balance and patterned movement on the large scale, artistic symmetry is evident also in smaller details. The narrator built two scenes involving Elijah and the woman out of chiastic relationships (cf. Cohn, 336, for a slightly different analysis).

Structural Element	**Action**	**Verses**
II.B.1	Command: "Give me your son"	19a
II.B.2	Action (withdrawal)	19b
	a. Child taken from mother	19bα[1]
	b. Move to upper chamber	19bα[2]-β
IV.A.1	Action (return)	23
	a. Move to lower chamber	23aα
	b. Child delivered to mother	23aβ
IV.A.2	Declaration: "Your son lives"	23b

The narrative has simple beauty and dramatic power. For in moving through thematic reversals—seen variously as illness to life; denial to affirmation; public to private to public; crisis, cure (divine intervention), and return to health—the narrator dramatizes the mystery of sacred power and one's ambivalent relationship to it. Sacrality is hedged about as it comes into the world of the merely human. It is met in private, in a thresholding moment between time and eternity. The woman senses the power and knows its ambiguity. But she finally affirms its goodness and Elijah's truth, and she speaks with emphasis: "Now for sure [*'attâ-zeh,* v. 24a] I know that you are a man of God, and that the word of the Lord in your mouth is truth." (Cf. Jethro's confession of Yahweh's power in Exod 18:11.) Structurally and thematically, the narrative comes to rest in this woman's recognition and confession. (Cf. 1 Kgs 18:39; 2 Kgs 2:15; 5:15; 9:13.)

Genre

As with 17:2-16, this unit is best identified as a PROPHETIC LEGEND, a story which seeks to edify by portraying wonderful attributes and/or wondrous actions of a prophet (Fichtner, *Könige,* 259). Attempts at greater precision have not achieved any noticeable consensus (e.g., Rofé, 149-50, "didactic legenda"; Hentschel, 95, "miracle story"; De Vries, 54, "prophet-legitimation story"; Schmitt, 473-74, "constructed prophetic narrative"). While these various designations offer important insights into the narrative, they restrict too much its multivalent character and its potential for diverse usage, depending on varying circumstances of telling and transmission.

An important generic element is PETITION, seen in vv. 20, 21. Form and style are typical. A rhetorical question makes a case for granting the petition; the petition itself begins with address to God, "(O) Yahweh, my God . . ." and develops the request in simple imperative style (v. 21). See fuller discussion with parallel texts at 1 Kgs 3:4-15.

Setting

Prophetic legend may have stemmed from prophetic groups or have had its provenance among the folk (→ discussion at 17:2-16). This particular example may derive from the northern kingdom, as many critics suggest. It is probably ethnocentric of Schmitt (p. 474) to speculate about a circle of theologians among prophetic groups (*"Theologenkreise der Prophetengruppe"*; cf. Bronner, 140 and passim, "theologian," but without definition). The occasions for telling such a story would have been varied. In its particular literary context, the legend forms a second major episode in Elijah's life between the announcement of drought and the looming confrontation with King Ahab.

Intention

Since we cannot see with certainty the societal settings behind the text in Kings, we must focus on the legend's function in literary context. Surely, the narrator wanted to demonstrate the legitimacy of this prophet, "man of God," Elijah (De Vries, 54). His power is like that of Moses (cf. Num 11:4-13, 15, 18-24a, 31-35; Exod 14:1-31; 15:22-25; Schmitt, 466-71). But looking more closely at the immediate context, one also sees that the legend rounds out a kind of indirect introduction of this man Elijah and his storied affairs. He is to be "troubler of Israel" (18:17) and champion of Yahweh (18:1-40). But here, he has appeared with the abruptness of epiphany (17:1). His deeds are his pedigree. Taken with vv. 2-16, two legends set up the approaching conflict with Ahab by gathering the forces on Elijah's side: he is provided for, given special care and knowledge (vv. 2-16), and then actively mediates Yahweh's benevolent power. In a word, he comes to "prophetic maturity" (Cohn, 336). We suspect the approaching contest even before Elijah the protagonist knows of it, and we comprehend the forces that are within Elijah's grip. In this context, the widow's reproach (v. 18) anticipates that of Ahab (18:17); Yahweh's control over food, water, events, even death and life, anticipates both the issue and outcome of the future confrontation with Ahab; the woman's confession that Elijah's word is truth foreshadows the people's confession, "the Lord, he is God" (18:39); and as though there might be some question in the reader about the reliability of a prophet's word that propels the main drama (17:1), the events in vv. 2-16 and 17-24 attest to Elijah's truth. His word is let loose amid wondrous deeds of power. In sum, the legends not only introduce Elijah, who rises like a specter in Ahab's kingdom, but they tell something of his place and power.

Bibliography

See bibliography at 17:1–19:21. B. Diebner, "Form-, gattungs- und traditionskritische Untersuchung alttestamentlicher Wundererzählungen" (Habilitationsschrift, Bonn, 1971); R. Kilian, "Die Totenerweckungen Elias and Elishas—eine Motivwanderung," *BZ* 10 (1966) 44-56; A. Schmitt, "Die Totenerweckung in 1 Kön xvii 17-24," *VT* 27 (1977) 454-74; idem, "Die Totenerweckung in 2 Kön 4:8-37," *BZ* 19 (1975) 1-25.

LEGEND: ELIJAH'S (AND YAHWEH'S) TRIUMPH, 18:1-46

Structure

I. Narrative setting 1

A. Prophetic word formula	1a
B. The divine word: commission	1b
1. Command: go to Ahab	1bα
2. Promise: rain	1bβ
II. Actualization of the divine word: rainstorm	2-45a
A. Elijah's appearance before Ahab	2-40
1. Execution of command: Elijah starts toward Ahab	2a
2. A meeting on the way	2b-16
a. Background: scene at Ahab's court	2b-6
1) Crisis: the famine	2b
2) Ahab's response to crisis	3-5
a) Obadiah summoned	3a
b) Digression: Obadiah the pious	3b-4
c) King's command: search for fodder	5
3) Execution of command	6
b. The meeting (Obadiah and Elijah)	7-16
1) Initial sighting and exchange	7-8a
2) Dialogue	8b-15
a) Elijah's command: announce Elijah to Ahab	8b
b) Obadiah's response: imputation speech	9-14
(1) Imputation question	9
(2) Elaboration	10-14
(a) Oath formula	$10a\alpha^1$
(b) Declarations	$10a\alpha^2$-12
(c) Rhetorical question: attestation of innocence	13
(d) Imputation: Elijah's command and its results	14
c) Elijah's counter-response	15
(1) Oath formula	15a
(2) Declaration of intent: appear before Ahab	15b
3) Outcome of dialogue	16
a) Obadiah to Ahab	16a
b) Ahab to Elijah	16b
3. Appearance before Ahab: confrontation and contest	17-40
a. Preparatory dialogue	17-19
1) Ahab's accusing query	17
2) Elijah's response	18-19
a) Denial	18aα
b) Counteraccusation	18aβ-b
c) Command: gather prophets	19
b. Execution of command	20

c. Contest on Mount Carmel: Elijah and prophets (people) — 21-40
1) Preparation for contest — 21-24
   a) Elijah's challenge to people: choose who is God — 21a
   b) Response: silence — 21b
   c) Elijah's proposal: a demonstration — 22-24a
      (1) Statement of position — 22
      (2) Proposal for contest — 23-24a
   d) People's response: statement of agreement — 24b
2) The contest — 25-39
   a) First invocation of Baal — 25-26
      (1) Command to prophets: invoke Baal — 25
      (2) Execution of command: ritual and petition — 26aα
      (3) Result: silence — 26aβ-b
   b) Elijah's taunt — 27
   c) Second invocation of Baal — 28-29
      (1) Ritual and petitions — 28-29a
      (2) Result: silence — 29b
   d) Invocation of Yahweh — 30-39
      (1) Command: gather people — 30aα
      (2) Execution of command — 30aβ
      (3) Preparations — 30b-35
         (a) Repair of altar — 30b-32a
         (b) Preparations for invocations — 32b-34
            α. Wood and water, first time — 32b-34a
            β. Wood and water, second time — 34bα
            γ. Wood and water, third time — 34bβ
         (c) Result: abundance of water — 35
      (4) Petitions to Yahweh — 36-37
      (5) Result — 38-39
         (a) Epiphany of fire — 38
         (b) Speech of acclamation — 39
3) Consequences: the slaying of prophets — 40
   a) Elijah's command: seize prophets — 40aα
   b) Command executed — 40aβ
   c) Prophets of Baal killed — 40b

B. Actualization of the divine word: rainstorm — 41-45a

1. Setting (Elijah and Ahab)	41-42a
a. Elijah's speech	41
1) Command: go up, eat, drink	41a
2) Explanation: sound of rain	41b
b. Command executed	42a
2. Ritual of conjuration (Elijah and servant)	42b-44a
a. Preparations: withdrawal to summit	42b
b. Watching, seven times looking	43
c. Results: a cloud rising	44a
3. Miracle of rain (Elijah and Ahab)	44b-45a
a. Command to Ahab: go down	44b
b. Rainstorm	45a
III. Departure	45b-46
A. Ahab to Jezreel	45b
B. Elijah before Ahab	46

This unit opens onto a new subject matter—the meeting between Elijah and Ahab, and the contest on Mount Carmel. Formally, the report of a divine communication with Elijah, v. 1, suggests continuity with 17:2-16. In fact, this opening builds only on a motif from 17:1 (*māṭār,* "rain"), moves the larger drama forward, but otherwise makes no direct link with ch. 17. The unit ends naturally at 18:46, since 19:1 turns in a new direction and assumes that the events at Carmel have found their resting place.

Persistent voices defend the unity of this tradition at a stage prior to the Dtr assemblage of Kings (e.g., Burney, *Notes,* 210; Eissfeldt, *Der Gott,* 32-33; Šanda, *Könige,* I, 454-59, taking all of chs. 17–19 as a unit; Gray, *Kings,* 384). Even so, it seems likely that an editorial unity, early or late, has been forged out of diverse materials, not all of which are of the same age and provenance (Fohrer; Alt; Würthwein; Hentschel; Steck; De Vries). No matter how much one seeks a smooth narrative in the present text, loose ends, somewhat contradictory trajectories, and lost motifs remain. The unit seems to have been based on several independent traditions, no longer completely visible, or perhaps upon a much fuller and more complex narrative now unavailable, but suggested by undeveloped motifs (e.g., famine and pursuit of Elijah, vv. 2-16 [implicitly relating to 17:1?], a theme dropped in favor of the great contest between Yahweh prophet and Baal prophets, vv. 20-40; yet this latter section in a way interrupts the confrontation between Ahab and Elijah, vv. 17-18, and relates only indirectly to famine and the rainmaking of vv. 41-46). Since consensus on the stages of composition eludes the grasp of scholars, it seems advisable to investigate the sense of unity for the final composite form.

The unit is governed by a broad movement of plot: the divine word spoken to Elijah (I, v. 1) finds its actualization in the coming of rain (II.B, vv. 41-45). Yet, this thematic rubric is epidermal, less related to narrative details than to prominent surface motifs: 17:1; 18:1; 18:41, 45 (but note the use of different words for "rain": *māṭār* [17:1; 18:1] and *gešem* [18:41-45]). Thus, the way to fulfillment seems strained and indirect. Of course, at the beginning the drought announced in 17:1 and presupposed in most of ch. 17 serves as backdrop (18:2-6). But new themes emerge which seem to live independently. We see Jezebel as a persecutor of Yahweh prophets, vv. 4, 13, and Ahab as a pursuer of Elijah, vv. 9-14. In something of a turnabout near the end, Elijah slaughters the Baal prophets and conjures up the mighty rainstorm. Between beginning and end stands the confrontation between Ahab and Elijah, climax and catalyst for the finale. Yet this very moment turns quickly into a contest between Yahweh and Baal, as well as between Elijah and the Baal prophets, and becomes an occasion for the people to confess Yahweh and deny Baal. The entire sequence terminates when Elijah conjures rain, he and Ahab depart from one another, and the dramatic energy drains away in Elijah's breathless run to Jezreel. Thus, if the way from divine word to its fulfillment is reasonably clear, nevertheless it remains a challenge to understand the exact sense of the stones that make the path.

As is typical of many biblical narratives, the main portion of this unit (II.A, vv. 2-40) is built of distinct scenes involving only two characters at a time: Ahab and Obadiah; Obadiah and Elijah; Elijah and Ahab; Elijah and the prophets (people). The scenes imply depth rather than state it, and most of the dramatic action occurs in dialogues (→ 3:16-18 and comments there). Following the divine communication to Elijah that acts as a narrative setting, the narrator shifts abruptly to Ahab's court, preparing us with a circumstantial clause: "Now the famine was severe in Samaria" (v. 2b). We learn of Ahab's remedial measures in his orders to Obadiah and also of Obadiah through a flashback, vv. 3b-4, which anticipates his later words (v. 13). Without stressing the matter, the narrator has also suggested an inner connection between famine and Jezebel's purge of Yahweh prophets. He conveys a sense of desperate struggle without telling the story. This first scene is thoroughly preparatory; it sketches the situation, introduces two characters, and just barely suggests depth beneath the glimmering surface. We move to the second scene (II.A.2.b, vv. 7-16) suspecting more than we know.

Here, Elijah meets Obadiah in a kind of proleptic evocation of the prophet-king confrontation to come. Obadiah's speech reveals a double sense of pursuit: Ahab searches for fodder and also has gone to extraordinary lengths to pursue Elijah—either because he is somehow deemed responsible for the troubles in the land (17:1; 18:17) or because he has escaped a Jezebel-inspired pogrom (vv. 3b-4; 13). The situation is serious enough to make Elijah's presence seem a disturbing, even unjust, demand upon Obadiah. He is not unlike the widow who imputed malevolent intentions to Elijah (cf. 18:9 and 17:18); and he is like Ahab, who with similar opening words (cf. vv. 7b, 17) will greet Elijah as "troubler of Israel" (v. 17). So Obadiah's first words and actions are entirely correct and outwardly respectful (v. 7). But his polite and circumspect language covers and reveals a biting imputation (vv. 9-14): Elijah wants to have *me* slain by catching *me* up in his devious escape from Ahab's net! The irony is exquisite. *We* know that Elijah is really on his way to meet the king (he has been commanded to meet Ahab [18:1], and because of his exemplary obedience in ch. 17 we have no cause to believe otherwise), but Obadiah knows nothing of these previous events and assumes the worst. Again, Obadiah anticipates, for when Elijah confronts Ahab, the king will not know that rain is on the way; and lacking Obadiah's courtly manner, the king will assume the worst, too: "Is it you, you troubler of Israel?" (v. 17).

This second scene does not finally advance the narrative action. Through oath (v. 15) and simple statement (v. 16) it reiterates what the reader already knows: in obedience to God's command, Elijah is on his way to meet Ahab (cf. vv. 2 and 15). The two scenes together, vv. 2b-6 and 7-16, retard the decisive action in the interest of narrative complexity and suspense. We now know how severe is the drought, and how thoroughly powerful is Elijah's word (17:1). We recognize how deadly earnest is Ahab's pursuit of Elijah, and how necessary was his secretive existence east of the Jordan (17:3). We sense the desperation in Jezebel's persecution of Yahweh's prophets; the narrator described her as "cutting off the prophets" (*bĕhakrît,* v. 4), and Obadiah saw her as "murdering" them (*bahărōg,* v. 13). It is clear that Elijah's pursuit of God's word threatens his own person as much as it does King Ahab and the land. Gradually, the contours of confrontation have taken shape, sketched in dialogue, suggested in circumstance, implicit, foreboding.

The main antagonists finally meet each other (II.A.3, vv. 17-40). Like the preceding section, this scene is built of two smaller vignettes: the initial meeting of Ahab and Elijah (II.A.3.a, vv. 17-19), and the ensuing contest in which Elijah challenges the people and the Baal prophets (II.A.3.c, vv. 21-40). Ahab is quick to affront: "Is it you, you troubler of Israel?" (v. 17). And Elijah answers, astonishingly, just as directly. Not at all powerless, hiding nothing in false civility, he accuses Ahab of apostasy; and as though to announce punishment (cf. the style of typical prophetic speeches, e.g., 1 Kgs 21:20b-21a; 2 Kgs 1:16), Elijah calls for the prophets to be gathered together. No purpose is given.

Somehow the little scene sets up the conditions for—we learn later—a demonstration of divine power. However, the trading of accusations is not in itself crucial for subsequent action. It seems more important that out of Elijah's "showing" himself to Ahab (cf. 18:1, 15), regardless of the words exchanged, comes the impetus to put the bloom on a drama seeded by Yahweh's promise: out of the showing, somehow, would follow rain (18:1). The mutual accusations take on another importance. They identify the somewhat shadowy "villain" and the underlying conflict in the narrative. After a cryptic beginning (17:1) which leaves much unspoken and retardations which suggest hostilities and dark motivations, but never so clearly as to ruin suspense (18:2-16), we now see the root opposition which powers the drama: Ahab himself and his pursuit of Baal—perfectly opposed to Elijah and *his* pursuit of obedience to Yahweh. Ahab is less a character than a symbol. By him we measure the depth of the conflict of will to which the surface action relates.

In this light, it is not surprising that Ahab disappears in the following scene (II.A.3.c, vv. 21-40). In his place stand the prophets of Baal, looming large in number, supported by the "people," who seem mute and sullen, demanding to be convinced of their implacable unfaith (v. 21b). Implicit, of course, in this confrontation is the opposition between Yahweh and Baal. Hence, the question put to the bystanders: "If the Lord is God, follow him; but if Baal, then follow him" (v. 21), and their answer finally in v. 39: "The Lord, he is God; the Lord, he is God." In between is the contest, now framed by the narrator's focus on witnesses and the raw struggle between Elijah and the Baal prophets. The narrator is dramatic. He exaggerates (Elijah is one, the prophets many—vv. 22, 25; cf. 1 Kings 22) while slowing the pace. The Baal prophets try to rouse their god two times, with the same result: "and no voice, and no answer" (vv. 26aβ, 29b). The silence gets added emphasis, "and no one heeded." These two silences, pregnant with irony and triumph, find space in sound, in Elijah's mocking taunt, v. 27. The narrator lingers over detail as though to savor ridicule and victory; there is plenty of repetition, vv. 25-26, 26aβ/29b; "cry aloud," vv. 27/28; also "call upon the name," vv. 24, 25, 26. And when Elijah takes his turn at invoking divine power, the scene builds slowly—gathering of witnesses, heaping up of preparations, repairing an altar with a pause to explain the symbolism of twelve stones, the thrice-repeated dispersion of water on the altar. Even granting the possibility that the text is disturbed in vv. 30-31, it remains true that the author builds toward a climax made of ironic, mocking contrasts. Elijah stands alone, the Baal prophets are many (and for good measure, though they play no part in the scene, there are prophets of Asherah as well, v. 19). Baal, the one god who is repeatedly called upon, even taunted, is silent over against Yahweh, one God, who answers decisively against spectacular odds. The Baalistic ceremony, characterized perhaps unsympathetically as "prophesying" (v. 29, *RSV* "raved on") and frenzied (v. 28, "They cut themselves . . . until the blood gushed out upon them"; Roberts notes a parallel in an Akkadian text from Ugarit), stands in contrast with Elijah's elaborate, deliberate, even methodical preparations. Even his petition is properly modulated and filled with encomium for Yahweh (v. 37).

Suddenly the contest is over. The narrative pace quickens, as though the better to characterize the life and power of Yahweh. As the fire of Yahweh fell (*wattippōl,* v. 38), so the people fell (*wayyippĕlû,* v. 39). No longer silent witnesses, perhaps awestruck, they confess Yahweh as their God in hymnic tones. The narrator's images rivet this moment to deeply traditional Israelite sensibilities. The coming of Yahweh's power is at the same time a "burnt offering" upon a proper Yahweh altar (vv. 32-33; cf. Exod 20:24), built of stones symbolic of Israel's covenantal constitution (v. 31; cf. Gen 35:10). The altar is doused twelve times (four jars, dumped three times) as though inundation offers up the twelve tribes along with the bull. The people become, symbolically, a Levitical-pure Israel again, even to the point of slaying without question the apostates among them (v. 40; cf. Exod 32:25-28; see F. M. Cross, *Canaanite Myth,* 192 [see listing at "Introduction to 1 Kings"]; and Cohn, 340-41). The defeated Baal prophets face their execution at the brook Kishon. It is a water extinction, and perhaps a final ironic contrast to that twelve-tribes-of-Israel water poured round the altar and consumed as perfect sacrifice along with the "burnt offering, and the wood, and the stones, and the dust" (v. 38). Nothing remains—not even Baal prophets—except an offering given and wholly, perfectly, received.

Ahab appears again in the final scene (II.B, vv. 41-45), which offers the miracle of rain, the final outworking of Yahweh's promise. Just as was done in reviving the dead child (17:17-24), and as will be done in giving sacral power to Elisha (2 Kings 2), so Elijah withdraws to the summit of Mount Carmel (v. 42b), apparently leaving Ahab behind. Here the powers known only to Yahweh and his prophet (and to the reader) are manifest (vv. 42-43a). Apartness is the natural habitat of the unnatural. And on either side of this center, like a tethered and vanquished foe, Ahab receives and obeys the prophet's commands. As he probably was during the great contest, the king is still a bystander, accepting his cues from Elijah. There is no sign that he has given up Baal. But now the expectation is that somehow Yahweh prophets will count for something. Protagonist and antagonist depart from one another. Ahab goes in haste, it is hinted, to escape the torrents of conjured water; Elijah runs in prophetic excess, suffering the demands of "the hand of the Lord" (v. 46; cf. Ezek 33:22; 2 Kgs 3:15). They go together, while separate.

We may now see that vv. 21-40 form another grand retarding moment in the larger narrative. Just as vv. 2b-16 slowed the pace between command and confrontation with Ahab, so vv. 21-40 retard the movement from that critical "showing" and the coming of rain. The pause enriches the understanding and increases the wonder. How much lay unsuspected in that simple command to Elijah, "Go, show yourself to Ahab" (18:1)! Indeed, manifestation—Elijah to Ahab, Yahweh to the crowds—is the climactic event in the drama presented in these long retarding moments. One might even say that the tradition gives us two plots: the one, action oriented, finding resolution in the advent of rain; the other, ideologically oriented, slowly building the dimensions of conflict in dialogic scenes, and finding resolution in religious confession (v. 39). The one plot is easy to see and fits the pattern of so many miracle events in the Bible: a crisis finds resolution through the intervention of divine power or its earthly intermediary. Developed in elaborate retarding moments, the second plot adds interest, subtlety, suspense, epic grandeur, and depth. On this level the narrator dramatizes the conflict of religious allegiances so intimately a part of the general picture of Ahab's reign, and Elijah's role in it. What might have been a simple narrative of divine word and its realization, similar in structure to 17:2-6, is really an epic-proportioned drama of the gods and their representatives and the ideal Israel. Religious destiny is focused on this one half day on Mount Carmel. It is curious that Ahab is essentially a bystander, with the exception of his accusing query put to Elijah in v. 17. The hero is clearly Elijah, and behind him, Yahweh—but not because of Elijah's dealings with Ahab so much as because of his putting the central epic question: "Who is God?" (v. 21). In this regard, Elijah is like Moses—a servant of Yahweh, v. 36, who advocates Yahweh, one might say *meets* Yahweh, on a Canaanite mountain, vv. 30-38 (cf. for Moses, Exod 24:3-8; Deut 11:29-32; Exod 3:1-12).

Genre

This unit is best defined as PROPHETIC LEGEND, a story which shows less interest in artistic development of plot or character than in emphasizing wondrous attributes and deeds of God's intermediary. Generally unhappy with such a broad designation, some critics have sought more precision by largely ignoring the totality of the text in favor of a focus on vv. 21-39, assuming these to have been originally independent and complete in themselves. It is doubtful that this section of the whole is more than a fragment. In any case, there is no consensus on a more specific generic identification. One hears, for example, of "sanctuary legend" (Steck, 79; Würthwein, "Erzählung"; Alt, *KS* II, 148), "supplicatory power story" (De Vries, 54-55), "decision narrative" (Tromp), and "Yahweh story with instructional tendencies" (Preuss, 82). Defining the unit somewhat differently as 17:1 and 18:26-46, Hentschel (pp. 112-15) speaks of a "story of political criticism." In view of the uncertainties and the proliferation of generic designations which emphasize unduly one or another aspect of the material, it seems wisest to retain the more open-ended and descriptive term legend. For all its limitations, even this is preferable to "prophetic story as part of Israelite history" (Plöger, 57).

Within the legend, we may identify smaller generic elements. The legend is opened by a prophetic COMMISSION, v. 1, consisting of the typical PROPHETIC WORD FORMULA, "And the word of the Lord came to Elijah," and a quoted private communication from God ordering the prophet to go to Ahab, and adding a PROPHECY of rain. Obadiah's address to Elijah, vv. 9-14, is an IMPUTATION SPEECH, a form of argument which belongs to DISPUTATIONS, either leading to trial proceedings (Boecker) or separate from legal contexts altogether. The speech begins with a question which implies that a wrong has been done to the speaker (cf. Judg 8:1, leading into a longer speech that seeks to appease; similarly, 1 Sam 20:1). Then follows an elaboration of the point, citing the wrong that is alleged to have been committed (so in Num 22:28-29; 1 Sam 26:18-20). We may note that in the midst of this imputation speech in Obadiah's mouth is an OATH with its typical formula, "As the Lord your God lives . . ." (v. 10; see discussion at 17:1). Also, Elijah responds with an oath in v. 15. Elijah's PETITION to Yahweh (vv. 36-37) has been noted for its pious modulation and encomium of God. The language is exalted, almost hymnic, and recalls the petitions ascribed to Solomon (see full discussion at 3:6-9; 8:23-26). In context, Elijah's petition asks for God to show himself. Not surprisingly, therefore, the following verses recall a familiar literary pattern for reporting THEOPHANY: a manifestation of God, followed by reactions of fear, awe, worship (see Lev 9:24; 2 Chr 7:1-3; cf. Exod 3:6; 34:6-8). The ACCLAMATION FORMULA, v. 39b, hymnic in character (cf. Ps 95:7; 100:3; 105:7), has its closest parallels in parenetic contexts offering demonstrations of Yahweh's power, e.g., Deut 4:35, 39; 7:9; and 1 Kgs 8:60, in the midst of a speech identified as PARENESIS (see full discussion at 8:54-61).

Setting

Answers to the question of setting reflect one's judgment about tradition and compositional history and carry all the liabilities associated with theories built on incomplete evidence. For example, among those who designate vv. 21-39 as an independent "sanctuary legend," Würthwein ("Erzählung," 135) located the story's provenance among Yahwistic prophets associated with a shrine on Mount Carmel. Tromp went further and postulated a ritual of periodic Yahweh affirmation at Mount Carmel during which this "decision narrative" would be told. On the other hand, De Vries (p. 54) asserted, vaguely, a setting among "prophetic circles in challenge to institutional authority" (cf. Hentschel, 326-27).

Generally speaking, prophetic legend would have had its origin and transmission among prophetic groups or among the folk who tell stories of their prophets. In this particular example in its final form, which probably is older than the assemblage of Kings, the special emphasis on religious struggle suggests a provenance among prophetic groups who were deeply interested in the triumph of Yahweh over rival gods, either as an accomplished, or aspired to, social condition. Steck (p. 146) locates the fixation on Elijah in this triumphant image among a prophetic "guild" tied to Elisha. Occasions of use would have been varied, however, according to circumstances. One may not overlook a range of possibilities, including the ideological defense of Yahwism when such allegiances were declining (Long) or rising, as, for example, in a time of Yahwistic triumph (cf. 2 Kings 9–10, the militant attempts of Jehu to establish Yahweh as the national god, alone without rival).

Intention

Given the uncertainties, we cannot really see much of the original intentions for supposed earlier forms of this legend. Even from its final form in 1 Kings, it clearly seems mistaken to look for a *single* intention. Against the background of Elijah's drought-breaking powers, the narrator portrays a deep conflict in religious loyalty, perhaps even a vivid polemic against Baal (Bronner). Of course, Elijah is the earthly hero—fully empowered by Yahweh (ch. 17) and amply justified in his solitary vigil for the heavenly hero. With these images and clash of wills, the exilic Dtr author-editor affirms single-minded devotion to the God who demands and exacts obedience in the catastrophe of a scattered body politic. Ahab and, to a certain extent, Jezebel are less real as antagonists than they are as symbols. The events of Mount Carmel make the king into a paradigm of Baalistic devotion, or at least benign support, without his ever taking an essential or forceful part in the drama. For the Dtr author-editor, this king—because of his historical connections with non-Jerusalemite worship in Samaria—could only be presented literarily as part of an age which called forth a fanatical religious zeal for Yahweh by a "kingdom of priests" (Exod 19:6), the absence of which must have been seen as sufficient cause for the monarchy's ultimate demise. It is by *not* being an important figure in this legend that Ahab can corroborate the editor's condemnation, first expressed in 16:30.

Bibliography

See bibliography at 17:1–19:21. A. Alt, "Das Gottesurteil auf dem Karmel," in *Fest. Georg Beer* (Stuttgart: Kohlhammer, 1935) 1-18 (repr. Alt, *KS* II [Munich: Beck, 1953] 135-49); H. J. Boecker, *Redeformen,* 26-34 (see listing at 2:36-46a); A. Jepsen, "Elia und das Gottesurteil," in *Near Eastern Studies in Honor of W. F. Albright* (ed. H. Goedicke; Baltimore: Johns Hopkins, 1971) 291-306; B. O. Long, "The Social Setting for Prophetic Miracle Stories," *Semeia* 3 (1975) 46-63; H. D. Preuss, *Verspottung fremder Religionen im Alten Testament* (BWANT 92; Stuttgart: Kohlhammer, 1971) 80-100; J. J. M. Roberts, "A New Parallel to 1 Kings 18:28-29," *JBL* 89 (1970) 76-77; H. Seebass, "Elia und Ahab auf dem Karmel," *ZTK* 70 (1973) 121-36; N. J. Tromp, "Water and Fire on Mount Carmel: A Conciliatory Suggestion," *Bib* 56 (1975) 480-502; E. Würthwein, "Die Erzählung vom Gottesurteil auf dem Karmel," *ZTK* 59 (1962) 131-44.

ACCOUNT OF EPIPHANIES IN THE WILDERNESS, 19:1-18

Structure

I. Account of Elijah's flight to Beer-sheba	1-3
A. Setting: Ahab's report to Jezebel	1
B. Jezebel's message to Elijah: oath of death	2
C. Result: flight to Beer-sheba	3
II. Account of epiphany beyond Beer-sheba	4-8
A. Narrative setting	4
1. Journey into wilderness	4a
2. Elijah's death petition	4b
B. Dream epiphany	5-8a
1. Narrative setting	5a
2. First dream sequence	5b-6

a. Opening: Behold!	$5b\alpha^{1}$
b. Angel's appearance	$5b\alpha^{2}$
c. Command	5bβ
1) Narrative introduction	$5b\beta^{1}$
2) Command proper	$5b\beta^{2}$
d. Appearance of food	6a
e. Elijah's response: takes food, sleeps	6b
3. Second dream sequence	7-8a
a. Angel's appearance	7aα
b. Command	7aβ-b
1) Command proper	7aβ
2) Motive	7b
c. Elijah's response: takes food	8a
C. Travel to Horeb	8b
III. Account of epiphany at Horeb	9-18
A. Narrative setting: journey to cave	9a
B. First audition	9b-11aα
1. Prophetic word formula	9bα
2. Dialogue	9bβ-11aα
a. Yahweh's question	9bβ
b. Elijah's answer: lament	10
c. Yahweh's reply: order	11aα
C. Epiphany	11aβ-13a
1. "Passing" of Yahweh	11aβ-12
2. Elijah's reaction	13a
D. Second audition	13b-18
1. Audition formula	13bα
2. Dialogue	13bβ-18
a. Yahweh's question	13bβ
b. Elijah's answer: lament	14
c. Yahweh's reply	15-18
1) Commission speech	15-16
2) Announcements	17-18
a) Concerning destruction	17
b) Concerning salvation for remnant	18

Save for the allusions in v. 1, this unit of tradition has little to do with the preceding chapter's dominant thematic structures, that is, with the movements from prophetic word to its fulfillment in the coming of rain and the victory of Yahweh (Elijah) over Baal (Baal prophets). Moreover, the conclusion is clearly marked by a vague connective, v. 19aα, and new themes in vv. 19b-21, localized away from the "wilderness" and Mount Horeb locations that are prominent in vv. 1-18. Nearly all critics suppose that the links with ch. 18 are mainly accomplished by a "join," vv. 1-3a, a piece of uncertain age, which looks back to some elements in the previous chapter and sets a motif of flight for ch. 19. Yet these verses do not carry much thematic force beyond v. 4 (see, e.g., Fohrer, *Elia,* 36; Steck, 20-21; Schüpphaus, 5-52; Gray, *Kings,* 373; Alt, 135; Smend, 541). Much more a matter of dispute is whether vv. 3b-18 are unified, and if not, what can be recovered of originally separate bits of tradition. There is no evident consensus (cf. esp. Würthwein, "Elijah"; Smend; Steck; Jeremias; von Nordheim). At least one recent critic has argued strongly on stylistic grounds for a unified composition in these verses and an original link with ch. 18 (Carlson; cf. Šanda, *Könige*). We should recognize the tensions in the material, as well as the itinerary-like divisions into scenes, vv. 1-3, 4-8, 9-18. Whatever its compositional history, there are signs of unity in the final text.

The overall structure is determined by two distinct features: an "itinerary" motif which has Elijah moving from one place to another (vv. 3, 4a, 8b, 9a), and a series of divine manifestations, angelic epiphanies (vv. 5-6, 7-8, 9-11a, 11b-18). Like items in a chain, these epiphanies are now linked together by the itinerary notices. Though his first move is interpreted as fleeing for his life from Jezebel (v. 3), Elijah's subsequent changes of location are simply geographical mileposts, with no hint of flight.

The structural analysis reflects these two main features of the text. Thus element I (vv. 1-3) is set off from II (vv. 4-8) by travel to Beer-sheba and beyond; the two scenes of dream epiphany near Beer-sheba (II.B, vv. 5-8a) are in turn separated from the next scene by a move to Horeb (v. 8b). Here, on this "mount of God," there is a further move beyond, into a cave on Horeb. V. 15 carries this itinerary motif further by implying that Elijah is about to move to yet another wilderness location. The language implies the resumption of a journey interrupted: "go again, on your way to the wilderness of Damascus" (*lēk šûb lĕdarkĕkā* . . . , v. 15a). Thus, the overall structure suggests a journey by stages, in a wilderness area only vaguely defined, with momentous events occurring at stopping points—Israel in the wilderness *redivivus*: divine disclosures on the way to a destination as yet untold (cf. Exodus 17–Numbers 10). It is a deeply biblical convention at work here, as though God, or his angels, chose to appear apart from organized, social space—deep in the wilderness (*midbār,* Exod 17:1; 19:1; 3:1), high on a mountain (Exod 19:3), in a cave (1 Kgs 19:9), in utter isolation (→ discussion of a similar motif of segregating sacred power in 17:17-24).

The unit begins with a transitional scene (I, vv. 1-3) which looks summarily back to ch. 18 and effectively opens onto the material which follows. The narrator's prose is terse, lacking special color or elaborate description. From our point of view his linkage to the events at Mount Carmel is minimal, and fixed on a relatively minor incident in the epic-proportioned drama. Ahab simply tells his queen that the Baal prophets are dead. But Jezebel views this as an event of *major* consequence. Her reaction is swift and severe, yet the confrontation with Elijah curiously indirect. She sends a messenger (*mal'āk*), an unnamed emissary of death (v. 2). The author must be speaking with irony, for Elijah is later to meet "messengers" (*mal'āk, RSV* "angels") of life, not death, in the trackless hills of Beer-sheba and Horeb. For his part, upon hearing the queen's oath, Elijah fears for his life and flees, as once before he must have done when facing Ahab's anger (17:1-2). Once again, from a position of triumphant power this man of God has become an outcast.

The scene at Beer-sheba consists essentially of two dream appearances (note the mention of "sleep," v. 5a, and the conventional description of images standing at the sleeper's "head," v. 6a; cf. Gen 28:13 and Oppenheim, 189). The accounts are balanced in both form and content. An angel appears (vv. 5b, 7a), commands Elijah to eat (vv. 5b, 7aβ), Elijah eats and drinks (vv. 6, 8). V. 7a links the double epiphany together: "The angel of the Lord came again a second time. . . ." There is only the slightest hint of dramatic tension. We know why Elijah has fled and finds himself in this situation (vv. 1-3); we watch him receive food and drink. But why must the scene be essentially repeated? Why must he eat and drink again? The answer is in a small variation to an otherwise unvarying pattern in this text. On the second occasion, the messenger, or angel (*mal'āk*), commands Elijah, "Arise and eat," and follows this order with an explanation which propels us forward: "for the journey is tougher than you are" (*kî rab mimmĕkā haddārek*, v. 7b).

The dream is over, not because Elijah obeys the specter's command to eat (for he does this much in v. 6b), but because the prophet changes location. The action fades from dream image to itinerary notice in keeping with the larger framework of the composition. Elijah moves from Beer-sheba to Horeb, the mountain of Moses, of God, of manifestation (Exodus 3; 19). He comes to a cave (v. 9a).

The narrator fills the stay at Horeb, like the sojourn at Beer-sheba, with two events, described in nearly identical ways. This time it is not dream, but strange audition which seizes Elijah. The first scene (vv. 9b-11a) opens with the familiar (→) prophetic word formula, introduced with "And behold!" (*wĕhinnēh*) as though Elijah still dreams somewhat (see vv. 5, 6). In fact, this opener is equivalent to the impersonally formulated audition phrase in a third scene: ". . . and behold, there came a voice to him" (v. 13b). Each formula begins the actual moment of audition (cf. Gen 15:4 for similar language in a passage which explicitly refers to the events as "vision" [*maḥăzeh*]). Immediately Elijah hears a question, identical in both scenes: "What are you doing here, Elijah?" (vv. 9bβ=13bβ); then comes the prophet's lament, in nearly identical words (vv. 10, 14), followed by a divine reply consisting of direct commands (vv. 11a and 15-18; cf. a similar analysis by von Nordheim, 159-60). Of course, these parallel audition scenes now frame the central epiphany, Yahweh's "passing by" (III.C, vv. 11aβ-13a; cf. Exod 34:6). The opening audition, therefore, seems clearly built to move us dramatically from a quietly understated mysterious manifestation of spoken word to an event that will upstage it—the elaborate, stately, measured cadence of natural upheaval as Yahweh himself appears. Here the language is descriptive: a string of participial or nominal clauses, repeating for sonorous effect three key words, wind, earthquake, fire, and a refrain, "The Lord was not in the (wind, earthquake, fire)." The Hebrew is succinct and forceful: *lō' bārûaḥ yahweh . . . lō' bāra'aš yahweh . . . lō' bā'ēš yahweh* (vv. 11aβ-12a).

The drama resonates on several levels. There is ironic contrast between the measured stateliness of this description and the violent upheavals to which it alludes, as though serenity is somehow sensed at the center of agitation. This nuance is nicely turned about when the "still small voice" (v. 12b) elicits a fearful, awestruck reaction from Elijah, as though God's calm becomes kinetic motion in the prophet. If the enigmatic phrase *qôl dĕmāmâ daqqâ* (v. 12b) means, on the other hand, a "thin, petrifying sound" (De Boer) or a "roaring and thunderous voice" (Lust), the suggestion of violent disturbance is carried forth. In any case, the effect is one of completely overwhelming intervention—a divine interruption which freezes human action between command (v. 11a) and its execution (v. 13) (against many critics who wish to treat vv. 11aβ-13 as intrusive). There is drama, too, in the striking contrast between those large events where Yahweh is *not,* and that small event (a quiet voice, or a shrill, awful sound) where Yahweh *is*. These "natural" phenomena counterpoint another set of contrasts: where Elijah *is* (fleeing in the wilderness) and where he *should be* (in the organized Israelite land, acting as Yahweh's spokesman; von Nordheim, 161).

In this light, it seems fitting that the second audition following epiphany focuses on renewed prophetic tasks (von Nordheim; Coote). Elijah hears a new commission which suggests that he cannot simply flee his prophetic calling (vv. 10, 14; cf. Jeremiah 15; 20; Jonah); he is to be part of the eventual end to this ideological conflict between Yahweh and Baal, Elijah and the Baal prophets, apostate people and Jezebel-Ahab partnership. For through Elijah's anointing of Hazael, Jehu, and his own successor Elisha, there is to be a purge of all those devoted Baalists and a plucking of seven thousand Yahweh loyalists from the scene of massacre.

Genre

It is difficult to specify a genre for this unit because of the varied literary affinities for different portions and the lack of clear parallels for the whole. A chain of "itinerary motifs" has decisively shaped the composition (→ discussion above and vv. 3, 4a, 8b, 9a; cf. v. 15; parallels in Exod 15:22-27; 16:1-36; 17:1-7; Coats, "Wilderness Itinerary," and his FOTL volume on *Exodus*; Davies). But "itinerary motif" does not define the substance of the events which occur by stages in the wilderness. Nor is (→) story appropriate to the whole, for essential dramatic tension and plot are simply lacking, or at most are left as embryos in the opening transitional scene (vv. 1-3a). Yet, at least for vv. 4-8, the form, content, and basic purpose of Legend are apparent. In these two Dream Epiphanies, Elijah is sustained by images which miraculously turn out to be physical food from God's angel—a wondrous deed provoking awe and admiration, not unlike the legend in 17:2-6. The sense of sustained story is quickly lost in vv. 9-18, however, where the narrator simply describes a divine manifestation in rather conventional ways: a show of power linked to divine speech which proclaims judgment on individuals and nations (cf. Isa 6:1-13; Ps 68:8-11 [*RSV* 7-10]; Isa 30:27-28).

Indeed, major parallels to portions of the unit are to be found in Reports of Theophany and Dream Epiphany. The latter is most evident in vv. 4-8. A narrative introduction mentions "lying down," "sleeping" (but no mention of "dream," a not uncommon omission); the dream sequence opens with the stereotyped "And behold" (*wĕhinnēh*), and the description of images (in this case, epiphany and divine speech) follows directly. Close, but not exact, parallels may be seen in Gen 28:11-17; 35:9-15; 20:3-7; 1 Kgs 9:1-9; 3:4-15 (→ full discussion and bibliography there). On the other hand, vv. 9-18 make no mention of narrative features associated with dreams (lying down, sleeping, etc.). The stress is clearly on audition and massive divine manifestation, not dreamscape. In the background may be the poetic report of theophany which typically describes the coming of Yahweh, along with accompanying disruptions of man and nature (Jeremias; cf. Judg 5:4-5; Psalm 29; 68:8-11 [*RSV* 7-10]; Isa 30:27-28; Nah 1:2-5; Hab 3:3-12; for a parallel in Ugaritic descriptions of Baal-Hadad, the Canaanite weather god, note the text in *Ugaritica* 5, 557; Eng. tr. in Walter Beyerlin, *Near Eastern Texts Relating to the Old Testament* [tr. J. Bowden; OTL; Philadelphia: Westminister, 1978] 220-21).

The OT narrative tradition of theophany associated with Moses may have been more important than this essentially poetic convention, however. Note Exod 33:12–34:8. In response to Moses' repeated request for signs of divine favor toward the people, Yahweh "passed before Moses" (*'ābar,* 33:19; 34:6; 33:22; exactly the verb used in 1 Kgs 19:11) and proclaimed the "name of Yahweh" in the form of heaped-up epithets (Exod 34:6b-7). The narrator insists that Moses be protected from direct encounter with theophanous visage: "you shall see my back; but my face shall not be seen" (33:23). After the theophany, Moses falls to the ground and worships (34:8), just as Elijah, on seeing Yahweh "pass by," wraps his face to blunt the force of the numinal presence (1 Kgs 19:13). We may compare Exod 3:2-12 and 19:10-25 for similar vocabulary and structure. In general terms, the traditions describe the theophany (cf. the imagery of "fire" and "earthquake" in Exod 19:18), a reaction of fear, awe, or worship, and out of this interaction comes divine message and/or dialogue. The similarity between the Moses narrative tradition and this unit in Kings contributes heavily to the supposition that Elijah is seen as a kind of second Moses. The prophet even receives a commission on Horeb, as did Moses (Exod 3:1).

In addition to the Mosaic narrative tradition of theophany, a literary convention for reporting human lament and divine answer is visible in this Elijah passage. Elijah's lamenting words, vv. 10, 14, and his petition, v. 4, are reminiscent of a COMPLAINT SONG OF THE INDIVIDUAL (cf. Psalms 3–7; FOTL volume on *Psalms* by Gerstenberger). This genre typically cites the innocence or righteousness of the supplicant, the sore straits in which he finds himself, and clearly implies that divine intervention is expected or desired, even directly sued. Literary reflexes of this cultic genre are well known in prophetic literature, e.g., Jer 11:18-20; 15:15-18; 17:14-18; 20:7-12, 14-18; Joel 1:15-20. Often these prophetic laments were followed, originally or in redaction, by a divine reply (cf. Jer 11:21-23; 15:19-21; Joel 2:19). A similar juxtaposition of complaint and divine answer is characteristic of Exodus 33, already cited as a possible model for the description of theophany. The author has Moses demand divine intervention (it is a scene of intercession), and theophany is God's decisive response. Similarly, Num 11:10-25, in its present form, casts Moses as one who disputes with God, imputing to him the injustice of the situation, demanding of God, "Kill me at once . . ." (11:15). The reply is divine speech (v. 23) and theophany (v. 25a). See further Gen 15:1-6, a report of (→) vision which includes a lament (15:2) about Abraham's lack of a suitable heir. God replies directly (v. 4) in audition ("And behold, the word of the Lord came to him . . ."), a formula exactly like that in 1 Kgs 19:9b.

These parallels hardly justify Hentschel's (pp. 102-3) designation "prophetic lament narrative." Formally speaking, the similarities are suggestive but fairly imprecise. Against Olmo-Lete (pp. 147-64), one should not speak of "narrative of vocation" here. Even though Elijah does receive a divine COMMISSION, vv. 15-18, it is surely not his first and primary election to the prophetic life, and the parallels with the classic texts such as Jeremiah 1 and Isaiah 6 are very remote. Even less grounded in literary evidence is the attempt to derive certain features from legal procedures (Steck, 120-21), and a similar postulated literary reflex from some vaguely defined public ceremony ("*Audienzzeremoniell*"; Seybold, 8-10). The most that should be claimed is that "stock scenes" involving lamenting, petitioning prophet and divine answer with patterns of reporting theophany, especially as seen in the Mosaic traditions, have shaped this text.

In sum, there is no easy generic designation for this unit. Influences from itinerary, report of dream epiphany, descriptions of theophany, especially as represented in the Mosaic narratives, compositional patterns of lament (dispute, complaints, petitions) followed by divine reply (word, theophany, dialogue) all seem to have had a weight worth mentioning. Certainly legend fits vv. 4-8 tolerably well, but hardly the entire unit (against Steck, 143; De Vries, 55, designates the unit as a subtype of legend, "theophanous commission story," but in this way restricts too much its range of meanings). We are left with a text that retains its unique qualities (cf. Fohrer, *Elia,* 38-42, who speaks of a "story of encounter with God at Horeb"). The unit finally seems closest to an account of epiphany or theophany because as a whole it lacks the requisite features of genuine story. The account seems to have been constructed out of diverse traditions and shaped according to a mix of literary genres.

Setting

In view of the literary complexity of this unit and the obstacles to identifying its generic type, it seems misguided to speculate in the usual manner about a typical social setting. The account may be unique, and it may have existed *only* as a written entity in the books of Kings. There is little real evidence to support Würthwein's contention that the account stemmed from prophetic groups active in a time when Hazael and Jehu were embroiled in events threatening Israel's (the northern kingdom's) existence (see v. 17 and Würthwein, "Elijah," 162-63). More to the point is the present literary setting for the account. It deeply breathes the air of Mosaic narratives, and thus encompasses a kind of thematic breadth that looks backward in time and evokes the literary heritage of the Pentateuch. At the same time, the account looks far forward into 2 Kings. Elijah's experience on Horeb comes as a slide from the emotional heights of Carmel. Yet, despair elicits its own hope, and the text looks toward a successor for both Elijah and his nemesis, King Ahab. It is the ghost of Victory-Future that raises its head and places this event at Horeb within the range of that dramatic collusion of those successors, Elisha and Jehu, in Yahweh's final victory over Baal (see 2 Kings 9–10).

Intention

In the light of all these considerations, it seems best to focus our thoughts on the question of literary intention in the books of Kings. One sees in the account the themes of fear and flight, even despair, and of course, Yahweh's response. The answer to Elijah's complaint is hardly consolation, however. It is miraculous provision in the wilderness—a second example in context after 17:2-15. It is as though a cycle evident in chs. 17–18 begins again in ch. 19. A similar dynamic controls the scene on Mount Horeb (vv. 9-18): flight, despair, answer from God. But this time the answer is commission and a promise: anoint successors (Elisha, prophet-successor, and Jehu, king-successor), and final victory in the struggle between Yahwists and Baalists will come. In this way, the author carries forward a theme at the center of those grand retarding moments in ch. 18 (18:3-15, 20-40; see discussion above). The virulent conflict between Yahweh and Baal, Elijah and the Baalists, *will* have its end, but not immediately (vv. 17-18).

Obviously, the author ties these broader concerns to his portrayal of Elijah as prophetic hero of the Yahwists. As in ch. 17, Elijah is favored and sustained by Yahweh's special care; he flees Jezebel, or is he *led* to God and renewed commission? Food and drink for the body and triumphant prophetic task for the soul—physical and spiritual nourishment. Taken with 17:2-16, this theme of divine provisioning, then, brackets the Mount Carmel episode in ch. 18. In both "brackets," the theme has its counterpoint in events which undermine and question Elijah's status and power for good. The widow (17:18) thinks he has come to kill her son; Jezebel (19:2) swears to seek his life. Perhaps Elijah himself sings this countermelody when he heads for the desert (17:5; 19:3) and ironically takes up Jezebel's fixation: ". . . take away my life" (v. 4). In both bracketing sections, Elijah is cared for and his position affirmed.

Two feedings (God's provision for Elijah)	17:3-6, 8-16	Mount Carmel	19:4-6, 7-8
Elijah's position in question	17:18 (17-23)	Episode	19:1-3, 4, 10, 14
Elijah confirmed	17:24	18:1-46	19:15-18

In effect the narrator surrounds and thereby emphasizes the magisterial Elijah of ch. 18. Carmel is where the prophet is fullest in control, enjoys his highest triumph, and consummately symbolizes the religious struggle. The hero is finally human because he is enclosed by physical cares and spiritual doubts.

Care and provisioning on the way and the theophany at Horeb finally mark out a second triumph to match the one on Mount Carmel. Envisioned for the future, it is nonetheless as palpable as those theophanous events swirling about Elijah's cloak-wrapped ears. Proleptic victory and vindication, reaching into the reign of Jehu, make of this unit a first prophecy of Jehu's militant purge of Baalism from Ahab's kingdom (see 2 Kings 9–10). A kind of legacy beyond his own death wish unfolds in Elijah's (and our) hearing. At the same time, Elijah's status as individual Yahwistic hero shrinks a bit. He is not, after all, so much a Moses *redivivus* as he is a prophet destined to stand aside for those who will come after. Or perhaps we have missed a nuance in the Mosaic archetype: *like* Moses, who was not to set foot on covenanted soil, Elijah is not to see the final triumph of Yahweh's partisans (cf. Childs).

From this perspective, we may now understand why King Ahab is so insignificant a character. He is secondary to the action of 19:1-3, a role which is consistent with his position of bystander in ch. 18 and his absence from ch. 17. More by implication than by direct statement do we hear the narrator's imputation of villainy to Ahab. It seems appropriate, therefore, that the solution to the problem which Ahab symbolizes lies not with Ahab himself, but with a foreigner (Hazael) and a successor to himself (Jehu) and to the "troubler" of his rule

(Elisha). The narrator's intention looks to 2 Kings 9–10 where he can celebrate the triumph of Yahweh (2 Kgs 10:28-31, 32-36).

In the light of such an ideological drama, an individual king or prophet, save as he may be reckoned on the side of the righteous, seems not to matter very much.

Bibliography

See the bibliography at 17:1–19:21. R. A. Carlson, "Elia à l'Horeb," *VT* 19 (1969) 416-39; G. W. Coats, "The Wilderness Itinerary," *CBQ* 34 (1972) 135-52; R. B. Coote, "Yahweh Recalls Elijah," in *Traditions in Transformation* (*Fest.* F. M. Cross; ed. B. A. Halpern and J. D. Levenson; Winona Lake, IN: Eisenbrauns, 1981) 115-20; G. I. Davies, "The Wilderness Itineraries: A Comparative Study," *Tyndale Bulletin* 25 (1974) 46-81; P. A. H. de Boer, "Notes on Text and Meaning of Isaiah xxxviii 9-20," *OTS* 9 (1951) 179; G. del Olmo Lete, *La vocacion*, 147-64 (see listing at 17:1–19:21); F. L. Hossfeld, "Die Sinaiwallfahrt des Propheten Elija. Gedanken zu 1 Kön 19,1-18 anlässlich der Sinaiexkursion des Studienjahres der Dormition Abbey 1978/79," *Erbe und Auftrag* 54/6 (1978) 432-37; J. Jeremias, *Theophanie. Die Geschichte einer alttestamentlichen Gattung* (WMANT 10; Neukirchen: Neukirchener, 1965); J. Lust, "A Gentle Breeze or a Roaring Thunderous Sound?" *VT* 25 (1975) 110-15; idem, "Elijah and the Theophany on Mount Horeb," *Bibliotheca Theologicarum Lovaniensium* 41 (1976) 91-100; Chr. Macholz, "Psalm 29 und 1 Kön 19," in *Werden und Wirken des Alten Testaments* (*Fest.* C. Westermann; ed. H.-P. Müller, H. W. Wolff, and W. Zimmerli; Göttingen: Vandenhoeck & Ruprecht, 1980); E. von Nordheim, "Ein Prophet kündigt sein Amt auf (Elia am Horeb)," *Bib* 59 (1978) 153-73; A. L. Oppenheim, *Dreams* (see listing at 3:4-14); M. Sekine, "Elias Verzweiflung—Erwägungen zu 1 Kön xix," *Annual of Japanese Biblical Institute* 3 (1977) 52-68; K. Seybold, "Elia am Gottesberg. Vorstellungen prophetischen Wirkens nach 1 Kön 19," *EvT* 33 (1973) 3-18; S. Weissmann, "Die Erzählung von der Theophanie am Horeb," *BethM* 11 (1965/66) 140-43 (Hebrew); E. Würthwein, "Elijah at Horeb—Reflections on 1 Kings 19:9-18," in *Proclamation and Presence* (*Fest.* G. H. Davies; ed. J. Durham and J. Porter; Richmond: John Knox, 1970) 152-66.

THE SELECTION OF ELISHA, 19:19-21

Structure

I. Narrative setting	19a
A. Journey from Horeb	19aα^1
B. Elijah's finding of Elisha	19aα^2-β
II. The selection of Elisha	19b-20
A. The sign of selection: Elisha's mantle	19b
B. Elisha's response: petition	20a
C. Elijah's counter-response	20b
III. Conclusion	21
A. Sacrificial meal	21a
B. Elisha's following and serving Elijah	21b

Most critics agree that this unit stands relatively independent of its present context. At its outer limit, 20:1, there is a complete shift of scene and subject matter, marked by inverted word order and a perfect (*qṭl*) verb. At the inner limit,

19:19, the connective itinerary phrase "So he departed from there" (*wayyēlek miššām,* v. 19a) continues the movement by stages (cf. 19:3, 4, 8) but offers only the vaguest link with the rest of ch. 19. In theme, the little scene may be connected with v. 16b. The link is imprecise, however. The verb in v. 16, "anoint" (*māšaḥ*), itself an unusual word to use for selecting a prophet (cf. for priests, Exod 28:41; 29:7; for holy objects, Gen 31:13; Num 7:1; for kings, 1 Kgs 1:34, 39; 2 Kgs 9:3, 6), does not occur in vv. 19-21. And the action there is indeed something other than one would expect for "anoint." Whether the connection with ch. 19 is original and how this unit along with 19:15-18 might relate to the traditions of Elisha are matters of some debate. At the least, a majority of commentators suppose that the unit 19:19-21 was originally independent of its present surroundings and that it stands unified now in itself.

The structure seems simple and clear: the narrative traverses a path from Elijah's finding Elisha (I, v. 19a) through a scene of meeting between the two men (II, vv. 19b-20) to a concluding action (III, v. 21), the outcome of which places Elisha in the service of Elijah. The style is terse, the plot minimal. Description is spare—only the circumstantial clause in v. 19a. Typically for Hebrew narrative, dialogue stands as the main action (v. 20).

The brevity makes full understanding of details and their function in the narrative very difficult. For example, what kind of an act or signal is the sending of Elijah's "mantle"? Or the meal? Despite many confidently stated opinions, evidence for the narrative's significance is totally lacking. It is designated "sacrifice" (*RSV* v. 21 obscures the sense of the Hebrew *wayyizbāḥēhû,* "and he sacrificed them [the animals]"). But in this case, the verb tells us very little. Finally, the dialogue in v. 20 remains obscure.

Apparently the narrator reaches his essential point in noting that Elisha went and served Elijah (vv. 20a, 21bβ: "Then he arose and went after Elijah, and ministered to him"). The verb "minister to" (*šrt*) means general service of a nonpriestly kind. Cf. *mĕšārēt,* said of a "youth" (*na'ar*) attached to a prophet (2 Kgs 4:43; 6:15) or used for a "servant" to the royal family (2 Sam 13:17-18; 1 Kgs 10:5) or to Moses (Exod 24:13; 33:11; Num 11:28; etc.). It is not a question of becoming a "disciple" (for this notion, perhaps *'ebed,* "slave, servant," suits better, as in 2 Kgs 2:16; 5:20), but of becoming an attendant to one of superior social rank.

In the context of 19:16b, however, the phrase "and he ministered to him" carries the nuance of Elisha's becoming a designated successor to Elijah. The Mosaic narrative traditions provide this meaning, too. But also, in Moses' case alone, the noun "servant" (*mĕšārēt*) refers to a specially legitimated successor, Joshua, who is tapped as the future prophetic-priestly-political-military leader (Deut 31:7-8, 14-23). As such, the traditions distinguish him as "servant (to Moses) from his youth" (Num 11:28; cf. Josh 1:1). So in the matter of choosing a successor, Elijah evokes—as he did on Horeb—the memories of Moses and his times.

Thus, a narrative setting (I, v. 19a) brings two characters together. The ensuing action (II, vv. 19b-20) indicates that Elisha interpreted the sending of the mantle as an invitation to service, but he demurs, provoking an enigmatic response from Elijah. Finally, with a sacrificial meal (III, v. 21), Elisha takes leave of his family and becomes Elijah's attendant. The immediate and wider Mosaic context adds the nuance of succession to a position of leadership.

Genre

This unit is an ANECDOTE or brief STORY. There is a minimal plot: the slight dramatic tension aroused by sending the prophet's cloak and the ensuing action, which seems to hint at a complication (Elisha seems to demur slightly), is resolved at the end when Elisha takes up service to Elijah. In theme, this anecdote is similar to the longer narrative in which David comes into the service of King Saul (1 Sam 17:31-58) and more distant, the traditions of ordinary men becoming "disciples" of Jesus (Luke 9:57-62; Mark 1:16-20 [= Matt 4:18-22; Luke 5:1-11]; cf. John 1:35-42). It is unsuitable to speak of a "prophetic call narrative" (De Vries, 54) or to assimilate this unit with the rest of ch. 19 to the general structure of accounts of prophetic vocation in Jer 1:4-10; Isa 6:1-13; Ezek 1:1–3:15 (Olmo Lete, 147-64). Both procedures rely too heavily upon meanings drawn from *literary* context and too little on the content and structure of the unit itself. Similarly, to see here an "installation" of a prophet as part of "prophetic biography" (Baltzer, 100-1) is unsupported by available evidence.

Setting

Originally, this anecdote may have found its setting, even its creation, among prophets—perhaps in the group headed by Elisha (see 2 Kgs 6:1). Not to be excluded, however, are the folk, who may have had equally keen interests in telling stories about famous prophets. The anecdote is of course now preserved in a special literary context. It comes at the close of the long complex of tradition involving Elijah in struggles against Baalism, and immediately after Yahweh's direct commission to this despondent Elijah that he anoint a king-successor and a prophet-successor (19:15-18).

Intention

Intentions that the anecdote may have served in oral transmission are hidden from us. In its literary setting, however, the narrative obviously describes how Elisha came into contact with Elijah, and began his "service," his successorship. But also, the anecdote functions as a kind of "sign" (although the word is not used): the author-editor of kings apparently meant it to suffice as the beginning of fulfillment. The divine commission given to Elijah (vv. 15-18) with its associated promise of eventual triumph of Yahweh over Baal finds its first, anticipatory realization in this strange action of one prophet "finding" an attendant. The anecdote confirms the proleptic victory imaged in Yahweh's words. Note the similar function of a prophetic "sign" in Isa 38:7-8 and 1 Kgs 13:3 (→ discussion at 1 Kgs 13:3). As abrupt and fortuitous as the incident appears, it nevertheless is in keeping with the sudden, mysterious character of Elijah's appearance and movements during Ahab's reign (17:1; 18:12, 46). The villain in the kingdom, from Ahab's (and Jezebel's) point of view, turns out not only to be under divine care (17:2-16; 19:3-8), but guaranteed an "heir" as well. The really important contextual significance is that the event is a foretaste of the longer story's end in Jehu's purge of Baalists (2 Kings 9–10).

Bibliography

See bibliographies at 17:1–19:21 and 19:1-18. E. Böklen, "Elisas 'Berufung' (I Reg 19:19-21)," *ZAW* (1912) 41-48, 288-91; C. A. Canosa, "Vocacion de Eliseo," *Est Bib* 29 (1970) 137-51.

WARS WITH SYRIA AND THE VIOLATION OF *ḤĒREM*: CANONICAL FRAMEWORK, 20:1-43

Structure

I. The wars with Syria (Ben-hadad)	1-34
A. Episode one: battle for Samaria	1-21
1. The situation	1
2. Complication: negotiations for spoils	2-11
3. Negative results: battle	12-21
B. Episode two: battle for Aphek	22-34
1. Preparations for battle	22-28
2. The battle	29-30
3. Aftermath: release of Ben-hadad (offense against Yahweh)	31-34
II. A prophet's confrontation with the king of Israel	35-43
A. Preparations	35-38
B. Confrontation (reveals the offense)	39-42
C. Aftermath: king returns to Samaria	43

This unit is demarcated on one side by (1) its abrupt shift in subject matter, from Elijah and Elisha (19:19-21) to Ben-hadad, Syrian king, and a scene of war; (2) by a change in style—from *waw*-consecutive narrative (*wyqṭl*) to a new beginning with simple perfect verb (*qṭl*) and inverted normal word order. At its conclusion (v. 43), another radical shift in subject takes place (21:1), with only the vaguest of linkage ("and after these things") and a typical opening line for independent narrative: "Now Naboth the Jezreelite had a vineyard . . ." (*kerem hāyâ lěnābôt*; cf. Judg 11:1; Exod 3:1; 1 Sam 2:12).

There are indications that this canonical unit was developed out of originally separate entities. Many of the older critics viewed all the prophetic materials (vv. 13-14, 22, 28, 35-43) as secondary (e.g., Wellhausen, *Composition*, 282-83; Hölscher, *Quellen*, 192), a hypothesis now updated with detailed reconstructions of the history of redaction (Schmitt, 48-51; cf. De Vries, 125). Other recent critics, following the early lead of Šanda (*Könige*, I, 508-10) treat the prophetic materials, save for vv. 35-43, as integral to the unit (e.g., Jepsen, *Nabi*, 90-91; Schüpphaus, 57-58; Gray, *Kings*, 414-18; Montgomery, *Kings*, 318-19; Zimmerli, *Erkenntnis*, 16-18). Very different is S. De Vries (p. 125), who views vv. 35-43 along with vv. 30b-34 as tradition originally independent of vv. 1-30a. Adding to these complications is the fact that the LXX places ch. 20 *after* MT ch. 21. Thus, tensions in the material suggest complicated development, but scholars do not agree on a reconstructed history of composition.

On the other hand, there are clear signs of at least some conscious redactional unity. The prophetic material in vv. 13, 22, 28 certainly need not be intrusive; moreover, vv. 35-43 presuppose the events narrated in vv. 29-34. Our sense of Ahab's transgression obviously depends on knowledge of those events. And the unnamed prophet (v. 38) disguises himself as a wounded soldier, as though the situation of war made the deceit believable, particularly *the* war (*hammilḥāmâ*, v. 39), meaning in context the war with Syria.

The key to this redacted unity lies in an interpretative association of events read through the ending, that is, through the prophetic voice in vv. 35-43. A rather straightforward account of military encounters with Syria, including a standard precampaign consultation with the oracles (vv. 13-14) that sets a theme of Yahweh's self-demonstration ("you shall know that I am the Lord," vv. 13b, 28b), leads to an act of diplomacy by King Ahab. He agrees to release the Syrian king. But this "covenant" (v. 34) turns out to be an offense against Yahweh. As Ben-hadad is *ḥērem*, war booty "devoted to destruction" (v. 42), so Ahab and his forces shall in time become sacrificial spoils in Ben-hadad's stead: "your life shall go for his life, and your people for his people" (v. 42b).

The canonical framework, then, offers really two narrative plots: the one dealing with the victory over the Syrians (note the reference to this "ending" at 22:1), the other, a hidden plot growing out of the prophet's (and the narrator's) private knowledge: what appears to be diplomacy on Ahab's part is, ironically, offensive to God—and the deed, like a blood violation against a tribe, must be satisfied by new blood.

Genre

Since the canonical text is very likely a redacted composition, we may not speak with any precision of a literary genre. The unit surely suggests (→) story. More important is to recognize earlier narrative models for the ruling thematic structures. In 1 Samuel 15 and 2 Samuel 11–12, we find two similar accounts: a king's action (the one case, Saul; the other, David) is revealed in retrospect to be an offense against Yahweh. A prophet (Samuel for King Saul, Nathan for David) confronts the king and announces divine punishment, as though to requite the dastardly deed. The parallel between 1 Samuel 15 and 1 Kings 20 is particularly close. Unlike the cases of Saul and David, however, Ahab's judgment is not mitigated (cf. 1 Sam 15:24-31; 2 Sam 12:13-14). Ahab stands alone, naked of defense, covered with offense, doomed from the start, it seems, by the editor's appraisal that he "did evil in the sight of the Lord more than all that were before him" (1 Kgs 16:30).

Setting

From these comments, it is apparent that the important setting is that of the Dtr editor of Kings who placed this unit within the account of Ahab's reign. The redactional unit follows hard upon those traditions that suggest continuing conflict between the Yahwists and the Baalists, even with promise of triumph. Our gaze shifts once more to the particularities of Ahab's reign and its "troubles" with prophetic minorities. It is a view reflective of the Dtr author-editor's exilic hindsight into the vagaries of monarchy in Israel and Judah.

Intention

The intention of this redactional storylike unit is apparent from the confrontation (II, vv. 35-43) at its end. Here, the thematic focus shifts from an account of

Ahab's wars with Syria, with its theological view of military victory as demonstration of Yahweh's presence and power (vv. 13b, 28b), to a particular focus on Ahab. With this comes a different theological point: Ahab the king is an offender against God who must be condemned without reprieve. In other words, the canonical unit intends to *evaluate* the monarch, or at least to relate only those events which contribute to a religious appraisal of him. The text adds another example of Ahab's misdeeds, and offers the first of two prophetic announcements which foretell his demise. The unit therefore connects less with the themes of ch. 19 than with those in chs. 21 and 22, where Ahab stands against Yahweh (or his prophet). Whether ch. 20 originally followed ch. 21, as the LXX orders the material, is irrelevant to this general point. The Dtr author-editor has chosen to present a series of incidents which clearly show Ahab as offender and prophet as one who confronts offender with his wrong and announces punishment.

Bibliography

See bibliography at 17:1–19:21. H.-C. Schmitt, *Elisa. Traditionsgeschichtliche Untersuchungen zur vorklassischen nordisraelitischen Prophetie* (Gütersloh: Gütersloher, 1972); W. Zimmerli, *Die Erkenntnis Gottes nach dem Buche Ezekiel* (ATANT 27; Zurich: Zwingli, 1954).

WARS WITH SYRIA: VICTORY OVER BEN-HADAD, 20:1-34

Structure

I. Episode one: battle for Samaria	1-21
A. The problem situation: Samaria besieged	1
B. The complication: negotiations for spoils	2-11
1. First exchange: Ben-hadad's demand	2-4
a. Narrative introduction	2
b. Official message	3
1) Messenger formula	3aα
2) Message proper: demand for wealth and family	3aβ-b
c. Ahab's reply: statement of agreement	4
2. Second exchange: Ben-hadad's new demands	5-9
a. Narrative introduction	5aα
b. Official message	5aβ-6
1) Messenger formula	5aβ
2) Message proper: demand for unlimited plunder	5b-6
c. Ahab's reply	7-9a
1) Preparatory consultation with elders	7-8
a) Narrative introduction	7aα
b) Ahab's statement of the case	7aβ-b
c) Elders' advice	8
(1) Narrative introduction	8a
(2) Statement of advice: refuse demands	8b

2) Reply to Syrians 9a
a) Narrative introduction 9aα[1]
b) Ahab's message for Ben-hadad 9aα[2]-β
(1) Commission for messengers 9aα[2]
(2) Message proper: accept first demand, refuse second 9aα[3]-β

d. Narrative conclusion: departure and reporting by messengers 9b

3. Third exchange: interruption of negotiations 10-11
a. Message from Ben-hadad 10
1) Narrative introduction 10aα
2) Message: boastful oath 10aβ-b
b. Reply from Ahab 11
1) Narrative introduction 11aα
2) Message: taunt 11aβ-b

C. Resolution of problem: battle for Samaria 12-21
1. Preparations 12-15
a. Concerning Syria 12
1) Ben-hadad's order: take positions 12a-bα
2) Execution of order 12bβ
b. Concerning Israel 13-15
1) Consultation with prophet 13-14
a) Unsolicited oracle for Ahab 13
(1) Narrative introduction 13aα
(2) Oracle of self-disclosure 13aβ-b
(a) Messenger formula 13aβ[1]
(b) Oracle 13aβ[2]-b
α. Rhetorical question 13aβ[2]
β. Conveyance formula (give it into your hand) 13bα
γ. Recognition formula (you shall know . . .) 13bβ
b) Oracular inquiry 14
(1) First query 14a
(a) Question: by whom? 14aα
(b) Oracular reply 14aβ
α. Messenger formula 14aβ[1]
β. Oracle 14aβ[2]
(2) Second query 14b
(a) Question: who begins? 14bα
(b) Oracular reply 14bβ
2) Results: mustering of Israel's forces 15

2. The battle 16-21
a. Confrontation of forces 16-19
1) Israelites: army goes out 16a

2) Syrians: drunkenness in camp	16b
3) Israelites: servants of governors go out	17a
4) Syrians: reconnaisance	17b-18
a) Report of scouts	17b
b) Ben-hadad's order: take alive	18
5) Israelites: all go out	19
b. Description of battle	20
c. Epitomizing conclusion	21
II. Episode two: battle for Aphek	22-34
A. Preparations for battle	22-28
1. Consultations	22-25
a. Concerning Israel: counsel from a prophet	22
1) Narrative introduction	22aα
2) Prophet's words to Ahab	22aβ-b
a) Assurance	22aβ^1
b) Counsel	22aβ^2
c) Motive clause (prediction)	22b
b. Concerning Syria: counsel from servants	23-25
1) Narrative introduction	23aα^1
2) Servants' words to Ben-hadad	23aα^2-25a
a) Advice	23aα^2-b
b) Proposal for battle strategy	24-25a
3) Execution of proposal	25b
2. Muster of forces	26-28
a. Syrian	26
b. Israelite	27-28
1) Mustering	27
2) Unsolicited oracle for king	28
a) Narrative introduction	28aα
b) Oracle of self-disclosure	28aβ-b
(1) Messenger formula	28aβ^1
(2) Oracle	28aβ^2-b
(a) Basis for oracle	28aβ^2
(b) Conveyance formula	28bα
(c) Recognition formula	28bβ
B. The battle	29-30
1. Confrontation of forces	29a
2. Description of battle	29b-30
C. Aftermath of battle	31-34
1. Negotiations for release of Ben-hadad	31-34a
a. Background: proposal of servants to Ben-hadad	31
b. Preliminary negotiations: Ahab and Syrian servants	32-33a
1) Narrative introduction	32aα

2) Official message	32aβ
a) Messenger formula	32aβ[1]
b) Petition from Ben-hadad	32aβ[2]
3) Ahab's response: hint of treaty	32b-33a
a) Reply to petition	32b
b) Servants' response	33aα
c) Ahab's command: bring Ben-hadad	33aβ
c. Main negotiations: Ahab and Ben-hadad	33b-34a
1) Meeting of principals	33b
2) The agreement	34a
a) Ben-hadad's statement of terms	34aα
b) Ahab's statement of agreement	34aβ
2. Epitomizing conclusion: release and treaty (covenant)	34b

An important key to the structure of this long unit is in its recounting of two battles: one in Samaria (I, vv. 1-21) and one at Aphek (II, vv. 22-34). The latter account is clearly linked to the first as a second phase of military campaigning (vv. 23-25), and both accounts now follow a similar plan:

(1)	Preparations for battle (muster of forces; consultations)	vv. 12-15;	22-28
(2)	Descriptions of battle (confrontation; battle; slaughter; pursuit; etc.)	vv. 16-20;	29-30
(3)	Results (summary statements; extended denouement)	v. 21;	31-34

Both episodes depict a crisis, which leads to preparations for battle. In the first, the narrator sets forth the crisis at length (the breakdown of negotiations between Israel and Syria, vv. 1-11), in the second episode, very briefly (the renewed campaign, v. 22b). In both accounts, a prophet's unsolicited oracle forms part of the preparation for battle (vv. 13, 22).

However, the second oracle, v. 22, assumes a pivotal position in the larger narrative structure, for it links the two battle episodes to each other. The definite article, *the* prophet (*hannābî'*), must refer to the prophet of v. 13, and both scenes of oracle giving open with the same phrase, "a (the) prophet came near [*ngš*]" to Ahab, the king of Israel. The second oracle also looks forward to a new situation, informing Ahab and the reader of a new battle looming "in the spring." In this way, v. 22 serves as transition and narrative setting for the second episode, sketching the characters, the situation, and the main conflict to be resolved in the ensuing action.

Despite the clear focus on military campaigns, the first and third prophetic scenes (vv. 13-14, 28) offer particular theological accents to the narrative (cf. the structural outline in De Vries, 83-84). The description in v. 14 recalls those scenes of inquiry before priests in which persons, usually kings, seek divine guidance on the eve of battle (→ reports of oracular inquiry; Judg 1:1-2; 1 Sam 23:1-5,

10-12; 2 Sam 5:19). The first oracle, v. 13, even contains a (→) conveyance formula typically found in traditions of inquiry during Yahweh-sanctioned warfare: "I (Yahweh) will give it (them) into your hand this day" (cf. Judg 1:2; 2 Sam 5:19). Accordingly, we have labeled this activity in the structural outline "Consultation" (before battle), I.C.1.b.1), vv. 13-14; cf. II.A.2.b.2), v. 28. Yet, the first of these scenes really begins as an unsolicited meeting with a prophet, in contrast to what one expects in the typical accounts of religiously motivated battle. Moreover, while announcing victory, the first oracle adds a theological stress: ". . . and you shall know that I am the Lord" (v. 13bβ). The motif suggests divine intervention and attaches importance to the outcome of events as though they are to fulfill Yahweh's spoken word and lead to the recognition of Yahweh's power (Zimmerli, "Das Wort"). The third prophetic scene (II.A.2.b.2, v. 28) offers a similar point. No one solicits advice, and the encounter with an unnamed "man of God" offers no tactical guidance. In form and content the oracle resembles a typical (→) prophetic judgment speech with the added nuance that events will fulfill prophetic prediction, disclose Yahweh's power, and lead to his recognition.

Both of these (→) self-disclosure oracles are more important for theological tone than for the dramatic structure of two battle episodes (against De Vries). They add a certain theological *Tendenz* to the material, but do not determine the larger structure with its center in two episodes of battle.

In this light, section II.C, vv. 31-34, the elaborate aftermath of the second battle, is a necessary part of the whole literary effect. The larger account begins and ends with negotiations between two kings hostile to one another. But their positions reverse. At the beginning, Ben-hadad controls events and Ahab reacts, even submissively to a point. At the conclusion, Ahab is victorious and Ben-hadad solicitous, the victim of a complete reversal of fortune. This dramatic turnabout is part of a broad chiastic structure:

A.	Negotiations between parties (Ben-hadad over Ahab)	vv. 1-11
B.	First battle (Samaria)	vv. 12-21
B'.	Second battle (Aphek)	vv. 22-30
A'.	Negotiations between parties (Ahab over Ben-hadad)	vv. 31-34

The narrator enhances this balanced effect with a series of symmetrical features. Ahab twice consults about the military situation (vv. 7-8, with advisers; v. 14, with a prophet), as does Ben-hadad (with advisers or "servants" [vassal-allies?], vv. 23-25a, 31). There are two special oracles of disclosure, one for each battle episode (vv. 13, 28), and each announcing Israelite victory while proclaiming events as Yahweh's self-demonstration to the people.

Despite these features which stress the recounting of battle, the narrator has developed his materials with artistic flair and suggestive portrayal of characters. He shows little interest in describing the actual military engagements. In both episodes, the description of battle is like a minor stroke on a large canvas: the first, vv. 16-21, leaves fifteen verses for events leading up to the actual battle; the second, vv. 29-30, leaves eleven verses for preparations and aftermath. In fact, real human drama and literary interest are apparent in the scenes *surrounding* the battles.

The first negotiation scene consists almost entirely of direct discourse. Descriptive prose mainly signals the flow of speech. The scene falls into three pairs of complete verbal exchange (vv. 2-4, 5-9, 10-11). The second dialogue, like a large centerpiece, carries within its bosom a fourth exchange, this one between Ahab and his advisers. Furthermore, the word "send" (*šālaḥ*) runs throughout (vv. 2, 5, 6, 7, 9, 10) and ties the whole scene together in an image of diplomatic messages shuttling to and fro. Identical phrases, "and the king of Israel answered" (*wayya'an melek yiśrā'ēl*), vv. 4 and 11, envelop the dialogue much like an outer frame. We may visualize the design as follows:

Ben-hadad to Ahab Ahab to Ben-hadad	vv. 2-4	*šlḥ/'nh*
Ben-hadad to Ahab	vv. 5-6	*šlḥ*
Ahab to elders Elders to Ahab	vv. 7-8	*šlḥ*
Ahab to Ben-hadad	v. 9	*šlḥ*
Ben-hadad to Ahab Ahab to Ben-hadad	vv. 10-11	*šlḥ/'nh*

The contrastive dialogue in this section is crucial to our impression of these kings and the events in which they are implicated. Ben-hadad's terms grow quickly into extortion, and when one might think of them as outrageous, Ahab shades the key word (*šlḥ*) into a nuance which captures the emotional turmoil: "all that you first demanded [*šālaḥtā*] of your servant" (literally, "all that you sent (for) to your servant at the first," v. 9). If he is to be measured by the words of his envoys, Ben-hadad seems arrogant and overbearing. His speech is point-blank, without sugaring of any kind; it asserts prerogatives of superior power, not requests: "your gold and your silver, it (they) is (are) mine and your wives and your sons, the best (of them), they are mine!" (v. 2). By contrast, Ahab seems almost compliant, and certainly behaving as a vassal should (see vv. 4, 9, "my lord the king"). Even when refusing Ben-hadad the license to plunder at will, Ahab manages only the simple "but this thing I cannot do" (v. 9). When tensions rise to their utmost Ahab finally drops this diplomatic containment of emotion and uses the direct imperative: "Say (to him) . . ." (v. 11).

Adding to this sense of character are the minimal bits of narrative prose which mention that Syrian messengers come and go. In fact, Ahab speaks to Ben-hadad *only* through them. These envoys (*mal'ākîm*) with their formal way of talking (vv. 2, 5) are a constant mediational presence in the scene. They represent bureaucracy hidden in our illusion of direct exchange between individuals. They seem to be a narrative realization of the overbearing situation and officious personality of Ben-hadad.

Throughout this exchange, the narrator's voice remains measured and matter-of-fact. Formal regularity carries steadily rising emotional tension until negotiations come to an impasse in Ben-hadad's boastful oath (v. 10) and Ahab's outright taunting refusal of *all* demands (v. 11). In its ironic play of form against strident outburst the scene suggests just that controlled realism which Ahab projects and which by contrast Ben-hadad lacks.

The second negotiations (II.C, vv. 31-34) following the accounts of battle are more briefly told. Still, the literary flair is apparent. There is patterned dialogue (three exchanges, vv. 32, 33, 34), but in this case it seems closely bound to narrative prose which encloses the whole (vv. 31-32a, 34b) and regularly interrupts the verbal exchanges (v. 33a, 33b). Here the bargaining is conciliatory, the tone subdued, and whatever Ben-hadad was in the first scene of negotiation, he now seems to be its opposite. His first words, again spoken through his messengers, are a model of courtly grace: "Your servant Ben-hadad says, 'Pray, let me live' " (v. 32aβ^2). The exchange that follows is tentative and elliptical; it barely hints that the parties might come to some agreement. Ahab declares, ". . . he is my brother" (*'āḥî hû'*), and the Syrian messengers, taking the words as an omen, reply, "Your brother (is) Ben-hadad" (*'āḥîkā ben-hădad*), v. 33aα. The exchange probably reflects informal declarations of agreement, mutuality, and friendship that would have preceded formal treaties between parties (E. Gerstenberger, "Covenant and Commandment," *JBL* 84 [1965] 41). Declarations such as "He is my brother (servant, friend)" are familiar ones between kings linked by official treaties (1 Kgs 9:13 [Hiram to Solomon]; Barrakib of Senjirli refers to his allies as "my brothers the kings," in *KAI*, no. 216, line 14; now from a third-millennium B.C. letter at Ebla, one royal official to another, making or administering a treaty on behalf of the king: "Thou art [my/our] brother, and I am [thy] brother . . ." [D. McCarthy, "Ebla, *hórkia témnein*, *ṭb*, *šlm*: Addenda to *Treaty and Covenant*," *Bib* 60 (1979) 248]. Cf. reports reflective of treaty making in 1 Kgs 15:18-19; 2 Kgs 16:7-9, and discussion there. See also P. Kalluveettill, *Declaration and Covenant* [AnBib 88; Rome: Pontifical Biblical Institute, 1982] 123-39).

From the first hint, or first declaration of mutuality, the scene moves to direct negotiations between principals (v. 34). The narrator pointedly removes from our view Ben-hadad's messengers (the kings meet in a chariot), and with them depart the symbols of imperious presence in the narrative. Ben-hadad's words to Ahab at this moment are in utter contrast to his staccato demands of the opening scene. He *offers* and *promises* benefits rather than seizes the spoils of superior power. Momentous decisions are taken, but pithily summarized: "So he made a covenant ["treaty," *bĕrît*] with him, and let him go" (v. 34b; a different understanding of this uncertain Hebrew text is given by E. Kutsch, *Verheissung und Gesetz* [BZAW 131; Berlin: W. de Gruyter, 1972] 57-58). With this brief note the turnabout is complete: Ahab the oppressed is now victorious, and Ben-hadad the oppressor is now solicitous. The covenant ratifies these kings' complete reversal in fortunes.

The preparations for battle (I.C.1, vv. 12-15; II.A, vv. 22-28) are also depicted rather fully. The narrator covers Syria in one verse. He emphasizes Ahab's preparations in only slightly more space (vv. 13-14), but nonetheless packs in an extraordinary number of narrative moments: unsolicited oracle, with full quote; then follows a two-stage oracular inquiry which concedes nothing of the typical form because of abbreviated content, v. 14b. In effect, the narrator has constituted an interruption in the midst of Ben-hadad's drink-crazed mustering of forces (vv. 12 and 16). He arrests our gaze on Ahab receiving, and seeking, guidance from God.

Characterization by contrast continues in the preparations for the second battle (vv. 22-28). There is a chiastic arrangement: consultations for Israel (v. 22), then for the Syrian forces (vv. 23-25); then in reverse order, mustering of Syrian troops (v. 26) followed by the Israelites (v. 27). Relatively more space is devoted to Syria's prebattle consultations than to Israel's; the reader must have been meant to relish the folly of Syria's way (they rely on themselves and their comical assumption about Yahweh's power being limited to the hills) in contrast to Ahab, who relies on God (vv. 13-14). The mustering of forces is handled with opposite proportions. The narrator notes briefly the Syrian gathering and interrupts the urgency of Israel's muster with a prophetic oracle. (Note how the speech is framed with identical images: the armies facing one another, vv. 27 and 29.) The oracle itself pointedly debunks the Syrians' counsel and signals once again the impending victory which belongs to Yahweh and his own self-demonstration (cf. vv. 28 and 13).

A similar fulness of description characterizes the confrontation between forces (vv. 16-19). The narrator rapidly alternates *loci* for the action—from the Israelite to the Syrian camp, back to the Israelite, and so on. Along with this goes a repetition of key words and phrases. The effect is to convey simultaneity of action.

a	Israelites go out *(wayyēṣĕ'û)*	v. 16a
b	A scene in the Syrian camp	v. 16b
a	Servants of governors (Israelites) go out *(wayyēṣĕ'û)*	v. 17a
b	A scene in the Syrian camp	vv. 17b-18
a	"These" went out, servants of governors (Israelites) *(yāṣĕ'û)*	v. 19

This literary device for simultaneous action has parallels in Gen 22:6, 7-8; 2 Sam 13:37-38 and is not a sign of clumsy editing of separate sources (against Schmitt, 46-51 [see listing at 20:1-43]).

In terms of military action, nothing much happens in these verses. Instead, the narrator permits a slower paced look at the Israelites on their way to confrontation. Meanwhile, their opponents wait (v. 12), drink (v. 16), and watch (v. 17). With the storyteller's omniscience, one cannot miss the irony: Yahweh's power gathers for Israel (v. 13), while Ben-hadad boozes confidently in his tents.

We are now able to summarize the more complex structural and thematic features of this material. The unit begins and ends by depicting the relationship between Ahab and Ben-hadad (the relations between states are not far from view, of course). Precisely this relationship will become the object of main attention in vv. 35-43. The kings are a study in contrasts. At the opening, Ahab is compliant, then resistant but with measured response, then taunting in his implacability; Ben-hadad is arrogant, demanding, imperious—a man who seeks conflict. Relations between the kings deteriorate and rupture into war between nations. At the end of the unit, Ahab stands victorious but conciliatory. And Ben-hadad meets him as a supplicant—vanquished, but with something left to give in the now face-to-face negotiations.

At beginning and end, Ahab acts not from religious motives, but according to the plain realities of the vassal-military situation (vv. 2-11) and perhaps the dictates of his heart (v. 32b). He is numbered by the Syrians among Israelite "kings of mercy" (*malkê ḥesed; RSV* "merciful kings," v. 31). Or perhaps one should understand it as "kings who will recognize and respect agreements" (so De Vries, "A Reply to G. Gerleman on *malkê ḥesed* in I Kings XX 31," *VT* 28 [1979] 151-64).

Nested between this contrastive character study are the two battles in which the narrator artistically explores the range of preparations and finally narrates Israel's complete rout of the Syrians. It is only in this section that a theological perspective emerges. Israel's (and Ahab's) confidence in Yahweh contrasts with Syria's (and Ben-hadad's) preparations without divine guidance. Left to the prophets' utterances and the narrator's building of implicit contrasts, the point seems to be less about personages than about events: victory is to be Yahweh's self-demonstration. This emphasis takes gradual steps: from the first mention of these matters in v. 13 to the fully expressed view that Yahweh is directly punishing the Syrians, v. 28. One sees that the Syrians act prudently from a military standpoint, but from the narrator's (and readers') standpoint, they behave comically. Their strategy was based upon arrogance, boasting, and superior power (vv. 1, 10). But in the second battle Ben-hadad acts upon a premise which must have seemed to a Yahwist absurdly foolhardy: Israel's God-space is limited to the hills, and like Samson without his hair, Yahweh is weak away from his mountain (v. 23). The narrative irony is exquisite. From inside knowledge, so to speak, Ahab goes forth, knowing the outcome. Lacking this knowledge, Ben-hadad twice suffers defeat, yet presuming each time to have had victory in hand. There is something "wise" about Ahab and Israel, or at least divinely empowered, and something "foolish" about Ben-hadad and the Syrians, or at least godlessly impotent.

Genre

This unit is clearly historical STORY. Because of its particular content and theological perspective on events, we may speak with some justification of a PROPHETIC BATTLE STORY, i.e., a story of battle in which prophets enunciate major interpretative themes. (Cf. 2 Kgs 19:1-37 [= Isaiah 37].) The essential elements of story are clear. An initial situation, the siege of Samaria, is complicated enormously by Ben-hadad's escalating demands for Israelite capitulation (vv. 2-11) and resolved when the Israelites break the siege in victorious battle (vv. 13-21). But victory is only temporary. It leads to a new narrative impulse, the looming battle for Aphek (v. 22), a crisis which finds resolution in decisive and climactic victory, vv. 29-30. Denouement comes in the reconciliation between the warring kings—draining away the boastful and hostile posturing assumed at the beginning (vv. 31-34). This prophetic battle story focuses on two themes: the battles for Samaria and Aphek, and the reversing relationship between Ahab and Ben-hadad, both seen through prophetic eyes, as though the events were guided and explained by divine oracle. De Vries (pp. 57-58) speaks of "historical demonstration narrative," but only for the presumed independent narratives vv. 1-21 and 26-29. Gray (*Kings*, 414-17) designates the story as a "prophetic adaptation of historical narrative," but it is unclear whether this phrase refers to a theory of composition or to a literary genre.

Clearly the schematic BATTLE REPORT lies in the background of this story. Typically such reports describe (1) the confrontation of forces, (2) the battle itself, and (3) the consequences of battle, usually with summarizing and characterizing statements (e.g., Josh 7:2-5; Judg 3:26-29; 2 Sam 10:15-19; Campbell, 68-69). Often the report will include a scene of consultation, prayer, or encouragement before the actual battle. The consultation takes several forms, but one in particular, report of ORACULAR INQUIRY, seems related to 1 Kgs 20:1-34. One hears of inquiry (*šā'al bĕyahweh*) to God (through a priest usually), followed by a simple tactical question which elicits a direct oracle in reply. See, for example, 1 Sam 23:2-4; 14:36-37; and full discussion at 1 Kgs 22:1-38.

Clearly, the story in 1 Kgs 20:1-34 is more than report of battle, and only v. 14 suggests the full schema of oracular inquiry. The prophetic material and perspective are major forces moving this story away from a simple report of battle, or even from the more complex (→) battle story (e.g., Josh 8:3-29; Judg 9:34-41). The prophets offer in vv. 13 and 28 SELF-DISCLOSURE ORACLES, a type of prophetic speech which announces salvation for Israel and disaster upon Israel's enemies, all done that Yahweh might be recognized and his power confessed. Typically, this oracle includes (1) a reason for God's intervention, (2) a declaration about the mode of God's action, and (3) a RECOGNITION FORMULA which reveals clearly the intent of God's work: "You shall know that I am the Lord." Although having their roots in the conceptual world of holy-war ideology, most examples of such oracles appear in later literature, e.g., Ezek 25:3-5, 6-7, 8-11, 15-17; Isa 41:20; 49:23, 26 (Zimmerli, "Das Wort"). In this prophetic battle story, these oracles flavor the telling of events and provide the important vehicle for the author's viewpoint that Yahweh guides historical events through the words of prophets.

Less important to the larger themes are other generic speech forms, such as BOAST, v. 10 (formulated as OATH), and TAUNT, v. 11, both favorites of Israelite storytellers. Finally, one should note the fragments of an OFFICIAL REPORT, vv. 2b-3, 5-6, and 32aβ, a communication from one person in authority carried by subordinates and reported to a designated recipient (cf. 1 Kgs 5:15-17; 2 Kgs 18:19-25). A report of COMMISSIONING OF A MESSENGER is frequently included, as in 1 Kgs 20:9. Of course, owing to spareness of narration and certain authorial intentions, commission and official message may be fully reported, repeated, or omitted in varying patterns, lending style and subtle emphasis to the narration (Vater, "Communication of Messages").

Setting

We lack sufficient evidence to suggest a typical social setting for prophetic battle story. It is hardly more than guesswork to locate supposed earlier stages of the present story among prophetic groups (De Vries, 54). One cannot easily rule out the possibility that this particular example and its main parallel, 2 Kings 19, existed only as part of a larger written document. (See W. O. E. Oesterley and T. H. Robinson, *Introduction to the Books of the Old Testament* [repr. New York: Macmillan, 1958], 97-98, for a hypothetical "Acts of Ahab.") In any case, the sympathetic portrayal of King Ahab would suggest a provenance for this particular example of prophetic battle story in northern Israel. The prophetic motifs may, but need not, indicate the involvement of prophets in its composition (Fichtner, *Könige*, 293-94). More to the point would be the present literary context of the story. It follows immediately Elijah's finding of his successor, that first taste of eventual Yahwistic triumph, and precedes the tradition in which Ahab is condemned for making a treaty with Ben-hadad. This last connection proves most important for our understanding.

Intention

From all these considerations, it is most important to consider the present literary functions above all. The author intends, of course, to recount the battles of Samaria and Aphek. Yet there is more than this purpose. In his studied portrayal of contrasts and reversed positions for these kings, the author also clearly intends to heroize Ahab. This Israelite king is dignified and courageous, even pious. He receives Yahweh's prophets with earnestness and solicits divine guidance (vv. 13-14, 22, 28); he saves Samaria, protects Aphek, and wins peace in the treaty with Ben-hadad. The story makes Yahweh a sort of hero, too. Clearly the Syrians are no match for this God of the Israelites (see De Vries, 54). In fact, the author ridicules the Syrians for their misapprehension (vv. 23, 28). In this regard, the story reinforces a point already made dramatically in chs. 17–18 (19): Yahweh will surmount any rival or any challenge. Finally, in the context of the final editor's selective recounting of Ahab's reign, this prophetic battle story must be seen in tandem with the following episode, vv. 35-43, where the ironic twist becomes clear. There is a hidden flaw in this image of triumph and heroism. Just as events can be guided by Yahweh's prophets, they can be judged and found wanting as well (see below at 20:35-43).

Bibliography

See bibliography at 17:1–19:21. A. F. Campbell, *The Ark Narrative* (SBLDS 16; Missoula: Scholars Press, 1975); A. M. Vater, "The Communication of Messages and Oracles as a Narration Medium in the Old Testament" (Diss., Yale, 1976); idem, "Story Patterns for a *Sitz*: A Form- or Literary-Critical Concern?" *JSOT* 11 (1979) 47-56; W. Zimmerli, "Das Wort des göttlichen Selbsterweises (Erweiswort), eine prophetische Gattung," in *Mélanges bibliques rédigés en l'honneur de André Robert* (Paris: Bloud & Gay, 1957) 154-64; idem, *Erkenntnis*, 16-18 (see listing at 20:1-43).

A PROPHET'S CONFRONTATION WITH THE KING OF ISRAEL, 20:35-43

Structure

I. Preparations for confrontation	35-38
A. First attempt at disguise	35-36
1. A prophet's meeting with another	35
a. Narrative introduction	35aα
b. Meeting	35aβ-b
1) The prophet's request	35aβ
2) Response: request refused	35b
2. Prophet's counter-response	36a
a. Narrative introduction	36aα[1]
b. Prophecy of punishment	36aα[2]-β
1) Reason	36aα[2]
2) Announcement of punishment	36aβ
3. Result: announcement fulfilled	36b
B. Second attempt at disguise	37-38
1. Prophet's meeting with another	37
a. Narrative introduction	37aα
b. Meeting	37aβ-b

1) Prophet's request	37aβ
2) Compliance with request	37b
2. Result: departure, disguise, waiting	38
II. Appeal before the king (confrontation)	39-42
A. Narrative setting	39a
B. Appeal (confrontation in disguise)	39b-40
1. Prophet's statement of the case (juridical parable)	39b-40a
2. King's statement of decision	40b
C. Prophet's response (confrontation out of disguise)	41-42
1. Recognition by king	41
2. Prophecy of punishment	42
a. Narrative introduction	42aα^1
b. Announcement of punishment	42aα^2-b
1) Messenger formula	42aα^2
2) Announcement	42aβ-b
a) Reason	42aβ
b) Punishment	42b
III. Aftermath: king's departure to Samaria	43

The pivotal point in the structure of this unit is in vv. 41-42 (II.C). The unnamed prophet unmasks himself in the midst of his fictional appeal before the king of Israel and declares Yahweh's punishment for the duped, and probably astonished, monarch. Rather elaborate preparations lead up to this climactic moment, and the author leads us quickly away, brilliantly sketching a sullen and resentful king trudging homeward (v. 43). (Cf. the somewhat different outline by De Vries, 135; and Mabee, 243.)

The first scene (I.A, vv. 35-36) seems at first glance only loosely associated with the longer narrative. A prophet, curiously and vaguely introduced as "a certain man of the sons of the prophets," at Yahweh's behest commands another to inflict a wound. When the other refuses to comply, the prophet strikes a blow of his own. He declares that the reluctant cohort will be killed by a lion. In the next moment, this fellow prophet ("his neighbor" [*rēʻēhû*, v. 35]) is killed by a wandering lion. The incident seems complete, anger satisfied, the lesson of power and obedience taught (cf. 2 Kgs 4:1-7). In context, however, this little scene is preparatory for the prophet's confrontation with the king of Israel. Curiously, it is abortive preparation on the way, and as such anticipates all the important aspects of that climactic moment in vv. 41-42. The prophet announces punishment for an individual, just as he will do before the king, and in a closely similar manner of speech (cf. vv. 36a and 42). The bizarre scene perfectly mirrors beforehand the divine word aimed at the monarch. Hence, the quick, effortless fulfillment, the startling death by lion, carries its own ominous quality. This prophet's word comes true, as though inevitable or prescient. And the destiny he will claim as the king's cannot fail to take its due.

Without this sense given by the story's end, however, we must read the second scene (I.B, vv. 37-38) as a less evocative step, strictly within the confines of a slowly opening plot. Quickly a wound is inflicted (the obedient man contrasts sharply with the disobedient, now dead, prophetic companion), and a disguise taken. We now see a hint of design. The prophet, looking like a soldier from the field of victory, "waited for the king by the way" (v. 38). We do not yet know his intentions. But one senses his power and seriousness. His actions suggest some careful, private design.

Carefully building on ruse and disguise, the final scene makes everything clear. Appearances are quite normal—an unknown commoner cries out to the king and states a problem (he apparently wants to disclaim responsibility for an escaped prisoner), appealing to the king to use his judgment to declare right and wrong and his power to enforce liability and restitution (cf. 1 Kgs 3:16-28; 2 Kgs 6:26-31; 8:3-6). But of course, the petitioner is a prophet bent on some secret mission, the appeal a ruse, the problem fictitious, the motives ulterior. Thoroughly deceived, the king states a quick decision: "So shall your judgment be; you yourself have decided it" (v. 40b). The terms by which the prisoner was held apply; the man should pay with his life or with a measure of silver. As the petitioner drops his disguise, the king's words turn back as self-condemnation. As Ahab let Ben-hadad, a royal prisoner, go, so Ahab must pay with his own life and with the life of his people (v. 42).

We now see the point of the beginning of this episode more clearly in its ending. The first prophet who disobeys and dies is like the king who has disobeyed a command to devote all battle spoils to Yahweh. The king will die by the hand of Yahweh, who is like a lion (Job 10:16; Hos 13:7). The prophet's ruse reveals the truth, but his earlier actions foreshadow it. The king is tricked, to be sure, and goes away sullenly. But the narrator suggests for the king an inevitable future. It will be another victory in its own time, but a triumph by Yahweh (and Yahweh's prophet?) over this king now suddenly shown to have misplaced his "mercy" toward Ben-hadad.

Genre

For all its incipient artistry, this unit does not go very far toward developing an independent dramatic plot. There is little or no tension to be resolved in the course of events. Essentially, we are given a narrative episode (cf. Mabee, 242) of an unnamed prophet coming to the king and cleverly manipulating events to expose the ruler's offense against his God. Vv. 1-34, or at least vv. 31-34, seem to be necessary conditions for our understanding. In this case, it seems best to speak of a storylike REPORT of PROPHECY OF PUNISHMENT. Essentially, we are given a brief narrative scene to make intelligible the prophecy delivered by this unnamed prophet. His speech is entirely typical of many examples found in the books of Kings (→ 13:20-22 with full discussion and parallels). Worth noting is the JURIDICAL PARABLE, vv. 39-40, a speech which puts a fictional case before the king for his adjudication. By analogy, the fiction illustrates an action already taken by the king, and so his judgment in the matter turns out to be a declaration upon his own behavior. Other examples of this favorite literary convention may be found in 2 Sam 12:1-4 and 14:5-7. The generic term, however, can hardly be applied to the entire unit, vv. 35-43 (against Simon).

Taking vv. 30b-43 as his unit for analysis, De Vries (p. 55) adopts the designation "regal self-judgment narrative," a subtype of prophetic legend. One need not agree with his term or his source and traditio-historical reconstructions to recognize the value in this suggestion. When read as part of the redacted unity in ch. 20 (→ discussion at 20:1-43), this report of a prophecy of punishment recalls a thematic structure evident in the final edited form of the David and Saul traditions. Saul's desperate sacrifice on the eve of a military engagement brings about direct confrontation with Samuel, who announces God's punishment on the hapless and unaware monarch (1 Samuel 15). Similarly, David offends Yahweh in the matter of Bathsheba (2 Samuel 11) and then faces Nathan, who—like the unnamed prophet dealing with Ahab—presents a fictional appeal so as to turn the king's judgment into self-condemnation. Nathan immediately announces the king's punishment in typical prophetic style (2 Sam 12:1-15). This same thematic pattern informs the redacted shape of 1 Kings 21, as well (→ the discussion at 21:1-29). Cf. also 2 Kgs 13:14-19. These canonical patterns help us see clearly that this storylike report of prophecy of punishment (whatever its ultimate source may have been) is no independent genre, but a scene in the larger redacted context of ch. 20.

Setting

Since its origins are obscure, and the unit now forms a scene within ch. 20, we should look carefully at the immediate literary context. In the glow of Ahab's victory and reconciliation with Ben-hadad, this prophecy is delivered, and only in this context can we identify the unnamed "king of Israel" as Ahab. At the same time, the unit issues in a sullen and withdrawn monarch, brooding like Saul at his disfavor with Yahweh. It is an image which will carry into ch. 21 in Ahab's dealings with Naboth (21:4) and forms an essential part of the exilic editor's selective rendering of Ahab's rule.

Intention

Obviously, the report announces Ahab's punishment and, in process, exposes his hidden transgression, the reason for God's judgment. The point offers an ironic twist to the story in 20:1-34. The hero of Samaria and the plains of Aphek, who rode the crest of that victory to a peaceful and apparently well-meant settlement with Ben-hadad, vv. 31-34, turns out to be, surprisingly, a transgressor. He knew nothing of God's prohibition on preserving enemy life, nor did *we* as readers. The author has exposed a hidden counterpoint to the otherwise sympathetic view of Ahab. But the king is doubly duped. Just as a prophet chose disguise to make plain the truth, so the story of triumph proves to be Yahweh's ruse: a situation, after the fact, revealed as offensive to God. It is enough to illustrate the Dtr editor's evaluation of this king (16:33) and to justify the first direct prediction of his eventual downfall.

Bibliography

S. J. De Vries, *Prophet* (see listing at 17:1–19:21); C. Mabee, "Problem," 239-56 (see listing at 3:16-28); U. Simon, "The Poor Man's Ewe Lamb: An Example of Juridical Parable," *Bib* 48 (1967) 207-42.

AHAB AND THE MURDER OF NABOTH, 21:1-29

Structure

I. Narrative situation	1
II. Complication: the vineyard desired	2-7
A. Dialogue: Ahab and Naboth	2-3
1. Narrative introduction	2aα^{1}
2. Dialogue proper	2aα^{2}-3
a. Ahab's offer: exchange or buy	2aα^{2}-b
b. Naboth's refusal	3
B. Results: Ahab's sullen withdrawal	4
C. Dialogue: Ahab and Jezebel	5-7
1. Narrative introduction	5a
2. Dialogue proper	5b-7
a. Jezebel's question	5b
b. Ahab's reply	6
1) Narrative introduction	6aα^{1}
2) Reply proper: report of impasse	6aα^{2}-b
c. Jezebel's response: promise of a solution	7
1) Narrative introduction	7aα
2) Response proper	7aβ-b
a) Rhetorical question	7aβ
b) Word of encouragement	7bα
c) Promise	7bβ
III. Resolution/new complication: the vineyard taken	8-16
A. Jezebel's plot for Naboth's murder	8-14
1. Forged royal instructions	8-10
a. Letters sent	8
b. Their contents: instructions for murder	9-10
2. Compliance with instructions	11-13
a. General summary	11a
b. Specific compliance: Naboth's execution	11b-13
3. Official report to Jezebel	14
a. Narrative introduction	14a
b. Official report: Naboth's death	14b
B. Result of Jezebel's plot	15-16
1. Jezebel's counsel to Ahab	15
a. Narrative introduction	15a
b. Counsel proper	15b
1) Order: take possession of vineyard	15bα
2) Reason for order	15bβ
2. Ahab's response: preparation for possession	16
IV. Climax: Yahweh's judgment on Ahab and Jezebel	17-26
A. Prophetic commissioning	17-19
1. Prophetic word formula	17

2. Commission proper	18-19
a. Commissioning formula	18
b. Charge: announce punishment for Ahab	19
1) Messenger formula I	19aα
2) Invective (accusatory question)	19aβ
3) Messenger formula II	19bα
4) Announcement of punishment	19bβ
B. Execution of commission	20-22, 24
1. Narrative introduction	20aα
2. Ahab's question	20aβ
3. Elijah's reply	20b-22, 24
a. Answer to Ahab's question	20bα
b. Prophecy of punishment	20bβ-22, 24
1) Reason	20bβ
2) Announcement of punishment	21-22, 24
C. Report of judgment on Jezebel	23
D. Summary theological appraisal of Ahab and Jezebel	25-26
V. Aftermath: mitigated judgment	27-29
A. Report of Ahab's penitence	27
B. Report of revelatory word	28-29
1. Prophetic word formula	28
2. Announcement of reprieve	29
a. Reason for reprieve	29a-bα^{1}
b. Reprieve proper	29bα^{2}-β

This text gives the impression of a clear break and new beginning, with a somewhat rough editorial transition. The style of v. 1 is typical of openers in Hebrew narratives: "Now Naboth the Jezreelite had a vineyard . . ." (*kerem hāyâ lĕnābôt hayyizrĕʿē'lî*). The very first phrase in v. 1, "after this" (placed in v. 2 by *RSV*), is probably a redactional link to ch. 20. Defining the end of the unit is more difficult and much more disputed. Surely 22:1 marks a break with the subject matter of ch. 21, but the unity of the immediately preceding material is doubtful. A majority of critics have held that vv. 1-20a belonged to an original narrative whose ending has been supplanted by a series of Dtr supplements in vv. 20b-29 (e.g., Fohrer; Šanda, *Könige*; Montgomery, *Kings*; Schüpphaus; Gressmann; cf. 14:7-11; 16:1-4; De Vries, 115n.6, takes vv. 27-29 as the original sequel to vv. 1-20a). Two redaction-critical studies (Steck, 41-43; Bohlen) have questioned this virtual consensus, looked at the possible relationships with 2 Kgs 9:21-26, and argued that a fragment of old tradition in vv. 17-20a (Bohlen and Steck differ only slightly on this point) was expanded with vv. 1-16 and the supplements in vv. 20b-29. (Cf. Gray, *Kings*, who views vv. 17-19 as a fragmentary second version of the tradition in vv. 1-16; and Würthwein, "Naboth," who takes vv. 1-16 as the basic unit which underwent expansion over time.)

Thus there is no consensus on what constitutes the original unit or on the history of composition and redaction resulting in the present text.

Whatever its prior history may have been, the canonical text seems for the most part thematically unified. At least as far as v. 20, the structure is clear. Thereafter, the flow becomes a bit confused (e.g., the commission given to Elijah, v. 19, is never explicitly carried out; v. 23, though related to the theme of punishment for Ahab, shifts the focus to Jezebel and adopts suddenly a third-person reportorial style; vv. 25-26, both in style and content, seem parenthetical). It is probably best to recognize that (1) a basic tradition has been supplemented, especially by the Dtr editor(s) in vv. 20b-28 (for vv. 21-22, 24, cf. the Dtr passages, 14:7-11; 16:2-4; for vv. 25-26, cf. 16:25-26; 16:30-31); (2) a clear understanding of the prior history of the text eludes us; and (3) the text is now a redacted unity, built along the lines of other canonical texts, as will be shown below.

The key to the overall structure is a double thematic movement. The first begins in Ahab's frustrated desire to own Naboth's choice vineyard (II, vv. 2-7) and moves to a resolution by means of Jezebel's plot to free the vineyard for the taking (III, vv. 8-16). But this outcome is itself a problem from the point of view of divine limits on royal prerogatives. Hence, a second thematic movement carries us forward through a confrontation between prophet and king in which transgression and punishment are announced (IV.A, B, vv. 17-24), and reprieve awarded (V, vv. 27-29). Thus, the narrative comes to its penultimate climax in the overt seizure of Naboth's property (v. 16) and to its main climax in vv. 17-24, the confrontation which answers a question unasked in the narrative: will simple justice be done in Yahweh's court? This turning point obviously is stressed, and its theme broadened to touch Jezebel's fortunes as well as the general canonical vision of Ahab's reign (vv. 23, 25-26). As if condemnation in ch. 20 were not enough, the unit heaps more condemnation on Ahab, relates a second prediction of disaster for this king (20:42; 21:21-22, 24), and for good measure adds a comment on his apostate religious conduct (vv. 25-26). The tension subsides a bit in the next scene, however, as Ahab repents (V.A, v. 27) and the reader overhears a private revelatory word from Yahweh to Elijah promising a mitigation of this terrible judgment (V.B, vv. 28-29). See a similar structural analysis for vv. 1-20, 27-29 in De Vries (p. 132 n. 18), and for vv. 1-16, see Bohlen (p. 145).

In the first major portion of this narrative (vv. 1-16), scenes of paired characters in dialogue alternate with action by a single character:

I-II.A	Ahab-Naboth	(Speech)	vv. 1-3
II.B	Ahab	(Action)	v. 4
II.C	Ahab-Jezebel	(Speech)	vv. 5-7
III.A	Jezebel	(Action)	vv. 8-14
III.B	Ahab-Jezebel	(Speech)	vv. 15-16

We know the characters mostly from their interaction with one another. Only at the beginning does Ahab initiate action. At first he seems disposed to act reasonably toward Naboth. When his offer to buy or trade for possession of the vineyard is refused, however, the king turns away, immobilized. He seeks refuge in self-doubt and sullenness, refusing food, his face turned away from human touch (v. 4; cf. 1 Sam 20:34; 28:23; Ps 102:5 [*RSV* 4]). Like a child hurt by another's abuse, he must be led out of his self-made downward spiral and made to assume the power of position which, in Jezebel's eyes, he has abdicated. The queen is strong willed, aggressive, large in the moment. She pulls Ahab from his despondency. Rhetorically reminding him of his position and commanding him to restore himself (v. 7; cf. 2 Sam 12:20-21; 1 Sam 1:18), she promises to give what she does not possess: "I will give you the vineyard of Naboth . . ." (v. 7). Later, in the next scene which pairs king with queen, Jezebel will again act decisively with the unscrupled strength that Ahab lacks. Again comes a command for the king: having been ordered to rise and eat, he is now commanded to take possession of the vineyard (v. 15). When Ahab goes down to the vineyard, the characterization has come full circle; the king has traveled an inner road, turning away and coming back. In course, what began as a matter for business negotiation between Ahab and Naboth became by Jezebel's devious design a sort of public exercise of royal "eminent domain."

In between these Ahab-Jezebel scenes is the long action-oriented section which highlights the queen in her own right (III.A, vv. 8-14). The woman who brings the king from his despair with a word, hinting at a plan as yet secret (v. 7), and the woman who stirs him to action when her plan is done (v.15) now in the middle of the narrative (vv. 8-14) seizes events as forcefully as she moves Ahab. She is devious and purposeful, intent on her design, methodical in its execution. The narrative pace is perfectly matched—rapid, with little description and no emotion, as though to suggest the queen's cold strength.

The next major portion of this redacted unit is arranged with less artistry. Two scenes of private communication between Yahweh and his prophet Elijah (IV.A and V.B, vv. 17-19 and 28-29) now bracket a major scene of confrontation between Elijah and Ahab (IV.B, vv. 20-24). With a suddenness that we have come to expect of Elijah (cf. 17:1), he abruptly comes into view. It is a scene of commissioning which offers a command from Yahweh to match those from Jezebel: "Arise, go down to meet Ahab . . . in the vineyard of Naboth. . . ." Yahweh charges Elijah with a word of judgment for this king who stands emboldened to take what Jezebel has given him. The real gift is unexpected, as startling as Elijah's appearance in the narrative. For Yahweh hands Ahab a platter filled with disaster. The initial dialogue (v. 20) recalls the antagonists' meeting on Mount Carmel (18:17). With a single stroke the narrator suggests that, Yahwist victory or no at Carmel, nothing much has changed. Immediately, Elijah frames his words and declares unequivocally the terrible slaking of God's thirst for justice. The moment is highly dramatic, but the text, in marked contrast to the more highly developed tradition in ch. 18, gives all attention to the prophet's words. They mark the Naboth incident as transgression against *Yahweh* (and ignore completely any other possible conclusion), assign full responsibility to Ahab (even though he had been pictured as merely compliant), and single him out as the one to bear punishment. The prophetic speech in confrontation thus forms the main climax to the overall action, the pitch from which tension can only subside.

This confrontation is also an occasion for the narrator (or the redactors, in this case) to stop the action, turn as it were to the audience, and comment (vv. 23-26). We, but not Ahab, learn that punishment is extended to Jezebel, almost as an afterthought; we, but not Ahab, hear a general theological evaluation of this king and his Phoenician queen. It seems a somewhat gratuitous excess. After all, to the Dtr author-editor of Kings, Jezebel was the consummate expression of Ahab's misguided ways (cf. 16:31).

Then, as though time stopped had begun to run on again, the action resumes

(V, vv. 27-29). Ahab repents. As at the beginning of the narrative, we are privy to a communication from God to prophet. A word comes to Elijah, offering mitigation of the judgment just announced. God will be satisfied in the next generation.

If the first portion of the narrative highlighted Jezebel's dominance over Ahab and events, so the second part emphasizes the power of God's and Elijah's word over this same king. The divine word of judgment delivered to Ahab (vv. 20b-22) is framed by divine word to Elijah. The king submits, just as he does to Jezebel's superior force. In the end, the Naboth incident seems transmuted into another image: a conflict of will and power between Israel's God, who demands all, and Israel's king, who cannot win.

Genre

In the light of their conflicting theories of composition and redaction, various scholars have presented differing generic designations for portions of this unit. For example, Bohlen (pp. 243-58) labeled vv. 1-16 as "artistic action narrative"; Würthwein called the same textual unit a "novelette," not very dissimilar from the judgments of others (cf. Welten, 26-27; Miller; Baltzer, "Naboth," 76-77). Eyeing the whole tradition, Plöger (pp. 39-41, 46-48) used the term "prophetic word-story"; Steck (pp. 143-44) settled for legend or didactive narrative (Legend). De Vries (p. 115) used the term "legend" for a good part of the entire unit, vv. 1-20a, 27-29, but tried for more precision in postulating a subcategory, "regal self-judgment story."

Obviously most of the disagreement over genre stems from differences over what constitutes the unit to be defined. For the redacted whole, it seems wisest to call the text PROPHETIC STORY, a narrative with developed plot (tension to its resolution) which places a prophet, his word, and/or action at the fulcrum of narrative interest.

To say more, we must begin at the end. In vv. 27-29 (V.A, B), the material apparently has been shaped according to a canonical SCHEMA OF REPRIEVE. The typical elements are (1) a description of penitence which follows upon divine punishment, or promise of such; (2) a prophecy or report of mitigated punishment, or reprieve.

The language of description is stereotyped. In 1 Kgs 21:27, Ahab "rent his clothes" (*qr' bgd*), fasted (*ṣûm*), dressed in sackcloth (*śaq*). These associated motifs widely depict grieving reaction to significant loss (Gen 37:29, 34; 2 Sam 1:11; 3:31; 13:31; Job 1:20) or deep emotion in grave circumstances or bad news (2 Kgs 5:7, 8; 6:30; 11:14; 18:37; 19:1 [= Isa 36:22; 37:1]). Naturally, because of the association of disaster with transgression against God, ripping at one's clothing is also a sign of penitence, as in Jonah 3:6; 2 Kgs 22:11, 19=2 Chr 34:19, 27—even in reaction to warnings of impending punishment (Jer 36:24). Thus, King Ahab's reaction to Elijah's prophecy of judgment suggests penitence. Even Yahweh recognizes the convention: "Have you seen how Ahab has humbled himself before me?" (*kî-nikna' 'aḥ'āb millĕpānāy* [v. 29]; cf. *kn'*, "humble oneself," in 2 Kgs 22:19; 2 Chr 7:14; 12:6, 12; 30:11).

Now the divine word which announces reprieve in this schema is similar to PROPHECY OF SALVATION. In context, the prophecy mitigates, limits, or lessens an expected punishment. The elements of speech typically include (a) allusion to penitent action, (b) reason for the mitigation of punishment, and (c) announcement of reprieve (or mitigation). See, for example, 2 Kings 22. The punishment which King Josiah expects on the basis of hearing *tôrâ* (v. 13) and prophetic oracle (vv. 16-17) are not to apply to him personally. The prophet speaks: because the king repents (v. 19), he is spared (v. 20). So, too, King David in 2 Samuel 12. He hears a prophecy (v. 13), and in return receives a word of reprieve which in effect transfers the punishment from king to unborn son (v. 14). Note the similar pattern in 2 Chr 12:7-8. Thus, in the story of Ahab, the full catastrophe expected on the basis of Elijah's (God's) words in vv. 20b-24 is averted by the king's penitent behavior (v. 27), and Elijah then receives a new revelation which announces reprieve: "I will not bring the evil in his days but in his son's days . . ." (1 Kgs 21:29).

Schemata of reprieve appear in the midst of larger narrative contexts that describe or announce calamity. The latter is then taken as punishment for transgression against Yahweh. The motivic sequence is always the same:

I. Calamity (punishment reported or announced for the future)
II. Schema of reprieve
  A. Reaction: description of penitence
  B. Prophecy or report of reprieve

(Cf. 2 Samuel 12; 2 Kings 22; 2 Chr 12:7-8.) This wider pattern does not seem to indicate an independent genre but rather a conventional thematic and formal pattern in the midst of longer narratives. Thus, 2 Kings 22, a heavily edited Dtr text having to do with Josiah's initiating religious reform, includes in its midst the schema of reprieve: description of penitence (v. 11) followed by a prophetic oracle announcing reprieve (vv. 18-20). Similarly, in 2 Sam 12:7-14, both a prophecy of judgment (vv. 7-12) and the schema of reprieve (vv. 13-14) sit as part of a longer narrative which graphically recounts David's wrong by Uriah, husband of Bathsheba (chs. 11–12). So too 2 Chr 12:2-12 alludes to calamitous judgment (vv. 1, 2, 3-5) and concludes with the schema of reprieve (vv. 6-8). One may observe the same pattern in a more general way in 1 Samuel 15. There the narrator tells of an offense against Yahweh (vv. 1-9, 10-16), reports a prophecy of judgment (vv. 17-23), and follows all with the schema of reprieve (vv. 24-31). Cf. further, 1 Kgs 20:1-34, 35-43; 1 Sam 28:4-19.

It should be clear that 1 Kings 21:1-29 in its redacted unity in large measure conforms to this canonical model. What may appear as loose editorial, clumsy supplementation of original materials turns out to be carefully ordered, even stereotypical. Judging from its importance in 2 Kings 22, one might suppose the schema of reprieve to be a favorite convention of the Dtr author-editors.

Within this constructed prophetic story, several smaller genres are worth noting. First, the PROPHECY OF PUNISHMENT, vv. 20b-22, 24, is thoroughly typical of those examples throughout the books of Kings and is shaped by the Dtr author-editor (→ 13:20-22, and full discussion with parallels; also 14:7-10; 16:2-4). In this particular example, there is a stylistic alternation from personal address, v. 21a, to impersonal formulation, v. 21b, back to personal address, v. 22, and finally to impersonal at v. 24. Such shifts are not uncommon. Cf. 16:3-4.

Second, in the midst of this prophecy of punishment stands v. 23, a short

SUMMARY OF PROPHETIC ORACLE. Disrupting both the style and focus of the main speech, the statement conveys summarily, without dramatic context, a prophetic word which was spoken concerning Jezebel. If an oracle is alluded to in v. 23b, it is done rather much in an impersonal, almost proverbial style, without the usual formulas for reporting a prophet's words. The verse is distinct, therefore, from the many (→) reports of prophetic word (cf. Jer 21:1-10) or reports of (→) prophetic revelation (cf. 16:1-4) and the frequent descriptions of various types of personally directed prophetic speeches in the books of Kings, such as (→) self-disclosure oracle (20:28) and (→) prophecy of punishment (13:21-22; 14:7-11; 21:20b-22).

Third, there is the special type of prophecy of salvation which we have designated as ANNOUNCEMENT OF REPRIEVE, v. 29. Its important elements include (1) an allusion to penitent action, leading into (2) the reason for the announcement, and finally (3) the announcement of reprieve. Parallels appear almost exclusively in the midst of larger narratives and as part of a schematic arrangement of diverse motifs into a schema of reprieve (→ discussion above; 2 Kgs 22:18-20; 2 Chr 12:7-8). Of course, this announcement of reprieve now occurs as the main part of a private communication between Yahweh and his prophet, or a REPORT OF PROPHETIC REVELATION (see 16:1-4 and full discussion at 17:2-16), typically introduced with the PROPHETIC WORD FORMULA, "And the word of the Lord came to Elijah . . ." (cf. 16:1-4).

Fourth, there is the report of PROPHETIC COMMISSION, vv. 17-19, a special type of the more generalized COMMISSIONING OF A MESSENGER. Such a prophetic report typically opens with a PROPHETIC WORD FORMULA, ". . . the word of the Lord came to so-and-so," includes the charge or commissioning formulas with imperatives, such as "Go!" or "Speak. . . ," and finally gives a MESSENGER FORMULA, "Thus says the Lord," followed by the message. See 12:22-24 and the full discussion with parallels.

Finally, we may note that vv. 25-26, though not in themselves a complete generic unit, seem to be typical of motifs found in the Dtr author-editor's (→) regnal resumé (→ full discussion of the literary device at 14:21-31). Picking up a phrase from v. 20b as a catchword, "sold himself to do evil," the author-redactor adds two special accents: (1) a new and specific interpretation of Jezebel's role in the events narrated in vv. 1-19; she *incites* Ahab to transgress; her crime is not against Naboth, but against Yahweh; (2) a generalized charge of apostasy against Ahab, similar to what we would expect in an introductory regnal resumé (cf. 16:31-33).

Setting

Given the uncertainties in our grasp of the earlier history of the traditions making up this unit, there is not much point in speculating on possible settings for reconstructed genres and shorter portions. As the strong literary patterns of punishment and reprieve would suggest, it is most important to see the context in which the unit now functions in the books of Kings. In this light, the prophetic story is set as a second incident of confrontation following the events on Mount Carmel. Perhaps more important, this particular story comes right after a prophecy of punishment has been delivered to Ahab by an unknown prophet (20:42) and before the decisive events which bring to an end his reign. It is entirely possible that the whole unit owes its particular arrangement to the later exilic author-editor of Kings.

Intention

In this literary context, therefore, the story provides a prediction of, and reason for, Ahab's demise. Thus it repeats a point made in 20:35-42, but unlike the prediction there, the king's demise is linked not only to a specific act, or inaction, one might say, but to a stereotyped evocation of those ideological charges contained in Dtr editorial summaries. As is often the case in the books of Kings, this particular prophetic story is subservient to ideology. It demonstrates how events moved according to Yahweh's determinations, regardless of any human motivations or strivings revealed in narrative details. For this last editor, it was probably not as important to see Ahab as a weak king, dominated by Jezebel and divine word, as it was to single him out as culpable and worthy of punishment. In context, then, the story portrays another incident in Ahab's series of transgressions and justifies again the summary evaluation given us by the editor in 16:30.

In this light, the element of prophetic judgment, as in ch. 20, is emphasized. Ahab is not just an Israelite king; he is the king who opposed Elijah (18:17) and Yahweh, and who in addition was responsible for the evils associated with his wife Jezebel (16:31-33). As on Mount Carmel, Ahab is a symbol of rebellion and of omission—allowing, even fostering, Jezebel's devious and insidious influence on the side of opposition to Yahweh (18:4, 13; 19:1-2). In this offense involving a wife of foreign origin, the redactor implicitly compares Ahab with Solomon (11:1-4).

Bibliography

See bibliographies at "Introduction to 1 Kings" and 17:1–19:21. K. Baltzer, "Naboths Weinberg (1 Kön 21): Der Konflikt zwischen israelitischem und kanaanäischem Bodenrecht," *WuD* 8 (1965) 73-88; R. Bohlen, "Alttestamentliche Kunstprosa als Zeitkritik," *TTZ* 87 (1978) 192-202; idem, *Der Fall Nabot: Hintergrund und Werdegang einer alttestamentlichen Erzählung (1 Kön 21)* (Trierer Theologische Studien 35; Trier: Paulinus, 1978); Alfred Jepsen, "Ahabs Busse. Ein kleiner Beitrag zur Methode literar-historischer Einordnung (1 Kön 1:27-29)," in *Archäologie und Altes Testament* (*Fest.* K. Galling; ed. A. Kuschke and E. Kutsch; Tübingen: Mohr, 1970) 145-55; J. M. Miller, "The Fall of the House of Ahab," *VT* 17 (1967) 307-24; H. Seebass, "Der Fall Naboth in I Kön 21," *VT* 24 (1974) 474-88; S. Timm, *Omri*, 111-36; M. Weitmeyer, "Nabots vingård (I Kong 21, 1-16). En traditionshistorisk kommentar," *Dansk teologisk tidsskrift* 29 (1966) 129-43; P. Welten, "Naboths Weinberg," *EvT* 33 (1973) 18-32; E. Würthwein, "Naboth-Novelle und Elia-Wort," *ZTK* 75 (1978) 375-97.

THE DEATH OF AHAB, 22:1-38

Structure

I. Narrative situation: peace between Syria and Israel	1
II. Complication: prospect of peace disturbed	2-4
A. Situation: meeting of the kings	2
B. Agreement to wage war	3-4
1. Narrative introduction	3aα

2. Proposal for war pact	3aβ-4a
a. Rhetorical question (pretext for war)	3aβ-b
b. Direct invitation for alliance to Jehoshaphat	4a
3. Jehoshaphat's reply: agreement (alliance formula)	4b
III. Preparations for battle: consultations with prophets	5-28
A. First consultation	5-6
1. Jehoshaphat's request for consultation	5
2. Result: oracular inquiry	6
a. Preparations: prophets gathered	6aα
b. The question put to prophets	6aβ
c. The reply: prophetic oracle	6b
1) Order: go up	6bα
2) Conveyance formula	6bβ
B. Second consultation	7-15
1. Jehoshaphat's request for consultation	7-8
a. Question concerning another prophet	7
b. Reply concerning Micaiah	8a
c. Jehoshaphat's rejoinder	8b
2. Result: oracular inquiry	9-15
a. Preparations	9-14
1) Command to summon Micaiah	9
2) Description of ongoing consultations	10-12
a) Kings "sitting," prophets "prophesying"	10
b) Report of Zedekiah's symbolic action	11
c) Epitomizing summary of consultations	12
(1) Prophets "prophesying"	12a
(2) Oracle	12b
(a) Order: go up	12bα
(b) Conveyance formula	12bβ
3) Command to summon Micaiah executed	13-14
a) Narrative introduction	13aα
b) Messenger's advice to Micaiah	13aβ-b
c) Micaiah's reply: oath	14
b. The question put to Micaiah	15a
c. The reply: oracle	15b
1) Order: go up	15bα
2) Conveyance formula	15bβ
C. Reactions to second consultation	16-23
1. Reaction of king of Israel: remonstrance of Micaiah	16

2. Micaiah's response: report of dramatic word-vision — 17
   a. Narrative introduction — 17aα[1]
   b. Vision — 17aα[2]-b
      1) Announcement of vision — 17aα[2]
      2) Vision sequence — 17aα[3]-b
3. King of Israel's counter-reaction: remonstrative question — 18
4. Micaiah's counter-response: report of dramatic word-vision — 19-23
   a. Narrative introduction — 19aα
   b. Report of vision — 19aβ-22
      1) Summons to attention — 19aβ
      2) Vision — 19b-22
         a) Announcement of vision — 19bα[1]
         b) Vision sequence — 19bα[2]-22
      3) Interpretative conclusion: evil on Ahab — 23

D. Consequences of consultations — 24-28
   1. Zedekiah's dispute with Micaiah — 24-25
      a. Zedekiah's challenge — 24
         1) Physical blow — 24a
         2) Verbal challenge — 24b
      b. Micaiah's rejoinder: announcement of evil for Zedekiah — 25
   2. Ahab's suppression of Micaiah — 26-28
      a. Orders to imprison Micaiah — 26-27
      b. Micaiah's repartee — 28

IV. Account of battle — 29-38
   A. Mustering of forces — 29-32aα
      1. Concerning the Israelites — 29
      2. Concerning disguises for battle — 30
      3. Concerning the Syrians — 31-32aα
   B. Description of battle — 32aβ-33
   C. Consequences — 34-36
      1. Death of Ahab — 34-35
      2. Israelite retreat — 36
   D. Epitomizing conclusion — 37
   E. Epilogue: prophecy fulfilled — 38
      1. Summary of events — 38a
      2. Oracle fulfillment formula — 38b

This unit clearly stands apart from the summary statements in vv. 39-40. When matched with 16:29-33, these latter verses complete the editorial framework surrounding all the material relating to Ahab's rule. Placing v. 38 is more difficult. The less-than-perfect connections with vv. 1-37 and the partial link to 21:19 may justify our thinking of v. 38 as a gloss on some original form of the main tradition. On the other hand, the structural connections between vv. 1-37 and v. 38 remain strong enough to consider the verse as a part of the unit for analysis. In any case, the form of the tradition is not altered significantly with or without v. 38. The beginning of the unit comes with vv. 1-2. While they may provide redactional linkage to ch. 20, they also seem typical of abrupt openings to folk narrative. As opening exposition, the verses sketch the necessary background to the sequence of events that follow.

Many critics have viewed vv. 1-37 (38) as essentially unified (e.g., Šanda, *Könige*, I, 506-10; Montgomery, *Kings*, 336; Schüpphaus, 59). In 1967 Würthwein challenged this view with considerable impact, since subsequent critics, while differing on details of the reconstruction, largely follow his lead in supposing that the canonical unit evolved when an original story about battle (largely preserved in vv. 1-4, 29-37) was supplemented in stages with prophetic additions (mostly seen in vv. 5-28; cf. Hossfeld, 27-36; Seebass, 109-24; Schmitt, 43, 50). Most recently, De Vries (pp. 25-30) argued for a connection between two originally independent narratives, most of which remain visible in (1) vv. 2b-9, 15-18, 26-37, and (2) vv. 10-12a, 14, 19-25.

There is no consensus on these matters. Among those scholars who support theories of two or more stages of development, one may find significant and embarrassing disagreements. Moreover, some stylistic and structural arguments for unity are not easily dismissed (Rofé; Long). Moreover, the text hangs on a typical and unifying literary skeleton, that is, schematic description of battle which contains (1) confrontation of forces, (2) description of battle, and (3) its consequences. Often such an account includes a scene of consultation with oracle-givers before the battle (cf. 1 Sam 4:1-2; Judg 4:12-16; 1 Kgs 20:26-30; Campbell, 68-71). It seems the wisest course, therefore, to admit a certain roughness in the narrative, to allow for prior developments no longer very clearly visible, and to highlight the structural and thematic integrity in the canonical unit (cf. Robertson; Rofé; Long).

In broadest terms, one may see that peace between two nations is interrupted by two kings plotting a war to regain lost territory (I, II; vv. 1-4). The kings seek tactical guidance in consultations (III.A, B, C, vv. 5-23) and march off to battle (IV.A-D, vv. 29-37), curiously ignoring the counsel of the prophet whose role the narrator emphasizes. An epilogue (IV.E, v. 38) reports prophecy fulfilled in these events and relates the narrative to a wider literary context, a prophetic judgment speech given in 21:19. This overall structure is misleading in its simplicity, however. There is more artistry than first meets the eye, and the narrator enriches the telling by consistently falsifying our expectations (Robertson).

Like many folk narratives, this one begins abruptly with an image of repose. Israel and Syria have been at peace for three years. Suddenly, premeditated design breaks the equilibrium. With extraordinary economy, the narrator takes us into the midst of that calm, intimates a desire, a plot conceived, an alliance sealed, and stability threatened. The pace is rapid, but the description restrained. The kings of Israel and Judah meet, and Ahab—whom we know by name at this point only in context—speaks twice. He poses a question to his "servants" (or his vassals?) that rhetorically justifies his plan. Then Ahab directs a second question to Jehoshaphat, king of Judah, proposing a joint campaign against the Syrians. Immediately Jehoshaphat agrees, concluding the alliance with a formula that pledges goods and people to the cause (cf. 2 Sam 5:1). Negotiations take place, but not at the expense of dispatch. This air of restrained haste, deliberately fixed by a single objective, the war, stands in contrast to the protracted consultations yet to come (vv. 5-28). The sense of control and calculation will seem ironic when subsequent events turn less on human designs than fortuitous, or fateful, circumstances. It remains now for the tension aroused in this opening scene to be resolved.

But the resolution is not immediate. A grand consultation with the prophets (III, vv. 5-28) in effect stops the action between preparations for war and the actual campaign. The scene shatters many other expectations too. Though requested and repeated, the consultations seem to have no real effect on subsequent events. The kings engage the enemy as though their oracles had all been favorable, or as though Yahweh had never been consulted. The prophets countermand each other, as though engaging in their own private war for authority and status. Yet Micaiah ben-Imlah, the obvious hero to the narrator (his "true" prophet), inexplicably utters a lie in v. 15 and overrules it with a twice reported vision and oracle in vv. 17-23. In short, what began as a narrative of two kings plotting war against Syria devolves to a story of one king and one prophet, counterpointed with disputing prophets, especially Zedekiah and Micaiah. It is a grand diversion which moves us not one step closer to the battle.

Nevertheless, the unit makes structural and thematic sense. We witness two scenes of consultation: one with four hundred prophets (III.A, vv. 5-6), the other with Micaiah ben-Imlah (III.B, C; vv. 7-23). The sequence of motifs in each scene is nearly identical. There is (1) a request for consultation ("inquire of [for the word of] Yahweh," vv. 5, 7-8) followed by (2) the scene of oracular inquiry (vv. 6, 15), involving a question put to the prophets and the answer in terms of divine oracle and victorious conveyance formula, "The Lord will give it into the hand of the king" (vv. 6b, 15b; cf. v. 12). Furthermore, both scenes and their oracles receive a similarly structured elaboration. The first consultation (v. 6) finds reaffirmation and reiteration in the circumstantial aside of vv. 10-12. So, too, Micaiah ben-Imlah's word to the king, though with more complexity. His oracle must be uttered first as untruth (v. 15b), then corrected in a first report of vision (v. 17), which in turn is reiterated in another vision adding up to a word of judgment upon the king: "The Lord has spoken evil concerning you" (vv. 19-23).

The second consultation, that is, the inquiry through Micaiah ben-Imlah (vv. 9-23), follows an artistic pattern of response and counter-response. Thus, Micaiah offers a first oracle (v. 15b), the king responds negatively (v. 16), Micaiah tries again with report of vision that amounts to oracle (v. 17), and the king responds negatively again (v. 18). This response triggers yet another and final oracle from the prophet (vv. 19-23). In the process, the narrator emphasizes enmity between the prophet and King Ahab (identified first in Micaiah ben-Imlah's words, v. 20), as well as dramatizes competing prophecies. For as counterpoint to Micaiah ben-Imlah's doomsaying ("evil") stand the words of victory ("good") on the lips of the four hundred prophets (v. 6), words that are reaffirmed in a kind of "meanwhile" scene describing symbolic action and oracles while the messenger fetches Micaiah ben-Imlah (vv. 11-12). In context, the words "good" and "evil" (*ṭôb, rāʿ*, or *rāʿâ*) serve as thematic catchwords (vv. 8b, 13b, 23), binding everything together and encoding the relationship of Ahab, the four hundred prophets, and Micaiah ben-Imlah. Inseparable from the contrast and ironies of "good" and "evil" is the opposition between Micaiah ben-Imlah on the one hand and the four hundred, whom presumably Zedekiah embodies, on the other.

What emerges, then, from this structured and thematic whole is verbal drama focused and personalized in paired relationships: Ahab-Micaiah and Zedekiah-Micaiah. Jehoshaphat, who in effect stirred the stew by pressing for consultation, is completely forgotten.

The details are illuminating. The two kings' exchange (vv. 5-8) provides the first main drama in dialogue. Their words highlight a motif new to the story, the long-standing enmity between the king of Israel and Micaiah ben-Imlah. Indeed, the narrator tricks us. He lingers to show contrasting opinions of Ahab and Jehoshaphat on this prophet, as though to better characterize the war *protagonists*. But the effect is rather to emphasize Ahab's hate (v. 8; cf. v. 18), thereby narrowing the scope of the drama and introducing the *antagonist*. The narrator gives us yet another point in the prophecies of victory (vv. 6, 11-12). Between the straightforward summons to fetch Micaiah (v. 9) and the prophet's appearance before the kings (v. 15) is placed a descriptive scene (vv. 10-12) marked off by inverted word order (in the Hebrew, the subject precedes participial predicates or circumstantial description, vv. 10a, 10b, 12). We learn that the four hundred prophets go on prophesying victory and that they are joined by Zedekiah, who is abruptly introduced through a rather truncated description of symbolic action (Fohrer, *Handlungen*). The effect is to stop the action (fetching Micaiah) and to focus the reader's attention on a second paired relationship. It is not only Ahab's hate for Micaiah that fuels the action, but also antagonism between prophets. We get an impression, undoubtedly exaggerated for dramatic effect, of unanimity among the four hundred prophets of Ahab. It is a single voice named and personified in Zedekiah and rising up in the shadow of Ahab's begrudging and hate-filled naming of Micaiah ben-Imlah (v. 8). When the action resumes, both paired relationships (Ahab-Micaiah, Zedekiah-Micaiah) touch. Like Ahab, the royal messenger expects the worst sort of discord from Micaiah ben-Imlah. He urges unanimous prophetic advice (v. 13) as though to reiterate the suspicion and hatred already given royal voice (v. 8) and to emphasize the distance between this Micaiah and the other characters so far introduced.

After this rather complex preparation (vv. 9-14) for the second consultation (vv. 15-23), we plunge directly to the point—or is it? The king asks for tactical guidance ("shall we go to . . . battle?"), and we hear from Micaiah the selfsame word of victory spoken by the four hundred other Yahwist prophets! Micaiah's first word, then, is some sort of ironic transition. We expect truth ("what the Lord says to me, that I will speak," v. 14) and something unflattering to the king ("he never prophesies good concerning me. . . ," v. 8). What we get is a word of encouragement—a lie, and Ahab knows it, to his credit. The oracle reveals the emptiness of that majority counsel in the ease with which it may be counterfeited. At the same time, Micaiah ben-Imlah's first words mark the beginning of an extended confrontation between prophet and king, the opening ironic prophecy in a series of blunt predictions of personal demise for Ahab. From this point the literary pattern of oracular inquiry dissolves into response and counter-response. Here, the issue for the king is not whether Micaiah ben-Imlah speaks the truth—he is assumed to have lied. Nor does Ahab doubt Micaiah's legitimacy. Rather, the king acts quite consistently to confirm his earlier assessment of this prophet ("he never prophesies good of me," v. 8) and to justify, certainly to reinforce, his hatred. The narrator allows us to see in this hapless monarch an enmity deeply held and a destiny firmly envisioned by God, who even sponsors lies. The train cannot be derailed. Like the words of victory, so the words of doom are given and reiterated. What separates the good from the evil, so to speak, is Micaiah's first oracle to King Ahab—a word of irony and ambiguity, countering our expectations, but not Ahab's, a lie that leads to truth.

In this drama of competing and conflicting words, we become aware of the deep contraries at work in the narrative. Micaiah ben-Imlah's truth, for which Ahab angrily asks, turns out to be a word of evil—precisely what Ahab expected and the narrator needed. It stands in contrast to the swelling prophetic accord among the four hundred. Presenting these contrasts entailed damming up the natural flow begun in vv. 1-4 with scenes of personal conflict (Ahab and Micaiah) and personal demise (Ahab). Ahab is confirmed and justified in his hatred for Micaiah. His attitude, unchanged from beginning to end, merely shows in different ways: a direct admission (v. 8), a distrusting demand for truth in Yahweh's name (v. 16), and overbearing self-assurance that his original assessment had been correct (v. 18). In the process, the conflict between Micaiah ben-Imlah and the other prophets moves into view. The latter's words, explicit and even personalized in the implicit contrast between Micaiah and Zedekiah, cannot be separated from Micaiah's troubles with Ahab. For the truth which Yahweh demanded of Micaiah (v. 14), which Ahab himself sought (v. 15), and which the reader knows is of God, is bolstered by its contrary in the oracles of the four hundred. But what an ambiguous vision of truth! Ahab's concern with hearing the truth and Micaiah's oath to speak the truth, that is, only what Yahweh tells him, are sharply juxtaposed with a lie and the vision of Yahweh's dispatching lying spirits to confuse the prophets (Robertson)!

The two main consequences that flow from this verbal drama are commensurate with the double focus in the scenes of consultation. God-duped and embodying a four-hundred-strong voice of victorious counsel, Zedekiah now physically and verbally accosts Micaiah ben-Imlah (vv. 24-25). Similarly, Ahab now acts on his harbored and reinforced hatred of this Yahweh prophet, undoubtedly seeing all too clearly that he is some kind of victim (vv. 26-27).

The two prophets dispute one another's legitimacy. This seems a natural consequence of introducing Zedekiah in vv. 10-12. But there, he was part of a literary foil which emphasized a thematic interest: contrasting the victory words of the four hundred with Micaiah's message. Here, despite a certain obscurity in the text, Zedekiah seems to play out the consequences of the thematic opposition, but concretely in action. In other words, the plot moves again. Conflicting messages communicated by narrator to reader through separate scenes now become personal dispute, even hostile outburst calling forth defense (vv. 24-28). The paired relationships (Ahab-Micaiah and Zedekiah-Micaiah) have reached their most strained point. At the same time, the scene turns toward the future. The conflicts so dramatically exposed are headed after all to a resolution of sorts in the impending battle. So, the narrative flow begun in vv. 1-4 is to be resumed after all, but carrying a personal mass of some weight. Ostensibly entered into as a part of normal preparations for war, those routine consultations actually became a display of personal and ideological conflict, grand military schemes filtered to personal dimensions. It seems no accident that Micaiah ben-Imlah's final challenge to King Ahab mirrors his first vision (v. 17b), as though what is sure for the troops—in the vision they return home in peace—is not to be for their leader.

The last major section of the narrative (IV, vv. 29-38) takes us quickly into the description of battle. The rather straightforward motivic sequence (mustering of forces, description of battle, results, including an epitomizing conclusion, v. 37) masks the subtleties within. In relation to our expectations aroused in vv. 1-4, a major shift has occurred, but a shift thoroughly prepared by the intervening vv. 5-28. The account of battle activity pinpoints the fate of two kings—the death of one and the escape of the other. Thus, the dramatic tension set up at the beginning (the plan to regain territory) is curiously resolved in the failure of the plan's agents, not of the plan. From this larger perspective, we may now catch something of the irony in the narrator's beginning. He set forth a situation which was not to be the essential dramatic point of the events to follow. It is as though he deceives the reader, just as the characters, including Yahweh, are parties to deceiving one another. The narrator conveys his interest in the personal fate of Ahab through ironic vision. The king-deceiver who disguises himself in battle meets his end, and one endangered by the deception is spared; one prophet, a deceiver who yet speaks the truth, triumphs over the four hundred prophets who spoke their truth while lying, having been deceived by Yahweh. The ironic twists are exquisite. The deceiver-king dies in battle, but apparently accidentally, with one set of circumstances undoing another. Ahab's deception does not work because reality lies far beyond his and Jehoshaphat's control. Or put another way, events lie in the hands of Yahweh, who sends both truth and falsehood with his prophets!

The oppositions and conflicts are thus resolved in the end, though with special irony and with focus on the fate of King Ahab. What began as a mission to regain territory digressed to explore enmity between king and prophet and between prophet and prophet; it now ends with the death of one man, as though that settled all. It is in the final canonical telling of this tale that circumstances lead to the death of Ahab in order to close out his reign. Thus, editorial purpose can be got from fortuitous events, logic from irony, vindication of Micaiah ben-Imlah from falsehood and truth. This same hand reaffirmed in prophecy fulfilled (v. 38) that events, really moved by Yahweh, are announced by his prophets. Yet, this view is almost an afterthought at the very end and simply adds another layer of ambiguity. To be sure, it offers an interpretation of sorts, but does not overcome the contraries which stand baldly before us without comment. Therein lies the narrator's vision—that fictional truth, or truthful fiction, will not be held by formulaic fences.

Genre

Depending on their various theories of compositional history, scholars have differed in their identifications of generic units. For example, Würthwein ("Komposition," 253) spoke of "*Sage*" or simply "story" for what he took as the oldest tradition dealing with the battle. He described the prophetic material (vv. 5-28) as a "dispute in narrative form over the issue of true and false prophecy," clearly less a generic term than a description of the text's evolution. Or again, De Vries (pp. 55, 63-64), resting upon his theory of two independent narratives lying behind the present text, described vv. 10-12, 19-25, as "word controversy narrative," and vv. 2b-9, 15-18, 26-28, 29-35a, 36-37 as "superseding oracle narrative," a type of prophetic legend in which a superseding oracle to a king is fulfilled in preference to another. Looking at more or less the unit as defined here, Campbell (p. 68 n. 1) designated it "battle narrative," but this term seems unsatisfactory because so little of the actual content of the unit is concerned with recounting military activity. Indeed, those events preliminary to battle seem enlarged upon and emphasized quite beyond what one would expect on the basis of parallels, say, in Josh 8:3-29; Judg 9:34-41. Rofé called the unit a "paradigm," meaning a tradition of real or imagined historical events introduced and recast to teach a lesson or illustrate a point. Such a reduction hardly does justice to the artistic ambiguities and ironic features in the text that confuse, perhaps by design, any simple point or "lesson."

In view of the wide disagreements, it seems best to use a more general and neutral designation, PROPHETIC STORY, so as not to restrict unduly the nuances of theme, structure, and literary function.

We may observe a few other literary genres within this prophetic story. Elements of the conventional BATTLE REPORT evidently were used in giving shape to the whole. Vv. 1-4, 29-37 (38) especially recall the schematic sequence of motifs: confrontation of forces, the description of battle, and its consequences, with concluding summary statements (Campbell, 68-73; cf. Josh 7:2-5; Judg 3:26-29; 1 Sam 4:1-4; → discussion at 1 Kgs 20:1-34). Often appearing as a part of battle reports is a scene of ORACULAR INQUIRY, in which people or commanders consult the deity for guidance before going into battle. Typically one goes to a priest to "inquire" (*šā'al*) of Yahweh, a question is put, and the answer comes through the intermediary priest, often with assurances of divine presence and a CONVEYANCE FORMULA, "The Lord (I) will give it (them) into your hand" (cf. 1 Sam 23:2-4; 14:36-37; Judg 1:1-2). In this story involving Ahab and his prophets, the pattern of oracular inquiry is not exactly that associated with holy wars and priests, since a prophet is sought out, and the key verb is *drš* ("search for, inquire"), not *š'l*. It may be that scenes of oracular inquiry before prophets, which are less schematic and usually portrayed as intercession during a crisis, may have been mixed with the typical priestly patterns here. In any case, the scene of consultation is entirely typical of battle accounts and obviously has helped to shape the prophetic story in 1 Kings 22. From prophetic traditions, one may also note the two VISION REPORTS in vv. 17 and 19-22. Both are examples of "dramatic word vision," a type which depicts a visionary scene, usually in first-person style, or dramatic action clearly taken as a portent of the future. Typically such reports open with an announcement of vision (cf. Jer 38:21b, "This is the matter which Yahweh showed me," or more simply, "I saw/looked" [*rā'îtî*], as in Isa 6:1). Then follows the vision sequence—a scene(s), sometimes with dramatic action, sounds, voices, often with the prophet participating in the visionary events. (Besides 1 Kgs 22:17, 19-22, see Amos 7:1-6; Ezek 9:1-10; Isa 6:1-10; Long.) How close such dramatic visions are to oracles is obvious from the introductory summons spoken by Micaiah ben-Imlah in v. 19: "Therefore, hear the word of the Lord" (typical for prophetic oracles; cf. Jer 10:1; Amos 5:1) and the oracular form of conclusion at the end of the account, v. 23: ". . . the Lord has spoken evil concerning you." Also from the prophetic traditions is the REPORT of SYMBOLIC

ACTION, v. 11. The full genre includes (1) Yahweh's instructions to perform an action understood to carry symbolic meaning, (2) a report that the instruction was carried out, and (3) a word of interpretation, usually cast as an oracle of God, but sometimes as a prophet's own word. 1 Kings 22:11 obviously shows only a truncated example, or better, a motif drawn from those normally associated with the genre (cf. Hosea 1; Jeremiah 13; Ezekiel 4; Fohrer, *Handlungen*).

Setting

Depending on their definition of the generic unit, scholars differ on their suggestions for the setting of this story. We have little or no evidence for what lay behind the present text. For the unit essentially as analyzed here, Rofé (p. 242) supposed that it (for him a "paradigm") would have been composed by disciples of Jeremiah. Würthwein ("Komposition") located its provenance among people in Judah who dimly remembered with some pain the time when Judah was a vassal of Israel and with some gleeful enmity portrayed Ahab as a "type" of Israelite king who met an ignoble end. It seems doubtful that we can be so specific with any confidence. However, the stress on prophets and almost incidental portrayal of royal military affairs might suggest prophetic groups or the folk remembering famous prophets and their exploits as a point or origin and/or transmission for the story. More to the point would be the present *literary* setting of the story. It comes at the very end of Ahab's reign, following a series of incidents which characterize him in various ways and offer foretellings of disaster for him and his dynasty (20:42; 21:21-24). This perspective surely stems from the exilic author-editor.

Intention

Original intentions are as obscure as origins. In its present literary context, however, this prophetic story obviously was meant to recount the death of King Ahab and so close out the selective summary of his reign. In doing so, however, the narrator presents a triumphant Yahweh prophet, whose word is vindicated in events, in contrast to a king and other Yahwist prophets who oppose him (to his and their disaster, presumably). Yahweh is clearly in control of events—which is why his strategy of sending a "lying spirit" works, and Ahab's strategy of "lying" by disguise in battle does not work (Robertson). Once again, it seems that not simply circumstances, but Yahweh's opposition is crucial to the way events turn out, that is, to Ahab's failure (cf. 20:42; 21:21). Ahab's hatred of a Yahweh prophet must have been seen by the storyteller as some kind of offense, meriting the ignoble end to which the king came. And if this were not enough justification, there is the explicit, though weak, link made in the oracle fulfillment formula, which ties events to those earlier prophecies of disaster (20:42; 21:19). Ahab, who after all is not treated as such a heinous figure in this story, is cast as a misguided opponent of Yahweh and therefore cannot but fail—even if it looks like fate or accident. For the exilic Dtr author-editor, the story is another illustration of the ways of God and of this king who "did evil in the sight of Yahweh" (16:30).

Bibliography

See bibliography at 17:1–19:21. A. F. Campbell, *The Ark Narrative*, 68-73 (see listing at 20:1-34); G. Fohrer, *Die symbolischen Handlungen der Propheten* (2nd ed.; ATANT 54;

Zurich: Zwingli, 1968); R. Halevi, "Micha ben Jimla, *the* Ideal Prophet," *BethM* 12/3 (1966/67) 102-6 (Hebrew); E. Haller, *Charisma und Ekstasis. Die Erzählung von dem Propheten Micha ben Jimla* (Munich: Kaiser, 1960); F. Hossfeld and I. Meyer, *Prophet,* 27-36 (see listing at 12:33–13:34); B. O. Long, "Reports of Visions Among the Prophets," *JBL* 95 (1976) 353-65; idem, "Beyond Atomistic Criticism: The Form and Function of 1 Kings 22," *Fest.* I. L. Seeligmann (forthcoming); D. Robertson, "Micaiah ben Imlah: A Literary View," in *The Biblical Mosaic: Changing Perspectives* (ed. R. Polzin and E. Rothman; Philadelphia/Chico: Fortress/Scholars Press, 1982) 139-46; A. Rofé, "The Narrative of Micaiah ben Imlah and the Question of Genres of Prophetical Stories," *Hagot BeMiqra* II (Tel Aviv: Don, 1976) 233-44 (Hebrew); W. Roth, "The Story of the Prophet Micaiah (1 Kings 22) in Historical-Critical Interpretation," in *The Biblical Mosaic: Changing Perspectives* (ed. R. Polzin and E. Rothman; Philadelphia/Chico: Fortress/Scholars Press, 1982) 105-37; H.-C. Schmitt, *Elisa* (see listing at 20:1-43); H. Seebass, "Micha ben Jimla," *KD* 19 (1973) 109-24; idem, "Zu I Reg 22:35-38," *VT* 21 (1971) 380-83; C. Westermann, "Die Begriffe für Fragen und Suchen im Alttestament," *KD* 6 (1960) 2-30; E. Würthwein, "Zur Komposition von I Reg 22:1-38," in *Das ferne und nahe Wort* (*Fest.* L. Rost; ed. F. Maass; BZAW 105; Berlin: W. de Gruyter, 1967) 245-54.

CONCLUDING REGNAL RESUMÉ, 22:39-40

Structure

I. Citation formula	39
II. Notice of king's death	40a
III. Notice of successor	40b

This unit is typical of those concluding summaries at the end of reigns in the books of Kings. The structure is nearly always straightforward and formulaic: a citation of other sources for regnal information, followed by mention of death and burial, then closing with a notice of the successor king. As in this unit, the citation offers the narrator an opportunity to expand slightly with brief mention of certain activities, the favorite of which has to do with achievements in construction (cf. 15:23).

Genre

This unit is a concluding REGNAL RESUMÉ. See 1 Kgs 11:41-43; 2 Kgs 10:34-35, and the full discussion at 1 Kgs 14:21-31.

Setting

Regnal resumé is an editorial device in the books of Kings and thus finds its setting in the editorial activity of the Dtr editor of Kings, working in the early exilic situation (post-587 B.C.). Characteristically, the concluding resumé is the last item relating to a particular king's reign and the transition to the next epoch in chronological order.

Intention

The intention of concluding regnal resumé naturally is to close out a particular reign and to look ahead to the successor king, whose reign will be selectively portrayed in subsequent materials. This resumé, as is often the case, sounds a calming note after events of violence and upheaval—the effect of a chronistic structure having been imposed on diverse narrative traditions.

Bibliography

See bibliography at 14:21-31.

THE REIGN OF JEHOSHAPHAT, 22:41-51 (*RSV* 41-50)

Structure

I. Introductory regnal resumé	41-44
II. Notice of concord with Israel	45
III. Concluding regnal resumé	46-51
A. Citation formula	46
B. Additional information	47-50
1. Concerning cult prostitutes	47
2. Concerning Red Sea trade	48-50
C. Notices of death, burial, successor	51

This unit is clearly distinguished from both the preceding summary of Ahab's reign, 22:39-40, and the opening of Ahaziah's rule, 22:52-54. Its structure shows the typical organizational pattern used by the Dtr author-editor in his coverage of each monarch. Introductory (I, vv. 41-44) and concluding (III, vv. 46-51) summaries act as a framework for special material dating to this particular reign, that is, for the brief note on the concord reached between Judah and Israel during the time of Jehoshaphat (II, v. 45). The *RSV* "also" (v. 44=MT 45) obscures the relationship of this note to the introductory summary, as though to suggest that the statement of peace were an aspect of the editor's theological appraisal given in the previous verse. Form-critically, the note of concord belongs to that section of a regnal period in which the author-editor speaks about specific events.

The concluding resumé, vv. 46-51, is somewhat unusual in that it breaks the typical sequence and offers additional information pertinent to Jehoshaphat's reign. Similar breaks may be seen in 1 Kgs 14:30; 15:23; 2 Kgs 15:16, 37. In the case of Jehoshaphat, we have a brief note about doing away with male cult prostitutes (cf. 15:12; 14:24) to which is added without obvious connection a slightly longer report about an attempt to revive trade expeditions in a time when Edom was too weak to resist. In both reports, the style is strictly reportorial with a minimum of narrative detail and no drama to speak of. Somewhat unusual in vv. 48-50 are the reportorial perfect (*qṭl*) verbs used to express sequential action (but cf. 6:29-35; 9:26).

Genre

Since this unit is a composite from the hand of the late Dtr author-editor, we may not specify a genre with precision. However, within the whole we see the typical introductory and concluding REGNAL RESUMÉS which summarize the accession and transition to the succeeding ruler in formulaic patterns (see full discussion and parallels at 14:21-31). Special material relating to this reign in vv. 45, 47, and 48-50 appears in the form of brief REPORT.

Setting

As a whole, the unit derives from the exilic work of the Dtr author-editor. The regnal resumé is likely his editorial creation, although one may not rule out the possibility that it, or elements of it, had their roots in native Israelite chronistic documents kept by royal scribes (see discussion at 14:21-31). The more particular reports carry tradition which may very well derive from such court records. In any case, the important setting now is a literary one—the position in the final redacted form of the books of Kings.

Intention

In this light, it is obvious that the author-editor intended to summarize the reign of Jehoshaphat, who had already been introduced into the ongoing account of Ahab (ch. 22). In the process, the author marks the end of hostilities between north and south (v. 45), a feature often mentioned in the period after Solomon's death (14:30; 15:6, 7, 16, 32). The note simply states in scribal record-keeping fashion what was already apparent in the preceding chapter (22:2-4, 29-36). It is difficult to guess what the intent of vv. 48-50 might have been, except to introduce proleptically the succeeding monarch, Ahaziah. Similar overlaps in the reigns may be seen in ch. 22 (Jehoshaphat in Ahab's rule); 12:1-24 (Rehoboam in Jeroboam's reign); 15:16-22 (Baasha during the time of Asa); etc.

Bibliography

See the listings for regnal resumé at 14:21-31.

THE BEGINNING OF THE REIGN OF AHAZIAH: INTRODUCTORY REGNAL RESUMÉ, 22:52-54 (*RSV* 51-53)

Structure

I. General information	52
A. Synchronistic accession formula	52a
B. Length and place of reign	52b
II. Theological appraisal	53-54

This unit opens a block of tradition which concludes at 2 Kgs 1:18 with the closing regnal citation formula for Ahaziah. The break between 1 and 2 Kings is therefore plainly artificial, arbitrary, and disruptive of the organization which the Dtr author-editor gave his materials.

The structure, style, and content of the unit are entirely typical of those introductory summaries given for most northern monarchs (cf., e.g., 16:29-33, 23-26; 15:25-26). See the detailed discussion at 14:21-31.

Genre

The unit is introductory REGNAL RESUMÉ, an editorial device of the Dtr author-editor of the books of Kings. See full discussion with parallels at 14:21-31.

Setting

Most critics assume that this kind of summary device stems from the exilic author-editor of Kings. Possibly similar resumés, or elements within them, may have had their original setting in scribal documents associated with the royal court (see full discussion at 14:21-31).

Intention

The author-editor clearly intended to introduce the reign of Ahaziah, to evaluate it, and to lead into a narrative about an event during that reign (2 Kgs 1:1-17).

Bibliography

On the regnal resumé, see the listings at 14:21-31.

GLOSSARY

GENRES

ACCOUNT (Erzählung, Bericht). A term nearly synonymous with (→) report. Generally longer and more complex than simple report, an account may consist of several briefer reports, statements, descriptions, or even fragments of (→) story, organized according to a common theme. Accounts may aim at some degree of explanation rather than simple narration of events. However, like reports, accounts show a matter-of-fact third-person narrative style and few literary, imaginative, or artistic features. Examples of account are Judg 1:16, 17; 1 Kgs 6:1–7:51.

ADMONITION (Ermahnung gegen . . .). A speech designed to dissuade an individual or a group from a certain kind of behavior. Thus, admonition is closely related to (→) exhortation, (→) parenesis, and (→) instruction, and not easily distinguished from statements which *prohibit* certain actions. Admonition is prominent in prophetic discourse (e.g., Isa 1:16-17; Jer 25:3-7; Amos 5:4-5, 6-7; and, in irony, Amos 4:4-5), but is equally at home in the didactic literature (e.g., Prov 6:20-21; 7:1-5). It is doubtful, therefore, that either prophets or wisdom teachers created this form of speech. Perhaps *both* groups drew upon a widely used genre of tribal discourse.

ANECDOTE (Anekdote). A particular kind of (→) report that records an event or experience in the life of a person. Anecdote may also show a tendency toward storylike features, such as conversation and imaginative description. It is the private "biographical" focus, however, as distinct from "public" events recounted in many reports, that is characteristic of anecdote. Examples are 1 Kgs 9:10-14; 19:19-21. Societal setting and intention for anecdote would naturally vary according to circumstances and content.

ANNALS (Annalen). A concise, year-by-year series of (→) reports, arranged chronologically and designed to record events pertaining to a particular institution, such as monarchy or temple. Although no Israelite examples exist, some OT texts may have been based on annals, but in ways finally unclear to us (e.g., 1 Kgs 3:1; 9:15-23; 2 Chr 11:5-12). Certain ancient Near Eastern (→) inscriptions may draw upon annals or even adopt annalistic style, but in themselves are not annals, since they aim at glorifying the king and commemorating his deeds (→ royal inscription; *ANET,* 234-41, inappropriately called "annals" of Thutmose III; A. K. Grayson, "Histories and Historians," *Or* 49 [1981] 150-52). A text very close to annal would be the ancient Palermo Stone (Breasted, *ARE* I, §§ 76-167). Annals would have had their typical setting among scribes who kept records pertinent to governmental affairs.

ANNOUNCEMENT OF JUDGMENT (Gerichtsankündigung, Gerichtsansage). An element of (→) prophetic judgment speech, but which often occurs separately as an independent type of (→) prophecy. Its essence is a statement that disaster, e.g., death, war, famine, is imminent as Yahweh's punishment for transgressions. For further details, → Prophetic Judgment Speech.

ANNOUNCEMENT OF REPRIEVE (Ankündigung von Strafaufschub, von Strafmilderung, von Begnadigung). A type of prophetic (→) oracle which states that God intends to mitigate a promised punishment to (an) individual(s). Typically, the elements include (1) an allusion to some act of penitence taken by the person in question, (2) the reasons for God's intended actions, (3) the reprieve or mitigated punishment. See 1 Kgs 21:29; 2 Kgs 22:18-20; 2 Chr 12:7-8. All these examples occur as part of a longer narrative now arranged into a stereotyped sequence called (→) schema of reprieve. The societal setting for announcement of reprieve is unclear, beyond the general one of prophetic activity. On the other hand, its history may only begin with written narrative traditions which seek to interpret royal and national affairs as religious, divine-human drama.

BATTLE REPORT (Schlactbericht). A schematic recounting of a military encounter typically organized around the following elements: (1) the confrontation of forces, (2) the battle, (3) the consequences of battle, whether defeat or victory, usually with summarizing and characterizing statements. Examples are: Num 21:21-24; Josh 7:2-5; Judg 3:26-30; 8:10-12; 2 Sam 10:15-19. Often, the report will include a scene of consultation with priests for divine guidance (as in 1 Sam 23:2-4; 14:36-37; [→] report of oracular inquiry) or words of encouragement (e.g., Josh 8:1-2). We have little or no evidence for the typical societal settings for this type of report. All the examples in the OT are now integrated into larger narrative contexts of varied contents.

BATTLE STORY (Schlachterzählung). A type of (→) story whose main theme and action serve to tell of a military encounter. It differs from (→) battle report in the sophistication of the narrative art: it shows narrative exposition, characterization, and plot. Like report, it tends to emphasize a "historical" aim: what the battle was and how it happened. Examples are Josh 8:1-29; Judg 9:34-41. → Prophetic Battle Story.

While some battle stories may derive from official literate circles, many belong to the folk and may incorporate motifs and techniques drawn from popular culture. Settings and intentions vary widely therefore, depending upon circumstances of origin, narrator, and occasions for telling.

BEATITUDE (Seligpreisung, Gratulation). At its simplest, beatitude is a short, formulaic speech which extols the fortunate or blessed state of an individual or whole people, such as Israel. Typically, the utterance begins with *'ašrê*, "fortunate" or "blessed," followed by the subject and any special qualifiers, often in the form of relative clauses. So 1 Kgs 10:8, "Happy [*'ašrê*] are your wives! Happy [*'ašrê*] are these your servants who continually stand before you. . . ." See Ps 2:12; Prov 8:34; 16:20. These basic elements can be expanded with the addition of elaborate clauses (e.g., Ps 1:1-2; Prov

3:13-14), or worked up into more lengthy collections of sayings, as in the NT (e.g., Matt 5:3-11). Beatitude is related to (→) blessing and (→) praise speech, but remains distinct. It does not invoke God's blessing or utter his praises, but describes one who is fortunate by reason of upright behavior or blessings already received from God. Egyptian parallels are known. Beatitude perhaps was originally a type of spontaneous exclamation. Most examples in the OT, however, suggest that it became a form of wisdom teaching, a description turned into didactic example or precept by those "wise men" whose instructions and learning live on in the books of Proverbs, Ecclesiastes, and certain of the Psalms.

BIOGRAPHY (Biographie). A type of (→) history which is concerned to record events of an individual's life over its duration. Biography may include evaluations of a person's achievements or importance in a larger view of a national history, and it may give its subject heroic or legendary proportions to some degree. Yet, the characteristic feature is that the narration purports to relate real events, organized and ruled by the chronology of a life. There are no genuine biographies in the OT—not even the narratives about Jeremiah (see Jeremiah 26–45), which claim that what the prophet experienced had didactic, edifying significance for others. The Jeremiah traditions live in a world of (→) legend, biography in the arena of (→) history.

BLESSING (Segen, Segnung). A pronouncement cast in either the imperative or indicative mode, designed to call down divine power through the spoken word. Blessing can be introduced or concluded with a formula employing the participle *bārûk,* "blessed," followed by the person who is to be blessed. Good examples are in Gen 24:60; Num 24:5-9. Blessing derives from a tribal ethos (so Gen 24:60; 27:27-29) but was also at home in organized cultic affairs (e.g., 1 Kgs 8:14). Blessing should be distinguished from (→) beatitude (e.g., Ps 2:12; 1 Kgs 10:8), which acclaims blessings already deemed to have been received and becomes a type of didactic saying—as indeed some formulas with *bārûk* have become (e.g., Jer 17:7). Blessing is also different from (→) praise speech (e.g., Ps 72:18; Exod 18:10), which, though beginning with a *bārûk* formula, always has God as its object, and so offers praise to *God* rather than invokes his blessing upon *people*.

BOAST (Prahlwort, Prahllied). An utterance which appraises some person or thing as superior to another. See 1 Sam 18:7; 1 Kgs 20:10; or Cant 6:8-9; perhaps also 8:11-12. Boast seems to have no fixed literary form; the term refers to the motivation, effect, or even the intent of one's speech. Thus, 1 Kgs 20:10 is in the form of (→) oath, but the effect is clearly to boast of one military commander's superiority over another. Or 1 Sam 18:7 takes the form of a proverbial saying, but means to boast of David's superior strength over against Saul.

CATALOGUE (Katalog). A list which enumerates items according to a systematic principle of classification. Decisive for the form is the scholastic and systematizing character of the material. Thus, catalogue is not simply a random (→) list, a summary, or a (→) register, which orders items according to the needs of governmental control. Nor is it simply a form of record keeping. Catalogue results from a particular kind of intellectual activity which seeks to order reality into systematic and classifiable bodies of knowledge. It probably was created by scribes and/or priests. Examples of catalogue in the OT are Leviticus 11; Exod 25:3-7. Texts which perhaps are based upon catalogues are Gen 6:19-21; 7:2-3, 8, 9; 1 Kgs 7:40b-44, 48-50. For ancient Near Eastern examples, cf. *ANET,* 205 (catalogue of gods), 276 (catalogue of tributes), 328-29 (catalogue of execrations).

CHRONICLE (Chronik). A prose composition consisting of a series of (→) reports, normally in third-person style, or selected events arranged and dated in chronological order. Chronicle differs from (→) annal in that the former may offer somewhat fuller prose, does not include entries for *each* successive year, and thereby moves away from record keeping toward selective recollection of history. Unlike commemorative (→) royal inscriptions, chronicles simply summarize events over discrete periods of time, whether for the purpose of genuine (→) history or for propagandistic "re-telling" of past events. There are no examples of chronicle in the OT (the books of Chronicles are better called [→] history), though references to "the book of the things of the days" (*RSV* "Book of the Chronicles," 1 Kgs 14:29; 15:7; etc.) may refer to Israelite writings of the type found in late Assyrian and Neo-Babylonian times. (For the latter, see Grayson, *Assyrian and Babylonian Chronicles*.) Perhaps 2 Kings 25 and Jeremiah 52 are drawn from Israelite chronicles. Clearly chronicle is a product of a centralized government which employed scribes to keep records and produce monumental inscriptions, king lists, and the like.

CHRONISTIC REPORT (Chronistischer Bericht). A type of brief (→) report explicitly dated by regnal year and thus having the character of (→) chronicle. One might speak equally of "annalistic" report, since (→) annals also characteristically employ regnal dating. Examples in the OT are 1 Kgs 14:25-28; 2 Kgs 12:7 [*RSV* 6]; 17:6; 18:9-12, 13-15; cf. the various units within 2 Kings 25, demarcated by regnal date formulas.

COMMISSION (Beauftragung, Sendung). An authoritative charge given by a superior to a subordinate. Commission may include a variety of elements such as direct command or specific instruction, depending upon the particular role which the order-giver envisions, e.g., military envoy (2 Sam 11:18-21, 25), messenger (Gen 32:3-5; 1 Kgs 14:7-11), royal official (2 Kgs 19:2-7). Commission is often found in narratives about prophets (e.g., Exod 3:7-10; 1 Kgs 12:22-24; 19:15-16; 21:17-19; Amos 7:15-17) and in the prophetic vocation accounts (e.g., Isa 6:9-10; Jer 1:4-10; Ezek 3:1-11). Thus, commission became an important way to represent the prophet as God's messenger and to organize collections of prophetic words. In this context, (→) reports of a prophet's commission typically show (1) the prophetic word formula, "the word of the Lord came to . . ."; (2) the commissioning formula, which often has the imperative, "Go, speak"; (3) the messenger formula, "Thus says the Lord"; and (4) the message itself, usually some kind of oracle addressed to individuals or nations. See Isa 7:3-9; Jer 2:1-3; 7:1-7; 26:1-6; 1 Kgs 12:22-24; 19:15-18; 21:17-19; cf. 2 Kgs 9:1-3.

COMMISSIONING OF A MESSENGER (Aussendung eines Boten). A narrative representation, usually as (→) report, which tells of the sending of a messenger with a message. The emphasis falls upon the (→) commission, which takes the form of direct instructions concerning where to go and what to say. Commissioning appears as part of a larger narrative in Gen 32:3-5; 1 Kgs 14:7-11; 20:9 and in (→) official reports, e.g., 2 Sam 11:18-25. It also takes on great importance in describing the prophet's (→) commission as messenger of God.

COMPLAINT SONG OF THE INDIVIDUAL (Klagelied des Einzelnen). A song sung by or on behalf of an individual in distress, complaining to God of the person's dire situation and petitioning for relief. Typically, such a complaint song will include (although not in any rigidly fixed order) the following elements: (1) invocation to God, (2) confession of transgressions or protestations of innocence, (3) affirmations of confidence in God's power, (4) complaints to God about one's condition, (5) imprecations of enemies, (6) petition to God for help, (7) vows. The petition for help is the center of the song; other elements may be expanded or omitted. Examples are: Psalms 3–7; 11–13; 17; 22. Presumably, such complaint songs would have been performed in cultic settings, at shrine or temple, or in the individual's home. A clear picture cannot be gained, however. The intent was to bring about a change in the person's situation by tapping into the divine powers made available through qualified cultic officials.

CONSTRUCTION REPORT (Baubericht). A type of (→) report which tells of building, manufacture, or fabrication of cultic and/or official state objects and edifices, along with descriptions of size, materials, ornamentation, etc. Simple verbs (e.g., *bnh,* "build"; *'śh,* "make") convey the action, and nominal clauses state in listlike fashion descriptive details. Examples are 1 Kgs 6:5-6, 8, 16-18, 20a, 23-26; 7:2-5, 6, 7; Exod 36:8-9, 14-15, 20-30; 37:1-9, 10-16. Related are the less specific reports of large-scale building activities associated with certain kings (e.g., 1 Kgs 12:25; 16:24, 34).

Archival records possibly stood behind these reports. In their present literary form, however, they seem to have been produced by scribes and priests whose aim was to record with prescriptive overtones many matters pertaining to cult and royal edifices. Probably some of these reports would have been included in the no longer extant (→) chronicles of the kings.

DEDICATORY INSCRIPTION (Weihe- oder Widmungsinschrift). A type of ancient Near Eastern (→) royal inscription written on an object dedicated by the king to a deity. The objects are of a cultic nature, such as ornamental mace heads, building bricks, door sockets, statues. Typically, the inscription includes (1) dedicatory address (e.g., "To the god so-and-so, his lord"), (2) royal name and epithets, identifying the giver of the object, (3) dedicatory statement (e.g., "He (I) dedicated (this XX) for his (my) life . . ."). See A. K. Grayson, *ARI* I, lxxxvi, 23; II, xcviii, 3. The OT may reflect the form of dedicatory inscription in Solomon's prayer, dedicating the temple (1 Kgs 8:13). Cf. Deut 26:10 and 1 Sam 2:28. See also → Prayer of Dedication.

DIRGE (Trauerlied, Grabgesang). A song bewailing the loss of the deceased, describing and praising his or her merits, and calling for further mourning. The most characteristic formulas employed are "How! Alas!" (*'êk* or *'êkâ*) and imperatives such as "weep!" "mourn!" The dirge was performed by hired women or gifted individuals and was sung in the presence of the corpse as part of the preparations for burial. Examples are 2 Sam 1:19-27; 3:33-34; 1 Kgs 13:30b (fragments). The prophetic books show adaptations of the dirge with new literary effects and purpose, e.g., Isa 14:4-23; Amos 5:1-3.

DISPUTATION (Disputationswort, Streitgespräch). A general term to designate a dispute between two or more parties in which differing points of view are held. Examples may be seen in disputes among wise men (e.g., the book of Job), parties in a legal proceeding (e.g., as reflected in Gen 31:36-43), or between prophet and people (e.g., Mic 2:6-11; Jer 2:23-28; 3:1-5). A particular example of disputation may include a variety of smaller literary genres, formulas, and stereotyped motifs. Obviously the settings vary according to circumstances and usage. Most OT examples appear in the prophetic literature, especially Deutero-Isaiah.

DREAM EPIPHANY (Traumerscheinung). A type of brief and schematic (→) report which mentions that God appears in a dream (Niphal of *rā'â,* "become visible"), gives a message, and/or otherwise engages in dialogue with a human being. Such reports are part of older and younger portions of the pentateuchal narrative (e.g., Gen 12:7; 17:1-21; 18:1-33; 26:2-5, 24; 28:12-16; 48:3-4) and the "historical" books (e.g., Exod 3:2-12; Judg 13:10; 1 Kgs 3:4-15; 9:1-9) and continue into NT times (e.g., Matt 2:19-20). Reports of dream epiphany may have originally been associated with shrines; some were rooted in (→) legends circulating among visitors in and about holy sites. However, such reports now assume greater literary importance as scenes in larger narratives or as bearers of themes important for continuity in the canonical materials (e.g., promise to the patriarchs, or wisdom for King Solomon).

DREAM REPORT (Traumbericht). A type of (→) report in the first- or third-person style that recounts the principal elements of a dream experience. Such reports use the verb "dream" (*ḥālam*) extensively, especially in the introduction, and demarcate major shifts in subject matter with the particle "and behold" (*wĕhinnēh*). Sometimes a conclusion will remark on the person's awakening and recognition that he or she was dreaming (e.g., 1 Kgs 3:15). The larger narrative contexts will often provide for a separate scene in which the dream will be interpreted. Examples of dream report are Gen 37:5-11; 40:9-11, 16-17; Judg 7:13-14. For ancient Near Eastern examples, see Oppenheim, *Dreams* (listed at 3:4-15). The primary setting for dream report in Israel would have been the situation in which one seeks understanding of the experience from a qualified interpreter (e.g., as reflected in Gen 41:1-8; Dan 2:1-11). Frequently, reports of dream center on an appearance of God to the dreamer and take on great importance in theological themes of canonical scope. For this aspect → Dream Epiphany.

ETIOLOGY (Ätiologie). A type of (→) story or (→) report set in primordial or historical times, involving god(s) and/or human beings, and designed to explain the origins of certain elements of knowledge, experience, practice, custom, and the like shared by a cultural group. Developed etiology (story) is rare in the OT, but brief reports and etiological motifs imbedded in larger narrative traditions are common. A common type, etymological etiology, explains a name by associating some event with that name by means of wordplay or folk etymology; the report concludes with a formula: "Therefore one calls the name of that place . . ." or "And he called her (its, his) name. . . , for he said . . . (explanation follows)." See Exod 15:23; 2:22. Other etiological motifs may be expressed in formulas, such as (1) "until this day" (e.g., Josh 4:9), (2) "it shall be a (memory) sign for you" (e.g., Gen 9:13; 17:11), or (3) a question-and-answer pattern: "What does so and so mean to you? (then follows the answer which explains origin and significance)," e.g., Josh 4:6-7. Etiology and etiological motifs are popular literary forms, and hence their settings would be with the ordinary people, in diverse circumstances.

ETYMOLOGICAL ETIOLOGY (Etymologische Ätiologie). → Etiology.

EULOGY (Lobrede). An utterance, often poetic, designed to praise a person, whether living or dead. In the OT, eulogy may appear as part of a (→) dirge, as in 2 Sam 1:19-27, or be reflected in eulogistic statements for the king and his accomplishments (e.g., 1 Kgs 5:9-14). In the ancient Near East, eulogy is regularly part of (→) royal inscriptions which commemorate the deeds of the king (e.g., *ANET,* 653-54; Breasted, *ARE* IV, § 47; cf. the stylized encomiums of courtiers who respond to a king's building plans, e.g., Breasted, *ARE* III, §§ 251-81; II, §§ 131-66).

EXHORTATION (Ermahnung zu . . .). → Admonition.

FAREWELL SPEECH (Abschiedsrede). A first person styled speech reported to have been delivered by a person near the time of his death. The contents follow a typical sequence: (1) references to advancing age or impending death, (2) admonition(s), and (3) directives to those hearing the speech. Farewell speech may occur in the context of a full report about testamentary activities and death (e.g., Gen 49:29-30, part of 47:29–49:33) or by itself (e.g., 1 Kgs 2:1-9), followed by report of death (2:10-11; Josh 23:1-16 [a highly theological example]; 1 Macc 2:49-70; T. 12 Patr., both later, very elaborate examples). Cf. Acts 20:18-35; John 13:1–17:26. Distant ancient Near Eastern parallels may be in the Egyptian (→) instruction (e.g., *ANET,* 418-19, 414-18). Originally, farewell speeches would have been delivered when a leader, family or tribal head, conscious of impending death, would have passed on his final words and bequeathed possessions to heirs. However, the OT examples deal with leaders who are prominent and important to the theological continuities in the canonical "story." In all these cases, biblical authors have depicted the passing of special figures as momentous events, weighted with religious, social, and historical significance.

GENEALOGY (Stammbaum, Genealogie). A type of oral or written (→) list which enumerates individual and tribal descent from an originating ancestor through intermediate persons down to the last, presumably contemporary with writer or speaker. OT examples may be linear (expressive of a single line of descent, e.g., Gen 5:1-32) or segmented (indicating multiple lines of descent, e.g., Gen 35:22b-26; 2 Sam 3:2-5). Genealogies are numerous in the OT, as well as in the ancient Near East; in the Bible they range in style and form from very simple lists (2 Sam 3:2-5) to more complex compositions which carry within them various bits of information and rudimentary narrative (e.g., Gen 10:2-32). Genealogies now appear variously integrated into wider canonical contexts. In late biblical times, genealogy seemed an appropriate literary form with which to introduce very large historical compositions (e.g., 1 Chronicles 1–9; cf. Matt 1:1-17).

HEROIC SAGA (Heldensage). A type of (→) saga which focuses on events in the life of one central figure who is significant for the people who remember him. Typically, heroic saga includes some account of the hero's birth, marriage, vocation, death—along with displays of virtue and heroic deeds. The intention is not simply to describe the hero as he really was, but to interpret him according to stereotyped, imaginative categories. An example in the OT of heroic saga is that of Moses, Exodus 1–Deuteronomy 34.

HISTORICAL STORY (Historische Erzählung). A self-contained narrative mainly concerned to recount what a particular event was and how it happened, but with more literary sophistication than is evident with simple (→) report. Typically, one finds at least a rudimentary plot running from a tension or problem to its resolution (→ story), along with dialogue and imaginative touches. The chief difference between historical story and (→) legend, fictional story or brief (→) tale, is not so much in content—which may contain fictional or even legendary elements—but in purpose. With historical story the narrator does not seek to edify, entertain, or instruct primarily, but to recount events as they occurred (whether or not, by modern critical standards, the evidence is sufficiently trustworthy). Examples of OT historical story are 1 Sam 11:1-11; 1 Kgs 12:1-20; Judg 9:1-21. A special type is the prophetic story, a developed prose narrative in which a prophetic figure plays a central role and carries themes and interpretative motifs expressive of the narrator's voice. See, e.g., 1 Kgs 20:1-43; 22:1-37. Some examples of historical story may have originated with the folk and been transmitted orally as traditional storytelling materials. For the most part, however, the biblical examples reflect literate scribal classes at work in the royal court or religious institutions.

HISTORY (Geschichtsschreibung). An extensive, continuous, written composition made up of and based upon various materials, some originally traditional and oral, others written, and devoted to a particular subject or historical period. The author of history links together his materials and unifies the whole by imposing overarching structural and thematic connections. History is dominated by a concern with chronology and cause-effect relationships; it seeks to place events and how they occurred within a framework of interpretation and in relation to the author's own time. For purposes of literary definition, it is not important whether, from our modern point of view, the events actually occurred as reported. Apparently neither Egypt nor Mesopotamia produced history, although both have left us many inscriptions of historical content. Examples from Greece are known (e.g., Thucydides or Herodotus). From the OT, one may cite 2 Samuel 9–20 and 1 Kings 1–2 as fairly early work. Less disputed examples would be the books of Kings, the books of Chronicles, and from much later times, 1–2 Maccabees. History writing presupposes literacy. For this reason, it developed in Israel most fully among those scribes whose business it was to record the affairs of the royal government. Writers of history intended to document, reflect on, and organize the past in order to understand, legitimate, or define in some way the institutional and social reality of their own time.

IMPUTATION SPEECH (Beschuldigungsrede). A speech by a person(s) charging another individual or group with a fault or crime. It is characteristic of (→) disputation, either leading to legal proceedings or quite unrelated to trials. Imputation speech follows no rigid form, and its contents vary according to the diverse occasions on which it was used. Frequently, however, a formula appears: "What is this you have done to me?" (e.g., Judg 8:1; Neh 13:17; 2 Sam 12:21). Imputation speech may also be quite convoluted and indirect, as in 1 Kgs 18:9-14. Other examples are Gen 12:18-19; 16:5; 26:9, 10; 29:25; 31:26-30.

INDICTMENT SPEECH (Anklagerede, Anklageerhebung). A formal statement handed down by a juridical authority charging a person with committing a crime. It may be presented upon approval of an accusation or in its own right, directly and probably orally. OT texts which probably reflect the form and substance of such indictments are 1 Sam 15:17-19; 22:13; 1 Kgs 2:42-43; 18:17; 22:18.

INSCRIPTION (Inschrift). Characters or words written, carved, or otherwise affixed to a surface, but not necessarily for public display. The OT probably alludes to such in 1 Sam 15:12; 1 Chr 18:3 (Hebr. *yād,* "monument," or victory stela?). Also, see 2 Sam 18:18 and Isa 56:5. Many examples are known from the ancient Near East, and even from Palestine (*ANET,* 320, 321); most are associated with the institution of monarchy. → Royal Inscription.

INSTRUCTION (Instruktion, Unterweisung). A fairly extensive writing or discourse, chiefly in the imperative mode, which offers distilled guidance on traditional matters to an individual or group. The form is somewhat flexible, but the contents rather fixed: broad values, traditional rules for conduct, aphoristic knowledge drawn from wide experience. Instruction tends to deal with the universal rather than the particular. In Israel, instructions were probably created by persons of some official, if not aristocratic, status, such as lawgiver, priest, or even prophet (Isa 8:16-20). But instruction could also be the work of scribes and "wisdom" teachers. In Egypt, the best examples derive from scribes who formulated didactic works to summarize accepted knowledge, or in some cases produced instruction in the guise of an after-the-fact testament from a king to his successor, with propagandistic overtones (*ANET,* 414-18; 418-19; more generally, see Lichtheim, *Ancient Egyptian Literature,* I, 58-80). Similarly, the clearest examples from the OT are in the didactic literature (e.g., Proverbs 1–9; 22:17–24:22). The settings and occasions of use for instruction must have been quite diverse. Closely related to instruction is (→) farewell speech, which often contains admonitions and specific directives appropriate to the speaker.

ITINERARY (Itinerar, Wegverzeichnis). A formal structure of (→) accounts or (→) reports, which relate movement by stages. Itinerary often includes special formulas, noting the point of departure ("set out from so-and-so") and/or the point of arrival in a journey ("encamped at so-and-so" or "came to so-and-so"), and thus may serve as a literary skeleton for larger collections of varied material (e.g., Exod 17:1–18:27; 19:1–Num 10:10; 1 Kgs 19:1-18). If the itinerary appears with little or no narrative materials between stages of movement, it should be understood as a type of (→) list, as, e.g., Num 33:5-37, 41-49.

JUDGMENT SPEECH (Gerichtswort, Gerichtsrede). → Prophetic Judgment Speech.

JURIDICAL PARABLE (Gerichtliche Gleichnis- oder Beispielerzählung). A prose narration, usually a (→) report, which relates a fictional though realistic violation of custom or law in order to induce the hearer, who has committed an analogous violation, to pass judgment on himself while adjudicating the fictional case. The best OT examples, all involving the king, are 2 Sam 12:1-4; 14:5-7; 1 Kgs 20:39-40. Each one is part of a larger narrative context, and in fact depends upon that context for its sense. Thus, it is difficult to know to what degree the literary device reflects customary social relations in ancient Israel.

KING LIST (Königsliste). A type of (→) list which enumerates successive rulers in a particular state. It consists of royal names, sometimes with the addition of epithets, regnal years, and filiation. Unlike (→) genealogy, which it may resemble in form, a king list need not express *kinship.* Its essential character turns on *succession,* which may or may not follow lines of kinship. King list is widely attested in the ancient Near East, where sometimes the stylistic distinction from (→) chronicle is hard to maintain (e.g., *ANET,* 265-66, 271-72, 564-67; other examples in Grayson, "Königslisten" [see listing at "Introduction to Historical Literature," pp. 2-3]). In Israel, king list may have been a literary model for Gen 36:31-39 as well as Judg 10:1-5; 12:7-15. King lists derive from bureaucratic circles in centralized governments, and aim to legitimate an orderly succession of rulers on a line extending back through many generations, even, on occasion, to primordial times when the gods first decreed kingship (e.g., *ANET,* 265-66).

LEGEND (Legende, Heiligen- oder Wundererzählung). A narrative concerned primarily with the wondrous, miraculous, and exemplary. Legend is aimed at edification rather than merely entertainment, instruction, or even imaginative exploration of the storyteller's art. Thus legends often encourage awe for a holy place (e.g., Judg 6:19-24), ritual practice (2 Macc 1:19-22), and holy men (e.g., Gen 22:1-19; 1 Kgs 12:33–13:34; 14:1-18; 17:1–19:21; 2 Kgs 1:2-16; 2:1-25) who may be models of devotion and virtue. Legend differs from (→) history and (→) historical story in its refusal to be bound by a drive to recount real events as they happened; it differs from the more artistic (→) story in giving less attention to developed points of narrative interest, such as description, artistic structure, and plot. Legend belongs to the world of oral folklore and storytellers. Legends took varied forms and were told in royal court, at religious shrines, in family and tribal settings, and on pilgrimages to holy sites.

LETTER (Brief). A general term for a written communication sent from one person to another. Typically, the letter would begin with a prescript which identified the sender and addressee along with a salutation or wish for blessing (e.g.,

Ezra 4:11, 17; 7:12). Then followed the body of the letter, opening with a transitional "and now . . ." (*wĕ'attâ*) and consisting of diverse contents and literary genres. See Ezra 4:12-16, 18-22; 7:13-26. Apparently Hebrew letters, like those in Egypt and Mesopotamia, contained no special conclusion. Allusions to letters and letter writing, along with quoted excerpts, may be found, e.g., in 2 Kgs 10:2-3, 6; Jer 29:1-28. Letters may stand behind the narrative convention of reporting diplomatic exchanges as direct dialogue, e.g., 1 Kgs 5:23 (*RSV* 5:8). Examples from the ancient Near East are plentiful (see *ANET,* 480-81, 482-92). Letters probably developed out of the custom of instructing and sending messengers with oral communications (see 2 Kgs 19:9-14), and they obviously presuppose scribes who can read and write. Particular settings and occasions for letter writing would naturally vary according to circumstances.

LIST (Liste). In its elementary form, a simple enumeration of items without any particular principle of order. In more developed forms, a list would be ordered systematically by a main idea or principle. Commonly, it would claim to reconstruct or preserve an order of things as they exist in reality. Examples of list are (→) genealogy, (→) king list, (→) itinerary. See also OT lists of booty (Num 31:32-40), votive offerings (Exod 35:5b-9), royal mercenaries (2 Sam 23:24-39), administrative officials (1 Kgs 4:2-6). The latter texts may have been drawn from administrative lists or (→) registers.

NOTICE (Notiz). A very brief (→) report not too different from a simple (→) statement. For example, 1 Kgs 3:1.

OATH (Eid, Schwur). A pronouncement, cast as either cohortative or indicative, which binds the oath taker to a particular course of action, attitude, or stance by invoking sanctions of the deity. Typically, an oath is introduced with the formula "As the Lord lives" (*ḥay-yahweh,* e.g., Judg 8:19) and/or a similar asseveration "by the life of" (*bĕḥê*) the person(s) to whom the oath is addressed (e.g., 1 Sam 20:3). Then follows what the oath taker will or will not do, the actual content of the oath. A fuller formula, and almost as common, runs "May God the Lord do so to me and more also, if. . . ," followed by the content of the oath (e.g., Ruth 1:17; 1 Sam 3:17; 14:44). The intention of oath is to impress upon parties their mutual obligations in various situations. Thus, the settings would differ according to circumstances. Some oaths would habitually be taken at shrines and associated with priests, others in various realms of social life. Literary reflexes of oath and oath taking are common in the OT and seen most commonly as (→) report(s) of oath in the midst of larger narrative contexts (e.g., 1 Kgs 1:29-30; 17:1).

OFFICIAL REPORT (Amtlicher Bericht). The representation of the transmittal of information or message by a person duly authorized and sent forth, such as a military envoy or royal messenger. Offical report amounts to a narrative sequence which recounts (1) the commissioning of a messenger, (2) the going forth and reception of the messenger, (3) the message, directly quoted, (4) the recipient's reaction. In the interests of narrative economy or special effects, some of these elements may be omitted, expanded, or abbreviated. In most cases, the message from one party to another is quoted, and so to be distinguished from (→) report, which simply narrates in third-person style, *for the reader,* the simple course of an event. Examples of official report are 2 Sam 11:18-25; 18:19–19:1 (*RSV* 18:33); Josh 2:1, 23-24. Fragments of, or allusions to, official report may be seen in 1 Kgs 20:2-3, 5-6, 32. Cf. 1 Kgs 5:15-16.

ORACLE (Orakel). A communication from the deity, often through an intermediary such as priest or prophet, especially in response to an inquiry (→ oracular inquiry). The OT also describes oracles as unsolicited. In all cases, the structure and content vary; oracles have to do with, e.g., salvation, healing, punishment, judgment, promise, encouragement, warning. Some oracles commission a prophet to his lifelong vocation, and frequently the prophet's speeches are presented as God's own words, hence as oracle. Settings and intentions vary, according to content and circumstances. Some clue as to solicited oracles comes from (→) reports which mention dreams, prophets, priests, as involved in procedures for obtaining divine communication. See, e.g., 1 Sam 28:6; Num 22:7-12, 19-20; Josh 7:6-15; Judg 1:1-2; 1 Kgs 20:13-14; 22:5-6, 15-17; Ezek 20:1-8.

ORACLE FULFILLMENT (Erfüllung eines Orakels). A type of (→) report that notes a situation or event and concludes with a formulaic expression that the circumstances have come about "according to the word of the Lord which he spoke by so-and-so." Normally, such reports are motifs in a longer narrative, sometimes indigenous to the narrative tradition, sometimes associated with various stages in the redaction. They intend in all cases to assert the correspondence between a divine word, spoken through a prophet, and events in the human realm. Examples are 1 Kgs 16:34; 17:16; 2 Kgs 1:17a; 2:22; 4:44. For this type of report as editorial remark see 1 Kgs 15:29; 16:12; 2 Kgs 9:36.

ORACULAR INQUIRY (Einholung eines Gottesbescheides). A type of (→) report which tells of seeking an oracle from God. The basic elements include: (1) report that an oracle was sought, usually at the request of a military leader; (2) the oracle in response to the inquiry. Two forms of the report occur, one associated with priests (cf. 1 Sam 23:9) and the other with prophets.

The normally brief priestly inquiry mentions "inquiring of Yahweh" (*šā'al bĕyahweh*), quotes the question put to the priest, and reports the answer as a word from God. Sometimes the question is omitted, and other minor variations occur. Examples are 1 Sam 23:2, 4; 14:37; 2 Sam 2:1. This procedure for seeking oracles had its setting in war making, in priestly divination by Urim and Thummim (Num 27:21). However, schematic representations of these activities belong to storytellers and history writers. The reports are usually scenes in longer narratives.

Inquiry for an oracle from a prophet is reported at greater length. The report typically recounts: (1) the problem to be addressed by divine word, (2) an audience with the prophet during which one requests an oracle (*dāraš 'et-dĕbar yahweh*), (3) the oracle, (4) report of its fulfillment. Examples are 2 Kgs 8:7-15; 1 Kgs 14:1-18; 2 Kgs 3:4-20. This sort of activity belongs to divinatory activities of prophets (cf. 2 Kgs 3:15-16). Reports of these activities are now mainly important as scenes in larger narratives which, in some cases at least, may derive from prophets and prophetic circles in Israel.

ORDER (Befehl, Verbot). A forthright, direct expression of personal will, which may be a speech of (→) command or (→) prohibition. Orders have several settings in social life and appear in many different literary contexts in the OT.

PARENESIS (Paränese, Ermahnung gegen oder zu etwas). An address to an individual or a group which seeks to persuade toward a definite goal. It may include several genres, such as (→) exhortation, (→) admonition, (→) instruction, (→) command, and (→) prohibition, arranged in flexible structures. Examples are Deuteronomy 6–11; Zech 1:3-6; Josh 24:2-15; 1 Kgs 8:56-61. Clear evidence for the setting of parenesis is unavailable.

PETITION (Petition, Bittrede, Bittschrift). A request or plea from one person to another asking for some definite response. In ordinary day-to-day expressions, a petition would almost always include: (1) the basis for petition, (2) petition proper, expressed directly or indirectly. (E.g., Gen 18:3-4; 1 Kgs 2:15-17; 5:17-20; Gen 23:4.) A highly stylized petition addressed to God, thus a prayer of petition, is common in portions of the OT shaped by Deuteronomic perspectives. The form is regular: (1) statements of transgression against God or of God's past dealings with important people serve as a basis for petition; (2) a transition formula, "and now" (*wĕʿattâ*), leads into the petition; (3) petition proper asks God for relief from distress (2 Kgs 19:15-19), forgiveness (Exod 32:31-32), divine favor (Exod 33:12-13; 2 Sam 7:18-29; 1 Kgs 3:6-9), and the like. See Jonah 4:2-3; Neh 9:6-37; Ezra 9:6-15. All these examples form representative images of ideal, heroic, divine-human dialogue that support thematic continuities in the wider canonical texts. These stylized prayers of petition represent a literary, theological development from ordinary petition. It is not possible to identify one primary societal setting for the genre, since petitions might be uttered by anyone in almost any situation.

PRAISE SPEECH (Lob und Dankrede). A brief or somewhat elaborate formulaic utterance which offers praise and thanksgiving to God for some good fortune or happy circumstance. Praise speech follows a typical, one-sentence structure: (1) formulaic opening ("Blessed be Yahweh" [*bārûk yahweh*]), followed by (2) a relative clause describing the event, deed, or circumstance which has called forth the praise. In form, the praise speech is much like uttering the name of God with certain epithets. Examples are 1 Kgs 1:48; 5:21; 8:15, 56; 1 Sam 25:32, 39; 2 Sam 18:28; Ezra 7:27. (Cf. 1 Sam 25:33 for an extension of the form into nonreligious speech.) Praise speech is related to (→) blessing (see 1 Kgs 8:14-15), but differs chiefly in function; it does not *pronounce* blessing upon someone, but *acknowledges* blessing from God. Although its usage was widespread in ordinary life, and its settings varied according to circumstances, praise speech would seem to have a special place in cultic affairs (1 Kgs 8:15; 8:56 is part of [→] parenesis in cultic ceremony).

PRAYER (Gebet). Any communication of a person toward his or her God. Ordinarily, prayer is direct address to God in the second-person singular and encompasses a wide variety of expression, motivation, purpose, and societal setting. Thus, prayer may take a number of different literary forms or genres depending on content, intention, and setting. For example, (→) complaint song of the individual, (→) hymn, (→) prayer of dedication, (→) prayer of petition. Besides the book of Psalms, which contains in effect many cultic prayers, we find mention of prayer in narrative contexts, e.g., Gen 24:10-14; 2 Kgs 20:3; Gen 18:23-32; and even in (→) vision reports, e.g., Amos 7:2, 5.

PRAYER OF DEDICATION (Weihegebet). A type of (→) prayer which is spoken on the occasion of dedicating an object, person, offering, or building to God. The examples in the OT are rather stylized. There is (1) a statement of background which provides context, and (2) a simple declaration, e.g., "I bring to you (God) . . ." (Deut 26:5-10) or "I have lent him to the Lord" (1 Sam 1:28) or "I have built you (God) an exalted temple" (1 Kgs 8:13). Now related in narrative contexts, these prayers probably reflect real cultic activities. Related to prayer of dedication is (→) dedicatory inscription, a genre not directly represented in the OT. But see *ANET,* 653-58, for examples from the Syro-Palestinian area.

PRAYER OF PETITION (Bittgebet). → Petition.

PROPHECY (Prophezeiung). A general term for any type of announcement by a prophet concerning future events or actions of God. Prophecy is different from (→) oracle since it refers to words of prophets, whereas oracle more broadly designates utterances, solicited and unsolicited, of priests and dream interpreters as well. There are many different genres of prophecy, as indicated by various contents, forms, and purposes.

PROPHECY OF PUNISHMENT (Prophetische Strafankündigung). A prophetic word which announces disaster to an individual or group because of some offense against God. The structure follows the procedure of two actions in a legal proceeding: indictment and verdict. Thus, prophecy of punishment typically contains: (1) an accusation, where the defendant or group is directly addressed and confronted with his (its) offense, and (2) the announcement of God's intervention in human affairs to bring about punishment. The latter usually begins with a messenger formula, "Thus says Yahweh," and is tied to the former with a logical connective, "Therefore" (*lākēn*). Thus, offense is reason for, or justification of, punishment. The literary structure is fairly flexible, especially in those forms which have a group, or even whole nation, in view. Examples are 1 Sam 2:27-36; Amos 7:14-17; Jer 20:1-6; 1 Kgs 13:21-22; 14:7-11; 16:2-4 (individual); Amos 2:1-3, 4-5; 4:1-3; Hos 2:7-9 (group). In Isa 3:1-11; Jer 2:26-28; Amos 9:8-10, all addressed to a group, one finds the basic components, accusation and punishment, reversed. The settings for prophecy of punishment varied according to the changing and diverse circumstances in which prophets were active.

PROPHECY OF SALVATION (Prophetische Heilsankündigung). A general term for those (→) prophecies which announce salvation, healing, health, restoration. It typically begins with a messenger formula, "Thus says Yahweh," or other introductions, and moves immediately to the announcement of salvation. The latter variously consists of statement(s) of God's intervention to save, the effects and results, and closing statements, sometimes with reasons for God's action. Examples are Isa 7:7-9; Jer 28:2-4; 34:4. Less constrained are Amos 9:11-12, 13-15; Mic 5:1-2 (*RSV* 2-3). Solomon's words to Shimei in 1 Kgs 2:42-45 seem to reflect both the prophecy of salvation (v. 45) and its corresponding opposite, the (→) prophecy of punishment (vv. 42-44).

PROPHETIC ANNOUNCEMENT OF SIGN (Prophetische Zeichenankündigung). An announcement in the context of (→) prophecies either of salvation or punishment that an event will occur in the future to confirm the main prophetic word. Normally, the announcement consists of three elements: (1) a declaration of an event as "sign" from God, e.g., "This is the sign (for you) from Yahweh"; (2) a subordinate clause which gives the significance of the "sign," e.g., "that the Lord has spoken" or "that the Lord will do this thing"; (3) the description of the event which is to be taken as "sign." Sometimes the second element is missing, as the context supplies the significance. Good examples of the genre are 1 Kgs 13:3; Jer 44:29-30; Isa 38:7-8 (=2 Kgs 20:9-10); 37:30-32 (=2 Kgs 19:29-31). The settings of such announcements would vary according to the circumstances in which prophets were active. In general, however, the main occasion seems related to the custom of soliciting (→) oracles from prophets, and also, by extension, asking for "signs" (Isa 7:10).

PROPHETIC BATTLE STORY (Prophetische Schlachterzählung). A type of (→) historical story focused on military encounter(s) in which one or more prophets assume important dramatic roles and enunciate for the reader those interpretative perspectives important to the author (→ battle story). Closely related is (→) battle report, which tells of military encounter but without those literary features characteristic of developed, imaginative (→) story, and often without reference to prophets. See, e.g., Josh 7:2-5; Judg 8:10-12. Examples of prophetic battle story are 1 Kgs 20:1-34 and 2 Kgs 19:1-37 (cf. Isa 7:1-9). Although the societal setting for this genre is uncertain, and may even have been quite varied, the intentions seem related to recounting an event in the past for historical, instructional, and explanatory reasons.

PROPHETIC JUDGMENT SPEECH (Prophetische Gerichtsrede). A speech in which the prophet as the spokesman for Yahweh announces judgment upon an individual, group, or nation. The main elements are: (1) statement of reasons for judgment, usually offenses against God; (2) logical connective, e.g., "therefore" (*lākēn*); (3) the announcement of judgment, often introduced with a messenger formula, "Thus says Yahweh." Additional elements occur frequently. Often, but not always, the reasons for judgment are presented as the prophet's own words, and the announcement as the words of Yahweh. Examples are Mic 3:9-12; Isa 8:6-8; Jer 11:9-12. The chief difference between this genre and the similar (→) prophecy of punishment is that the latter includes direct accusation to an individual or group, and thus preserves something of literary parentage in juridical procedures.

PROPHETIC LEGEND (Prophetenlegende). A type of (→) legend which focuses chiefly on the prophet as main character and exemplar of virtue, goodness, piety, and divine favor. Its purposes would be multiple, but chiefly to edify or inculcate religious devotion. Some prophetic legends would have originated among prophets, but some also among the people who dealt with prophets. Occasions of telling, the societal settings, were varied, as for legends in general. → Legend.

PROPHETIC REVELATION (Bericht einer Prophetenoffenbarung). A type of (→) report which recounts a private message from God to a prophet. Typically, such reports open with a prophetic word formula, "And the word of Yahweh came to so-and-so" (*wayĕhî dĕbar-yahweh [hāyâ] 'el*-PN), and then quote the message, which may be variously command, commission, prediction, warning, and the like. Examples in narrative are 2 Sam 7:4-16; 1 Sam 15:10-11; 1 Kgs 16:1-4; 17:2-4, 8-9; 21:28-29; cf. 1 Kgs 6:11-13. In the later literature, features of this narrative reporting style came to shape prophetic words intended to stand alone as a kind of public revelation. In these cases, the introductory formula became autobiographical in form ("And the word of the Lord came to me . . .") and functioned as a superscription to the divine message. The entire report now was much like an independent poem, a testimony revealed, rather than—as in the narrative contexts—a telling of what the prophet experienced or did. See, e.g., Jer 21:1-10; 32:1-44; 34:8-22; Ezek 14:1-11; 20:1-44.

PROPHETIC STORY (Prophetenerzählung). A type of (→) historical story in which a prophetic figure plays a central role and carries interpretative motifs expressive of the narrator's interest. For further information → Historical Story.

QUESTION-AND-ANSWER SCHEMA (Frage und Antwort Schema). A literary device which projects a question and its answer as a means of describing a future situation. One type assumes a disaster and assigns reasons and responsibility for it, thus elaborating on implicit admonitions to avoid the behavior which will lead to such an end. Typical are Jer 22:8-9; 1 Kgs 9:8-9; Deut 29:21-24 (*RSV* 22-25), all from the Dtr writers who placed national destruction in the context of broken covenant and realized covenantal curses. Parallels are in the commemorative (→) royal inscriptions of Ashurbanipal (e.g., *ANET,* 300). A second type appears as a divine speech addressed to a prophet, envisions a situation in which someone will ask a question, and suggests the answer that will be given. Examples are Jer 23:33; 5:19; 13:12-14; Ezek 21:12 (*RSV* 7); 37:18-19. Literary function, of course, varies according to biblical context. Models for this device apparently derive from situations in which a person sought oracles through a prophet. → Oracular Inquiry.

REGISTER (Register). An administrative (→) list, or even a book, which records for official purposes items or persons according to the means by which they are subject to administration by institutions or corporate bodies. The purpose of a register is to record and document the basis on which persons or items can be administered. Depending on the content, the forms of a register vary. OT texts either based on a register, or themselves a register, are citizens for labor recruitment (Nehemiah 3), or for military service (Num 1:17-47); officials to administer the state (1 Kgs 4:2-6, 7-19; Num 1:5-16); booty for support of religious shrines (Num 31:32-47). Cf. references to making registers in Num 1:2-4; 2 Samuel 24. Parallels appear frequently in Mesopotamian and Egyptian (→) royal inscriptions designed to commemorate the king and his deeds (e.g., *ANET,* 242-43, 249, 260-61, 278-79). Register originated with the scribal classes whose jobs included keeping administrative records of a centralized state. If such activity did not actually begin with the monarchy, it surely grew enormously with the consolidation of the Israelite state.

REGNAL RESUMÉ (Abriss einer königlichen Regierungszeit). A formulaic summary in the books of Kings which provides information about the monarchs of Israel and Judah. Regnal resumé normally appears in two parts, as an introductory and concluding summary which forms a framework around other materials relating to a particular reign. The introductory resumé typically includes: (1) name of the king and a synchronistic formula giving the date of accession; (2) the age of the king at accession (for Judah only); (3) the length of reign and capital city; (4) name of the queen mother (for Judah only); (5) a theological evaluation, variously worded, but in general highly stylized and stereotyped. Occasionally some elements, or even the entire resumé, may be missing for a particular reign. The concluding resumé, sometimes omitted, carries: (1) a citation formula, referring the reader to other sources for regnal information; (2) notice of death and burial of the king; (3) notice of succession. Examples are 2 Kgs 13:10-13 (the complete regnal resumé); 1 Kgs 15:1-5, 33-34 (introductory); 1 Kgs 14:19-20; 2 Kgs 10:34-35 (concluding). Regnal resumé is a literary device invented by the author-editor of 1–2 Kings, though it is possible that some elements at least were drawn from his sources.

REPORT (Bericht). A brief, self-contained prose narrative, usually in third-person style, about a single event or situation in the past. There is no developed plot or imaginative characterization (contrast [→] story). In that there is usually action, however, report is different from a statement or description. Report also differs from (→) official report, which is a narrative representation of a message being transmitted from one person to another. Varying in length from the very short (→) notice to the longer, even composite (→) account, reports carry diverse contents, e.g., settlement (Judg 1:16-17), royal construction (1 Kgs 6:2-38), name (→) etiology (Gen 35:8), a leader's (→) farewell speech (1 Kgs 2:1-9), diplomatic concord (1 Kgs 5:15-26 [*RSV* 5:1-12]), or (→) prophecy of punishment (1 Kgs 20:35-43). Certain types of report as defined by structure and content take on special importance in the OT (e.g., [→] dream, [→] theophany, [→] vision, [→] battle, [→] symbolic action). Naturally the setting for report would vary according to content and purpose.

REPORT OF PROPHETIC COMMISSION (Bericht einer Prophetensendung). A type of (→) report which tells of a prophet's being commissioned by God to speak or act. For full discussion, → Commission.

REPORT OF PROPHETIC WORD (Bericht eines Prophetenwortes). A type of (→) report developed rather late in association with the making of literary collections of prophetic (→) oracles. Even though the report may begin with a (→) prophetic word formula and include possibly secondary narrative elements of situation, date, and circumstance, the intent is not to convey a private (→) prophetic revelation, or what the prophet has done or experienced, but to preserve what the prophet has said publicly. The report stands apart from (→) story or (→) legend about the prophet, and emphasizes a word of God for its own sake. Examples are Jer 21:1-10; 32:1-44; 34:8-22; 35:1-19; Ezek 14:1-11; 20:1-44.

ROYAL INSCRIPTION (Königsinschrift). A general term for those ancient Near Eastern (→) inscriptions which commemorate historical kings and/or their deeds or record their gifts dedicated to the gods. There are Sumerian, Babylonian, Assyrian, and Egyptian examples, and several different types. All are products of centralized monarchies and aim in various ways to support and preserve strong royal government. (See Grayson; Sollberger; Hallo in bibliography at "Introduction to Historical Literature.")

ROYAL NARRATIVE (Königsnovelle). Narrative portions of Egyptian (→) royal inscriptions that present the king as an ideal figure of strength, piety, and success. Literary content and form vary considerably, and examples are known from ca. 1900 through 300 B.C. The accounts present the king in a variety of flattering ways: interacting with worshipful courtiers to plan and build great temples and monuments; quelling rebellions and going on military campaigns with glorious success; renowned from birth and youth, chosen by the gods to rule, given beauty, talents, special prowess. Examples may be found in Lichtheim, *Ancient Egyptian Literature*, I, 115-18; II, 57-72; Breasted, *ARE* II, §§ 131-66; III, §§ 251-81 (see A. Hermann and full information in bibliography at "Introduction to Historical Literature"). Since these accounts for the most part are portions of commemorative inscriptions carved on temple walls, their principal aims are to glorify the king and commemorate his deeds so as to accrue divine favor and afterlife for him. Possibly something like this type of royal inscription stands in the background of 1 Kings 3–11.

SAGA (Sage). A long, traditional narrative, composed of episodic units built around typical themes or topics. Saga may include originally independent shorter pieces, such as (→) legend, (→) story, (→) anecdote, and various types of poetry. These episodes tell of deeds, virtuous ancestors, and heroic events which contribute to the narrator's cultural world. Though saga may include fanciful elements, that world for the narrator is the real world, when the earth was pretty much as it is now (contrast [→] myth). OT examples are Exodus 1–Deuteronomy 34 (saga of Moses); Gen 12:1–25:10 (saga of Abraham). The settings for saga are diverse. It belongs to popular literature and thus would be composed, transmitted, and told in a range of circumstances and on many occasions. The intentions of saga would likewise vary according to the situation. Chief among the storyteller's aims would be to entertain and to educate members of the audience into the ways of their particular culture.

SCHEMA OF REPRIEVE (Schematische Darstellung von Strafaufschub, Strafmilderung, oder Begnadigung). A pattern of literary motifs characteristic of the final shape of certain heavily redacted portions of the OT. Typically, one reads: (1) a description of penitence which follows upon an event of divine punishment, or the promise of such; (2) a (→) prophecy of salvation which mitigates the punishment, or a report of such an event. The language is stereotyped. Penitents "rend" their garments (*qr' bgd*), dress in sackcloth, and fast (*ṣûm*). The prophecy, which typically includes an allusion to penitence, gives the justification for reprieve, and then announces that the punishment has been set aside or mitigated in some way. Examples are 1 Kgs 21:27-29; 2 Kgs 22:19-20; 2 Sam 12:13-14; 2 Chr 12:7-8. Although schema of reprieve may be a kind of "stock scene" at home with Israelite storytellers, it appears more likely that this literary schema had its origin in the redacting and shaping hands that organized large blocks of OT tradition.

SELF-DISCLOSURE ORACLE (Prophetisches Erweiswort). A prophetic word of salvation for Israel that at the same time announces disaster for her enemies and is the means by which Yahweh shows himself to be God. The characteristic elements are: (1) the reason for God's intervention; (2) the means of God's intervention; (3) a formula of recognition, "And you (they) shall know (recognize, *yd'*) that I am Yahweh," or "By this you (they) shall know. . . ." Thus, this oracle intends to announce not only salvation, but also that Yahweh be recognized as God. The earliest setting may have been in the cultic institution of holy war (cf. 1 Kgs 20:13-14, 22, 28, 35-43). With many variations, self-disclosure oracle is found in Ezekiel and Deutero-Isaiah, e.g., Ezek 25:3-5, 6-7, 8-11, 15-17; 26:2-6; Isa 41:20; 49:23, 26.

STATEMENT (Mündliche oder schriftliche Aussage). A brief prose-word or -writing which simply notes or describes a situation or circumstance. Unlike (→) report, it does not relate action, and it differs from direct speech. Examples are 1 Kgs 3:2, 3; 5:2-3, 4-5.

STORY (Erzählung). A narrative of some literary sophistication that creates interest by arousing tension and resolving it during the course of narration. Its structure is controlled by imaginative plot. The narrator moves from exposition (background and setting for the action) to a problem, sometimes complications in relationships (tension), to a climactic turn of events from which the resolution flows. Finally, narrative tension drains away into a concluding sense of rest.

Since literary structures are flexible and contents varied, one may not think of rigid definitions of type. Nevertheless, it proves useful to make certain distinctions. When a narrator emphasizes less his imaginative creation and artistic plot than what an event was and how it happened, we speak of (→) historical story. On the other hand, when a brief content is structured simply and its purpose centered on entertainment, we are dealing with folkloristic (→) tale. If the story dwells on the wondrous qualities and exemplary character of a person or place, it is a (→) legend, the primary purpose of which is religious edification. Finally, a story that moves in a fantasy world unlike that of ordinary experience is a (→) fairytale; if its content centers on primordial times when gods and men dealt directly with one another, it is (→) myth. Examples of story are Exod 2:1-10; 1 Kgs 1:1-53.

With the exception of some (→) historical stories, most OT examples of story derive from and belong to the folk. They are folktales which incorporate motifs, scenes, and narrative techniques out of popular culture and oral tradition. Settings and intentions vary widely, therefore, depending on the story type, narrator, and occasions for storytelling.

SUMMARY OF PROPHETIC ORACLE (Kurzbericht eines Prophetenspruches, zusammengefasster-). A statement in third-person reportorial form that aims to summarize very briefly the content of a prophet's (→) oracle. Occasion, circumstance, and scene are unimportant; the prophet is usually unidentified. Emphasis falls upon the generalized content which floats free of narrative moorings somewhat like a commonly known or invented saying. Examples are 1 Kgs 21:23 (cf. 2 Kgs 9:36); 2 Kgs 10:30; 14:25-27; 17:13; 21:11-15. Such summaries are literary devices and stem from the writing and collecting activity of scribes who put together the books of Kings.

SYMBOLIC ACTION (Symbolische Handlung). A type of (→) report in first- or third-person style that recounts incidents in which the prophets accompanied their pronouncements with actions understood to be symbolic demonstrations of their messages. Typically, such reports of symbolic action contained: (1) God's instruction to perform a certain act, (2) report of that act being executed, (3) an interpretation, usually cast as a word from God. Very often, the second element is omitted, and other minor details may be added. Examples are Isa 8:1-4; Jer 13:1-11; Ezek 4:1-8; cf. 1 Kgs 11:29-39; 22:11. Reports of symbolic action evolved from early accounts of magical activities. In their present literary contexts, however, they are similar in function to (→) reports of prophetic words. They communicate an oracle from God to men spoken by and enacted through the prophet.

TALE (Volkstümliche Geschichte). A short, folkloristic type of (→) story. Originally a part of oral tradition, a tale is characterized by a minimum number of characters, one or two scenes, and a simply constructed plot. Typically, a tale briefly sets out the circumstances for its action (exposition) and develops a point of dramatic tension as the problem to be resolved in the narration. Length varies somewhat, but in all cases the plot remains uncomplicated. Tale derives from popular storytellers and the varied situations of storytelling. Hence, the OT examples still show their relative independence, being incorporated into longer collections of narrative, (→) saga, or still resisting full integration into their written context. Examples are Gen 12:10-20; 26:6-11; Exod 4:24-26.

TAUNT (Verspottung, Verhöhnung). An utterance which derides a person or thing as inferior to another. Closely related to (→) boast, taunt often appears in similar circumstances: a battle of words between opponents. Taunt has no fixed form. The term refers to the rhetorical motivation, effect, or even intent of one's speech. See 1 Sam 17:43, 44; 1 Kgs 12:10b; 20:11; Jer 22:14-15; Isa 23:15-16.

THEOLOGICAL REVIEW (Theologische Beurteilung). An editorial statement in the books of Kings which reviews, states offenses of, and evaluates a king. The structure is somewhat flexible, but the language is flat, stereotyped, and aimed at measuring a king according to his religious orthodoxy. The language and style is related to that in the (→) regnal resumé, but limited to only a portion of what resumé covers. Theological review is dominated by evaluative tones, innuendos, and statements. It is characterized by generalization and lacks action or narrative interest. Theological review may incorporate (→) oracles as warning or as messages of salvation or punishment, though without narrative detail. They are oracles really carrying the author's omniscient perspective in the interest of religious evaluation. Examples are 1 Kgs 11:1-13; 2 Kgs 10:28-31; 17:7-18. Cf. Judg 2:11-15; 3:7-8. Theological review is a literary device of the author-editor of 1–2 Kings.

THEOPHANY (Gotteserscheinung). A type of (→) report, occasionally poetry, which recounts the manifestation of God, as distinct from (→) epiphany, which refers more generally to the appearance of any kind of divine being, e.g., angels, cherubim, etc. Two elements are characteristic: (1) description of Yahweh's approach, (2) accompanying natural upheavals (wind, fire, storm, etc.), along with reactions of fear and awe. Examples are Judg 5:4-5; Deut 33:2; Amos 1:2; Mic 1:3-4; Ps 68:8-9 (*RSV* 7-8). The genre was probably influential in shaping 1 Kgs 19:9-14. Either member may be expanded with additional motifs (e.g., Isa 19:1; 26:21; 30:27-33; Nah 1:2-6; Hab 3:3-12). Possibly originally set in celebrations of military victory, and hence aimed at praising the God who gives victory, these reports are now found in various literary contexts, such as (→) hymns (Ps 97:2-5) and (→) prophecy of punishment (Isa 19:1-4; 26:21).

THRONE CONSPIRACY (Verschwörung gegen den Thron). A type of (→) report which tells briefly and schematically of conspiracy against the king and its outcome. Typically it includes: (1) mention of conspiracy (the verb *qšr*); (2) the king is struck down and murdered (Hiphil of *nkh*, "struck/killed," and the verb *mwt*, "die"); (3) mention of conspirator who assumes the throne, often with a succession formula, "And X reigned in his stead." Examples are 2 Kgs 15:10, 14, 25, 30; 21:23. See also the more didactic, moralizing form of the report in 1 Kgs 15:27-30; 16:9-13. Similar reports appearing as part of Babylonian (→) chronicles and (→) king lists suggest that the OT examples may have been drawn from royal records or selected excerpts from such.

VISION REPORT (Visionsbericht). A type of (→) report which recounts what a prophet or seer (cf. Numbers 23–24) hears and/or sees in an inner perception. Varied in content and mostly cast in autobiographical style, a typical report includes: (1) announcement of vision, reporting essentially that the visionary "sees" (*r'h*), or was "made to see" (Hiphil of *r'h*); (2) transition to the vision: "and behold" (*wĕhinnēh*); (3) the vision, usually beginning with juxtaposed images and continuing with scene(s), sounds, voices, dialogues, movements (sometimes the prophet is drawn into the drama).

The OT offers three main types of vision report: (1) oracle-vision, dominated by question-and-answer dialogue wherein a simple visionary image provides an occasion for oracle (e.g., Amos 7:7-8; 8:1-2; Jer 1:11-14; 24:1-10; Zech 5:1-4); the report aims at oraclelike proclamation; (2) dramatic-word vision depicting a heavenly scene taken as a portent of some future event on earth (e.g., Jer 38:21-22; 1 Kgs 22:17, 19-22; Amos 7:1-6); the report recounts a private omenlike revelation, which may or may not be acted upon; (3) revelatory-mysteries vision, aimed at conveying veiled secrets of divine activity and future events; imagery is symbolic and bizarre, and always a pattern of dialogue between divine "guide" and prophet interprets the esoterica (e.g., Zech 2:1-2, 3-4; 4:1-6a; cf. Daniel 8; 10–12).

Vision reports belong to those situations in which persons would ask a prophet or seer to divine information about God's purposes (1 Kgs 22:13-23; 2 Kgs 8:7-15; Ezekiel 14; 20; Jer 38:21-22). → Oracular Inquiry. However, most examples now are important as literary vehicles for theological claims.

FORMULAS

ACCESSION AGE FORMULA (Formel für das Thronbesteigungsalter). Part of the introductory (→) regnal resumé, this formula simply states the age when a particular king began to reign. Allowing for minor variations, it appears as: "X years old (was) RN when he began to reign" or "RN (was) X years old when he began to reign" (literally, "a son of X years (was) RN at his reigning" or "RN (was) a son of X years at his reigning"). The formula is used only for Judean kings, but occasionally is missing in the resumé. For examples, see 1 Kgs 14:21; 22:42; 2 Kgs 8:17; 12:1; 14:2.

ACCLAMATION FORMULA (Akklamationsformel). A short utterance acclaiming that Yahweh alone is God, as in 1 Kgs 18:39b: "The Lord, (he) is God" (*yahweh hû' hā'ĕlōhîm*). Its roots seem to be in Israelite worship activities (cf. Pss 95:7; 100:3; 105:7), including religious (→) parenesis (cf. Deut 4:35, 39; 7:9; 1 Kgs 8:60).

CITATION FORMULA (Zitationsformel). Part of the concluding (→) regnal resumé, this formula refers the reader to other sources of information about a particular king's reign. Typically, the citation consists of three elements: (1) introduction, "and the rest of the acts of RN" (*wĕyeter dibrê* RN); (2) a brief epitomizing allusion to the reign, e.g., "and all he did," "and the conspiracy he committed," "his wisdom," etc.; (3) citation, usually as a question, "are they not written in the chronicles of the kings of (Judah) Israel?" Examples are 1 Kgs 11:41; 14:29; 15:7; 16:14; 2 Kgs 20:20.

CONVEYANCE FORMULA (Übergabeformel). A stereotyped statement that God did, or will, hand over Israel or Israel's enemies to defeat. A typical form for the defeat of Israel is "Yahweh gave/sold (will give/sell) them (Israel) into the hands of X." See the Deuteronomic summaries in Judg 3:8; 4:2. Conversely, formulated as direct address to Israel the formula appears as part of a prophet's or priest's (→) oracle and functions to assure Israel of victory over her enemies. Here the typical form is "I (Yahweh) will give X (it/them) into your (our) hand." For examples, see 1 Kgs 20:13, 28; 22:6; Josh 6:2; 8:1, 18; Judg 1:2; 4:7.

DEATH AND BURIAL FORMULA (Todes- und Bestattungsformel). Part of the concluding (→) regnal resumé, this formula states in two parts that a king died and was buried. The actual wording may vary slightly from case to case. Most frequently, one reads that "he (the king) slept with his fathers and was buried (they buried him)" (e.g., 1 Kgs 11:43a; 14:31). Occasionally, one or the other element is missing (e.g., 1 Kgs 14:20; 2 Kgs 15:22). Sometimes both may be absent or supplanted by a narrative which tells of the circumstances of death (e.g., 1 Kgs 16:9-10; 2 Kgs 12:21-22).

MESSENGER FORMULA (Botenformel). A stereotyped introduction to a message in which the speaker identifies the one who ordered the message transmitted. The most frequent form is "Thus says X [*kōh 'āmar* X]" (e.g., Gen 32:5 [*RSV* 4]; 2 Kgs 1:11 [cf. v. 9]; 2 Kgs 18:29). The formula frequently occurs in the prophets' (→) oracles as "Thus says Yahweh" (e.g., 1 Kgs 21:19; 2 Kgs 1:16; Jer 6:16; 8:4; Ezek 16:59), and shows that the prophet was understood in analogy with the practice of commissioning, instructing, and sending a messenger. → Commission.

ORACLE FULFILLMENT FORMULA (Orakel- oder Worterfüllungsformel). Part of a report of (→) oracle fulfillment, this formula asserts that something happened "according to the word of Yahweh" (*kidbar yahweh*), sometimes adding the clause "which he spoke by his servant PN" or, more simply, "which PN spoke." Examples are 1 Kgs 16:34; 17:16; 2 Kgs 1:17; 2:22; 4:44.

PROPHETIC WORD FORMULA (Prophetische Wortereignisformel). A statement that "the word of Yahweh came to PN (him, me)" (*wayĕhî dĕbar-yahweh [hāyâ] 'el*-PN . . .). The formula usually introduces a report of (→) prophetic revelation and belongs to (→) stories and (→) reports about prophets. It serves to convey the beginning of a private communication from God to the prophet and is thereby distinct from narrative introductions to prophetic words which have a public audience. Examples are 2 Sam 7:4; 1 Kgs 16:1; 17:2; 18:1. The formula became a device to introduce collections of prophetic (→) oracles in the prophetic books, e.g., Jer 2:1; 14:1; 24:4; 25:1; 30:1.

RECOGNITION FORMULA (Erkenntnisformel). Part of a (→) self-disclosure oracle, this formula expresses the purpose of Yahweh's action. The typical form is "And you (they) shall know [*yd'*] that I am Yahweh," e.g., 1 Kgs 20:13, 28. Cf. Exod 7:17, "By this you shall know [*tēda'*] that I am Yahweh." The formula occurs in Ezekiel, e.g., Ezek 25:5, 7, 11, 17; and Isaiah, e.g., Isa 41:20; 49:23, 26.

SUCCESSION FORMULA (Sukzessionsformel). The last element in the concluding (→) regnal resumé, this formula states the identity of the person succeeding to the throne. Typically, the expression is "And RN . . . reigned in his stead" (*wayyimlōk* RN . . . *taḥtāyw*). Where circumstances warrant, the words "his son" or other explanatory statements are added. Examples are 1 Kgs 14:31b; 15:8b; 2 Kgs 1:17; 20:21. The formula does not appear for every monarch in the books of Kings.

SYNCHRONISTIC ACCESSION FORMULA (Synchronistische Thronbesteigungsformel). Part of the introductory (→) regnal resumé, this formula states the date of accession to the throne of one monarch with reference to the regnal year of his counterpart in the northern or southern kingdom. For Judean kings the usual form is "In the nth year of RN, king of Israel, RN king of Judah began to reign" (*bĕ* + year *lĕ* + RN *melek yiśrā'ēl mālak* RN *melek yĕhûdâ*). For example, 1 Kgs 15:9; 2 Kgs 8:25; 14:1; 15:1. For northern kings, a slightly different formula occurs: "In the nth year of RN, king of Judah, RN began to reign (over all Israel) at X (for x years)" (*bĕ* + year *lĕ* + RN *melek yĕhûdâ mālak* RN . . . (*'al yiśrā'ēl*) *bĕ* + place X + number of years). Examples are 1 Kgs 16:8, 15; 2 Kgs 13:1, 10.